Disputatio

An International Transdisciplinary Journal
of the Late Middle Ages

Volume 3: (trans)
Translation, Transformation and Transubstantiation
in the Late Middle Ages

1998

Disputatio

An International Transdisciplinary Journal
of the Late Middle Ages

Volume 3: (trans)
Translation, Transformation and Transubstantiation
in the Late Middle Ages

edited by Carol Poster and Richard Utz

Northwestern University Press
Evanston, Illinois 1998

Northwestern University Press
625 Colfax
Evanston, Illinois 60208-4210

ISBN   0-8101-1646-4

Editorial Note

Disputatio is an international transdisciplinary annual of the late middle ages (ca. 1300-1550). Each issue provides exhaustive and diverse treatments of one significant example of late medieval culture by scholars representing various nations, approaches, and disciplines. We feature scholarly articles, inclusive review essays, and/or a comprehensive bibliography on the topic of each issue.

This volume shows the many ways in which constructions of (trans) are deployed in the late middle ages. Individual essays focus on translation, transformation, and transsubstantiation, including work on the medieval notions of translation and transformation, discussions of the problems faced by modern translators and editors of medieval texts, an essay on the various linguistic manifestations of (trans) in Middle English texts, and a substantial bibliography on transsubstantiation.

We would like to thank the members of our advisory and editorial boards and also our reviewers. Special thanks go to Eugen Seiterich (Librarian), and Christine Baatz of the University of Tübingen, Anne-Françoise Le Lostec, and Sara Jayne Steen, English Department Chair, and the College of Letters and Sciences of Montana State University for their support of *Disputatio*. We are especially glad to welcome two new members to our staff, Georgiana Donavin as Book Review Editor and Gwendolyn Morgan as Managing Editor.

Carol Poster and Richard Utz,
Editors

Contents

Burton Raffel, *Gawain, Chaucer, and Translatability* 1

Jean Dorat. *I: To Henry de Mesmes: A Horoscope.* Trans. David Slavitt..... 16

Gerald Seaman. *The French Myth of Narcissus: Some Medieval Refashionings* 19

Nancy B. Warren. *Saving the Market: Textual Strategies and Cultural Transformations in Fifteenth-Century Translations of the Benedictine Rule for Women* 34

Jean-françois Kosta-Théfaine. *La ballade XI de Christine de Pizan et la ballade 59 des Poésies Anglaises de Charles d'Orléans: adaptation, traduction ou simple coïncidence?*..51

James A. Knapp. *Translating for Print: Continuity and Change in Caxton's Mirrour of the World* 64

David Metzger. *St. Catherine, Lacan, and The Problem of Psycho-History* 91

Stephan Grundy . *Shapeshifting and Berserkergang* 103

Cynthia Brown. *Variance and Late Medieval Mouvance: Reading an Edition of Georges Chastellain's "Louange a tresglorieuse Vierge"* 123

Fritz Kemmler. *Entrancing "tra(u)ns/c": Some Metamorphoses of 'Transformation, Translation, and Transubstantiation'*....................................176

Richard J. Utz and Christine Baatz. *Transsubstantiation in Medieval and Early Modern Culture and Literature: An Introductory Bibliography of Critical Studies* 223

Gawain, Chaucer, and Translatability

Burton Raffel

Two basic linguistic truisms underly this discussion:

1) all human languages are culturally-evolved and culturally-shared systems for communication
2) any meaningful communication framed in one human language can be translated into another human language, provided that the prerequisites for determining meaning in the first language can be understood in the second.

These relatively abstract formulations will here be tested, and applied, in the context of two late medieval poetic texts written in Middle English, the anonymous *Sir Gawain and the Green Knight* (*Gawain*) and Geoffrey Chaucer's unfinished *Canterbury Tales* (*CT*). Translatability, and the necessity for translation, of these late fourteenth-century texts into Modern English is the central issue. It will be argued that, as *literary* texts, *Gawain* and *CT* incorporate not only the sorts of language-problems generally classified as semantic, but also culturally-determined and therefore chronologically-limiting literary significations (*inter alia*, stylistic, structural, prosodic). In both these Middle English texts, virtually all of these language problems (semantic) and embedded literary significations can be resolved, with some study and effort, and the texts rendered quite fully comprehensible; both texts are therefore translatable, in the technical sense of that word. In *Gawain*, however, the degree of difficulty -- that is, the distance between late-medieval meanings, semantic and literary, and those of Modern English -- is sufficiently large that this becomes not simply a difference in degree but in kind, and translation for the reader of Modern English is no longer merely an option, but (except for distinctly advanced-level scholars) is required. In *CT*, on the other hand, the distance between the various sorts of late-medieval meanings and those of Modern English is sufficiently close for reasonably ready comprehension without any necessity for translation, though to be sure one may for assorted reasons choose to translate. Chaucer being on the whole not much more difficult for the reader of Modern English than Shakespeare, I think it a serious mistake to translate *CT* -- but that is the subject of another and very different essay.

Gawain

The poem opens with a nineteen-line "fitt."[1] And these opening lines present, in small, the characteristics and difficulties of the entire poem:

> Siþen þe sege and þe assaut watz sesed at Troye,
> þe bory[2] brittened and brent to brondez and askez,
> þe tulk þa þe trammes of tresoun þer wroŷt
> Watz tried for his tricherie, þe trewest on erthe:
> 5- Hit watz Ennias þe athel, and his highe kynde,
> þat siþen depreced prouinces, and patrounes bicome
> Welneŷe of al þe wele in þe west iles.
> Fro riche Romulus to Rome ricchis hym swythe,
> With gret bobbaunce þat burŷe he biges vpon fyrst,
> 10- And neuenes hit his aune nome, as hit now hat;
> Tirius to Tuskan and teldes bigynnes,
> Langaberde in Lumbardie lyftes vp homes,
> And fer ouer þe French flod Felix Brutus
> On mony bonkkes ful brode Bretayn he settez
> 15- wyth wynne,
> Where werre and drake and wonder
> Bi syþez hatz wont þerinne,
> And oft boþe blysse and blunder
> Ful skete hatz skyfted synne.   (Davis, 1)

There is nothing quite like this in all of English literature. Anyone familiar with Old English verse recognizes, at once, the derivation of the poetic techniques (as well as some of the vocabulary) here employed, and at the same time is obliged to label this a highly altered, even arguably a debased, version of Old English poetry. Not only is the alliteration vastly overdone, by Old English standards -- 13 of the 14 alliterating lines feature a methodically, uniformly pounding three- or even four-stressed alliteration (3 and perhaps 4 of the lines begin with prosodically unbalanced half-lines, featuring 3 alliterations in the first half-line and 2 in the second) -- but line 5 seems to reflect inadequate understanding of the Old English procedure for the alliteration of vowels. The first half-line of line 5 alliterates "Ennias" and "athel," which follows the old rule. But "highe" breaks this alliterative pattern, in which all vowels can alliterate with all other vowels, leaving the second half-line with no alliteration at all. (The juxtaposition of "highe" and "kynde," in fact, is a good deal more like assonance than alliteration.)

At the same time, the last 5 lines of the fitt embrace, simultaneously, both very heavy alliteration and also a kind of gimpy quatrain in rough iambic trimeter, introduced by a single iambic foot (variously of two or three syllables, throughout the poem) that sets the "A" or main rhyme, which is then repeated in the second and fourth lines of the quatrain proper (which thus rhymes, including the brief introductory line, or "bob," A B A B A). Known as the "bob and wheel," this quatrain, effectively a five-line affair, is historically of immense interest.

Although it is not known precisely how the elements of Old English poetry were transmitted, across what is to us a gap in an exclusively written record, it is I think obvious and almost uniformly agreed that unrecorded oral transmission was the process. Clearly, the poet purposefully combines features of the two prosodic modes he knows and practices, one being the more ancient Old English stress-alliteration, the other being the more recent and French-influenced "Chaucerian" counting of metrical feet (see Raffel 1992, xiv-xv.) But precisely what the poet intended by his use of the "bob," and exactly how he perceived both the meter and the poetic weight of the "wheel," remain uncertain. I have referred to the bob and wheel, elsewhere, as a "rhymed tag" (Raffel 1970, 16); despite its many substantive contributions to the narrative, the bob and wheel, as practiced in *Gawain*, is neither technically so secure nor aesthetically so compelling as the poem's primary prosodic mode. To speak of "insistent rhymes and tight meter," as Benson does, and to praise the bob and wheel for creating "an emphasis that the Gawain-poet exploits to build narrative units in which 'the sting is in the tail'" (116), is distinctly to distort our perspective on the poem. Both Benson's metrical and narrative pronouncements need correction. "Each line of the wheel contains three stresses," notes Norman Davis much more accurately, "usually separated by one or two unstressed syllables" (152). Nor does the generalized, rather bland rhetoric of the wheel -- in this first exemplar, we are informed that Britain has been blessed with "war and distress and marvelous deeds," as well as "happiness and sorrow, each in its turn" -- deserve to be thus over-praised. As Cottle notes,

> *Gawain* is an original poem in which diverse traditions are brilliantly fused and made interdependent; but it will be agreed that even when there is

translation from French involved in an English alliterative poem, the process of adapting the rather trivial octosyllabic couplet to the drumroll of the alliterative line shows far more poetic pressure than its mere adapatation into an English short couplet such as Gower or the young Chaucer could have turned. (43)

Let me emphasize that this is a good deal more than an issue of critical appraisal, or what might be thought of as simply a different degree of reader-appreciation. Poetry which like the bob and wheel is prosodically uncertain and aesthetically generalized, and often rather flat, is on the whole harder to understand, as well as to react to: a poet necessarily sacrifices significant measures of poetic authority by demonstrating poetic inadequacies. Poetic authority, like authority in all the arts, is deeply influential on what might be called audience motivation. And though the sometimes thunderous alliterations of the "long line" can be and usually are both supported and cushioned by line-length and complexity, as well as by the strong narrative impetus, the short-lined, essentially narrative-free bob and wheel is provided with no such counterbalancing forces. Over-hefty alliteration sounds far more loudly in such a reduced space. The ear is buffeted by "*b*oth *b*lysse and *b*lunder/ Ful *s*kete hatz *s*kyfted *s*ynne," as it is by the undoubted "insistence" of the rhyming. It is I think not a specious arithmetic which points out that, of the 23 words in this bob and wheel, 13 are involved in its three alliterative patterns (3 on /b/, 3 on /s/, and no less than 7 on /w/), and that the tolling of five rhyme-words over a span of only 23 words is heavy rhyming indeed. Note that the six-line "Dedication" to George Herbert's *The Temple* employs six rhyme-words over a span of 52 words (Herbert 1994, 3), and even so inveterate a rhymster as Robert Herrick, writing in his favorite couplet form in an eight-line lyric, "Cherrie-Ripe," spreads eight rhymewords over a total of 48 words (Patrick 1968, 30). The Gawain-poet thus exhibits very much lessened sensitivity to the danger of rhyme-abuse, as do such later -- but not *so* much later -- poets as John Skelton (see Raffel 1992, 22-23).

In a somewhat different context, Marie Borroff has put the matter extremely well:

A work which belongs, as does *Sir Gawain and the Green Knight,* to a period remote in time and to a literary tradition which has not descended requires historical study as a preliminary to the criticism of style. We cannot intuitively recognize the stylistic qualities of the language of a Middle English poem as we do those of our contemporary language; and while

dictionaries of Middle English and the glossaries to individual texts provide information on meanings in almost all cases, they rarely include comments on style. *The intuitive impression of style may, in fact, be actively
misleading* (27, emphasis added).

Let me put *Gawain* to the side, for a moment, though the discussion
of its translatability, and in particular of the non-semantic literary significations involved therein, will need to be continued. What Borroff calls
the "actively misleading" quality of the merely "intuitive impression of
style" is, viewed in the present context, directly relevant to any evaluation of the desirability, even the necessity (*vel non*), of translating a
Middle English poem into Modern English. Chaucer's *CT*, in a word,
provides the Modern English reader with a far more reliable "intuitive
impression of style":

> Whan that Aprill with his shoures soote
> The droghte of March hath perced to the roote,
> And bathed every veyne in swich licour
> Of which vertu engendred is the flour;
> Whan Zephirus eek with his sweete breeth
> Inspired hath in every holt and heeth
> The tendre croppes, and the yonge sonne
> Hath in the Ram his halve cours yronne,
> And smalle foweles maken melodye,
> That slepen al the nyght with open ye
> (So priketh hem nature in hir corages);
> Thanne longen folk to goon on pilgrimages ...   (Robinson, 17)

Comparative ease of reading, for the Modern English reader, is not
produced, here, by spelling normalizations: Robinson's edition "follows
the spelling of the scribe" (Robinson, xliii). And neither the higher recognition a Modern English reader perforce accords to "the London
speech of [Chaucer's] time" (Robinson, xxx) -- it being the direct ancestor of Modern English, in a clearly documented line -- as contrasted to
the reduced recognition accorded by a Modern English reader to the
northwest county speech of *Gawain*, nor even the much greater famil-
iarity of the lines themselves, much affects the comparison of *CT* and
Gawain. Indeed, the *CT* lines are more familiar in good part precisely
because they are so much more accessible to the reader of Modern English. Significantly, even a spelling normalization of *Gawain* does not
change this:

> Sithen the sege and the assaut watz sesed at Troye,
> The borgh brittened and brent to brondez and askez,
> The tulk that the trammes of tresoun ther wroght
> Watz tried for his tricherie, the trewest on erthe ...

The first four lines of *CT* contain only one word on its face impossible for a reader of Modern English to understand, "soote," which also appears in *CT* spelled "swote" or "swete" and means, of course, "sweet." (Dressed in its alternative and today more recognizable garb, the word is easily understood by Modern English readers.) The first four lines of *Gawain*, on the other hand, contain not merely one but three words impossible on their face for a reader of Modern English to understand, "brittened" ("destroyed"), "tulk" ("knight, man"), and "trammes" ("machinations"), plus a number of spellings far more likely than in Chaucer to confuse such a reader. That is a threefold (or three hundred percent) increase: the fact that the absolute numbers are necessarily, in such a calculation, small ones does not change the significance of the marked difference in their amplitude.

Let me now turn to consideration of the various levels of non-semantic literary signification ("meaning") in the two poems. To the extent that matters largely (a) stylistic, (b) structural, and (c) prosodic can be separated, I will deal with them separately.

(a) *Stylistic significations*: Like the Old English poetry from which it ultimately derives, *Gawain* frequently precedes in essentially nonlinear ways. Line 1, e.g., informs us that there was a "sege" at "Troye." But it immediately goes on to inform us that there was an "assaut," which is sufficiently non-incremental (especially for a medieval audience accustomed to such patterns of warfare) to mark only a bare minimum of forward movement. In line 2, however, the poet pretty much repeats this information, substituting "borÿ" for "Troye": the medieval audience would already have known (and not only from "sesed," in line 1) that the victors had burned Troy to the ground, but would have taken pleasure in *Gawain*'s adornment of that fact with "brittened," "brent," "brondez," and "askez." (Aesthetic pleasure, to be sure, does not require, nor would it here have been accompanied, by linear progression.)

Indeed, though the grammatical subject of line 3, as Davis and others have maintained (Davis, 70), must be and surely was understood by the poem's original audience to be the "tulk," Aeneas, the Gawain-poet's stylistic predilections so favor nonlinear movement that he postpones the verb associated with this subject until line 4. This plainly aligns the syntax of line 3, in good part, not with what is yet to come in the poem, but with what has already been presented. Although in fact we are given new matter to deal with -- the "tresoun" of Aeneas -- the poet's presentation of it is made to seem as much circular-repetitive (nonlinear) as it is incrementally forward-moving (linear). But in Modern English, with its fully analytical syntax, the verb "is the grammatical motor of the sentence" (Stageberg, 170). The Gawain-poet features such linear progression, too; lines 4 through 7 employ it. But the Gawain-poet simply can not abstain from nonlinear syntactical movement; it is part and parcel of the stylistic conventions by which he operates. He weaves non-linear syntactical movement into (or on top of) the linear syntax of lines 8, and 9, and in the first half of line 11 so relying on it that he quite abandons that basic "motor," the verb. "Tirius to Tuskan," consisting only of noun-preposition-noun, is presented to us very much as if it were a free-standing grammatical clause (an "independent" clause being Modern English's usual label). And for Modern English readers this gulf between stylistic expectation and stylistic practice is difficult to deal with: English has long since evolved away from such constructions.

CT, though roughly contemporaneous with *Gawain,* demonstrates that the main line of the development of English had already taken the linear road. "Perced," "bathed," "engendered," "inspired," "hath ... yronne," and the other verbs of the famous opening lines, are in fact the "grammatical motors" of Chaucer's poem. The birds "maken," and the birds "slepen"; nature "priketh" them, as people "longen ... to goon," and thereafter "wende" "to seke" him who "hath holpen" them. Just as in Modern English, it is consistently the verbs which stir the pot. Indeed, the first occurrence in *CT* of anything that might even arguably be taken as the circular-repetitive movement of *Gawain* -- "holt and heeth" in line 6 -- is doubly undercut by being both the rhyme-word and being enjambed, the enjambement serving to emphasize the phrase's grammatical role as the direct object of the verb "inspired." "Kowthe in sondry londes," in line 14, is the next such putative occurrence of nonlinear syntactical movement, and it too is tugged out of the circular-repetitive role by being plugged into service as an integral part of the relentlessly linear movement of the rhyme, marching on in A A B B C C D D profusion.

(b) *Structural significations:* It may seem either fortuitous or trivial that while modern editions of *CT* often print the Middle English text in double columns, modern editions of *Gawain,* no matter how small the type-size employed, tend to present us with standard single-column pages. But this is neither accidental nor unimportant: the fact is that *CT can,* if desired, be set in double columns, and the extraordinarily lengthy lines of *Gawain*'s main, alliterative portions can not. And the significance of this fact is that Modern English readers are accustomed, *tout court*, to *read* -- to use their eyes, silently, to take what they are reading off the pages in front of them. *Gawain* surely had such readers, too. But the aetiology of *Gawain* is far more profoundly connected to oral traditions than is that of *CT*. As Benson notes, conceding sensibly that "obviously more study of this problem is needed, ... a continuous oral tradition accounts for both the survival and the continuing development of alliterative verse in Middle English" (118). And Boroff's refutation of the theory that *Gawain*'s alliterative lines rest on a seven-stress norm, rather than one of four stresses, shows in detail what any reader can see, namely, that *Gawain*'s alliterative lines are fairly packed with unstressed syllables (172-88). Though this is not in any way a difficulty, for the *listener*, it does present the Modern English *reader* of these alliterative lines with rather a lot for both eye and inner ear to take in. It is self-evident, too, that (as R. A. Waldron notes) the poet's "most obvious method of description, and perhaps the least efective for the modern reader, is to saturate the text with detail. This is the rhetorical counterpart of the ornamental detail which was such a prominent feature of contemporary manuscript illumination, painting, architecture and the visual arts generally" (7).

The length and weight of individual lines is also a necessary component in whatever interior formal structures a poem employs. Written mostly in free-flowing rhymed couplets, *CT* is only occasionally divided into formal stanzas ("The Man of Law's Tale," "The Clerk's Tale," "The Prioress's Tale,' "The Monk's Tale," and of course the jocular and abortive "Sir Thopas"); only one tale is written, not in verse, but in prose ("The Parson's Tale"). That is, both in the long and wondrous "Prologue," and in most of the tales that follow it, *CT*'s formal shape is dictated organically by the narrative being told, by its characters and content, by its tone. This is very much what Modern English readers have become accustomed to in the narrative modes with which they are familiar. As Stephen Knight has said of one of the almost universally praised narratives in *CT*, "The Franklin's Tale" (though he addresses the tale, again, in a somewhat different context from that under discussion here), "the poem develops the crucial action ... with great fluency" (195). "Fluency" is exactly what readers of Modern English perhaps prize most highly.

And the "fitts" (or "strophes", or even less accurately, "stanzas") into which *Gawain* is divided are dictated by no principle we have been able, or are ever likely, to understand. That is, not only are the individual lines longer and weightier than Modern English readers are used to, but the formal subdivisions correspond to no known rationale. It is entirely self-serving to argue, as Dorothy Everett has, that although "there is a danger, with a stanza that ends so emphaatically [i.e., with the bob and wheel], that the narrative might seem to move in a series of jerks, ... this effect is minimized by varying the length of the stanzas so their ends can ofen be made to coincide with natural pauses ..." (13). This is in truth to say no more than that the "stanzas" often end when they ought to.

Basil Cottle has observed, with considerable justice, that *Gawain* "is ostensibly narrative" (43). For the Modern English reader, confronting incomprehensibly stanza-like subdivisions in the poem is surely a clog on narrative momentum. An impediment, to paraphrase Gertrude Stein, is an impediment is an impediment.

(c) *Prosodic significations*: It is difficult, not to say impossible, to separate prosody from style and structure. Benson -- the best critic the Gawain-poet has yet had -- explains this in highly useful, far-ranging terms:

> The literary relations of *Sir Gawain* are complicated by the fact that it is both a [French-derived] romance and an alliterative poem. ... [B]ut England provided the poet with his style, and the art of *Sir Gawain* is essentially the art of the alliterative tradition.... [Few critics] recognize that an alliterative poem differs from a nonalliterative work in more than vocabulary and meter, that this style is a mode of discourse which in generations of use had developed its own way of designating objects and concepts, of describing places and events, and of building a narrative. Consequently, one must read *Sir Gawain* not only with a sympathetic awareness of its traditional meter and diction but with a set of syntactic, semantic, and even structural expectations much different from those one brings to the works of Chaucer .... (110-11)

Consider the prosodic difficulty raised in the very first line: "Siþen þe sege and þe assaut watÿ sesed at Troye." The heavy sibillant alliteration is too obvious to need comment. But just how heavy did the poet mean it to be? Did he intend this as a four-stress or a five-stress line? That is, the combined prosodic stress and alliteration clearly occur in "*s*ege," "*s*aut," and "*s*esed." They just as clearly do not fall on the second syllable of "*s*esed," which is unarguably not stressed, or on the terminal consonant of the first syllable of "*s*aut," also unarguably unstressed (through both /s/ sounds were probably pronounced, as they no longer would be in Modern English, which has -- in pronunciation as opposed to spelling -- no doubled consonants). But what of the first syllable of the very first word, "siþen"?

John Gardner is not only sure that it too is stressed, but contends that "the lines are simply pentameter, much like blank verse, but rhythmically more flexible than normal iambic pentameter, for the poet may use more unstressed syllables than the writer of blank verse would be able to use (cf. Hopkins' 'riders')'; or he may, on the other hand, drop out unstressed syllables we would normally expect ... Moreover, the tradition of alliterative poetry gives him the ability to shift, whenever he wishes to *break the pentameter effect*, to a classical [i.e., Old English] four-stress line" (Gardner, 87; emphasis added).

Burrow aptly says that *Gawain* "is a poem for the ear rather than the eye" (1). And Cawley confirms that "the alliteration is more strictly functional in *Sir Gawain*" than in other work attributed to the same anonymous poet (150). But what does the Modern English ear tell us about the poem's first line? There is quite simply no definitive standard to which we can hold either ourselves or the Gawain-poet: this first line is *either* composed of two balanced half-lines, adding up to a total of four combinations of stress and alliteration, *or* quite as probable it is composed of two unbalanced half-lines, the first with three combinations of stress and alliteration, the second with two. Note that, in either case, the first syllable of "siþen" alliterates with the /s/ sounds which follow in the line. The only question is whether the alliteration in "siþen" is accompanied by stress. And there is no way of knowing, in this line, or in a good many of the two thousand five hundred and twenty-nine lines which follow.

Prosodic uncertainty is, to be sure, a relatively minor matter, compared to other problems created for the Modern English reader by *Gawain*'s free-swinging, sometimes tub-thumping alliteration. The semantic and syntactic complexities of line 8 are difficult enough to unravel, without there being primary alliteration on four of the eight words in the line, plus a secondary, medial /r/ and more or less reverse-echoic alliteration in "Fro," which is clearly not stressed. "Fro riche Romulus to Rome ricchis hym swyþe," taken sequentially (as Modern English readers have been trained to read our now fully analytic syntax), means "After rich (high-ranking) Romulus to Rome made-his-way (proceeded) quickly," the "hym" being reflexive and thus contained in what modern readers perceived to be the verb. Unwary modern readers will be initially flummoxed by "ricchis," which to them seems (but is not) clearly a nominal; the apparent (but nonexistent) link to "riche," which is an adjective, will add to the possibility of confusion. (Just as "wele," in line 7, means "riches (wealth)" but has no link other than alliteration to "welneÿe," meaning "almost"; the first is a a noun, the second an adverb, and they have only distant etymological connections.) Alliteration this strong may not directly add to modern readers' semantic problems -- but it cannot add to their sense of comfort or ease. In the bob and wheel, as I have already noted, alliteration this heavy seems to the reader of Modern English almost unbearably heavy.

How then does one translate *Gawain*, recognizing that the process is virtually an obligatory one, in addition to one containing fearsome difficulties? Let me set out and then annotate the first fitt of the translation I published in 1970 (Raffel 1970, 49):

> Once the siege and assault had done for Troy,
> And the city was smashed, burned to ashes,
> The traitor whose tricks had taken Troy
> For the Greeks, Aeneas the noble, was exiled
> 5- For Achilles' death, for concealing his killer,
> And he and his tribe made themselves lords
> Of the western islands, rulers of provinces,
> And rich: high-handed Romulus made Rome
> Out of nothing, built it high and blessed it
> 10- With his name, the name we know; and Tirrus
> Father of Tuscan founded towns;
> And the Lombards planted a land; and Brutus
> Split the sea, sailed from France
> To England and opened cities on slopes
> 15- And hills,
> Where war and marvels
> Take turns with peace,
> Where sometimes lightning trouble
> Has struck, and sometimes soft ease.

The general strategy here is to sufficiently modify the stylistic as well as the purely semantic and syntactic significations, so that readers of Modern English can simultaneously get some clear sense of the original and derive some roughly equivalent aesthetic satisfaction from the reading. It has always been my position that crude, awkward, unlovely renditions of powerful and (as here, though more notably in later passages) lyrical poems are in a sense not translations at all. That is, to translate, in my professional lexicon, means to recreate, to produce some more or less equivalent simulacrum of the original in a different culture, time, and language. Bad cannot represent good, in translation, just as prose cannot represent verse.

That said, I am obliged to say that, almost thirty years after making this translation, I would not do it, today, exactly as I did earlier. In line 1, e.g., "had done for" is both a translation and an explanation, what I then liked to call an "embedded footnote." It is even truer in 1997 than it was in 1970 that not everyone recognizes even the name of Troy, let alone summons up the necessary historical information possessed by Middle English readers and listeners. "Had done for" seems to me, in addition, perhaps too contemporary; I might translate, now, "Once the siege and assault had ended at Troy."

I might also preserve more of the circular-repetitive nonlinearity of line 2, eliminating the "And" which begins the line and shapes a linearity not completely true to the original, though without much question easier for the reader of Modern English to accept. (My axiom of axioms, in translation, remains however: "The translation is not the original.") The point to translations, I now believe, is often precisely the stretching of the reader, the forcing (but in palatable fashion) of modern minds and sensibilities into older frameworks. But I would preserve the rest of the line unchanged. The reader of Modern English has no need to wade through, say, "burned to embers and ashes," when (a) "burned to ashes" is in fact the Modern English idiom of choice and (b) "the city was smashed, burned to ashes," by its use of internal rhyming both alerts the reader to the bob and wheel, before it arrives, and also softens the shock of its arrival.

Lines 3 through 5 are, as I have said, dependent on one rather than another scholarly reading. If one thinks that the "tulk" is Antenor, as a signiicant minority of both scholars and translators do, one will of course translate differently. I have not one but two embedded footnotes, in these three lines: "the Greeks," an addition which I perpetrated regretfully but still believe usefully, and the whole of line 5, about Achilles and his killer, Polyxena, who had been deceitfully hidden by Aeneas. It is not an easy choice: does one or does one not provide background so esoteric as to be meaningless to most modern readers? And if one does supply that background, is it better done in embedded footnotes or in the more traditional variety? I have no definitive answers; my own practice, over the years, has pretty much varied from case to case -- few traditional footnotes in Rabelais (Raffel 1990), where too many would be needed and one risks, as translators have done, turning a translation into an encylopedic commentary, but many more in *Don Quijote* (Raffel 1995), where fewer are required and the information conveyed is distinctly more important to, as well as more closely woven into, the meaning of the original text. Is it necessary to explain, as I have done in line 4, "exiled," that Aeneas was tried and then exiled by the Greeks? I still think it is, though I may well be in error. The Gawain-poet gives the reader only "watz tried" ("was tried"). But his readers and listeners knew the result of that trial. Precious few modern readers can make that statement.

There is considerable syntactic rearrangement in these lines, too, in part to accomodate embedded footnotes, in part to partially linerarize the unlinear. Aeneas and his kin "depreced" ("subjugated") provinces, in the original text; I translate "made themselves lords ... [and] rulers of provinces," assimilating "patrounes" into "lords and rulers," and creating a Modern English scale of events, (1) "lords/Of the western islands," (2) "rulers of provinces," and (3) "And rich" -- which last phrase assimilates "al the wele" ("all the wealth").

"High-handed" as the adjective for Romulus, in line 8 of the translation, assiimilates "riche" ("rich, noble, high-ranking") and "gret Bobbaunce" ("great pomp, pride"). It may seem that "Romulus made Rome/ Out of nothing" has no source in the original -- but "þat burȝe he biges vpon fyrst" means, in fact, "he built that city from the beginning/ from the ground up." Like the Gawain-poet, I wanted the alliteration of "*no-thing*," as well as the whip-snapping crack of the word. "Built it high" thus is an expansion of "biges vpon fyrst," as well as the substitution of one nonlinear expression for others which fell by the way. So too "neuenes hit [the city] his aune nome" ("gave it his own name") is expanded into "blessed it/With his name." It may be slightly stronger than is required: I am still not sure. But I am sure that "called it after his name" would not do any more than would "named it after himself."

"Tirrus/Father of Tuscan," in lines 10-11 of the translation, stems from an emendation and a seventeen-line footnote by Norman Davis, editor of the text from which I translated the poem (Davis, 71n.). "Teldes bigynnes" means, literally, "built buildings" -- but "founded towns" is I think exactly what *that* means, in Modern English. And since, as Davis notes, "Langobardus was the legendary ancestor of the Langobardi or Lombards," I feel no compunctions about having compressed "Lanagaberde in Lumbardie" into "the Lombards" (Davis, 71n.). "Planted a land," simply enough, stems from the Gawain-poet's decision to use as his verb "lyftes," in the phrase "lyftes vp homes" ("builds homes").

"Felix Brutus," in the Middle English, is almost certainly not a first name and a last name, as it may appear, but the addition of a thoroughly conventional appelation to Brutus' name: "felix" is of course Latin for "happy." Line 12 of the translation drops the appelation, which had a conventional place, then, but has none whatever, now. Brutus is described as having "split the sea," in line 13 of the translation, as a rendering of "fer ouer þe French flod" ("far over the French sea"). He is described as having "opened cities on slopes/And hills" as a rendering of "On mony bonkkes ful brode Bretayn he settez" ("he founds/establishes on many very broad British slopes/hillsides," where the Middle English places "settez" ("founds/ establishes") at the end rather than, as in Modern English, at the beginning of the sentence).

I said of the bob and wheel, in my long introduction to the translation, that it "has been, in about equal proportions, a delightful challenge and an affliction. My practice has been to come as close to the rhyming pattern of the original as I could, but never knowingly to sacrifice other qualities to the rhyme pattern." I then added, in parentheses, the comment that "I have been even freer with the meter" (Raffel 1970, 40). Metric-al freedom, it seemed to me (and still so seems), was necessary, to keep from falling into the sometimes rigidly, simplistically oversimple prosody of the original. The poem's first bob and wheel, in lines 15-19, can reasonably well stand for the rest: it is I suspect about as good and about as bad. It would be pleasant to think that, presumably riper in my craft and defter in my skills, I would do better, were I to tackle the translation again. But I am not at all sure that is true, nor am I about to put the assumption to the test.

Southwestern Louisiana University

Notes

1. Sometimes referred to as a "stanza," though it has no fixed length and is thus devoid of the replicative structures a true "stanza" requires; I have in the past substituted the term "strophe," used loosely to mean a non-replicative form of unspecified length, but "fitt," though today a less familiar term, is clearly more accurate, with etymological roots that go back to King Alfred. "Fitt" has also been used to describe the four "parts" or "sections" or "books" into which *Gawain* may or may not have been meant to be divided, as indicated by the large capital letters occurring at four points in the sole surviving manuscript.

2. Technological insufficiencies compel me to use the character "ẏ" for the scribe's multi-functional but unreproducible voiced front spirant or semivowel (also sometimes a voiceless back fricative).

Works Cited

Benson, Larry D. *Art and Tradition in Sir Gawain and the Green Knight*. New Brunswick NJ: Rutgers, 1965.

Borroff, Marie. *Sir Gawain and the Green Knight:A Stylistic and Metrical Study*. New Haven: Yale UP, 1962.

Cawley, A.C., ed. *Pearl, Sir Gawain, and the Green Knight*. London: Dent, 1962.

Cottle, Basil. *The Triumph of English, 1350-1400*. London: Blanford, 1969.

Davis, Norman. Ed. *Sir Gawain and the Green Knight*. Ed. J. R. R. Tolkien, and E.V. Gordon. 2nd ed. Oxford: Clarendon Press, 1967.

Everett, Dorothy. "The Alliterative Revival." *Twentieth Century Interpretations of Sir Gawain and the Green Knight*. Ed. Denton Fox. Englewood-Cliffs: Prentice-Hall, 1968.

Gardner, John. *The Complete Works of the Gawain-Poet*. Chicago: Chicago UP, 1965.

Herbert, George. *Works*. Hertfordshire: Wordsworth, 1994.

Knight, Stephen. *Rymyng Craftily: Meaning in Chaucer's Poetry*. Atlantic Highlands: Humanities, 1976.

Patrick, J. Max, ed. *The Complete Poetry of Robert Herrick*. Norton: New York NY, 1968.

Raffel, Burton, trans. *Miguel de Cervantes: Don Quijote*. New York NY: Norton, 1995.

---. *From Stress to Stress: An Autobiography of English Prosody*. Hamden: Archon, 1992.

---. trans. *François Rabelais: Gargantua and Pantagruel*. New York NY: Norton, 1990.

---. trans. *Sir Gawain and the Green Knight*. New York NY: Mentor, 1970.

Robinson, F.N., ed. *The Works of Geoffrey Chaucer*. 2nd ed. Boston: Houghton, 1961.

Stageberg, Norman C. *An Introductory English Grammar*. 2nd ed. New York NY: Holt, 1971.

Waldron, R.A., ed. *Sir Gawain and the Green Knight*. London: Arnold, 1970.

I To Henry de Mesmes: A Horoscope

Jean Dorat

The ghastly pang of dreaded dropsy
within an invalid's belly tears
with no worse force; the exotic goddess,
Cybélé, bangs the drum she bears
    with no worse racket than what we heard
    from my own Marguerite . . . My word!

Her belly stretched and wracked with the pains
of labor, she cries out at the top
of her voice to all the saints in heaven
imploring that her suffering stop,
    but most of all to her name saint --
    to Marguerite -- she makes complaint.

To you she calls out, and calls again,
to come, as Lucina used to do
in pagan times to accouchements,
in her time of need and get her through
    this trial, and the saint complies, and the mother
    is suddenly quiet -- but there is another

fainter cry -- of the newborn babe
announcing itself to a world that knows --
as any father does -- those tears
the child sheds in advance of the blows
    it must receive from a life on earth.
    Am I wrong, perhaps? At this baby's birth

are the omens otherwise? Do I dare
dream for my daughter a better fate
than most of us face? There are some signs
by which one might prognosticate
    in a more optimistic mode. I see
    the infant the midwife holds out to me,

bright red, still wet from the birth canal,
odd-looking as newborns are, and my heart
leaps up to behold this sudden increase
in my house and fortunes. And on her part,
    the mother is fine. She is smiling and
    Henry de Mesmes has offered to stand

godfather! The glory of his noble
house, he will be for her what the King
of Navarre was for him when he was born.
Holding her in his arms, he will bring
    blessings, luck, or call it grace,
    intelligence, charm, and a handsome face.

At every step of your life's way
from that beginning, you have known
kindness and warm welcomes. Princes
smile as you approach the throne.
    You have found all men to be polite,
    to you -- who assumed it was your right

to be treated well, and the world complied.
Royalty out of a fairy tale
were your companions in a real life
beside which children's stories pale.
You were at ease with them, and they,
beside which children's stories pale.
    You were at ease with them, and they,
    delighted, treated you the way

you clearly deserved. That puissant king,
when he took you in his hands, put by
the scepter they were accustomed to.
He crooned to you to hush your cry,
    while the Holy Spirit's whisper came
    to inspire as men spoke your name.

When Jupiter endowed his child
Apollo with godly powers, he
apeared in diminished glory, lest
with all his usual panoply
    he frighten the boy. And now you bring
    such favors to me as that great king

bestowed on you. Thrice happy, I
am grateful to you as you do
us honor, passing on that light
your benefactor shone on you --
  such graces as must gratify
  the most demanding parent's eye.

On her delicate cheek, Lucina has put
that mark of lovely gentleness
we love in little girls, but I
shall educate her, nonetheless,
  and she shall have in hand, instead
  of the sewing basket's needle and thread,

Apollo's lyre and she shall learn
to pluck from its strings a tune to lift
our spirits as they resonate.
Sappho of Lesbos had that gift.
  She is said, I know, to have been depraved;
  my child, I trust, will be better behaved,

but like her, my daughter shall learn to weave
in words instead of wool such fine
fabrications as make mankind
suppose Latona bore divine
  triplets: Diana, Apollo, and then,
  if less well known, my Madeleine

in whom all Cynthius' qualities
and Cynthia's combine in splendor
of such degree as to surpass
our expectations of her gender,
  excelling in her father's art,
  the apple of his eye and heart.

I pray the fates be kind to her,
and give her health and happiness
so that one day she may join with me
in song and may herself address
  her odes (I shall delight in them)
  to you, my dear M. de Mesmes.

Translated from French by David Slavitt

The French Myth of Narcissus: Some Medieval Refashionings

Gerald Seaman

For a boy without a lover, Narcissus has had a history of strange bed-fellows. Earlier this century, Freud diagnosed Narcissism as a condition of perverts and homosexuals (45) while, more recently, medieval schol-ars like Frederick Goldin called Narcissus the paradigm of courtly man (212). As an emblem of the human condition, therefore, Ovid's fair boy could be either our spleen or our ideal. Debased or dignified, healthy or ill, aspiring toward greatness or falling from grace, Narcissus, for his various readers, could be said to typify contrary human impulses toward madness or perfection. In medieval French literature, however, Narcissus has been deployed both as a character type and as a protagonist in what were ostensibly exemplary, but cautionary, contexts. In this respect, Ovid's original character has shown himself to be impressively malleable and enduring. The subject of Old French narrative refashionings from the twelfth through the fifteenth centuries, Narcissus appeared in such works as the *Narcisus*, Robert de Blois' *Floris et Liriope*, the *Ovide Moralisé*, and the *Jeu de Narcisse*. As I will argue here, with particular emphasis on the *Narcisus* and *Floris et Liriope*, each of these reinter-pretations of Ovid denoted an attempt to uncover the moral significance of the Narcissus character and thus to edify the reader. Medieval proces-ses of narrative invention provided some basic tools in the refashioning process and at the same time affected the outcome and message of these individual texts. For this reason, modes of literary invention are an im-portant component of our discussion. Combined with an analysis of the paratextual support that each medieval author generated for his tale, an understanding of these modes as gestures of narrative appropriation, as-similation, transformation, and production, therefore, will help us to assess the success or failure of these didactic projects. In this connection, the following questions will provide a backdrop to our inquiry: Did these tales partake of a conservative discursive practice that simply repeated the tragedy of Ovid's Narcissus? If so, what did this repetition mean? How should we interpret it? Were any new morals or new ideas generated? Or, was Narcissus simply used as a foil for the author's narrative practices and social concerns?

Is There A Moral To This Story?

In its narrative structure (i.e. the exposition and reasonably faithful translation of discrete elements of the *Metamorphoses* followed by extensive gloss) the fourteenth-century *Ovide Moralisé* gives every evidence of the quintessentially medieval effort to discover not just an allegorical significance in Ovid, but also moral examples, and even religious truths. Indeed, in its method of translation and interpretation, the *Ovide Moralisé* shifts alternatively between the historical level of the text (as it is represented by the Old French translation) and its allegorical, tropological, and anagogical levels (given in the gloss). This is generally indicative of a common method of reading Ovid in the Middle Ages. Concerning Narcissus in particular, Vinge's study points out that allegorical and symbolic interpretations were already being offered in the twelfth century by thinkers such as John of Salisbury, Arnolphe d'Orléans and Alexander Neckam (72-76). Among the shared points of reference in the extensive tradition of medieval Ovidian exegesis, there was a typical (and not surprising) understanding that the life of Narcissus furnished the reader with a powerful statement either against worldly vanity, individual arrogance, or excessive pride. By contrast, Boccaccio's *Genealogia Deorum* (used by Chaucer and others) was an exceptional case where the author limited himself to a personal allegory and thus avoided any religious interpretation of the text, glossing Narcissus and Echo positively as figures of perduring reputation (Vinge 102-104).

It is obvious, then, that the *perception of a moral* guided and perhaps inspired medieval French readings and rewritings of Ovid's tale of Narcissus. Whether a moral was ever intended by Ovid, and what it might have been, are more difficult questions that merit a pause for conjecture. Following Eitrem, Goldin has shown that, in classical and preclassical times, "Narcissus was conceived as the anti-Eros, whom the God of Love had to destroy as his enemy and the greatest danger to the continuation of life" (42). To the extent that his death removed obstacles to reciprocal love and the habits of procreation, Narcissus might therefore have been a necessary foundational character in Ovid's personalized vision of history, love, and the course of human affairs. With respect to the medieval reception of the text, Goldin has argued that Narcissus' fate furnished courtly lovers with a model transformational moment. Particularly in courtly lyric, Goldin discovered Narcissus as an exemplary character whose tragic demise was meant to persuade all lovers to spare themselves a similar fate (27). Not merely a negative exemplum, however, Narcissus offered all those who heeded his message the promise of "the birth of self-consciousness through love" (22) and a subsequent release from "the terror of self-admiration" (58). In other words, confronting the life and fate of Narcissus was perceived by Goldin as a necessary stage in the evolution of the perfect courtly lover. Before there could be devotion and deference to the inaccessible and ideal lady, the obstacle of self-love had first to be recognized and subsequently overcome. From there, courtly self-consciousness could develop and the lover could direct his affection to his chosen lady.

One realizes, of course, that medieval efforts to create an exemplary character were bound by processes of narrative invention that intentionally altered, embellished, abbreviated and amplified their original materials. In reference to John of Garland, the seminal work of Douglas Kelly has elucidated the essential elements of such invention, some of which warrant citation: "The author in quest of suitable *materia* 'materiam queret, quesitam inveniet, inventam ordinabit, ordinatam exornabit, exornatam in publicam proponet et in lucem' (seeks matter, finds what he seeks, arranges what he finds, embellishes what he arranges, and publishes what he has embellished)" (36). It is important to note here that, in essence, the search for material for invention could imply an elementary segmentation of an original author or text, a segmentation which would then be transformed into the medieval author's own *materia*. Once placed in the service of the author's designs, moreover, this segment would become the vehicle for a new *figura* and the source of a new ethical truth. Both of these latter elements necessarily emerged from the medieval author's balance of *intentio* and *materia* (see Kelly 32-67), a fact which places subsequent interpreters in an unenviable position. For, inasmuch as one attempts to find a moral in the medieval variations of the Narcissus story, one also contributes (and this must be acknowledged outright) to the potential erasure of any lesson Ovid might have himself intended.

In the early literary production of the French Middle Ages, Narcissus was frequently deployed as a cameo foil for conventional descriptions of beauty or, predictably, for stock depictions of excessive pride. Thanks to Kelly's research, we know that these attributes (beauty, pride, and others like them) are what Matthew of Vendôme would have called *colores operum*, or characteristic qualities. Through them, an author could incorporate character "types" into his narrative style by deploying proper names (such as Narcissus) in a topical and illustrative manner, without necessarily using them to refer to particular, historical, personages (Kelly 52-56). For example, in his second romance, Chrétien de Troyes chose Narcissus as a point of reference for the perfect beauty of his eponymous hero, Cligés:

Por la biauté Clygés retreire	To relate the beauty of Cligés
Vuel une description feire,	I wish to make a description
Don molt sera bries li passages.	Whose length shall be very brief.
En la flor estoit ses aages,	He was in the flower of his youth
Car ja avoit prés de quinze ans;	For he was nearly 15 years old;
Mes tant ert biax et avenanz	And he was as handsome and arousing
Que Narcissus, qui desoz l'orme	As Narcissus, who under the boughs
Vit an la fountainne sa forme,	Saw his shape in the fountain,
Si l'ama tant, si com an dit,	And loved himself so much, as they say,
Qu'il an fu morz, quant il la vit,	That he died when he saw his form,
Por tant qu'il ne la pot avoir.	And despite everything he could not possess it.
Molt ot biauté et po savoir,	He was very beautiful, though not very wise
Mes Clygés en ot plus grant masse,	But the wealth of Cligés' wisdom surpasses his
Tant con li ors le cuivre passe	Like the weight of gold surpasses copper
Et plus que je ne di encor	And much more than I choose to say.
(vv. 2721-2735)	(All translations in this essay are my own).

As has been remarked by critics such as Alice Colby (115-16), this passage is noteworthy for its abrupt shift from praise to blame, but one also senses here an almost triumphant evocation of type on Chrétien's part. Indeed, in a description that is laconic by most narrative standards, medieval and otherwise, Chrétien elides Cligés and Narcissus in body but divorces them in spirit. As a character who "Molt ot biauté et po savoir" (v. 2732), Narcissus thus assumes the operative role in Chrétien's text of a beautiful fool, an image of physical perfection covering a profound spiritual defect. Played off against the Narcissus type, therefore, Cligés is quickly and effectively illustrated for the reader as a knight who embodies a kind of celebrated beauty that is redeemed by knowledge and virtue.

Though effective, the use of Narcissus as a readily recognizable figure of consummate masculine beauty was not widespread in early medieval French romance. In fact, in the courtly tradition, Narcissus as type has most commonly been treated by scholars like Goldin "as an analogue to the courtly lover" who could not "attain what he most desires (the Lady)" (Hult 263). This certainly was the case in Benoît de Sainte-Maure's *Roman de Troie* where Achilles (Achille) equated his suffering for the love of Polyxène to the suffering of Narcissus:

Narcisus sui, ce sai e vei	I am Narcissus, this I know and can see
qui tant ama l'umbre de sei	Who so loved his own shadow

qu'il en morut sor la funteine.	That he died at the fountain.
Iceste angoisse, iceste peine	This same anguish, this same pain
sai que je sent: je raim mon onbre,	I know that I feel it; I love my shadow
je aim ma mort e mon enconbre	I love my own death and my obstacle
(vv.17691-17696)	

Tiels iert ma fins, que que il tart,	Thus will I die, sooner or later
car je n'i vei nul autre esgart.	For I see no other way
Narcisus por amor mori,	Narcissus died for love
e je refarai autresi	And so I shall repeat the same.
(vv. 17707-17710)	

For Benoît and his audience, Narcissus was most definitely a ready-made cultural icon of the tragedy of love, one that emphasized the deadly synergy of the lover's desire, his pain and anguish, and his beloved's inaccessibility. As the superlative expression of this synergy, however, Narcissus also emblematized a fate that was powerful enough to transform Achilles from ruthless fighter (the assassin of Hector) to helpless lover (the suitor of Hector's sister). As the quintessentially thwarted lover, then, the Narcissus type in the *Roman de Troie* served in some important ways to provoke empathy for a kind of heroic emotional experience, one whose ultimate issue and expression could possibly have been the death of Achilles. Contrary to the depiction in Chrétien de Troyes' *Cligés*, therefore, the Narcissus type in Benoît's romance was not foolish at all. Indeed, his character was illustrious rather than defective; he was for Achilles the faultless symbol of love in its most powerful form.

In depicting Narcissus as a character type, Chrétien and Benoît, though they differed in narrative emphasis, did not stray far from the original Ovidian material. Roughly contemporary to *Cligés* and the *Roman de Troie*, however, the first full-length narrative rewriting of Ovid's tale in Old French (the *Narcisus*) abandoned such use of cameo types and significantly remodeled Narcissus. This remodeling occurred throughout the 1010-verse text and was obviously the result of a process of narrative embellishment and amplification (Ovid's original is 174 verses) whose global intent was to adapt the Narcissus character to medieval realities (by making him a twelfth-century aspirant to knighthood, for example). As Martine Thiry-Stassin has pointed out, moreover, this remodeling may have also resulted in part from the author's use of a combination of Ovidian sources for the *materia* for his work. (There is in fact no other credible way to account for the author's decision to place Dane [Daphne] in the position of Echo). Nonetheless, for our purposes, the most significant refashioning of the Narcissus tale was expressed in the paratextual support of the *Narcisus*. In the prologue especially, the author, drawing on rhetorical tradition dating from Cicero and Quintillian, clearly announced his own peculiar didactic project and in so doing challenged his readers to assess the moral implications of Narcissus' actions. In such wise, he transformed his narrative into a cautionary tale for medieval lovers and effectively severed his own story from Ovid's original:

Mais neporquant quant il [a]vient	For nevertheless it comes to pass
Ke cil qui fole amore maintient	That when a man persists in mad love
[En est sorpris et bien destroiz]	He is alienated and destroyed by it
En est il bien raisons et drois	Thus is it reasonable and right
que cele en oie sa proiiere	That the woman hear his supplications
Ne ne soit pas vers li trop fiere,	And not be too proud toward him
Ke tost en poeut avoir damage	For she herself could soon suffer
Par son orgeul, par son outraige	From her pride and her offensiveness.
(vv. 17-24).	

The reverse correlative of this rejection was also possible:

Et s'il avient que fenme prit	And if it happens that a woman in love
Qui que il soit qui l'escondit	Is rejected by whomsoever she loves
Je voel et di sans entreprendre	I say and affirm without hesitation
Que on le doit ardoir u pendre	That he should be burned or hanged.
(vv. 29-32)	(All citations taken from Pelan and Spence)

That the Narcissus story could have a universal (i.e. masculine and feminine) application has been noted by David Hult in his work on the *Roman de la Rose* (288). Hult has also postulated that, because Narcissus could be viewed as a lady or a male lover, his character defies the standard courtly model (288). These are both provocative observations and, to the extent that they also apply to the *Narcisus*, they should significantly influence our investigation into the implied moral of these citations and of the Narcissus tale.

Let us therefore briefly consider the courtly model. Since the hypothesis of courtly love was first formulated by Gaston Paris, and later extended by C. S. Lewis, scholars have occasionally (and sometimes contentiously) debated the authenticity of its medieval origins and meaning. In response to critics of Paris, who have averred that he simply invented "amour courtois," Jean Frappier has argued that the term coined by Paris could just as easily be replaced by the incontestably medieval "fin amor" without diminishing the thesis of the nineteenth-century French master. Further, on this same question, there have been reasonably comprehensive and fair investigations made into the so-called twelfth-century "courts of love" and their main cast of characters (Eleanor of Aquitaine, Marie of Champagne, and Andreas Capellanus) by reputable scholars such as John W. Baldwin, John F. Benton, William W. Kibler, and June Hall Martin McCash. To judge these studies, I believe it safe to say that they have furnished us with enough evidence to contend that something akin to courtly love was indeed a genuine source of literary interest and cultural focus in medieval France. What remains open to question, however, is the extent to which courtly love can be used as a hermeneutic overlay for uncovering the ethical value of Narcissus' plight for the medieval French public.

To that end, it may be helpful to summarize Paris and Lewis briefly. To begin with, although they do not paint their discussions of courtly love with the same stroke, it should be noted that conspicuous to each of their discussions are the tenets of courtly love as first set forth by Paris (518-519). These tenets are: (i) courtly love is secret, risky, illegitimate, and adulterous; (ii) the status of the courtly lover is inferior to that of his beloved; (iii) the beloved lady has a capricious and somewhat disdainful nature; (iv) the lover (and the poet) idealizes the inaccessible courtly lady; and (v) the courtly lover serves the lady in a way that, in Lewis' terms, is "closely modeled on the service which a feudal vassal owes to his lord" (2). In addition, Lewis' neat enumeration of the characteristics of courtly love as Humility, Courtesy, Adultery, and what he calls the Religion of Love aptly demonstrates another of Gaston Paris' fundamental conclusions: that courtly love was a kind of virtue or set of virtues that animated and supported all other social virtues (Paris 522).

Narcissus was unquestionably disdainful and inaccessible to his suitors. They in turn certainly idealized him, and may have found him capricious. Adultery, the inferiority of the lover, and service after the feudal model, by contrast, played little or no part in Ovid's tale or in its medieval refashionings. One could of course argue that these missing pieces are relatively unimportant (especially when one considers the vital presence of inaccessibility and idealization), but this would be misguided. For, if one were to accept this argument, one would also be obliged to dissolve Lewis' dual virtues, Humility and Courtesy, a gesture that would be tantamount to dismantling the system of courtly love altogether. In fact, if courtly love were ever to be bereft of such crucial virtues as these, its ennobling impulse would be inevitably suppressed. That these virtues, however, are clearly absent from the twelfth-century *Narcisus* cannot be disputed. For this reason, logic compels us to concur with Hult and differ with Goldin on this delicate issue: as a paradigm of the medieval lover, Narcissus does not in fact support the courtly model.

To return to our analysis of the prologue of the *Narcisus*, it is evident that the author intended to present Narcissus to his public as a negative exemplum, that is, as a model of behavior that should not, under any circumstances, be emulated. In this context, it is significant that he made no reference to Narcissus' beauty, as did Chrétien, nor did he insist on the intensity and depth of his emotional suffering, as did Benoît. In fact, his didactic thrust was curiously focused on one single element from Ovid's text: the rejection of the lover by the beloved. Given that focus, one easily ascertains that this particular poet was attempting to reduce the whole of Ovid's story to a narrative of the perils of unrequited love. The *materia* may perhaps be suitable to such an *intentio*, but the resulting message bears no semblance to any ethical truth whatsoever. In lieu of any real lesson, we are offered then instead a twisted discourse on suffering. "Raison" and "drois" (v. 20) provided the author with an apparent justification for such suffering. But, to use such lofty categories as "reason" and "rectitude" as a means to justify an act so base as punishing ladies who do not oblige their suitors, is equivalent to voiding the didactic statement of any true moral significance. In the end, what the prologue offered ladies was not in fact justice, but rather persecution. In this connection, one might contend that this was indicative of that unique brand of misogyny prevalent in the Middle Ages. This contention may be partially valid, but one should not overlook the fact that the poet reserved for men a fate that was explicitly worse than the women's. Indeed, should they deny their ladies, men were threatened with burning at the stake or hanging: "Je voel et di sans entreprendre / Que on le doit ardoir u pendre" (vv. 31-32).

This insistence on punishing Narcissus as if he were a criminal is unique among all the medieval rewritings of this text that we have studied. Even the farcical *Jeu de Narcisse* (15th century) avoided taking such a stance, and the texts from the intervening centuries, including *Floris et Liriope* and the *Ovid Moralisé*, treated his death more symbolically than literally. Needless to say, the twelfth-century author's sentence was more than unusually harsh. In reality, one would expect these types of executions (hangings, burnings at the stake) to be reserved for heretics, traitors, murderers, or other violent offenders, but not for Narcissus or any other lover who did not requite the love of his or her suitor. As a principle of right conduct, then, it would of course be absurd to maintain that all lovers, men and women alike, should be able to possess the objects of their affection. Moreover, it would be equally absurd, in fact perverse, to exhort all men and women *to yield* to their suitors. It is more than reasonable to conclude, therefore, that, despite its expressed didactic intent, the twelfth-century *Narcisus* contains absolutely no moral resolution. Far from being an edifying tale, this text amounts in the end to little more than a veil for repressive social practices.

Punishing Pride and Beauty: The Strange Case of *Floris and Liriope*

In the thirteenth-century, Guillaume de Lorris, in his *Roman de la Rose*, repeated the repressive rhetoric of the *Narcisus* in the gloss to his own Narcissus story:

Dames, cest essample aprenez,	Ladies, learn by this example,
qui vers vos amis mesprenez;	You who mistreat your lovers;
car se vos les lessiez morir,	For if you leave them to die,
Dex le vos savra bien merir	God will certainly punish you for it.
(vv. 1505-1508)	

That "this tale is meant to point to the ladies in the audience" (Hult 273) is true beyond any doubt, and this observation greatly buttresses the claim that the life of Narcissus in the Middle Ages had applications that crossed gender lines. One particularly intriguing and illuminating case occurred in Robert de *Blois' Floris et Liriope*. As its title suggests, this curious text was as much concerned with elucidating the moral implications of Narcissus's fate as it was with tracing the origin of his flaws to the members of his family. This is indicative of what R. Howard Bloch would call the poet's "genealogical consciousness" (*Etymologies* 80) and it also demonstrates a parallel between lineage and etymological grammar. Using what Bloch calls "a common representational model" and "similar set of representational practices" (*Etymologies* 83), Robert's narrative thus sought to establish the historical and cultural meaning of Narcissus by founding his behavior in the invented, mythic and pseudo-historical past of his ancestors (see *Etymologies* 80-81).

In his genealogical operation, Robert began by creating a prestigious lineage for Narcissus wherein the memory of illustrious ancestors served as the guiding principle of invention. Thus, in the description of Narcissus' newly invented, and still living, grandfather, an entire history of noble accomplishments could be realized and continued:

Mout fut proisiez et renomez	He was greatly praised and renowned
De largesse, de cortesie,	For his generosity, courtesy,
De biautei, de cheualerie.	Beauty, and chivalry.
Preudome furent sui ancestre,	His ancestors were brave men
Et il ne pout plus vaillans estre;	And there were none more worthy;
Et tant estoit cortois de cuer,	He was so gentle hearted

Que il ne vousist a nul fuer	That he would never for any reason
Avoir chose dite ne faite	Have said or done a thing
Q'en vilonie fust retraite	That might be construed as ill-bred
(vv. 106 - 114)	

In this short excerpt (the actual description approaches 50 verses in length), we clearly have an arch description of the perfect and timeless courtly lord. In terms of narrative invention, its "syntagmatic multiplication of attributes" (Kelly 56) is remarkable for its fidelity to Matthew of Vendôme's prescription for interpretatio / expolitio, or "elaboration by repetitive or incremental statement" (Kelly 56). This grandfather was indeed a good man in every sense, in body, mind, soul and reputation. He was, moreover, successful in all things; he was the lord of Thebes and, although he married late, he was the father of a beautiful daughter (vv.161-174).

It is somewhat shocking, then, to discover that this man was actually named Narcissus, but such an onomastic choice is not inconsistent with what Bloch has discovered about genealogical consciousness. It is also not inconsistent with Chrétien de Troyes' acknowledgment of Narcissus' beauty, nor with Benoît de Sainte-Maure's judgment that the life of Narcissus expressed a depth and intensity of feeling that bordered on the heroic. What the grandfather's name and his excellent pedigree suggest to us, in fact, is that Narcissus the grandson -- because of his beauty, because of his emotional experience, and because of his lineage -- *should have been* an exemplary medieval knight, lover, lord, and husband, in the poet's estimation. That he did not become any of these things, however, was primarily a function of an intervening tragedy of his genealogy. In fact, Narcissus' mother was to blame.

According to Robert de Blois, then, Narcissus (the grandson) was a second-generation defective lover whose death marked the ultimate stage in the disintegration and dissolution of his grandfather's prestigious feudal family. The family's decline had already begun with the birth of Narcissus' mother, Liriope. Born to beauty unsurpassed (vv. 184-258), she had hair blonder than Ysolde's (vv. 221-223) and was eloquent and well learned (vv. 260-268). She was proud, however, and lacked the virtue of humility (vv. 269-284). Most significantly, she was a living model of the behavior that would bring her family to ruin and eventually cost Narcissus his life:

Si fu ele souent requise	Thus, she was often asked
De toz les millors a devise	By the very best of men
Et d'amor et de mariaige;	For her love and for her hand;

Mais tant par avoit fier coraige,	But she had such a proud heart
Qu'ele cuida ke nuns ne fust	That she did not find a single one of them
Si vailans, qu'auoir la deust.	Worthy enough to have her.
En sa biautei tant ce fia,	She placed so much trust in her beauty
Que touz chevelaiers mesprisa	That she disdained all knights.
(vv. 293 - 300)	

Within the context of the continuity of the dynastic family, Liriope clearly recalls the image of the Narcissus from remote classical and preclassical times with which this paper began. Enemy of Eros and a threat to the continuation of life, she, like the original Narcissus, was the dangerous and threatening product of coupling beauty with pride. Robert was explicit about confronting this threat in his prologue to the *Floris et Liriope* and, as we shall see, his response to Liriope's refusal to take a husband and produce an heir led him to a strange and startling resolution:

Or m'estuet de biautei parler,	Now must I speak about beauty
Que blamer la wel et louer;	Which I should like to praise and blame;
De l'un et de l'autre dirai	I will speak to one and all
Raison selonc ce ke i'en sai;	The truth as I know it
L'orgeul we ie sanz espargnier	I wish not to spare pride
Forment blamer por chastoier	But to blame and chastise it as well.
(vv. 1 - 6)	

In addition to its subtle links to the classical and pre-classical Narcissus, the general textual attack on beauty and pride may also contain distant echoes of early Christian theology. In this connection, Bloch has shown that the first-century Church fathers "were obsessed by the relation of women to decoration. They were fascinated by veils, makeup, hairstyle, and hair color -- in short, by anything having to do with the cosmetic" (*Misogyny* 39). Women, in fact, were "conceived as ornament" and thus irrevocably "associated with artifice and decoration" (*Misogyny* 40). Similarly, Alan of Lille, in his *Plaint of Nature*, associated the sin of pride with "womanish adornments" (187) and condemned the futility of such ornamentation because life was "the matter of a moment" (187). Robert de Blois echoed Alan on this point when he asked in his prologue, "De sa biautei ke remanroit?" (v. 37), and the *Ovide Moralisé* gave added emphasis to the ephemeral nature of beauty when it transformed the looks of fair Narcissus into a "samblance laide et hideuse" (v. 1832) that, after his death, was reflected in the black and shadowy waters of hell. Robert likewise illustrated beauty as a deceptive mask, claiming

La biautez cuevre la puor,	Beauty masks what is rotten
Mais ades est li pardesous	And its underside is always

Et lais et puans et hidous.	Ugly, foul, and hideous.
Ensi est biautez orguillouse,	Thus is beauty supercilious
Defors apert mout sauerouse,	It appears delightful on the outside
Mais par dedens l'ordure gist	But within waste lies in wait
Qui la biautei trop evellist	Which is veiled over by beauty.
(vv. 94-100)	

Such imagery of beauty covering rotten flesh was common to the perspectives on women that Bloch discovered in his work on the origins of medieval misogyny. Indeed, because it helps us to establish an illuminating parallel, one of Bloch's citations of Chrysostom on women bears full citation in this context: "'For the groundwork of this corporeal beauty,' Chrysostom writes, 'is nothing else but phlegm, and blood, and humor, and bile, and the fluid of masticated food'" (*Misogyny* 27). From this perspective, one could easily concur with Bloch that women in general were viewed as embodying "the material corruption of the flesh" (*Misogyny* 27) and for that reason were subject to persecution based in large part on nothing more than gender.

If beauty and pride constituted crimes against God for the early Christian fathers, they also contributed, in the *Floris et Liriope*, to defining the figure of Narcissus as a crime against nature, an emblem of forbidden homoerotic love. In Robert's poem, as in Ovid's tale, the end of Narcissus' life was marked by the arousal of his desire for what he believed to be the apparition of a beautiful young boy in the waters of the fountain. Consistent with the genealogical consciousness of the *Floris et Liriope*, however, the fate of Narcissus was as much a function of his own desire as it was the logical outcome of his sad family history. In this sense, the text that precedes the death of Liriope's son can be read as a persecution of his mother for her choice not to marry and also as an additional indictment of her peculiar sexual practices. As Duby has shown, the ritual and custom of marriage "inserted procreation into an order of things" (6) and "regulated the sexual impulses" of medieval society "in the interest of a patrimony" (7). Liriope's sexual impulses, as we shall see, were certainly not intentionally directed toward the interest of any patrimony. Worse, as Robert's text makes perfectly clear, they were irregular and against the "order of things."

Although the work of William Burgwinkle has shown that "the intermixing of male and female and homo- and hetero-sexuality was far more prevalent" (5) in the Middle Ages than it is in our times, it would still be accurate to say that Liriope displayed what we would call lesbian tendencies. Though she obviously conceived (out of wedlock) the boy

Narcissus with the man Floris, Liriope had her own erotic desire initially aroused by a person she assumed to be Floris' sister, Florie (who was actually Floris himself, in drag). As Robert's text further indicates, when Liriope first began having amorous (but not sexual) relations with the transvestite Floris, she in fact had no idea that her lover was truly a man. As she herself said to her presumed girlfriend, Liriope could never have even imagined feeling the same kind of love for a man:

Onkes mais nen oi noueles,
Que tant s'amaissant .II. puceles;
Mais n'ameroie tant, ce croi,
Nul home tant com ie fas toi,
Ne tant, ce cuit, ne me plairoit
Li baisers, s'uns hons me baisoit
(vv. 1003-1008)

I have never heard news
Of two girls who loved each other so much;
I believe that I would never love
Any man the way that I love you
Nor do I believe that kisses would please me as much
If I received them from a man.

Rather than provide any form of resolution to the narrative and conceptual conundrum of a man in drag copulating (and consequently procreating) with a lesbian woman, Robert added an ellipses to his text at this point ("Del sorplus riens ne vos dirai, / Car nule veritei n'en sai," vv. 1043-44) and thereby deferred judgment to the end of his tale where the traditional death of Narcissus was reenacted. If our hypothesis about the genealogical consciousness of the author is correct, and this death can be explained in terms of the boy's defective lineage, then Robert had clearly innovated on previous medieval French depictions of the Narcissus story. Like the twelfth-century *Narcisus*, however, his reinterpretation of Narcisus' fate and behavior was unspeakably cruel. To support this contention, it should suffice to point out that Robert's reinvention of Ovid's original tale culminated in an act of retributive justice against the boy's parents and family, one which, from the perspective of the poet and his public, was not only necessary but also abundantly deserved:

Dolans pere, chaitiue mere,
Com ceste mors vos iert amere!
Apres ce ke sa mort savrez,
A nul ior mai ioie n'avres.
Mors est; ensi perdi la vie,
Par orgoil l'ai ensi fenie.
He, orguez, honis soies tu!
Maint mal sont par toi avenu.
(vv. 1741-1748)

Sad father, sorrowful mother
How this death must be bitter for you!
Once you have learned of his death
You will never have joy again
He is dead; and lost his life
Through pride, which did him in.
Hey, proud one, shame on you!
For much that is evil comes from you.

In the end, the use of Narcissus as a foil for punishing pride and beauty in the *Floris et Liriope* reflected two prevalent medieval cultural realities associated with feudal genealogy and sexuality: First, the compelling necessity of marriage and procreation to dynastic succession and continuity made any narcissistic refusal a kind of impermissible violation of the future. Second, the official and unofficial interdictions against homosexuality, as expressed either by the Church (in the Third Lateran Council, for example) or by thinkers such as Alan of Lille (whose *Plaint of Nature* was predicated on the eradication of homosexuality), turned even the solitary moment of homoerotic insight into a potentially criminal act, one which neither God nor nature could abide. By refashioning Ovid's play of reflection and reflexivity into a thin allegory of the confusion of gender identities and the perversion of sexual roles, Robert de Blois' *Floris et Liriope* therefore transformed what was a rich mythical narrative into a mundane discourse of persecution with dubious moral significance.

University of Evansville

Works Cited

Alan of Lille. *The Plaint of Nature*. Trans. James J. Sheridan. Toronto: Pontifical Institute of Mediaeval Studies, 1980.

Baldwin, James W. *The Language of Sex Five Voices from Northern France around 1200*. Chicago: Chicago UP, 1994.

Benton, John F. "The Court of Champagne as a Literary Center." *Speculum* 36.4 (October 1961): 551-91.

Bloch, R. Howard. *Medieval Misogyny and the Invention of Western Romantic Love*. Chicago: U of Chicago P, 1991.

---. *Etymologies and Genealogies: A Literary Anthropology of the French Middle Ages*. Chicago: U of Chicago P, 1983.

Burgwinkle, William. "Knighting the Classical Hero: Homo/Hetero Affectivity in *Eneas*." *Exemplaria* 5.1 (1993): 1-43.

Chrétien de Troyes. *Cligés*. Ed. Alexandre Micha. Paris: Champion, 1982.

Colby, Alice M. *The Portrait in Twelfth-Century French Literature: An Example of the Stylistic Originality of Chrétien de Troyes*. Genève: Droz, 1965.

Das mittelfranzösische Narcissusspiel (L'istoire de Narcisus et de Echo). Ed. Alfons Hilka. *Zeitschrift für Romanische Philologie* 56 (1936): 275-321.

Duby, Georges. *Medieval Marriage: Two Models from Twelfth-Century France*. Trans. Elborg Forster. Baltimore and London: John Hopkins UP, 1978.

Frappier, Jean. "Sur un procès fait à l'amour courtois." *Romania* 93 (1972): 145-93.

Freud, Sigmund. "On Narcissism: An Introduction." Trans. Joan Riviere. *Collected Papers 4*. New York: Basic Books, 1959.

Goldin, Frederick. *The Mirror of Narcissus in the Courtly Love Lyric.* Ithaca: Cornell UP, 1967.

Guillaume de Lorris. *Le Roman de la Rose.* Ed. Félix Lecoy. Paris: Champion, 1973.

Hult, David F. *Self-Fulfilling Prophecies: Readership and Authority in the first "Roman de la Rose."* Cambridge: Cambridge UP, 1986.

Kelly, Douglas. *The Art of Medieval French Romance.* Madison: U of Wisconsin P, 1992.

Kibler, William W., ed. *Eleanor of Aquitaine.* Austin and London: U of Texas P, 1976.

Lewis, C.S. *The Allegory of Love.* New York: Oxford UP, 1958.

Martin McCash, June Hall. "Marie de Champagne and Eleanor of Aquitaine: A Relationship Reexamined." *Speculum* 54.4 (1979): 698-711.

Narcisse: Conte ovidien français du XIIe siècle. Edd. Martine Thiry-Stassin and Madeleine Tyssens. Paris: Belles Lettres, 1976.

Narcisus (poème du XIIème siècle). Edd. M.M. Pelan and N.C.W. Spence. Paris: Belles Lettres, 1964.

Ovid. *Metamorphoses.* Trans. Frank Justus Miller. Third edition, revised by G.P. Goold. Loeb Classical Library 42. Cambridge: Harvard UP, 1984.

Ovide Moralisé: Poème du commencement du quatorizième siècle. Ed. C. de Boer. Wiesbaden: Martin Sändig, 1966.

Paris, Gaston. "Etudes sur les romans de la Table Ronde: Lancelot du Lac. II. *Le Conte de la Charrette.*" *Romania* 12 (1883): 459-534.

Robert de Blois. *Floris et Liriope.* Ed. Wolfram v. Zingerle. Wiesbaden: Martin Sändig, 1968.

Le Roman de Troie de Benoît de Sainte-Maure. Ed. Emmanuèle Baumgartner. Paris: Union Générale d'Editions, 1987.

Thiry-Stassin, Martine. "Une autre source ovidienne du Narcisse?" *Le Moyen Age* 84 (1978): 211-26.

Vinge, Louise. *The Narcissus Theme in Western European Literature up to the Early 19th Century.* Trans. Robert Dewsnap et al. Lund: Gleerups, 1967.

Saving the Market: Textual Strategies and Cultural Transformations in Fifteenth-Century Translations of the Benedictine Rule for Women

Nancy B. Warren

In the debate over Biblical translation, which raged in the early years of the fifteenth century, the anti-translation faction argued:

> translation into the mother tongue will allow any old women (*vetula*) to usurp the office of teacher, which is forbidden to them (since all heresies, according to Jerome, come from women); it will bring about a world in which the laity prefers to teach than to learn, in which women (*mulierculae*) talk philosophy and dare to instruct men. (Watson 843)[1]

This dire prediction highlights ecclesiastical authorities' anxieties about the impact of the vernacular and the influence of women in religion in later medieval England. The clergy historically enjoyed a virtual mono-poly on sacred knowledge since they had the greatest access to Latin learn-\ing and Latin sacred texts. As the envisioned social consequences of vernacular translation reveal, the clergy feared encroachments on their privileged territory by lay people, especially by women. Susan Signe Morrison observes, "Since the learning of Latin constituted the entry into an exclusive male realm, separate from the lower-status female home, any attempt to translate and disseminate information from Latin would be seen by educated men as potentially threatening" (Morrison 102).

Translation is a process which "changes an existing boundary" (Ellis 3), and by undermining the foundations of the clergy's authority -- that is, their position as sole possessors and interpreters of Latin sacred texts -- translation shifted boundaries delimiting hierarchies. As a result, the clergy's privileged access to cultural and material resources, which followed from their monopoly on spiritual knowledge, was threatened. The socially-transformative properties of translation put the English clergy in the position of having to, in Pierre Bourdieu's terms, "save the market."[2] Translation appeared, from a clerical perspective, as the source of diverse dangers, and so the struggle to preserve all the conditions of the social field which afforded the clergy the greatest access to symbolic and material capital likewise focused on translation.[3]

One market-saving strategy was Arundel's Constitutions of 1407-1409, which sought to control the spread of the vernacular, and the social disruption perceived as accompanying it, by requiring episcopal authorization of all translations of texts containing scripture. The requirement of episcopal authorization of translations attempts, by means of the vernacular itself, to replace boundaries displaced by the spread of the vernacular. Translation becomes a vehicle to assert clerical authority rather than a threat to that authority. Osbern Bokenham's *Mappula Angliae*, a fifteenth-century translation of Ralph Higdon's *Polychronicon*, exhibits a different strategy. In what he calls a "shorte epiloge excusatorie," Bokenham writes:

> þys seyde tretis be not so convenyently nor so eloquently expressid & spokyn yn englyssh tounnge as þe excellence of þe auctours latyn stile requirithe. For, certenly þe natyff rudnesse of my modur-tounnge hathe so infectyd & cankeryd my speche & my language wyt þe barbarisme of þe soyle þe wych I haue be fostryd & brought forthe yn of youthe.... (qtd. in Serjeantson xvi)

The Austin friar Bokenham's association of the "englysshe tounnge" with the feminine, and with the accompanying qualities of inadequacy and contamination, works to reinstate hierarchical relationships -- that of superior, masculine Latin and inferior, feminine vernacular, and, by extension, that of male, clerical authorities and female, lay subjects. To "save the market" and their position in it, clerics engaged in textual strategies like those of both Arundel and Bokenham. In other words, the clergy used the mother tongue for their own benefit, manipulating transation, the source of instability, to recuperate the vernacular for the status quo. Simultaneously, they devalued the mother tongue, marking it (and those who speak it) as inferior.

Ecclesiastical authorities' textual, market-saving strategies are of particular interest in relation to women religious because literate culture expanded among non-noble women in the fifteenth century (Bartlett 13), and nuns were in one of the best situations available to women for gaining literacy skills. The Latin literacy of later medieval nuns has been generally considered lacking; however, vernacular literacy was another story altogether. Financial accounts and court records indicate nuns' act-

ive participation in business affairs which would have required significant literacy skills.[4] As women religious achieved levels of pragmatic
and professional literacy, "their social visibility and power" increased
(Bartlett 17). Presumably, their potential as a source of disruption also
increased from a clerical point of view.[5]

Burgeoning vernacular literacy among women religious was clearly
not the only vernacular literacy which posed a problem in the eyes of
clerical authorities. In fact, the vernacular literacy of nuns may have been
somewhat less a source of ecclesiastical anxiety than the vernacular literacy of secular women (as in the case of Lollard women) and of rebellious
lay men, since women religious were, at least theoretically, cloistered and
less able to make trouble. The Church's already conflicted attitude toward
female spirituality, though, made ecclesiastical authorities ever vigilant,
as the *Northern Prose Version* and the *Northern Metrical Version* of the
Benedictine Rule reveal.[6]

These translations of the Benedictine Rule for women strain very
hard to make translation serve historical, hierarchical relations of masculine and feminine, Latin and vernacular, sameness and difference. Just
as the text of the rule is translated into the vernacular for women, later
medieval English Benedictine monasticism for women is itself a "translation," adapted not only linguistically but also ideologically for women
in order to fight social and religious boundary shifts by enforcing a
rigorously hierarchical sex/gender system. Like Arundel's Constitutions,
these texts seek to "save the market" by manipulating the vernacular to
control its transgressive power and that of the women who read it, putting both firmly under the control of reaffirmed clerical authority. The
translations, like Bokenham's epilogue, do their utmost to construct the
vernacular as feminine and, correspondingly, as inferior and lacking,
qualities the texts also attribute to the female audience.

In the two Middle English versions of the Benedictine Rule the
vernacular, the very source of disruption, reasserts the legitimacy and
authority of Latin. Putting the vernacular "in its place," that is, under the
authority of Latin, is a step in a larger movement to put women religious
firmly in their place vis-à-vis the male clergy. In many clerical circles in
later medieval England, a "set of associations" existed "between a barbar-
ous mother tongue, an uneducated readership with a 'carnal understanding of the truth,' and the danger that this readership will rebel"
(Watson 844). The corollary was that "a lack of grammatical regulation
in the vernacular...impl[ied] the unruliness of those who speak it"
(Watson 844). One way the prose translation of the rule asserts the

strong authority necessary to avert such danger is to introduce all of the chapters (except VIII-XVII, LXII, and LXV) with an introductory phrase of some kind indicating that what follows is said by, spoken by, or commanded by St. Benedict.[7] These introductory phrases are not included in the Latin text, and they place a figure of ecclesiastical authority in a position of preeminence and priority. The figure and voice of St. Benedict serve as substitutes for the authoritative Latin text itself; they work to shore up clerical authority and the value of Latin in order to reinforce the system of social relations in which the clergy and Latin are dominant.[7] At the beginning of chapter VII, significantly a chapter addressing meekness, the masculine authority of St. Benedict and Holy Scripture coalesce as they are said to speak together, and to speak Latin: "Of mekenes spekis sain benet in þis sentence, & sais with hali scripture: 'Omnis qui se exaltat &c.'" (Kock, *Prose* 11) The introductory phrases remind the female audience that this text advocating meekness is legitimate and should be believed, respected, and obeyed precisely because of the Latin, masculine authority that is prior to it.

Ralph Hanna III writes, "Perhaps most distressing for the conservative, Englished Latin had been cut free from the Latin tradition.... It had become 'open'" (11). The insertion of the figure of St. Benedict links the vernacular firmly to the Latin tradition, reasserting closure. The insertion of the figure of St. Benedict, like the episcopal authorization of vernacular scriptural texts required by Arundel's Constitutions, puts a strong authority figure in place as a prophylaxis against rebellion, as a way of ruling the potentially unruly.

The brief prayers which conclude most of the chapters in the prose translation of the Benedictine Rule may not initially appear to replace boundaries by reasserting hierarchical relations of languages and genders as the introductory phrases do.[9] In fact, though, the prayers set up a dynamic in which the voice of masculine authority speaks to and subordinates passive, feminine hearers and readers. These prayers, which are typically only one or two lines long, request help, aid, knowledge, or mercy in connection with the topic discussed in the chapter. For example, chapter XLVIII on labor and study ends with the prayer, "Lauerd for his pite giue vs sua to wirk, and sua vre lescuns at vnderstande, þat we at te ende til heuin be broght. Amen" (Kock, *Prose* 33). The prayers almost all speak in first person plural.[10] The "we" of the prayers reflects the monastic convention of praying communally and for all Christians, but the "we" is never one of full solidarity. The sameness and unity of the "we" put forth in the prayers is actually difference masked as sameness, and when this difference is unmasked, the inferiority of those who are "other" emerges.

For instance, Chapter XXXVII addresses provisions for the elderly and children. The introductory phrase, "Of þe alde & of þe barnis spekis sain benet in þis sentence" (Kock, *Prose* 27), serves as a reminder of masculine, ecclesiastical authority and the right to speak. However, no prayer ends the chapter, and there is no use of the first person plural. There is no assertion by the voice of masculine authority of unity and same-\ness with these most "feminized" members of the community. Chapter LXII on the ordination of priests also lacks a prayer.[11] There can be no "we" here because the female audience cannot participate in the role of the priest treated by the chapter. Women's very bodies, "other" and, like those of the elderly and the young, less than perfect, bar them from clerical status.

Perhaps the most striking indication of the way the withdrawal of the first person plural in the prayers functions to "save the market" and replace boundaries occurs in chapter VI. This chapter, which addresses silence, begins with the introductory phrase, "Sain benet spekis in þis sentence of silence, how 3e sal it halde" (Kock, *Prose* 10). Not only is there no "we" in a prayer in this chapter, but the text also repeatedly addresses its female readers or hearers as "3e":"he bidis þat 3e do als þe prophete sais.... loke wheþer 3e wil take to. þe maistires aw at speke for to lere hyr discipils wisdom. þe decipils sal here þar lesson & understand it." (Kock, *Prose* 10) This is a significant departure from the Latin, which speaks with a participatory first person plural in prescribing restrained speech: "Faciamus quod ait propheta: Dixi: *Custodiam vias meas, ut non delinquam in lingua mea.*" (Fry et al. 190)[12]

The language and grammar of the translated passage set up a hierarchy which is absent in the Latin, which goes beyond daily monastic practice of silence, and which is important in considering issues of gender, power and authority. St. Benedict, a male, clerical authority figure, commands the female hearers or readers to be passive and silent. In contrast to the female listeners, "þe maistires," a group of those (male) individuals with sufficient authority and knowledge, are authorized to speak. Included among these knowledgeable, authoritative "maistires" is the translator, who has access to the original text and who, being by virtue of his knowledge and gender exempted from the requirement of silence put forth by the chapter, "leres" the hearers of the text's wisdom through the translation. "Sain benet spekis," as does the translator, but the nuns do not. The text does its utmost to constrain the feminine vernacular and contain the female voice which would speak this language with potentially disruptive consequences.

The verse translation in MS BL Cotton Vespasian A.25 sets up the same hierarchical relationship in which a voice of male authority subordinates passive female hearers and readers. It makes the requirement of silence apply more to women than to men. On the ladder of meekness, the eleventh step of humility concerns speaking few words. The Latin ends the section with the verse, "Sapiens verbis innotescit paucis" (Fry et al. 200). The English verse translation reads:

> "Sapiens in paucis verbis expedit --
> He þat is wise in word & dede,
> His wark with fone wordes wil he spede."
> And naymly women nyght & day
> Aw to vse fune wordes alway.   (Kock, *Verse* 1081-84)

While it is an indication of virtue, a sign of wisdom, for a man to use few words, women in particular (*naymly*) have an obligation to (*aw to*) use few words. This emphasis reflects clerical attitudes about women and speech, considering that "[a]side from carnality in general, the vice most frequently assigned to women was loquacity" (Newman 24).

> Differing ecclesiastical attitudes toward silence for men and women religious appear in episcopal injunctions to male and female houses and build on the differences indicated in the verse translation of the Rule. In his 1432 injunctions to the male Benedictine house of Ramsey Abbey, Bishop Gray en-\joins that: silence be kept henceforward in the cloister, church, dorter, and frater, under pain of one penny to be paid out of the commons of every monk who shall transgress herein, towards the work of the floors aforesaid.... (Thompson 104)

Bishop Flemyng, in his 1421-1422 injunctions for the female Benedictine house of Elstow Abbey, enjoins:

> silence be kept by all without distinction at the due times and places, to wit in the house of prayer, the cloister, and the dorter, under pain of fasting on bread and water upon the Wednesday and Friday following; and, if any nun shall make default in this particular, let her be constrained to that penalty: the second time, let the same penalty be doubled; and, if she be proved to have made default in this matter a third time, let her be from that time enjoined to fast on bread and water every Wednesday and Friday for the next

40

half year, and on Monday and Thursday, let her be content with bread and beer. (Thompson 52)

Notably, the penalties for women who break silence are from the outset more severe than those for men (for whom a simple fine suffices), and the punishments mandated for women escalate with repeated offenses. The bishop, however, does not envision that the monks might engage in repeated transgressions. His description of second and third offenses by nuns manifests the general ecclesiastical perception that faults of speech were especially common for women. The bodily punishments for women, contrasted with the financial punishments for men, underline concerns about female carnality, pointing to a desire to punish the unruly female flesh which is the source of the problem. Significantly, the system of monetary fines in the male community does not chastise the flesh but rather ultimately contributes to the physical improvement of the house (i.e., the work of the floors), leading to better living conditions for all.

Silence and regulation of speech are clearly important parts of monastic life for both men and women.[13] The verse and prose translations, however, construct a system of social relations in which male authorities (significantly, in both texts those with access to Latin) have the right to speak while female hearers are commanded to listen rather than speak. This particular framing of monastic silence, like that evident in the injunctions, recalls the cultural desires evident in anti-translation rhetoric -- that is, the desire to prevent keep dangerously carnal women silent and obedient.

The verse translation does not include chapter introductions and concluding prayers as the prose version does, but it attempts to minimize the potentially disruptive power of the vernacular and of women in other ways. For example, it contains a translator's prologue which precedes the Rule's prologue beginning "Ausculta o filia." This additional translator's prologue explicitly explains that the text is a translation for women who do not know Latin:

> Monkes & als all lernyd men
> In latyn may it lyghtly ken,
> And wytt þarby how þay sall wyrk
> To sarue god and haly kyrk.
> Bott tyll women to mak it couth,
> Þat leris no latyn in þar 3outh,
> In ingles is it ordand here,
> So þat þay may it lyghtly lere.   (Kock, *Verse* 9-16)

This passage illustrates the translator's connection of Latin with a masculine, learned elite and the vernacular with a feminine, unlearned, inferior group. The repetition of the word *lyghtly* sets up apparent sameness that is actually difference. The prologue indicates that both men and women can easily (*lyghtly*) learn the doctrine of the Benedictine Rule; however, monks and all educated men learn it easily in Latin while women only learn it easily in English. The passage implies that the English of this version will say the same thing as the Latin, an implication proved false by a comparison of the translation with the Latin. What monks and educated men learn from the Latin is not at all the same as what women religious learn from the vernacular verse translation. The Latin and English versions of the Benedictine Rule do not shape men's and women's work, their service to Holy Church, as either the same or equal in spite of the theoretical sameness the passage implies. In the verse translation of the Benedictine Rule, language difference in fact marks gender difference, and difference is, in the course of this version, once again an indication of the lesser perfection of the feminine.

Although the verse translation lacks any references to "sain benet" that position him as a figure of masculine, clerical, Latin authority, it does retain Latin chapter headings. It also contains many more full lines of Latin in the body of the text than the prose version does. The general practice of the prose version is to include one or two words of a Latin quotation followed by a fuller version of the passage in English.[14] The verse translation, on the other hand, contains 55 full verse lines in Latin, and only once does it employ the technique so common in the prose translation of abbreviating with "&c."[14] The Latin lines in the verse break both meter and rhyme, standing out from the surrounding English. Thus, the Latin language of patriarchal authority, the language of the original Rule as well as of the Scriptures, stands in a place of distinction from the feminine vernacular. This positioning works to assert Latin's priority, power, and authority over the vernacular. The Latin chapter headings, together with the lines of Latin included within the body of the text, attempt, like the figure of St. Benedict in the prose version, to ground the translation in a hierarchical relation with the Latin text, prioritizing the authoritative original.

The Latin chapter headings and lines suggest a correspondence between original and translation while simultaneously revealing, as in the added translator's prologue discussed above, differences that highlight the lesser perfection and subordinate position of both the feminine vernacular and the female audience. The English translations given for the Latin lines included in the text enact this strategy by sometimes altering the meaning of the passage. For example, "Ego sum vermis & non homo" is rendered, "I am a worm & no woman" (Kock, *Verse* 1030a-31). The rendering of *homo* as woman is on one level a simple concession to the text's stated audience. On another level it signals more substantial, gender-based changes that occur when Latin passages are stated and then rendered into the mother tongue, or, perhaps even more powerfully, when the Latin is not included but simply rendered in English with words that have a very different meaning. If the presence of Latin suggests at least some ability to read the language or some knowledge of the original text, which, in spite of pessimistic views of women's Latin literacy, would not be entirely unlikely in a female monastic community, then the changes would have had an even greater impact on the female audience.[16]

In the verse version, alterations from Latin to English tend to involve issues of authority. The vernacular text reduces the scope of women's authority in religion as part of the strategy to contain potentially disruptive forces and prevent women religious from asserting newfound power. The new opportunities for independent participation in spiritual life offered to women by the spread of vernacular literacy and the increased availability of vernacular texts proved particularly disconcerting for ecclesiastical authorities, coinciding as they did with the late medieval "feminization" of sanctity.[17] This process, like that of vernacular translation, presented new spiritual possibilities to women. The paradigm of the "virile woman," in which women made themselves masculine in their pursuit of a spiritual life, gave way to one which Barbara Newman has aptly termed "womanChrist," that is, "the possibility that women, qua women, could participate in some form of the *imitatio Christi* with specifically feminine inflections and thereby attain a particularly exalted status in the realm of the spirit" (3). In the model of womanChrist, then, female particularity and difference came into their own as sources of spiritual power.

Chapter 2 of the verse version concerns the qualities and responsibilities of the superior, who in the masculine Benedictine tradition is said to hold the place of Christ in the monastery since he is addressed by a title of Christ as the Apostle indicates. The Latin reads: "Christi enim agere vices in monasterio creditur, quando ipsius vocatur pronomine, dicente apostolo: *Accepistis spiritum adoptionis filiorum, in quo clamamus: abba, pater.*" (Fry et al. 172)

John E. Crean Jr., who has examined Middle High German translations of the Benedictine Rule for women, describes this passage as "pivotal in evaluating any feminine RB version. In question is the persona of the abbess as perceived by the editor" (169). As Crean says, the way a translator deals with "Christi Pronomine" is "a kind of litmus test of how intimately the abbess may be understood to 'hold the place of Christ in the monastery'" (169). The Middle English verse does not describe the prioress holding the place of Christ at all. Rather, it says:

> And to be honored euer hir aw;
> Bot in her-self sche sal be law,
> Pryde in hert for to haue none,
> Bot loue god euer of al his lone
> And wirschip him werld al-wais,
> Als þe apostel plainly sais
> Vn-to all folk, who so it be,
> Þat takes swilk staite of dignite:
> "Accepistis spiritum adepcionis."
> He sais: :"Ʒe take þe gaste of mede,
> Þat lele folk vnto lif suld lede,
> In pe whilk gaste we call & cry
> Vnto our lord god al-myghty,
> And 'fader, abbot' þus we say." (Kock, *Verse* 327-39)

While the verse version does include the first line of the scripture passage in Latin connecting the superior with Christ, the English changes the passage's meaning. The father abbot in the English is identified with God the Father rather than with Christ as in the Latin, but the female superior herself, who is made subordinate, receives no such validation of her position.[18] The three Middle High German versions Crean examines, which range from the fourteenth century to 1505, all identify the abbess with Christ to a greater or lesser extent. The Middle English verse, however, instead instructs the abbess to be meek and to love and worship God. The translator thus constructs her persona to be consistent with current, sanctioned ideals of female religious life. The identification of the abbess with Christ would have made the radical possibilities inherent in the image of womanChrist all too real and would have been dangerously counterproductive to clerical strategies to "save the market."

Other important differences between the Latin and English treatments of the superior arise in Chapter 64, which discusses the election of a superior and outlines the qualities that make a person an ideal candidate. Significantly, the need for learning, described as desirable for an abbot but perceived at this period as so problematic for women, is absent from the English description of the female superior. Textual knowledge and education for the abbot become simply knowledge of proper conduct for the prioress. In describing the desirable traits of an abbot, the Latin reads: "Oportet ergo sum esse doctum lege divina, ut sciat et sit unde *proferat nova et vetera*, castum, sobrium, misericordem, et semper *superexaltet misericordem iudicio* ut idem ipse consequatur." (Fry et al. 282) The English verse reads:

> Al if scho be highest in degre,
> In hir-self lawest sal sche be.
> Hir aw to be gude of forthoght
> What thinges to wirk & what noght,
> Chaste & sober, meke & myld,
> Of bering bowsum os a child.   (Kock, *Verse* 2263-68)

Beyond the shift from a male superior who has textual learning to a female superior who knows how to behave properly, the different emphases in these passages exhibit a desire to neutralize the potential threat of female authority.[19] Lines 2263-64 echo chapter 2's previously discussed stress on meekness for the female superior in accordance with contemporary ideals of female spirituality. While both the abbot and the prioress should be chaste and sober, the desire that the prioress be "meke & myld" is a departure from the Latin account of the abbot. The abbot is to be merciful (*misericordem*) rather than meek, and having mercy implies having power and authority. Earlier in the Middle Ages, twelfth-century Cistercian abbots used maternal imagery in discussing the exercise of authority out of a need "to supplement their image of authority with that for which the maternal stood: emotion and nurture" (Bynum, *Jesus* 154). However, the description of the prioress's meekness and mildness does not participate in this tradition, for indeed, she is not described here as a mother. She is not to be maternal (emotional and nurturing) but "[o]f bering bowsum os a child;" she is to be the lowest in order to hold the position of superior.

The prose translation also contains passages which change the sense of the Latin and reveal a configuration of female monasticism aimed at limiting the dangers of the feminine. In this text, the perceived dangers do not seem to be those posed by female authority, since it does not emphasize the superior's meekness to the same extent as the verse translation, but rather those posed by potentially unruly women themselves. In chapter IV the rule sets out the "Instruments of Good Works." After the instruction to deny oneself and follow Christ, the Latin instructs the monk "corpus castigare" (Fry et al. 182). However, the prose translation advises the nun to "halde þe in chastite, and iuil langingis do away" (Kock, *Prose* 8). The shift from a command to chastise the body to a command to keep the body chaste harmonizes with late medieval ecclesiastical emphasis on a particularly enclosed kind of chastity in women's spirituality.[20] Rather than engaging in active physical asceticism which might lead to excesses in corporeal spirituality so distrusted in late medieval holy women, women religious are to preserve their chastity and expel desires that might lead to its breach.[21] The change in the prose translation manifests the "static perception" of female monasticism which follows from ecclesiastical stress on the importance of chastity (and in particular, the importance of intact virginity) for women. Unlike a monk, who undertakes a "quest" to attain his spiritual ideal, a nun, in this male conception of female monasticism, ideally begins and ends in the same state.[22]

Another subtle change made by the prose translation to the sense of the Latin points to negative clerical attitudes about the ways in which female spirituality and female nature differ from male spirituality and nature. Chapter XX concerns the proper way to pray. Both the Latin and the English prose version say prayer should be brief and devout; both, however, make exceptions to this rule. The Latin makes the exception "nisi forte ex affectu inspirationis divinae gratiae protendatur" (Fry et al. 216), but the English says, "Bot yef it sua bi-tide, þat any falle in mistrouz; þan sal scho pray gerne to god" (Kock, *Prose* 19). According to the *Middle English Dictionary*, "mis-trouz" means doubt, disbelief, suspicion or mistrust, quite a departure from the exception of "affectu inspirationis diuinae gratiae" for which the Latin allows. The Latin envisions the positive possibility of the inspiration of divine grace leading to prolonged prayer for men; the English envisions the negative possibility of a fall into doubt necessitating especially fervent prayer for women. The feminine is once again stigmatized as inferior in its difference.

The two English translations of the Benedictine Rule for women engage in diverse textual strategies to "save the market" for the pre-eminence of Latin in order to shore up masculine, clerical authority and the clergy's continued, privileged access to material and symbolic resources. These texts are only a single manifestation of a much wider phenomenon as they manipulate language and gender to restore the boundaries keeping Latin and vernacular, masculine and feminine, and, ultimately, clerical authority and female spirituality in their traditional hierarchies. In spite of a period of success, however, Arundel's Constitutions ultimately did not halt the spread of vernacular religious texts. Similarly, the attempts of writers such as Bokenham to assert the preeminence of Latin and the feminine inferiority of English did not irretrievably stigmatize the vernacular. The textual strategies to "save the market" at work in the fifteenth-century English versions of the Benedictine Rule likewise did not fully translate into monastic practice. Obedientiaries' accounts, court records, and documents from episcopal visitations reveal that fifteenth-century English Benedictine nuns were not the silent, enclosed, meek, and unquestioningly obedient women the prose and verse translations seek to create. Rather than being entirely subjected by clerical attempts to "save the market," women religious could and did "play the market," taking advantage of the social and religious opportunities available to them, opportunities enhanced by the rise of the vernacular.

University of Michigan

Notes

1. This passage comes from Richard Ullerston's pro-translation *determinatio* in which he summarizes his opponents' attack on translation. The passage is translated by Nicholas Watson in his article "Censorship and Cultural Change in Late-Medieval England." My argument in this article takes as its starting point the important work on religion and the rise of the vernacular done by Watson and his predecessors, in particular the work of Anne Hudson in *The Premature Reformation: Wycliffite Texts and Lollard History* and *Lollards and Their Books* and that of Margaret Aston in *Lollards and Reformers*.

2. The concept of "saving the market" comes from Pierre Bourdieu's article "The Economics of Linguistic Exchanges."

3. Put simply, symbolic capital is material resources stored in non-material form but redeemable in the future for material benefits. On symbolic capital, see Pierre Bourdieu, *Outline of a Theory of Practice*, 171-83.

4. For instance, Anne Clark Bartlett argues that the translation of the Godstow nuns' records into English does not indicate a decline of learning but rather represents the nuns' desire to take charge of their business practices. She says that the translation ought to be seen as an indication of "the expansion of women's authority and knowledge" and as evidence for the increase, rather than the decrease, of female literacy in the later medieval period (25). Roberta Gil-

christ and Marilyn Oliva also address the "substantial administrative talents" needed by women religious to run their houses. They note, "In addition to the organizational skills necessary to provision their houses within allotted revenues, the nuns had to know how to read, write, and keep the financial records of income and expenses" (55-56).

5. Further enhancing the potentially advantageous and potentially threatening position of women religious was the dearth of textual production and engagement in fifteenth-century male monasteries. In his analysis of the librar-ies of nuns, Bell finds that "the interest of the nuns in fifteenth-century books and literature stands in marked contrast to the unimpressive record of their male counterparts..." (76). He puts forward the possibility that due to "what most men would have seen as their limitations, the spiritual life of the English nuns could have been richer, fuller, and, one might say, more up to date than that of their more numerous brethren, who, for the most part, were still mired in the consequences of a conservative and traditional education" (Bell 77).

6. The *Northern Prose Version* appears in MS BL Lansdowne 378, and it dates from the beginning of the fifteenth-century (Kock x). The *Northern Verse Version* appears in MS BL Cotton Vespasian A.25 and dates to "the former part of the 15th c" (Kock x). I cite all quotations from the prose version (hereafter *Prose*) by page number from the Kock edition and all quotations from the verse version (hereafter *Verse*) by line number from the same. I refer to chapters in the prose version using Roman numerals and to chapters in the verse version using Arabic numerals. Because the translators and houses with which the texts are associated are currently unknown, I will focus on how the texts themselves work in later medieval English culture.

7. Chapters VIII-XVII, which lack introductory statements, concern divine service, and in these chapters untranslated Latin appears as in the verse version discussed below. The Latin of the divine service, standing untranslated, and the institution of divine service itself, require nothing additional to secure their positions of authority. In other chapters, Latin quotations are translated, but here, since the Latin itself is present without "inferior" vernacular representation, the legitimizing aspect of the figure of St. Benedict is unnecessary. Chapter LXII discusses priests and the Church hierarchy. Since this passage deals with the masculine ecclesiastical hierarchy, clerical authority needs no support or reinforcement from the insertion of the figure of St. Benedict. This chapter additionally appears to conceive of the abbess as male, beginning, "Yef þabbes prais for preste ouþir for dekin at be ordainde til hymselfe, *He* sal loke, þat þai be digne þerto at be preste" (Kock, *Prose* 40, my emphasis). Chapter LXV concerning how to choose a prioress does not contain an introductory phrase properly speaking; however, the figure of Saint Benedict is introduced within the chapter.

8. Bishop Fox places similar insertions of the figure of St. Benedict in his sixteenth-century translation of the Benedictine Rule for the nuns of the Windsor Diocese. Joan Greatrex notes that Fox's text contains "frequent

repetitions of phrases like 'Be holde susters (sayth seint Benet)' or 'O dere susters (sayth seynt Benet)'" (227-28). Greatrex, however, does not comment on what the function of these insertions might be beyond saying that they reveal "the homely touch of a fatherly hand" (228).

9. Chapters VIII-XVII on divine service lack prayers as well as intro-ductory passages.

10. The one chapter containing a prayer which does not state directly or at least imply a "we" is chapter XXXI on the cellaress, which ends, "Lauerd, for þi merci giue hir sua hir office at do, þat so may haue þanc o god and of þe cuuent" (Kock, *Prose* 24).

11. Chapter 52 in the Latin original addresses the oratory, and chapter 60, which covers the admission of priests to the monastery, stresses that they are to observe the discipline of the order. Since in Benedict's time few monks were priests, it is not surprising that ordination of priests is not explicitly addressed in the original.

12. In all of the Latin quotations, the emphasis is present in the original.

13. Newman writes, "Because the discipline of silence played such a large part in monastic life, exhortations to avoid wicked or idle speech occur frequently in the literature. These are not aimed particularly at women or at men; both sexes are instructed in the virtue of silence and the vice of an unbridled tongue.... But while idle words were considered a peril for all religious, the proverbial chatterbox was always female.... Writers who viewed all speech with a professional suspicion employed misogynistic rhetoric on this point even if they were not, in other respects, notably hostile to women" (24-25).

14. The prose version has brief (3 words or fewer) Latin headings for the prologue, primum capitulum, secundum capitulum, tercium capitulum, and cap-itulum IIII. Chapters I-IV are the only ones with Latin headings. Except for "Qui viuis & regnas deus per omnia secula" in chapter VII, the only full phrases of Latin occur in the chapters about divine service. In contrast, the verse trans-lation has Latin headings, many extended, for 42 of its chapters.

15. "Si greges meos faciam &c" (Kock, *Verse* 2300a).

16. M. T. Clanchy discusses degrees of ability in Latin among those not fully literate in Latin in chapter 7 of *From Memory to Written Record*.

17. Dyan Elliott discusses this process in *Spiritual Marriage*. She takes the terminology of "feminization of sanctity" from André Vauchez, *La sainteté en occident aux derniers siècles du moyen age*. As quantifiable evidence for the feminization of sanctity as the Middle Ages progressed, Donald Weinstein and Rudolph M. Bell show that the percentage of female saints rose from 11.8% in the twelfth century to 22.6% in the thirteenth century, continuing to increase to 23.4% in the fourteenth century and 27.7 % in the fifteenth century (220-21).

18. In fact, the reference to God is perhaps more scripturally exact than the association with Christ, as Fry points out. "The biblical text invoked here does not actually give the title *abba* to Christ but to God the Father" (Fry et al. 172

n.22). Chapter II in the prose version is not really comparable because it is definitely masculine, referring to the abbot. The connection of the. abbot with Christ is made, although without the inclusion of the Scripture passage in either Latin or English: "For he sal be in haly kirke in godis stede for to lere his munkis wisdom and charite" (Kock, *Prose* 5).

19. In Chapter LXIV of the prose version, the English seems much closer to the sense of the Latin; the abbess is required to be "wise in goddis law, þat sho dra3e til witnes baþe to þe new law and til þe alde testament" (Kock, *Prose* 42).

20. On the importance of enclosed chastity in female spirituality, see Karma Lochrie, *Margery Kempe and Translations of the Flesh*.

21. See Caroline Walker Bynum, *Holy Feast and Holy Fast: The Religious Significance of Food to Medieval Women*. Bynum explores the complexities of women's ascetic spirituality and clerical attempts to contain what they perceived as excesses of asceticism.

22. Newman writes, "The newly professed nun, unlike the monk, had the dubious advantage of beginning in the same state where she would ideally end" (44).

Works Cited

Aston, Margaret. *Lollards and Reformers: Images and Literacy in Late Medieval Religion*. London: Hambledon, 1984.

Bartlett, Anne Clark. *Male Authors, Female Readers: Representation and Subjectivity in Middle English Devotional Literature*. Ithaca: Cornell UP, 1995.

Bell, David. *What Nuns Read: Books and Libraries in Medieval English Nunneries*. Kalamazoo: Cistercian Publications, 1995.

Bourdieu, Pierre. "The Economics of Linguistic Exchanges." *Social Science Information* 16 (1977): 645-68.

---. *Outline of a Theory of Practice*. Trans. Richard Nice. Cambridge Studies in Social and Cultural Anthropology 16. Ed. Ernest Gellner et al. Cambridge: Cambridge UP, 1977.

Bynum, Caroline Walker. *Holy Feast and Holy Fast: The Religious Significance of Food to Medieval Women*. Berkeley and Los Angeles: U of California P, 1987.

---. *Jesus as Mother: Studies in the Spirituality of the High Middle Ages*. Berkeley and Los Angeles: U of California P, 1982.

Clanchy, M. T. *From Memory to Written Record*. London: Arnold, 1979.

Crean, John E., Jr. "Voces Benedictinae: A Comparative Study of Three Manuscripts of the Rule of St. Benedict for Women." *Vox Benedictina* 10.1 (1993): 157-78.

Elliott, Dyan. *Spiritual Marriage: Sexual Abstinence in Medieval Wedlock*. Princeton: Princeton UP, 1993.

Ellis, Roger. Introduction. *The Medieval Translator: The Theory and Practice of Translation*. Ed. Roger Ellis. Cambridge: Brewer, 1989. 1-17.

Fry, Timothy et al., eds. *RB 1980: The Rule of St. Benedict in Latin and English with Notes.* Collegeville, MN: Liturgical P, 1989.

Gilchrist, Roberta and Marilyn Oliva. *Religious Women in Medieval East Anglia: History and Archaeology c. 1100-1540.* Studies in East Anglian History 1. Norwich: Centre of East Anglian Studies, University of East Anglia, 1993.

Greatrex, Joan. "On Ministering to 'Certayne devoute and religiouse women': Bishop Fox and the Benedictine Nuns of Winchester Diocese on the Eve of the Dissolution." *Women in the Church: Papers Read at the 1989 Summer Meeting and the 1990 Winter Meeting of the Ecclesiastical History Society.* Ed. W. J. Sheils and Diana Wood. Studies in Church History 27. Cambridge: Blackwell, 1990. 223-35.

Hanna, Ralph III. "*Compilatio* and the Wife of Bath." *Latin and Vernacular: Studies in Late-Medieval Texts and Manuscripts.* Ed. A. J. Minnis. Cambridge: Brewer, 1989. 1-11.

Hudson, Anne. *Lollards and Their Books.* London: Hambledon, 1985.

---. *The Premature Reformation: Wycliffite Texts and Lollard History.* Oxford: Clarendon, 1988.

Kock, Ernst A., ed. *Three Middle-English Versions of the Rule of St. Benet and Two Contemporary Rituals for the Ordination of Nuns.* EETS o.s. 120. Millwood, NY: Kraus, 1987.

Lochrie, Karma. *Margery Kempe and Translations of the Flesh.* Philadelphia: U of Pennsylvania P, 1991.

Morrison, Susan Signe. "Don't Ask, Don't Tell: The Wife of Bath and Vernacular Translations." *Exemplaria* 8 (1996): 97-123.

Newman, Barbara. *From Virile Woman to WomanChrist.* Philadelphia: U of Pennsylvania P, 1995.

Serjeantson, Mary S. Introduction. *Legendys of Hooly Wummen.* By Osbern Bokenham. EETS o.s. 206. London: Oxford UP, 1938. xiii-lxxx.

Thompson, A. Hamilton. *Visitations of Religious Houses in the Diocese of Lincoln.* Vol. 1. Lincoln Rec. Soc. 7. Lincoln Rec. Soc., 1914.

Watson, Nicholas. "Censorship and Cultural Change in Late-Medieval England: Vernacular Theology, the Oxford Translation Debate, and Arundel's Constitutions of 1409." *Speculum* 70 (1995): 822-64.

Weinstein, Donald and Rudolph M. Bell. *Saints and Society: The Two Worlds of Western Christendon, 1000-1700.* Chicago: U of Chicago P, 1982.

Vauchez, André. *La sainteté en occident aux derniers siècles du moyen age.* Rome: Ecole Française de Rome, 1981.

La ballade XI («Seulete suy et seulete vueil estre»)1 de Christine de Pizan et la ballade 59 («Alone am y and wille to be alone») des *Poésies Anglaises*² de Charles d'Orléans: adaptation, traduction ou simple coïncidence?

Jean-françois Kosta-Théfaine

> *«Of these sayynges Christine was the aucteuresse,*
> *Whiche in makynge hadde such intelligence*
> *That therof she was mireur amd maistresse;*
> *Hire werkes testifie the experience*
> *In Frensch languaige was writen this sentence*
> *And thus Englished doth hit rehers*
> *Antoin Widevylle, the earl Ryvers.»*

On connaît, grâce aux travaux de P. G. C. Campbell,³ quels étaient les liens qu'entretenait Christine de Pizan avec l'Angleterre. Deux types de relations se font jour. Le premier, somme toute personnel, relie Christine à ce pays par l'envoi de son fils, dès 1397, auprès du comte de Salisbury qui vint en France en 1396 pour négocier le mariage de Richard II avec Isabelle, fille de Charles VI – qui, elle-même, comme l'on sait, deviendra par la suite la première femme de Charles, duc d'Orléans. Christine de Pizan relate, du reste, le départ de son fils dans *L'Avision-Christine* en ces termes:

> «Comme ycellui gracieux chevalier amast dictiez et lui meismes fust gracieux dicteur, apres ce qu'il ot veu des miens dictiez, tant me fist prier par plusieurs grans que je consentis, tout le feisse envis, que l'aisné de mes filz, assez abille et bien chantant, enfants de l'aage de .xiii. ans, alast avec lui ou pays d'Engleterre pour estre avec un sien fils auques de l'aage.»⁴

Par ailleurs, le second rapport qu'elle entretient avec l'Angleterre, est constitué par la réception dont a joui, de son vivant, son oeuvre Outre-Manche de son vivant. En effet, il semble incontestable que celle-ci a été à la fois et largement appréciée et source d'inspiration pour certains auteurs anglais.⁵

D'autre part, le nombre des manuscrits contenus dans les biblio-thèques britanniques, constitue un témoin de la réputation de Christine dans ce pays. De plus, il nous faut rappeler, comme le notait P. G. C. Campbell, que certains manuscrits contenant les oeuvres de la poétesse ont été transportés Outre-Manche, comme c'est le cas de celui conservé à la British Library sous la cote Harley 4431 et qui contient une grande partie de la production de Christine de Pizan.[6]

Quant aux autres manuscrits, qui étaient aux nombres de douze à la British Library et quatre à la Bodleian lorsque P. G. C. Campbell rédigea son article en 1925, on observe que certains d'entre-eux, toujours selon cet exégète, auraient été exécutés en Angleterre. Cette hypothèse se trouve justifiée par les sommaires descriptions qu'il donne des manu-scrits qui, d'après lui, paraîssent être d'origine anglaise: il s'agit des manuscrits B.L. Harley 219, Royal Ms. 19 B XVIII, Harley 4605, Royal 15E VI[7] et le Royal Ms. 14 E II.[8]

Dès lors, il semble clairement établi que l'oeuvre de Christine a été l'objet d'un réel intérêt en Angleterre. De fait, on ne saurait s'étonner de l'existence de traductions et d'adaptations de ses textes en moyen ang-lais.[9] Cependant, il existe une ballade composée par Charles d'Orléans, lors de sa captivité en Angleterre, intitulée «Alone am y and wille to be alone», qui s'avère être d'une étrange ressemblance avec la célèbre ballade XI, qui fait partie intégrante du cycle des *Cent Ballades*,[10] de Christine de Pizan: «Seulete suy et seulete vueil estre». L'existence de ce que l'on peut qualifier avec prudence, d'une «traduction» moyen anglaise d'une ballade de Christine de Pizan est d'autant plus surpren-ante qu'elle a été écrite par un auteur qui est lui-même français et dont l'anglais n'était pas la langue maternelle, même si, comme l'on sait, il la connaissait parfaitement.

L'attribution à Charles d'Orléans de ces *Poésies Anglaises*, con-tenues dans un unique manuscrit: le ms. B.L. Harley 682, a, en un temps, divisé la critique.[11] En effet, pour Sergio Cigada,[12] conférer la paternité de ce recueil à Charles d'Orléans était à considérer avec circonspection car elle lui apparaissait, à la fois, comme gratuite et injustifiée. Daniel Poirion,[13] quant à lui, rejetait cette attribution à Charles d'Orléans en se fondant sur des arguments axés sur le fond et la forme des pièces contenues dans le ms. B.L. Harley 682. Cependant, ces deux exégètes, tout comme ce fut le cas de Kenneth Urwin,[14] s'accordaient sur le fait qu'il existait une frappante ressemblance entre la ballade 59 des *Poésies Anglaises* de Charles d'Orléans et la ballade XI de Christine de Pizan. Par ailleurs, si tous trois assimilent les pièces de ce manuscrit à des «traductions» en moyen anglais des poèmes français de Charles d'Orléans, il faudra attendre les travaux de John Fox,[15] pour que la question soit reconsidérée et qu'apparaisse le terme qui, semble-t-il, est le plus adéquat si l'on porte une attention minutieuse aux textes français et anglais. Il préféra, en effet, employer le terme d'«adaptation» en moyen anglais plutôt que celui de «traduction».

Dans un article publié en 1943, John Fox démontre clairement ce travail d'«adaptation» sur lequel il est, semble-t-il, inutile de revenir et qui se fonde, selon lui, sur: «Un travail de patience qui a exigé toute une technique et toute une recherche. [Car] par les trois voies du sens, des sons et de l'orthographe, le poète s'est efforcé de capter en anglais l'âme même des vers français.»[16] Les exemples cités par cet exégète sont significatifs, de même ceux de Robert Steele, dans le second volume qui complète son édition des *Poésies Anglaises* de Charles d'Orléans.

On ne peut dès lors que refuser le terme de «traduction» s'agissant des pièces contenues dans le manuscrit B.L. Harley 862, en admettant de manière définitive qu'il s'agit bien d'une «adaptation» en moyen anglais de poésies françaises. Cependant, il nous faut maintenant nous intéresser à ces deux ballades, car si toutes les pièces rédigées en moyen anglais sont des adaptations de poèmes français de Charles d'Orléans, cette ballade 59 semble bien être unique en son genre puisque l'on doit l'original français à Christine de Pizan.

Si le terme d'adaptation ne fait plus de doute, on est encore en mesure de se poser certaines questions quant au fait qu'un des poèmes de Christine de Pizan ait pu faire l'objet de ce type particulier de travail, et qui plus est par un Français.

Dès lors, deux questions majeures se posent à nous: comment comprendre que Charles d'Orléans ait pu connaître cette pièce de Christine? Et pourquoi avoir choisi ce poème plutôt qu'un autre? Pour répondre à la première question, il est possible d'émettre deux hypothèses. La première est celle que proposait déjà Kenneth Urwin à savoir que: «Charles was always strongly under the influence of Christine's personality.»[17]

Influence qui d'une part, si l'on en croit Pierre Champion, serait dûe au fait que «dans la maison de son père [=celui de Charles d'Orléans], il avait pu rencontrer Froissart, Christine de Pisan, Boucicaut, Eustache Deschamps.»[18] Et d'autre part, au fait que les lectures de Charles d'Orléans comprenaient les «écrits des Pères, ouvrages de droit, livres de médecine, rhéteurs ou poètes de l'Antiquité (...), chroniques, Roman de la Rose, oeuvres de Christine, de Froissart, d'Eustache Deschamps, d'Alain Chartier...»[19] A cela s'ajoute, également, rappelons-le, un autre élément d'importance, constitué par le fait que les parents de Charles d'Orléans – Louis d'Orléans et Valentine Visconti – étaient tous deux , comme l'on sait, des patrons de Christine de Pizan. Ainsi, cette dernière a, comme le souligne à juste titre Charity Cannon Willard dans sa biographie consacrée à la poétesse,[20] assidûment fréquenté la cour d'Orléans de 1399 à 1404, c'est-à-dire, précisément, durant la période pendant laquelle Christine de Pizan a composé la plus grande partie de son oeuvre lyrique.

La seconde hypothèse consisterait à imaginer que Charles d'Orléans aurait pu, lors de sa captivité en Angleterre,[21] avoir entre les mains le manuscrit B.L. Harley 4431 qui, rappelons-le, contient les oeuvres poétiques de Christine de Pizan, dont cette ballade XI et qui fut acquis en 1425 par le duc de Bedford.

Cependant, bien que les deux hypothèses soient pleinement plausibles, on doit avouer qu'il est, somme toute, impossible de savoir, avec certitude, quelle a été la voie de transmission par laquelle Charles d'Orléans à bien pu connaître l'existence de ce texte. Néanmoins, au vu du succès que connaissait l'oeuvre de Christine de Pizan en son temps, tant en France qu'en Angleterre, il ne nous semble pas impossible d'affirmer que la connaissance par Charles d'Orléans de cette pièce n'est très certainement pas le fruit d'une pure coïncidence.

Quant à la seconde question, il ne nous paraît pas invraisemblable d'imaginer que son choix se soit porté sur cette pièce car elle est, et c'est encore le cas aujourd'hui, certainement la plus connue de toutes celles composées par Christine de Pizan. En d'autres termes, cela signifie donc que son choix n'a pu être déterminé que par la fortune qu'a connu cette ballade XI.

Maintenant qu'il est possible d'évacuer cette idée de coïncidence d'une part, mais aussi celle qui consiste à conférer à la ballade 59 des *Poésies Anglaises* de Charles d'Orléans le statut d'une simple «traduction» d'un modèle français d'autre part; il nous faut aborder ces deux poèmes afin de voir quel est le mode de fonctionnement de l'adaptation moyenne anglaise. Afin d'illustrer de manière significative notre propos, nous donnons ci-après une transcription de ces deux ballades:

Seulete suy et seulete vueil estre,	Alone am y and wille to be alone
Seulete m'a mon doulz ami laissiée,	Alone withouten plesere or gladnes
Seulete suy, sanz compaignon ne maistre,	Alone in care to sighe and grone
Seulete suy, dolente et courrouciée,	A[l]one to wayle the deth of my maystres
Seulete suy en languour mesisiée,	Alone whisch sorow wille me neuyr cesse
Seulete suy plus que nulle esgarée,	Alone y curse the lijf y do endure
Seulete suy sans ami demourée.	Alone this fayntith me my gret distres

Seulete suy a huis ou a fenestre,
Seulete suy en un angle muciée,
Seulete suy pour moy de plours repaistre,
Seulete suy, dolente ou apaisiée,
Seulete suy, riens n'est qui tant me siée,
Seulete suy en ma chambre enserrée,
Seulete suy sanz ami demourée.
Seulete suy partout et en tou estre.
Seulete suy, ou je voise ou je siée,
Seulete suy plus qu'autre riens terrestre,
Seulete suy de chascun delaissiée,
Seulete suy durement abaissiée,
Seulete suy souvent toute esplourée,
Seulete suy sanz ami demourée.
Princes, or est ma dou
lour commenciée:
Seulete suy de tout dueil menaciée,
Seulete suy plus tainte que morée,
Seulete suy sanz ami demourée.

Alone y lyue an ofcast creature
Alone am y most wofullest bigoon
Alone forlost in paynfulle wildirnes
Alone withouten whom to make my mone
Alone my wrecchid case forto redresse
Alone thus wandir y in heuynes
Alone so wo worth myn aventure
Alone to rage this thynkith me swetnes
Alone y lyue an ofcast creature
Alone deth com take me here anoon
Alone that dost me dure so moche distres
Alone y lye / my frendis alle are foon
Alone to die thus in my lustynes
Alone most welcome deth do thi rudenes
Alone that worst kan pete lo mesure
Alone come on / y bide but thee dowtles
Alone y lyue an ofcast creature
Alone of woo y haue take such excesse
Alone that phisik nys ther me to cure
Alone y lyue that willith it were lesse
Alone y lyue an of-cast creature.

Si l'on examine tout d'abord ces deux pièces d'un point de vue formel, il est possible d'émettre plusieurs remarques qui font émerger quelques différences entre elles. En effet, la ballade de Christine est composée selon le schéma classique, que l'on connaît bien, et qui est le suivant: 1 str. + R + 1 str. + R + 1 str. R + Envoi facultatif;[22] et il en est de même pour celle de Charles d'Orléans. Cependant, on observe que la première pièce renferme 7 vers par strophe contre 8 pour la seconde. D'autre part, le texte français est composé de vers de 9 syllabes, alors que son adaptation moyen anglaise comporte des vers de 10 syllabes. Par ailleurs, si Christine utilise encore l'envoi (qui, comme l'on sait, est facultatif à partir du XIVème siècle) en l'introduisant de manière très classique par le substantif «princes», sa version moyen anglaise en propose, quant à elle, une adaptation, somme toute, assez libre, rédigée sur quatre vers et faisant l'économie de la formule consacrée qui l'annonce. Enfin, certaines disparités se font également jour en ce qui concerne les rimes. Ainsi, la ballade de Christine suit le schéma: ababbcc ababbcc ababbcc bbcc, alors que celle de Charles: ababbcbc ababbcbc ababbcbc bcbc. En revanche, l'anaphore «seulete» est fidèlement traduite par «alone» et conservée d'un bout à l'autre de l'adaptation moyen anglaise, y compris dans le premier vers de l'envoi.

Dès lors, il est évident que sur un plan formel, l'adaptation moyen anglaise prend une certaine ampleur, mais aussi une certaine liberté, du point de vue de la longueur, par rapport à l'original français. En outre, avec l'allongement du nombre de syllabes, mais aussi de celui de la strophe, Charles d'Orléans semble vouloir conférer à son poème un nouveau souffle. D'autre part, cela lui permet également de montrer son indépendance par rapport à son modèle, et de donner à l'adaptation qu'il en fait une touche personnelle, qui lui permet de se démarquer, en quelque sorte, du texte qui lui a servi de moule.

En ce qui concerne le fond, on observe que les disparités entre les deux poèmes sont beaucoup plus importantes qu'elles ne l'étaient pour la forme. En effet, si le premier vers de la ballade de Charles d'Orléans est une «traduction fidèle» du premier vers de celle de Christine de Pizan: «Alone am y and wille to be alone» de «Seulete suy et seulete vueil estre» on doit avouer que les choses se compliquent très rapidement lorsque l'on continue de progresser dans la lecture de l'adaptation moyen anglaise. Ainsi, le second vers de la Ballade de Charles d'Orléans: «Alone withouten plesere or gladness» trouve sa correspondance dans le vers 4 de la pièce de Christine: «Seulete suy, dolente et courrouciée». Quant au quatrième vers du poème de Charles d'Orléans: «Alone to wayle the death of my maystres» il correspond au vers 3 de la ballade de Christine: «Seulete suy, sanz compaignon ne maistre».

On note au passage que dans l'adaptation moyen anglaise, le substantif féminin «maystres» se substitue au profit du substantif masculin «maistre» du modèle. Ce qui signifie que les deux poètes orientent leur composition selon leur propre identité. Ainsi, Christine, à travers cette pièce qui fait partie intégrante du cycle des poèmes dits de veuvage,[23] fait référence à son défunt époux, Etienne du Castel;[24] tandis que Charles, quant à lui, fait allusion à une dame dont il est séparée; peut-être s'agit-il, tout simplement, de Bonne d'Armagnac, sa jeune femme demeurée en France.[25]

Par ailleurs, les deux premiers vers de l'envoi de l'adaptation qui traitent des effets physiques causés par la douleur: «Alone of woo y haue take such excesse/Alone that phisik nys ther me to cure» reprennent les vers 23 et 24 de son modèle français: «Seulete suy de tout dueil menaciée,/Seulete suy plus tainte que morée». Ainsi, une même thématique se retrouve développée, celle de l'isolement du poète face au monde: isolement que Christine vit de manière symbolique à travers son veuvage mais également le deuil qu'elle doit accomplir sans l'intervention d'aucune aide extérieure; et isolement bien réel de Charles d'Orléans, qu'il subit à travers son emprisonnement en Angleterre.

Enfin, pour ce qui est du refrain, qu'il s'agisse du modèle français (vv. 7, 14, 21 et 25) ou de son adaptation moyen anglaise (vv. 8, 16, 24 et

28), il reste identique: «Seulete suy sanz ami demourée» et «Alone y lyue an ofcast creature». Cette reprise, mot pour mot, d'un refrain similaire dans les deux ballades ne fait, dès lors, que renforcer cette violente image de la solitude dans laquelle se trouvent plongés les deux poètes. Par ailleurs, la construction circulaire de cette forme fixe qu'est la ballade permet une amplification significative du désespoir dans lequel se trouvent les deux poètes, puisque ce refrain réapparaît, dans les deux cas, à quatre reprises.

Pour ce qui est des autres vers, il n'est possible d'établir aucune correspondance entre eux. Ainsi, sur un total de 28 vers pour le poème de Charles d'Orléans, contre 25 pour celui de Christine de Pizan, on ne peut en mettre en rapport, de manière cohérente, seulement 7 entre ces deux pièces. Dès lors, il est plus qu'évident que nous nous trouvons, avec cette ballade 59 des *Poésies anglaises* de Charles d'Orléans, en présence d'une adaptation très libre de la ballade XI de Christine de Pizan. Cependant, on n'aura de cesse d'observer, dans ces deux poèmes, la permanence de thèmes communs et, somme toute, classique dans la lyrique des XIVème et XVème siècles. En effet, il est incontestable qu'à travers ces deux ballades, se donnent à lire des images saisissantes de la mélancolie qui, comme l'on sait, ont été plusieurs fois reprises et développées dans une grande partie de l'oeuvre de Charles d'Orléans, tout comme chez Christine de Pizan et bien d'autres poètes du Moyen Age tardif. Ainsi, cette mélancolie, générée par la solitude qui est, dans la pièce en moyen français, celle de la veuve éplorée, retrouve certaines affinités dans celle du prisonnier de la version moyen anglaise. Dès lors, tous deux s'inscrivent dans le sillage des victimes des assauts de Fortune. De fait, affligés par les coups du destin, ils n'ont plus d'autre ressort que de chanter la solitude, la souffrance mais aussi la mélancolie qu'ils éprouvent au plus profond d'eux-mêmes.

De la confrontation de ces deux textes, il semble clair qu'émergent plusieurs éléments importants. D'une part, que la célébrité de l'oeuvre de Christine de Pizan était, de son vivant, incontestable Outre-Manche, élément d'autant plus justifié avec l'adaptation moyenne anglaise par un français d'un de ses poèmes qui est, soulignons-le une fois de plus, très certainement le plus connu de tous. D'autre part, si l'on a pu constater que certains vers étaient littéralement traduits en moyen anglais, on doit avouer que la ballade 59 des *Poésies anglaises* de Charles d'Orléans est une remarquable adaptation de son modèle français. Tout d'abord, les rares vers traduits ne sont pas redonnés dans le même ordre qu'ils l'étaient dans l'original, mais aussi Charles tente, en y réussissant brillam-

58

ment, de donner un nouveau souffle à son poème, et donc de s'éloigner, de la manière la plus subtile qui soit, de son original, par le biais de l'allongement du vers et de la strophe. Ainsi, cette adaptation peut également ment apparaître comme un véritable travail de réécriture, sinon de recomposition, dont seuls quelques éléments du modèle original sont conservés. Ce beau travail d'adaptation rend bien la tonalité générale contenue dans son modèle de départ, de la façon la plus judicieuse possible dans une langue qui n'était pas, rappelons-le, la langue maternelle du poète. Ainsi, nous avons, une fois de plus, une preuve du génie poétique de Charles d'Orléans.

Notes

1. Ed. Roy, tome I, p. 12 [Pour une vue d'ensemble sur les travaux consacrés à Christine de Pizan, voir Kennedy 1984 et 1994].
2. Ed. Steele, p. 70. [Bien que cette édition constitue notre texte de référence, signalons, à titre indicatif, l'existence d'une édition antérieure: Ed. Watson Taylor. Cf. Hausknecht, 445-447. Par ailleurs, il existe une nouvelle édition critique des *Poésies anglaises* de Charles d'Orléans: Ed. Arn 1995. [Pour un panorama des travaux consacrés à Charles d'Orléans, voir Hubbard Nelson et Kosta-Théfaine 1997, 159-164].
3. Campbell, 659-670.
4. Ed. Towner, p. 165.
5. En ce qui concerne les influences des textes de Christine de Pizan sur ceux d'auteurs anglais, on consultera: Bühler 1949, Laidlaw, Curnow, Toynbee, Bornstein 1977, 1979, et 1980-81, Mombello, Quinn, Braden, Eadie, Wareham et Wilkins 1983.
6. A propos de ce manuscrit, Campbell, p. 663, nous apprend que «ce manuscrit, offert par Christine à Isabeau de Bavière, femme de Charles VI, vers 1407, s'est trouvé parmi les livres de Charles VI achetés en 1425 par le duc de Bedford, qui l'a donné à sa femme en secondes noces, Jaquette de Luxembourg. Le fils aîné de Jaquette, Anthony Wydeville, comte Rivers, l'hérita de sa mère et à sa mort, en 1483, le manuscrit passa entre les mains du seigneur de la Gruthuyse, Louis de Bruges. Après la mort de ce dernier en 1492, nous le perdons de vue pour presque deux siècles, jusqu'à ce qu'on le trouve dans la bibliothèque d'Henri, duc de Newcastle; par le mariage de sa petite-fille à Edouard Harley, comte d'Oxford, la manuscrit entra dans la collection Harleyenne, acquise en 1753 par le Musée Britannique». [Voir également *Archaeologia*, XXVI, 1836, 271 et suiv., et éd. Roy, tome III, xxi-xxiv].
7. Campbell, p. 664, nous signale que ce manuscrit «fut offert à Marguerite à l'occasion de son mariage en 1445. Même, si nous ne connaissions pas l'histoire de ce livre, il y a un autre fait qui permet de supposer que cette copie a été exécutée pour des yeux anglais. Dans l'original de Christine, il y

a un passage assez connu où elle s'étend sur la perfidie des Anglais; ce passage, qui eût naturellement blessé l'amourpropre de cette nation, manque entièrement dans cet exemplaire».

8. Selon Campbell, p. 665, «L'origine de ce manuscrit est encore une preuve de la faveur dont jouit Christine jusqu'à la fin du XVème siècle, car Edouard IV le fit copier entre 1473 et 1483, à ce qu'il paraît, d'après quelque original qui se trouvait en Flandre».

9. Il s'agit des textes suivants (nous signalons entre crochets les rééditions): *L'Epistre au Dieu d'Amours* (1399): T. Hoccleve, *The Letter of Cupid*, éd. Urry, 534-537 [éd. Furnivall, 79-92, éd. Skeat, pp 217-232, éd. Pollard, 13-31, éd. Fenster et Carpenter, 175-203]. – *L'Epistre d'Othea* (ca. 1400): Wyer, éd. Gordon 1904 [éd. Bühler 1970], éd. Gordon 1942. – *Le Livre de la Cité des Dames* (1405): Anslay, [éd. Bornstein 1978]. – *Le Livre des fais d'Armes et de Chevalerie* (1410): Caxton, 1489-1490, [éd. Byles, Caxton 1968]; *The Boke of Noblesse: addressed to King Edward the Fourth on his invasion of France in 1475*, London: Nichols, 1860 (Roxburghe Club, LXXVII). – *Le Livre du Corps de Policie* (1407): Skot 1521, [Skot 1971], éd. Bornstein 1977. – *Proverbes moraux* (1400-1401): Caxton 1478, [Woodville, 1526; 1810; 1815, 218-224; 1859; 1970]. – A ces traductions en moyen anglais s'ajoute une traduction portugaise du *Livre des Trois Vertus* (1405): *O espelho de Christina*, Lisbonne: Hernao de Campos, 1518. [Ed. Carstens-Grokenberger].

10. Ed Roy, 1-100.

11. Cf. *The Retrospective Review*, 3ème série, vol. I, 147-158; Bullrich, Stemmler, Cellini, Simmons, Clark 1971; Clark 1976, et Arn 1978.

12. Cigada.

13. Poirion.

14. K. Urwin.

15. Fox.

16. *Idem*, p. 438.

17. Urwin, p. 129.

18. Champion 1923, p. 21.

19. *Idem*, p. 33.

20. Willard, p. 51.

21. Charles d'Orléans, comme l'on sait, fut fait prisonnier à Azincourt, en 1415, puis emmené en Angleterre, où son exil durera jusqu'en 1440.

22. Au sujet de la construction des poèmes à forme fixe au Moyen Age, on consultera: Wilkins 1969, Bagoly, Ferrand 1986, 23 et suiv.; Ferrand 1993, 14-18 et Kosta-Théfaine 1997 (sous presse).

23. Il s'agit des pièces suivantes: Ballades I, V à XX et Rondeaux I à VII et XI, in éd. Roy, 1 et 5-21; 147-151 et 153-154. A propos de ces poèmes, voir Altmann.

24. En effet, Etienne du Castel, parti en voyage à Beauvais en 1389 avec Charles VI, contracta une maladie contagieuse et ne revint jamais.

60

25. Cette hypothèse a également été suggérée par Pierre Champion en 1911 (Cf. Champion 1911). Cependant, selon lui, seule une partie de la pro-duction du poète du temps de sa captivité pouvait être adressée à Bonne d'Arm-agnac. Une autre partie, toujours d'après cet exégète, aurait pu être destinée à la femme de Suffolk -- qui avait lui-même Charles en garde -- c'est à dire Alice Chaucer, la petite fille du poète. Cf. à ce propos Champion 1923.

Ouvrages cités

Altmann, B. K. «Les poèmes de veuvage de Christine de Pizan.» *Scintilla* 1, 1984, 24-47.

[Anslay, B.]. *The Boke of the Cyte of Ladyes*, tr. B. Anslay, London: H. Pepwell, 1521.

Archaeologia, XXVI, 1836.

Arn, M. J. «The English Poetry of Charles d'Orléans.» *Dutch Quarterly: Review of Anglo-American Letters* 8 (1978): 108-121.

--- (éd.). *Fortunes Stabilnes: Charles of Orleans' English Book of Love: A Critical Edition*. Binghamton: Medieval and Renaissance Texts and Studies, 1995.

Bagoly, S. «Christine de Pizan et l'art de ‹dictier› ballades.» *Le Moyen Age* 92 (1986): 41-67.

The Boke of Noblesse: addressed to King Edward the Fourth on his invasion of France in 1475. London: Nichols, 1860 (Roxburghe Club, LXXVII).

Bornstein, D. «French Influence on Fifteenth Century English Prose as Exemplified by the Translation of Christine de Pisan's *Livre du Corps de Policie*.» *Mediaeval Studies* 39 (1977): 369-386.

--- (éd.). *The Middle English Translation of Christine de Pisan's «Livre du Corps de Policie» ed. from ms. C.U.L. Kk. 1.5*. Heidelberg: Winter, 1977.

--- (éd.). *Distaves and Dames: Renaissance Treatises for and about Women*. Delmar, NY: Scholar's Facsimiles and Reprints, 1978.

---. «Sir Anthony Woodville as the Translator of Christine de Pisan's *Livre du Corps de Policie*.» *Fifteenth Century Studies* 2 (1979): 9-19.

---. «An Analogue to Chaucer's *Clerk's Tale*.» *Chaucer Review* 15 (1980-1981): 322-331.

Braden, G. «Beyond Frustration: Petrarchan Laurels in the Seventeenth Century.» *Studies in English Literature 1500–1900*, 26 (1986): 5-23.

Bühler, C. F. «Wirk alle thyng by conseil.» *Speculum* 24 (1949): 410-412.

---. (éd.). *The «Epistle of Othea» Translated from the French Text of Christine de Pisan by Stephen Scrop*. London: Oxford UP, 1970. (Early English Texts and Studies, CCLXIV).

Bullrich, G. «Über Charles d'Orléans und eine ihm zugeschriebene englische Übersetzung.» *Wissenschaftliche Beilage zum Programm der städtischen Realschule zu Berlin*. Ostern, 1893, n° 119.

Byles, A. T. P. (éd.). *The Boke of Fayttes of Armes and Chyualrie*. Translated and printed by William Caxton from the french original by Christine de Pisan. London: Oxford UP, 1932 (Early English Text and Studies, CLXXXIX). Rééd., 1937.

Campbell, P. G. C. «Christine de Pisan en Angleterre.» *Revue de Littérature Comparée* (1925): 659-670.

Carstens-Grokenberger, D. (éd.). *Christine de Pisan: «Buch von den drei Tugenden» in portugiesischer Übersetzung*. Münster: Aschendorffsche Verlagsbuchhandlung, 1961. (Portugiesische Forschungen der Görresgesellschaft, zweite Reihe, Band I).

[Caxton, W.]. *The Boke of the Fayt of Armes and of Chyualrye*, tr. W. Caxton, Westminster: W. Caxton, 1489-1490.

---. *The Fayt of Armes and of Chyuatrye*. Ed. facsimile de la traduction de W. Caxton, Amsterdam/New York: Da Capo Press, Theatrvm Orbis Terrarvm, 1968 (The English Experience, XIII).

Cellini, B. «Le Poesie inglesi di Charles d'Orléans.» *Studi in onore di Italo Siciliano*, 2 vol., Firenze 1966 (Biblioteca dell'Archivum romanicum Serie 1. Storia, letteratura, paleografia, 86).

Champion; P. *Vie de Charles d'Orléans*. Paris: Champion, 1911.

---. «La dame anglaise de Charles d'Orléans.» *Romania* 49 (1923): 580-584.

---. *Histoire poétique du XVème siècle*. Paris: Champion, 1923.

Cigada, S. «Christine de Pisan e la traduzione inglese delle poesie de Charles d'Orléans.» *Aevum* 32 (1958): 509-516.

Clark, C. «Charles d'Orléans: Some English Perspectives.» *Medium Aevum* 40 (1971): 254-261.

---. «Postscript.» *Medium Aevum* 45 (1976): 230-231.

Curnow, M. C. «*The Boke of the Cyte of Ladyes*, an English Translation of Christine de Pisan's *Le Livre de la Cité des Dames*.» *Les Bonnes Feuilles* 3:2, 1974, 116-137.

Eadie, J. «A New Source for the Green Knight.» *Neuphilologische Miteilungen* 87 (1986): 569-577.

Fenster, Th. S. et M. Carpenter Erler (éds. et trs.). *Poems of Cupid, God of Love: Christine de Pizan's «Epistre au Dieu d'Amours» and «Dit de la Rose», Thomas Hoccleve's «The Letter of Cupid» with George Sewell's «The Proclamation of Cupid»*. Leiden: Brill, 1990.

Ferrand, F. (éd.). *Chansons des XVème et XVIème siècles*. Paris: U.G.E.-10/18, 1986.

---. «Les formes poétiques.» *Quatre siècles de poésie. La lyrique médiévale au Nord de la France*. Ed. et tr. F. Ferrand et F. Suard. Troësnes: Corps 9/ Limonaire, 1993.

Fox, J. «Charles d'Orléans, poète anglais?» *Romania* 86 (1965): 733-462.

Furnivall, F. J. (éd.). *Hoccleve's Works I: The Minor Poems in the Phillips ms. 8151 (Cheltenham) and the Durham ms. III.9*. London: Kegan Paul, Trench, Trübner, (Early English Texts and Studies, Extra Series, LXI), 1892.

Gordon, G. F. (éd.). *The Epistle of Othea to Hector, or the Boke of Knyghthode: translated from the french of Christine de Pisan, with a dedication to Sir John Fastolf, K.G., by Stephen Scrop esquire.* London: J.B. Nichols and Sons, 1904 (Roxburghe Club, CXXXXI).

Gordon, J. D. (éd.). *The Epistle of Othea to Hector: a «Lytil Bibell of Knyghthod», edited from the Harleian Manuscript 838,* tr. attribuée à A. Babyngton. Philadelphia, 1942.

Hausknecht, E. «Vier Gedichte von Ch. d'Orléans.» *Anglia. Zeitschrift für Englische Philologie* 17 (1895): 445-447.

Hubbard Nelson, D. *Charles d'Orléans: An Analytical Bibliography.* London: Grant & Cutler, 1990. (Research Bibliographies and Checklists, 49).

Kennedy, A. J. *Christine de Pizan: A Bibliographical Guide.* London: Grant & Cutler, 1984. (Research Bibliographies and Checklists, 42).

---. *Christine de Pizan: A Bibliographical Guide. Supplement I.* London: Grant & Cutler, 1994. (Research Bibliographies and Checklists, 42.1).

Kosta-Théfaine, J.-F. «Charles d'Orléans: bibliographie récente.» *Le Moyen Français* 38 (1997): 159-164.

---(éd.). «Les *Virelais* de Christine de Pizan.» *Speculum Medii Aevi* 3:2 (1997) (sous presse).

Laidlaw, J. C. «Christine de Pizan, the Earl of Salisbury and Henry IV.» *French Studies* 36 (1982): 129-143.

Mombello, G. «J.-M.-L. Coupé e Horace Walpole: gli amori di Christine de Pizan.» *Studi Francesi* 46 (1972): 5-25.

O espelho de Christina. Lisbonne: Hernao de Campos, 1518.

Poirion, D. «Création poétique et composition romanesque dans les premiers poèmes de Charles d'Orléans.» *Revue des Sciences Humaines* 90 (1958): 185-211, [Rééd., in D. Poirion, *Ecriture poétique et composition romanesque.* Orléans: Paradigme, 1994, 307-337].

Pollard, A. W. (éd.). *Fifteenth Century Prose and Verse.* Westminster: Constable, 1903.

Quinn, W. A. «Hoccleve's *Epistle of Cupid.*» *Explicador* 45 (1986): 7-10.

The Retrospective Review, 3ème série, vol. I, 147-158.

Roy, M. (éd.). *Oeuvres poétiques de Christine de Pizan.* Paris: Firmin Didot, 1886, Rééd., New York: Johnson Reprint, 1965.

Simmons, A. «A Contribution to the Middle English Dictionary. Citations from the English Poems of Charles, duc d'Orléans.» *Journal of English Linguistics* 2 (1968): 43-56.

Skeat, W. W. (éd.). *The Complete Works of Geoffrey Chaucer.* Oxford: Clarendon Press, 1897.

[Skot, J.]. *The Body of Polycye,* tr. J. Skot, Londres, J. Skot, 1521.

---. *The Body of Polycye.* Ed. facsimile de la traduction de J. Skot, Amsterdam/ New York: Da Capo Press, Theatrvm Orbis Terrarvm, 1971 (The English Experience, CCCIV).

Steele, R. (éd.). *The English Poems of Charles of Orleans edited from the Manuscript Brit. Mus. Harl. 682*. London: Early English Text Society, (Original Series, 215), 1941, p. 70.

Stemmler, T. «Zur Verfasserfrage der Charles d'Orléans zugeschriebenen englischen Gedichte.» *Anglia. Zeitschrift für Englische Philologie* 82 (1964): 458-473.

Towner. M. L. (éd.). Christine de Pizan, *L'Avision-Christine*. Washington, D.C.: The Catholic University of America Press, 1932. Rééd., New York: AMS Press, 1965.

Toynbee, P. «Christine de Pizan and Sir John Maundville.» *Romania* 21 (1892): 228-239.

Urry, J. (éd.). *The Works of Geoffrey Chaucer*. London: B. Lintot, 1721.

Urwin, K. «The 59th English Ballade of Charles of Orleans.» *Modern Language Review* 38 (1943): 129-132.

Wareham, T. E. «Christine de Pisan's *Livre des Fais d'Armes et de Chevalerie* and Its Fate in the Sixteenth Century.» *Seconda miscellanea di studi e ricerche sul Quattrocento Francese*. Ed. F. Simone, J. Beck et G. Mombello. Chambéry: Centre d'Etudes Franco-Italien, 1981, 135-142.

Watson Taylor, G. (éd.). *Poem written in English by Charles duke of Orleans, during his captivity in England after the battle of Azicourt*. London: Shakespeare Press, 1827.

Wilkins, N. «The Structure of Ballades, Rondeaux and Virelais in Froissart and in Christine de Pizan.» *French Studies* 23 (1969): 337-348.

---. «Music and Poetry at Court: England and France in the Late Middle Ages.» *English Court Culture in the Later Middle Ages*. Ed. V. J. Scattergood et J. W. Sherbonne. London: Duckworth, 1983, 183-204.

Willard, Ch. C. *Christine de Pizan: Her Life and Works*, New York: Persea Books, 1984.

[Woodville, A.]. *The Morale Prouerbes of Christyne*, tr. A. Woodvill, Westminster: W. Caxton, 1478.

---. *Morall Prouerbes of Christyne*, tr. A. Woodville, in Chaucer, *Here begynneth the boke of fame*. London: R. Pynson, 1526.

---. *The Morale Prouerbes of Christyne*, tr. A. Woodville, in T.F. Dibdin, *Typographical Antiquities*, London: Printed for William Savage, 1810.

---. *The Morale Prouerbes of Cristyne*, tr. A. Woodville, in T.F. Dibdin, *Bibliotheca Spenceriana*, London: Shakespeare Press, IV, 1815.

---. *Morale Prouerbes, composed in French by Christyne de Pisan, translated by the Earl Rivers, and reprinted from the original edition of William Caxton, A.D. 1478, with introductory remarks by William Blades*, London: Blades, East and Blades, 1859.

---. *The Morale Prouerbes of Christyne*, tr. A. Woodville, Amsterdam/New York: Da Capo Press, Theatrvm Orbis Terrarvm, 1970 (The English Experience, CCXLI).

Wyer, R. (tr.). *The .C. Hystoryes of Troye*. London: Robert Wyer, 1530.

Translating for Print: Continuity and Change in Caxton's *Mirrour of the World*

James A. Knapp

> *...the relationship between the individual text and the series of texts formative of the genre presents itself as a process of the continual founding and altering of horizons.*
> Hans Robert Jauss, *Toward an Aesthetic of Reception.*

When, in 1481, William Caxton chose to translate a popular French encyclopedia known as *L'Image du Monde* and publish it *as The Mirrour of the World*, a new community of readers was beginning to take shape. The demand for texts to occupy his recently established Westminster press required a form of translation that, while formed in the complex context of medieval translation, began to resemble the more modern function of linguistic translation -- to make texts written in one language available to a group of readers literate in another. Unlike many medieval translators who claimed to be interested in re-presenting authoritative texts in vernacular languages, but were committed to a form of translation marked by rhetorical intervention in the academic tradition,[1] Caxton seems to have taken the task of translation as would many modern translators -- as a matter of linguistic accuracy. The question as yet undecided by modern scholars is whether Caxton's "accurate" translations resulted from an honest desire to replicate non-English language texts in English or from his inadequate skill as a literary translator compounded by the hurried schedule set by the demands of a commercial printing house. The extent to which he followed his copy texts suggests that his conception of translation differed from that employed by academic translators interested in actively shaping the medieval textual tradition; for this reason Caxton has been characterized by some as little more than a scribe, one whose texts are marked by an "unashamed transference of French words and idioms into English...and...frequent misunderstanding of the French" (*World* 126). But at the same time his detractors admit that Caxton's

translations are fairly typical when compared to those of his contemporaries. The similarities between Caxton's style of translation and
other fifteenth-century efforts together with the subsequent conclusion
that he was not a pioneer in English letters have overshadowed the ways
in which Caxton adapted his translations for the press.

Like modern translators, Caxton was faced with an unanswerable
question concerning translation: Which is better: a "free" translation
which captures the "essence" of the original while bearing little linguistic
relation to the source text, or a close replica of the linguistic character of
the source, which ignores the relation living languages bear to the
cultures in which they are formed? Different answers to this question
dominate in different cultures and at separate times depending on where
a culture locates value in relation to authorship and textual authority.
The purpose of this essay is not to offer an answer to this question, but
rather to examine how one fifteenth century translator attempted to
honor what Walter Benjamin identified as the central goal of all translation: "the purpose of expressing the central reciprocal relationship between languages" (Benjamin 72). Behind Benjamin's description is the
assumption that to translate a text one must first believe that the act of
translation is potentially productive, that by translating a text it is possible to bring a different (but related) culture's linguistic experience to
bear on one's own "purposeful manifestations of life" (Benjamin 72). For
Caxton, the act of the cultural translation of texts involved more than just
the linguistic text. As a publisher, printer, and bookseller, in addition to
being a translator, Caxton had to choose books that he knew would sell,
that he knew he could transform from manuscript to print, and that
would appeal to both noble patrons and the newly literate readers of
printed books. In his presentation of *The Mirrour of the World*, it is
possible to see a medieval thinker grappling with the demands of a
market driven by a new kind of reader. In response to the challenge of
print, Caxton chose a text recommended for its moral value, and he
crafted his edition both in visual appearance and textual integrity in the
hope that "euery man resonable may vnderstonde it."[2] Caxton's role as
the translator, editor, and publisher of the *Mirrour* reflects both the emergence of a vernacular print tradition and the indebtedness of that
tradition to the late medieval culture in which it developed. Moreover,
Caxton's decisions concerning how closely to follow his copy in this and
his other editions helped to shape the character of the early English
printed book and, subsequently, early English literary culture.

I. "Imago," *L'Image, Mirrour.*

The Mirrour of the World is the first book printed in England (and in English) with significant illustrations[3]. In his preface, Caxton states that his book:

> waz translated out of latyn in to ffrensshe by the ordynaunce of the noble duc Johan of Berry and Auuergne the yere of our lord .M.CC.xlv., And now at this tyme rudely translated out of ffrensshe in to Englissh by me symple persone William Caxton, at the request, desire, coste and dispense of the honourable & worshipful man Hugh Bryce Alderman and Cytezeyn of London, entendyng to present the same vnto the vertuous noble and puissaunt lord, Wylliam lord hastynges, lord Chamberlayn vnto the most Crysten kynge, kynge Edward the fourthe kynge of England and of ffraunce.... (a4[v])

From this preface and various MS evidence it is possible to determine that Caxton's edition consists of his own translation (completed between January 2 and March 8, 1481)[4] of an Old French encyclopedia entitled *L'Image du Monde.* Caxton made his translation from a French MS produced in Bruges in 1464.[5] Most scholars find strong evidence suggesting that this working MS is now in the British Library, MS Roy.19A IX, although George Duncan Painter has argued that discrepancies in the illustrations for Caxton's *Mirrour* indicate that he used a similar, but not identical, MS.[6]

The French MS can similarly be traced to an earlier source, in the Bibliotheque Nationale (Fonds fr. 574), on the evidence that the ascription of the *Image* to Jean de Berry, in both Caxton's *Mirrour* and Roy.19A IX, is the result of a unique scribal error.[7] As Jean de Berry lived in the fourteenth century, and could not have written the French version in 1245, Oliver Prior, the only modern editor of Caxton's book, concluded that the Roy.19A IX scribe mistook the textual claim of ownership (in MS Fonds fr. 574) for authorship (Prior viii). In fact, Roy.19A IX is a copy of a prose encyclopedia which is likely to have appeared first in verse form. The poem appears to have been quite popular and still exists in two substantive versions, one written in 1245 (6594 octosyllabic verses) and the other in 1247 (expanded by some 4000 verses, with the order of chapters altered).[8] As the prose version seems to be closer to the first edition, Prior concluded that they were probably written around the same time (Prior x).[9] From the use of the Lorraine dialect it has been determined that the work was written in the city of Metz, probably by a man called Gossouin de Metz.[10] As the Old French text consists of a compilation of the work of various Latin authorities, Gossouin, the "author," did something more than "translate out of latin" an existing text, and something less than "author" the text in the modern sense of the word.[11]

Rita Copeland has argued persuasively for the two-fold nature of medieval academic translation as descended from classical models:

> Medieval vernacular translation of the classical auctores emerges from [the] historical intersection of rhetoric and hermeneutics, and carries the chief features of the academic practice from which it arises. It takes over the function of commentary on the auctores, and in so doing replicates the characteristic move of academic exegesis, that of displacing the very text that it proposes to serve. Like commentary, translation tends to represent itself as 'service' to an authoritative source; but also like commentary, translation actually displaces the originary force of its models. (*Rhetoric* 4)

The double nature of commentary can be seen as a central characteristic of medieval translation even beyond the realm of academic discourse, though the ratio of "service" to "displacement" tends towards the former in the case of more popular texts.[12] Gossouin's role in producing the *Image du Monde* can be seen as standard practice for the dissemination of "popular" texts in a period when national languages had yet to be firmly established. The relation of popular to academic translation is clear in J. D. Burnley's description of late medieval English translation: "There was no reason why [the translator] should think of his action as translation in the narrow sense we now use the word: that is, as a process by which a text existing in one language and culture is transferred into linguistic items with a corresponding function in a second language and culture. Rather, if he thought in technical terms at all, he might consider himself as involved in the business of inventio, seeking subject matter from sources which had not previously been exploited within his own cultural sphere" (Burnley 41). The translators of which Copeland and Burnley speak were to varying degrees actively engaged with the intellectual movements of the period, their rhetorical interventions crafted in a context of continual textual negotiation. The extent to which they inserted themselves into the textual tradition determined their disciplinary identity variously as scribes, compilers, commentators or authors, though the lines between these categories are not always clear.[13] Gossouin's text thus constitutes an individual work, though almost none of its content originated with him.

The textual history of the *Mirrour* points to a strangely hybrid book. As an example of the medieval compendium or encyclopedia, Caxton's edition seems a backward-looking effort to preserve, unquestioned, the cumulative knowledge of a medieval Europe we now know to have been on its way out. Yet as a handbook of practical knowledge it seems a precursor of the Almanacs and "how to" books which would become so popular in the 16th and 17th centuries. This latter point is supported by the choice to publish the prose version (as opposed to the verse which was still available, and likely more widely known) indicating the desire to associate the book with other prose encyclopedias such as that of Bartholomaeus, a work that had been translated into English by Trevisa. Considering that Bartholomaeus' *De Proprietatibus Rerum* was the book Caxton produced while learning to print in Cologne, his choice to publish the *Mirrour* is quite interesting. As Prior pointed out: "Caxton's choice was in every way a happy one. He could have selected any one of many Latin works of great value, which contained the sum of the knowledge of the times. But these were too learned or too cumbersome for the use of ordinary readers and laymen....The French *L'Image du Monde* alone fulfilled the necessary conditions of a popular encyclopaedia" (Prior v-vi). This point works to dispel the belief that Caxton simply catered to aristocrats; an English translation of a well known Latin text, such as Bartholomaeus', would appear to be a more appropriate gift from an aspiring merchant (Bryce) to a lord (Hastings) than that of a "popular" French encyclopedia.

If the choice to publish the *Mirrour* was at least in part Caxton's own, it offers insight into both his own intellectual leanings and his intended market. Caxton's mention of the month in which the Bruges MS of the *Image* was written may indicate that he knew of the MS and intended to print it before he had been approached by Bryce.[14] Russell Rutter points out that in the epilogue "Caxton gently refocuses attention on his own efforts, addressing the general public, the Lord Chamberlain, and even his Sovereign," going on to conclude that "[t]he *Mirrour of the World* was his responsibility and Bryce but a shadow in the background" (Rutter 464). Rutter may be exaggerating somewhat as Caxton states in both the prologue and the epilogue that Bryce was responsible for the "request, desire, cost and dispense" of the *Mirrour* (a4,ᵛ n3ᵛ). This statement is important, as financial backing, especially in the case of an illustrated book, was of no small order.[15] Still, it is likely that Caxton chose the text himself, and that by the very nature of commissioned printing (as against the commissioned manuscript), he envisioned an audience beyond that of his backer and the court. Barbara Belyea has identified Caxton's ability to balance the demands of traditional patronage with those of the public market: "Like the pattern of his prologues and epilogues -- the disparity between their impressive dedications to noble patrons and their actual appeal to a wider public -- Caxton's achievement was to innovate within traditional forms, to appeal to a newly literate public with the same delicacy and respect that earlier writers had lavished on their courtly audiences" (Belyea 19). It is clear that he took great care in both choosing what to print and the way he presented his editions.[16]

Even such a brief account of the context surrounding Caxton's production of the *Mirrour* reveals a curious combination of careful economic planning, political positioning, and historical accident. This is further emphasized by Caxton's treatment of the text. He does not, for example, correct the Roy.19A IX scribe's misattribution of *L'Image du Monde* to Jean duc de Berry, or the statement that it was translated from an earlier Latin work.[17] These "mistakes" are not necessarily surprising, especially considering that Blades would also fail to correct the reference to de Berry and later catalogers of the *Mirrour* (de Ricci and Duff, copied by Pollard and Redgrave) would list the edition as a translation of an unknown Latin work of Vincentius entitled *Speculum vel Imago Mundi*. Moreover, it is doubtful that Caxton shared the interest in authorship displayed by these bibliographers.[18] More likely is the possibility that this sentence from the French served a purpose that had little to do with an individual author and everything to do with the relationship of the text to a tradition of authority. Following N. F. Blake's description of Caxton's prologues and epilogues as "publisher's blurbs," it is possible to imagine that Caxton saw the value in advertising the book as the work of a Latin authority which had been sanctioned by a French duke (*First Publisher* ix).[19]

As if in anticipation that such errors would be caught, Caxton was careful to describe himself as "ryght vnable and of lytil connyng," thus justifying the universal disclaimer: "repute not the blame on me, but on my copie whiche i am charged to folowe as nyghe as god wil gyue me grace"(a5ʳ). In a translation of a compendium framed by Caxton's embellished prologue and epilogue, this disclaimer carefully locates Caxton as a producing agent without accountability. For the reader there can be no doubt who produced the translation and the book, "me simple personne William Caxton," and yet the same reader is called upon to reserve any criticism for the original writer, now absent and unnamed. This latter writer, accountable for textual flaws, is conveniently left out of Caxton's translation -- he does not translate the reference in the French preface to "le commandement de Jehan le clerc libra rier & bourgois dicelle ville de bruges" (fol. 4^v), the occasion upon which his MS copy was produced. Leaving out this reference to the Burgundian bookseller while retaining the reference to Jean de Berry and adding the mention of Bryce and Hastings effectively anchors the text in an older aristocratic authority while replacing the Burgundian setting with an English one. The stage thus set, Caxton carries out an act of cultural translation while at every turn evoking the trope of the innocent translator.

II. Englishing the *Mirrour*.

In his Epilogue to the *Mirrour* Caxton states that he not only followed his "copye," but that he "made it so playn that euery man resonable may vnderstonde it yf he aduysedly and ententyfly rede or here it" (n4^v). This statement, which is not in MS Roy.19A IX, allows Caxton to advertise his English version as "new and improved" without undermining the authority given the text by its French and Latin history. His presentation of the *Mirrour* resembles that of a modern publisher: he identifies his role as a disseminator of classic and essential texts in a new and accessible format. In fifteenth century terms the novelty of his new format is that it is suitable for a wide audience: "euery man." Caxton's intended audience is so wide, in fact, that literacy is not even a requirement: his translation is "so playn" that one only need to "here" it to understand. This is not an audience comprised of medieval scholars; it is, instead, a "popular" audience, and one that is specifically English.[20]

By addressing his volumes to a readership beginning to form outside the bounds of the medieval European intellectual community, Caxton not only capitalized on an untapped market, he also contributed to its formation. Hugh Bryce's decision to commission the *Mirrour* suggests that a new class of book owners and lay readers was emerging. Though the agreement between Caxton and Bryce would have held political as well as intellectual promise (the edition was intended as a gift for a nobleman), it also indicates how the rising social position of merchant and other non-aristocratic classes, the increased availability of books (thanks to printing), and the movement of book production from monastic to university and commercial centers, helped to foster interest in (and resources to purchase) books for a whole new sector of society. Caxton's choice of texts to print and the material he saw fit to include with those texts reflects a desire to draw out English-only speakers who were England's newest book owners.[21] Though Lotte Hellinga cautions that "[i]t would not be right to generalize from these few instances [of evidence of ownership] and conclude that tradesman and merchants made up Caxton's public," she also makes the point that "it seems logical that this printer who worked so much in the vernacular found his readers among those who could not read Latin....[W]e may say that merchants, who would not have attended university and thus would not have read languages other than English (although there were exceptions), became owners of English books" (Hellinga 218). Compared with the Latin readers in England who acquired both their taste for books and the books themselves from the continent, these owners of English books constituted another class of book owners, one that formed their reading habits in the course of business and domestic life, rather than at university or in the monastery.

By 1481, there had only been two significant movements toward a standard use of English strong enough to establish a reading constituency that favored non-Latin readers: the Wycliffite standard spread by Lollard preachers, and the "Chancery" standard initiated by royal Signet of King Henry V. Both of these developments were relatively new when Caxton began work at Westminster; the Lollard movement only originated in the last quarter of the fourteenth century, and it was not until 1417 that Henry V ordered that England's official correspondence be in English (Fisher 161). John Fisher describes the development of the Chancery standard as, "beginning in the Signet of Henry V and moving outward from the Chancery to the municipalities, guilds, and bookshops" (Fisher 163). Historically, Caxton appears at the intersection of government and commerce at precisely the time when Chancery English was becoming firmly rooted in both areas of English society. Arguing for the likelihood that Caxton was trained in the Chancery standard as a part of his apprenticeship in the Mercers' company, Fisher has identified the influence of Chancery forms on Caxton's own prose. In Fisher's view, the characterization of Caxton's prose as pragmatic, described by Blake as the result of stylistic ineptitude, rather supports that his style was that of a man trained in Chancery standard and writing for others versed in the same: "Linguistic variation may be the soul of poetry; it is anathema to a law or contract, where words have exact denotations established by precedent and legal decisions. Blake's description of Caxton's personal vocabulary as 'limited and generally of a prosaic, practical nature' is an accurate characterization of the vocabulary of the Chancery documents" (Fisher 165).[22] If Caxton had confined himself to laws or contracts, his role in the development of literary English may not have been significant. But, his choice to print and edit English-language literature and to translate, edit and print foreign language texts identifies him as a participant in that development, and leads to the question of why a cloth merchant would become the first publisher of Chaucer and Lydgate.

Accepting that Caxton identified a newer readership without traditional education and language training, and that this readership was likely accustomed to a form of standardized English designed for efficiency of communication, helps to explain his presentation of the *Mirrour*. His instructions to the reader are simple: there is no need for formal education, rather if one is "reasonable" and as long as care is taken in the study of the book, its contents are available. Caxton embellishes the French call "excerser en lisant & estudiant les fais des sages Jadiz traueillant en vertus prouffitables" (fol. 4^r) by stressing the importance of "redyng, studyng & visyting the noble dedes of the sage and wysemen," as a way of "eschewyng ydlenes at such tyme as they have none other vertuouse ocupacion on hand" (a4^r). This call for virtuous action not only fits in nicely with the Christian elements of the edition, it echoes the moral code of the Mercers' company.[23] Blake points out that Caxton repeats his call to "echew idleness" in more than one of his other prologues, and that this was generally accepted as a good thing to do in England at the time (*World* 158). Even if the strict work ethic and moral code of the Mercers' Company were not always followed, the company line and the opinion of the moral majority, were in tune with Caxton's statement here. Despite his continual recourse to a rhetorical defense of his translation as a transparent copy of his source, Caxton was inevitably involved in what Renaissance translation theorist Lawrence Venuti has called "the translator's crucial intervention in the foreign text." This intervention, which Caxton tries to downplay, is a necessary function of all translation in which the translator "actively rewrites [the text] in a different language to circulate in a different culture" (Venuti 4-5). But, unlike the earlier medieval translators working to displace the "master" text through rhetorical strategies of commentary, Caxton's intervention seems to be a function of his desire to make certain foreign language texts available to English-only speakers, texts that he found personally valuable. In the case of the *Mirrour*, his volume not only revealed the system of the world to its readers, it reflected a cultural model to which they could relate.

Throughout the prologue and epilogue, Caxton's contributions to the edition have a dual emphasis: first, that the reader "ought" to study the present volume (to eschew idleness, because it tells of God's marvels, because it includes the "situacion" of the firmament, etc.), and second, that the volume is easy to understand, that it openly declares its truths. The moral advice is Caxton's; the French version merely states that nobles have often studied "les fais des sages" contained in the volume. But, when Caxton promoted the edition as required reading, he apparently felt obligated to also make it accessible. Blake points to Caxton's expansion of single French verbs to doublets and triplets as a method intended to add weight to the prologue as an advertisement for the book, one that had to be "fashionable and striking" in style (*World* 158). But Prior also points out that Caxton created word pairs throughout the edition, most often when he retained a French word and offered an English equivalent in addition. Such a strategy allowed him to claim accuracy (by including the actual French word) while also presenting an understandable English supplement.[24] On this account, it appears that in one move, Caxton both creates the need for his volume and tailors it to the abilities of his potential readership. However, this description is too modern, as neither market capitalism nor a modern concept of textual authority had yet displaced their medieval precursors. Rather, it is in the clash between Caxton's response to modern pressures brought on by the printing press (the need to sell books in volume) and the still medieval character of his reading public that the uniqueness of the *Mirrour* is most pronounced. The more modern aspects of the edition that would have appealed to a non-Latin reading public -- the plainness of the English translation, its connection to a merchant -- could have compromised the book's medieval authority, the Ducal sanction and its status as a reflection of God's truth. Thus, Caxton is forced to carry out his editorial modernization and "Englishing" of the text under the guise of the copyist. If the delicacy of this balancing act does not tell the whole story behind Caxton's conservatism, it does much to explain his reluctance to make significant textual changes.

Scholars have described Caxton's most obvious textual contributions to the *Mirrour*, aside from those in the prologue and epilogue, as the work of "a good Kentishman" (Crotch cxiv), who was "thoroughly patriotic" (Prior vii). The most significant of Caxton's changes included the omission of a French reference to the fact that the English have tails, the addition of Oxford and Cambridge to Paris as centers of learning, the addition of Bath to the health-giving resorts of Europe, a comment doubting the truth of St. Patrick's Purgatory, and a revision of the French writer's geography concerning the countries of Europe and Africa. In addition to these larger interpolations, Caxton makes various other minor additions and omissions. Although patriotism is an obvious explanation for many of the changes, it is not the only explanation, and even when no other motive seems plausible it is important to remember that whatever patriotism Caxton demonstrated in print would have been influenced by a desire to please potential buyers. The alterations can be separated into three basic categories: (1) nationalistic (tails, Oxford & Cambridge, Bath), (2) corrective from experience (geography, St. Patrick's Purgatory), and (3) clarifying (Caxton omitted some passages from the French that he found confusing). Yet, in no case is there only one clear reason for the changes; even in the case of the tails, what seems to be straightforward nationalism could be defended as correction from experience (being from England, Caxton noticed that people did not have tails).[25]

In every case where the authority of the French text could be retained, Caxton did so. Throughout his translation Caxton is careful to reserve his alterations for aspects of the French text that are obviously wrong (confirmed so by personal experience) or obviously offensive to an English audience; clarity was a lesser, but by no means insignificant, concern.[26] In cases where his experience revealed an error, Caxton still did his best to maintain the authority of the original. Not surprisingly, in addition to preserving the authority of the French text, this strategy often also served to confirm Caxton's self-presentation as a conscientious editor. Thus, in the section on Africa, he both translates the French error and identifies it as such: "After thenne cometh Grece, Cypres, Cecyle, Toscane, Naples, Lombardye, Gascoyne, Spayne, Cateloyne, Galyce, Nauarre, Portyngal and Aragon. And how be it that the Auctour of this book saye that thise contrees ben in Affryke, yet as I vnderstonde alle thise ben within the lymytes and boundes of Europe" (g1^v). And, after translating the full French account of St. Patrick's Purgatory Caxton adds: "Hit may wel be that of auncyent tyme it hath ben thus as a fore is wreton, as the storye of Tundale & other witness, but I have spoken with dyuerse men that have ben therin. And that one of them was an hye chanon of Waterford whjche told me that he had ben therin v or vi tymes. And he saw ne suffred no suche thynges" (g4^v). In both cases Caxton includes the original description despite his belief that it is in error. His contributions operate as a kind of in-text marginal gloss: their relationship to the copy text is additive rather than substitutive. The reader is given the text as Caxton had seen it, and then offered a guide by which to read it. In this way, Caxton can maintain the appearance that his version is a true representation of the volume authorized by Latin authorities, Jean de Berry, and a courtly tradition, while simultaneously demonstrating that he is on the lookout for possible scribal mistakes.

Though there is no doubt that he shared a belief in medieval textual tradition -- he retains most of the traditional encyclopedic "knowledge" without comment -- Caxton's respect for his copy text was not so complete that he was above outright changes. Just as he removed the reference to the Burgundian bookseller responsible for the commission of his copy text, Caxton does not mention that he is responsible for adding Oxford and Cambridge to Paris as the seats of European learning or that he has omitted a reference to the English having tails. In these cases, where nationalism was of primary concern, no attempt to respect the original was made. Even if this textual tampering fails to make the edition a different book -- it is conceivable that even contemporary readers saw these production-specific references as ornamental extras -- the manner in which Caxton combed his translation and the simple fact that it was a printed "edition" and a translation set it apart from the group of texts represented by a medieval manuscript tradition. The fact that this volume would be reproduced in quantity, for a recognizable English speaking audience, shaped its textual character; the desire to imitate the illuminations in the original and the demand for printed books resembling manuscripts helped to shape its material appearance.

III. Reproducing a Copy: Illumination to Illustration.

There is nothing particularly unusual about the illustrations to the Bruges MS from which Caxton worked. By 1464 manuscript illumination was an established part of the process of manuscript production, and many medieval encyclopedias, including most extant editions of the *Image du Monde*, were illustrated.[27] Further, it is likely that Caxton's decision to commission woodcuts for the *Mirrour* was simply the result of his desire to produce a close approximation of his MS copy. However, the process by which the illustrations for Caxton's edition were produced differed greatly from that of MS illumination, and, regardless of the similarities in the final products, thus significantly changed the appearance of the book. Not only was the technique of woodcutting for book illustration fairly new, in Caxton's case (in English printed book production) it was untried. It may have been for this reason that Caxton's first use of illustrations came in an edition to which he considered the illustrations essential for an understanding of the text.

The author of the French prologue to MS Roy.19A IX describes the relationship of the illustrations to the text in a description of the book's structure: "Si contient cinquante cincq chapitres et vingt sept figures sans lesquelles il ne porroit estre de legier entendu" (fol. 4ᵛ). Caxton translates this statement quite closely: "Whiche booke conteyneth in alle lxxvij chapters & xxvij figures without whiche it may not lightly be understande" (a4ᵛ). This line suggests that the illustrations should be read along with the text if the "whole meaning" is to be revealed. This specific use of illustration points to an engagement with his product that goes beyond Blake's assessment that "Caxton now realized that illustrations could help to sell his books" (*English Literary Culture* 26). The possibility that Caxton considered the illustrations a necessary part of the text is even more likely considering the context of fifteenth century illustrated book production. As C. V. Langlois noted (in the form of an apology for the sparse illustrations to his third volume of *La Vie en France au Moyen Age*), the illustrations to medieval books in this genre were often more functional than decorative: "L'exposé du 'Système du monde' ne prêtait guère qu'à des figures schématiques, qu'il n'était pas facile d'agrémenter" (Langlois xxxi). Thus, if Caxton simply wanted to capitalize on the market for illustrated books, why did he not choose to reproduce a book from one of the many genres already known for their illustrations?

Though several factors may have influenced his decision to commission illustrations for the *Mirrour*, the financial risks known to be involved in printing illustrated books suggests that he would not have made this decision lightly. Thus, while it is possible that Bryce specifically requested an illustrated volume or that Caxton was influenced by the fact that he already had access to MS Roy. 19A IX, it seems unlikely that he would have based his decision to try illustration solely on the notion that pictures would help sell his books. On the other hand it does seems likely that Caxton considered the French illustrations an integral part of the text rather than an ornamental extra. As recent assessments of the production of illustrated books during this period have begun to show, the introduction of illustrations into a printer's editions destroyed more than one printer's business. Moreover, it is becoming clear that the survival of an early printer's business was based primarily on how accurately one identified the local market.[28] In assessing the role of illustration in Caxton's success, then, it is less important that he began to include illustrations than that he was able to use them in a manner that appealed to his audience. A closer look at the woodcuts for the *Mirrour* confirms that Caxton's success with illustration was, at least in this case, the result of the same kind of balance seen in his treatment of the text: he is simultaneously conservative (in his choice of text, and in the scope and execution of the illustrations) and forwardlooking (in his use of the "revolutionary" process of printing).

The relationship of the illustrations to the text not only varies from illustration to illustration but is often altered in the translation from MS to print. In order to get at the way the illustrations differ in the MS and the printed version, it is helpful to distinguish between "representational" and "schematic" illustrations, and those which share characteristics of both groups. The illustrations to the first part of the book are all of the representational type -- they are thematically related to the text, but do not break down the processes it describes in terms that could be learned. For example, an illustration in a section describing the art of music depicts two musicians, and though possibly illuminating how they look and how they might stand, the woodcut does not indicate how the instruments are played, or how music in general is made.[29] The illustrations in the third part are all schematic: referred to as diagrams by many commentators, these images illustrate ideas or principles discussed in the text through the use of abstract figures. The second part of the *Mirrour* includes illustrations displaying characteristics of both types, and these "hybrid" images are in some ways the most interesting in the volume. Using these categories to compare the MS and the printed version helps to reveal Caxton's attitude towards the book's illustrations.[30]

Because illustrations of the "representational" type are the most detailed, it is here that the most significant differences between cultural setting and graphic medium become visible. Though Caxton's illustrations are clearly modeled on those in the MS copy, the styles and the designs themselves differ in important ways. For example, both versions include an illustration of a master and scholars on the first page of the text (illustrating the prologue). Right off Caxton changed the book's appearance by substituting a different illustration, also depicting a master and scholars, for the woodcut that was probably based on the first illustration in Roy. 19A IX. The woodcut copy of the first illustration actually appears later in Caxton's text, illustrating the section on logic (figure 3). In the MS illustration (figure 1), the master, seated before four kneeling scholars, writes in a book set on a lectern. The illustration is appropriate to the opening words of the French prologue: "Considerant que parolles sont & demeurent vaines et escriptures premanentes ont les fais des anciens esté mis par declaracion en beaulx & aournés volumes. Affin que des sciences acquises et choses passées fust perpetuelle memoire..." (fol. 4'). The MS illustration thus compliments the text by offering a visual representation of "writing making words permanent." In Caxton's version,[31] the opening woodcut is also of a master, seated, lecturing to four scholars (figure 2). Yet, there is no lectern and no book. As Caxton had, but did not use, a fairly accurate copy of the first MS illustration (figure 3), it seems plausible to conclude that he chose to illustrate his prologue with a different scene, a choice that changed the relationship between the text and image. While the MS image literally illustrated the opening words of the prologue, Caxton's depicts the words of the prologue as if they were part of a lecture: there is the appearance that the master is actually introducing the book by "speaking" the prologue to the scholars. This interpretation of the image was shared by at least one of the book's early readers who added in ink the Latin "audita pereunt, scripta manent" within a scroll issuing from the mouth of the master.[32] This written addition echoes Caxton's textual addition to the original French prologue: "as I rede Vox audita perit, littera scripta manet" (a4^r).

By changing the illustration, Caxton is able to adjust the appearance of the book to fit its new context -- in printed rather than MS circulation, and in England rather than France or the Low Countries. Just as his version of the prologue stresses the "commandement" that the reader should "suffre nothyng to passe but that he vnderstand it right well" (a5^r), the choice of illustration invites an active participation from the reader (active enough to have prompted one reader to annotate the illustration). The difference in illustration points to a different use, by a different audience. Though the *Image du Monde* had been "popular" in manuscript form in France, Caxton needed to entice a readership that had probably had limited access to manuscripts, a group just beginning to develop its relationship to books. Consequently, while the meaning of a writing figure would have been easily recognized as self-referential in the context of a manually copied MS, in a printed book, detached from any writing hand, an orator seems to have made more sense to Caxton. As a guide for the use of the book, this illustration may have appealed to the portion of the *Mirrour*'s audience who could only see and "here" (rather than "rede") the work, a kind of illustrated invitation to an illiterate or newly literate group coming into contact with books for the first time. And, as the discussion of the next group of illustrations will show, the style of this and other woodcuts (though clearly constrained by the medium and the skill of the artists) further helps to move the action to Caxton's England.

The translation from MS illumination to English woodcut had a similar effect on images in the second category, those I am calling "hybrid." In both versions, the images of this "hybrid" type appear more quaint than others in the book as they often merge science and art -- something seldom done today.[33] In Caxton's edition they act as a bridge between the early illustrations and the later diagrams. Schematic enough to illustrate abstract concepts, they also include representations of the human agents that might engage with the concepts described, and ornamental features which seem unrelated to the topic at hand. The most interesting of these illustrate the section in which the shape and nature of the earth are described. Several differences between Caxton's illustrations and his MS copy occur in this section, including changes in design and the inclusion of an entire illustration not present in the MS. In the Caxton woodcut copy of a MS design illustrating the (theoretical) human ability to circle the Earth (figure 4), the woodcut designer has made several alterations. The most significant change is the introduction of a temporal element to the illustration. In the MS version (figure 5), the two figures are shown at the four corners of the Earth, illustrating that they could reach these places by walking in a straight line. Caxton's designs add the element of time: by giving the figures first longer hair (at the mid-point of the journey) and ultimately full beards, the illustration suggests that walking around the Earth would take a long time. Unlike the Burgundian travellers, Caxton's walking men age while they walk. Such a change not only suggests that the illustrations were produced with care, but that they were expected to be "read" by those who would use the volume.

Caxton also added a design to this section that does not appear in the Bruges MS. This design (figure 6) illustrates both the roundness of the Earth and a medieval conception of gravity. The design shows four figures at the four corners of the Earth, apparently holding stones over holes. Only from reading the text does it become clear what is actually being depicted in the design: "And yf the erthe were perced thurgh in two places, of whiche that on hole were cutte in to that other lyke a crosse, and foure men stoden right at the foure heedes of thise ii holes, on aboue and another bynethe, and in like wyse on both sides, and that eche of them threwe astone in to the hoole, whether it were grete or lytyl eche stone shold come in to myddle of therthe wythout euer to be remeuid fro thens, but yf it were drawen away by force" (d6ᵛ-d7ʳ). Like the travellers of the previous illustration, the figures in this design appear to be average people, and again the emphasis is on action: the people in the illustration are actually dropping the stones in the holes, as if the reader and three friends could go out and do the same if they so chose.

The "men-with-stones" is the last hybrid illustration in Caxton's edition. Apparently Caxton's artist could not easily conceive of a way to illustrate the book's most abstract points in terms of human action. While the travellers could age as they walked and the men could drop their stones, the concepts in the remainder of the book are even more abstract. The design immediately following the men-with-stones illustrates the order in which bodies are drawn to the center of the Earth (figure 7): "And yf the stones were of like weight, they shold come thereto alle at one tyme, as sone that one as that other" (d7^r). The human action related to this concept is negligible, and accordingly Caxton's woodcuts minimize ornament and move quickly to the schematic mode.

When the decision to abandon the representational and ornamental elements is made (for whatever reason), the relationship of the text to the illustrations takes on a different character. Not only may the text "not be lightly understande" without the figures, but the figures become completely incomprehensible without the text. While the illustration of the simplified little men dropping stones to the center of the Earth represents a visual version of the textual account, enhancing one's viewing experience (and possibly even making its point without words), a schematic figure indicating the arrangement of differently weighted stones in relation to the center of the Earth has no value apart from its role as an aid in drawing out the meaning of the text. When Caxton refers to this figure with his stock phrase, "as ye may playnly see by this fygure" (d7^v), the use of "playnly" stands out. For by this point in the text, it is the relationship of the text to the images, and not the images themselves, that is at all "playn." Even the "playnness" of the relationship between word and image does not equal obviousness or clarity: for the twentieth century viewer (at least), it is often easier to determine the meaning of the illustrations that include active human figures.

Caxton's schematic illustrations call upon the reader's ability to connect abstract conceptual principles to abstract schematic figures, without reference to recognizable mimetic representations. As this was not a requirement in most of the earlier illustrations, Caxton's *Mirrour* demands that readers increase their attention to the relationship between text and image as they make their way through the volume. Only a close reading of the text allows the schematic illustrations to become comprehensible. What little there was that could be "playnly" seen without the textual explanations, in the earlier illustrations -- clothing styles, human action, etc. -- is completely absent from these later images. Caxton's manipulation of some of the earlier images allowed him to give his edition a welcoming appearance necessary to sell books: one can imagine potential buyers identifying with the figures in the illustrations. Like all good salesmen, Caxton ensured his readers that no prior experience was necessary in order to understand his text; the book would increase rather than rely on the knowledge of its readers. At the same time he is able to retain the necessary level of diagrammatic abstraction required by the form of the original text, thus preserving the medieval authority of the text as well suggesting the general appearance of a manuscript.

Though a closer comparison of the images would undoubtedly reveal additional variants between Caxton's *Mirrour* and his MS copy, these examples suggest that this text is positioned between two eras and at least two countries. A careful examination of the features of such texts is possibly the only way to gain an understanding of a process of historical and cultural (ex)change to which these texts are the only surviving witnesses. Rather than trying to force transitional texts to fit modern descriptions of one period or another, it is possible to stress qualities indicative of both historical continuity and revolutionary cultural change. Though Caxton's readers may not have read this book in the manner I am suggesting, it seems clear that they could not have read it in the same way that French speakers read the *Image du Monde*, or used it in the same manner as others had the Bruges MS. However, as Caxton issued a second edition in 1490, it does seem that they read it, and their reading represents an extremely interesting moment in the larger history of English language texts. If we can avoid the temptation to define Caxton's moment, it will be less difficult to focus on the vagaries of a fifteenth-century English reading practice, which, like that of every other era, continued certain traditional practices while breaking with others. While it is helpful to map out the aspects of Caxton's editions that are "more medieval" in relation to those that are "more modern," it is just as important to remember that he did not see his world through these terms. That which has come to represent contradiction for the modern reader, was for Caxton more likely the stuff of a fully realized world, and it is that world into which he brought this interesting and eclectic book.

Eastern Michigan University

Notes

1. See for example, Pratt, "Medieval Attitudes": "Despite the somewhat conservative statements found in the prologues and epilogues of many translators, in practice they indulged in the type of rhetorical rewriting recommended by the classical and medieval artes. While claiming that the content and meaning of their model was paramount, the meaning which they actually elaborated rhetor-

ically was often the new sense which the translator subjectively found (or perhaps one should say invented) in his source" (26).

2. *The Mirrour of the World*, Sig. n4ʳ. Caxton's book is catalogued in *A Short Title Catalogue of Books Printed in England, Scotland, & Ireland and of English Books Printed Abroad, 1475-1640* Ed. A. W. Pollard and G. R. Redgrave rev ed. W. A. Jackson, F. S. Ferguson and Katharine F. Panzter (London: Bibliographical Society, 1986), # 24762. All references, hereafter will be given in the text and will be to the printer's signatures in the copy microfilmed by University Microfilms International for the series *English Books before 1640*. The book has been reprinted with the illustrations (but not the original page layout) once this century, see O. H. Prior, Ed. Caxton's *Mirrour of the World* (London: Kegan Paul, Trench, Trübner & Co., LTD. for the Early English Text Society, 1913).

3. Technically the first book printed by Caxton with an illustration was *The Recuyell of the Historyes of Troye*, printed in Bruges in 1475, which contains as its frontispiece a metal etching of a book being presented to Margaret, Duchess of York. As only one edition of this book includes the illustration, it is likely that it was included only in certain "presentation" copies. Beyond this, there is some question as to which is the first of Caxton's Westminster editions to contain illustrations. N. F. Blake believes it is *Cato*, others have argued that the *Mirrour* came first. As *Cato* only includes two illustrations, it seems safe to consider the *Mirrour* the first of Caxton's editions with "significant" illustrations. See Blake, *England's First Publisher*, 135-38 and Hodnett 1.

4. Painter 102.

5. Caxton states this fact in his preface (a5ʳ).

6. Painter disputes that this is the actual MS, but grants that it is a close relative (pg.108). Blake argues that the case is still strong that this is the actual MS, see *First Publisher* 138, *World* 154, and *Literary Cuture* 110.

7. MS Fonds fr. 574 has been reprinted by Oliver Prior as *L'Image du Monde de maitre Gossouin redaction en prose*. Texte du manuscrit de la Bibliotheque nationale, fonds francais no. 574. (Lausanne: Payot, 1913).

8. The existence of many MSs of this work has led many scholars to conclude that it was a popular book. Caution must be used with the term "popular," however, as ownership of any MS from the 13th to the 16th century was reserved for certain social classes. Texts which have survived in larger numbers were often those intended for elite markets and consequently housed in the libraries of lasting institutions (university and aristocratic libraries) -- see Paul Needham, *The Printer and the Pardoner*. It is only when texts come into print, a process begun by Caxton, that the work can begin to be viewed as popular in a more modern sense. And, by printing his editions, even Caxton only sightly increased the number of book owners.

9. C. V. Langlois disputed this claim: "[Prior] a présenté quatre arguments à l'appui de cette opinion. Mais aucun n'est décisif, car toutes les circonstances alléguées s'expliquent aussi bien dans l'hypothèse d'un anonyme opérant, à une époque indéterminée de la seconde moitié du XIIIᵉ siècle, sur un exemplaire

conforme à ceux de la première rédaction qui nous sont parvenus" (Langlois 3: 147-47). [Prior has presented four arguments to support this position. But none is decisive, for all of the circumstances that allegedly confirm his hypothesis can also support the theory that an anonymous figure based the prose work on a copy of the first [verse] edition at some unknown time in the second half of the 13th century.] (My translation.)

10. The identity of the author has been disputed. See Prior ix-x.

11. Prior discusses many of the sources used by Gossouin in the introduction and notes to his edition of the *Mirrour*, among the sources are: Jacobus de Vitriaco, Honorius Augustodunensis, and Neckam (Prior x).

12. Copeland stresses that her description of medieval translation is based on the evidence of vernacular translation as practiced in an academic context: "My arguments do not necessarily extend to the emergence of "popular" translation in genres such as the lai or the metrical romance from one vernacular language into another, nor to hagiographical or devotional writings, nor to translation of scientific works. The important question of biblical translation is also outside the scope of this study. My chief concern here is the question of academic critical discourse in Latin and vernacular traditions" (*Rhetoric* 5).

13. See Millett, "Chaucer," 95.

14. Blake supports this view. See *Caxton and His World* 35-36.

15. See Tedeschi, "Publish and Perish."

16. Blake would not agree. The following is typical of his assessment of Caxton: "As Caxton paid scant attention to the textual quality of the works he produced, it might be thought he would make the products of his press aesthetically satisfying. Nothing could be further from the truth, for a glance at Continental books or at later English ones will show how primitive and utilitarian his are....When all is said and done they [his books] are neither textually accurate nor aesthetically appealing" (*First Publisher* 120). For the opposite view see note 21 below.

17. This may be the result of a difference in usage: as the work was translated from various Latin sources, the fact that it was not an individual text may not have occurred to Caxton, or the Bruges scribe.

18. This point is strengthened by the fact that Caxton showed no interest in identifying the author of the French version, though much of the modern bibliographical debate over the text has been concerned with just this aspect.

19. Blake comments that the mention of the Burgundian bookseller, "would add nothing to the esteem of the book" (*World* 160), but fails to mention that omitting it also allowed this edition to take on a specifically English identity.

20. Again, the use of the word popular is tricky in this period. I am using it here merely to indicate a shift in readership from the medieval MS to the Caxton printed edition, the latter being available to many who would not have had access to the former. See note 8 above.

21. The most extensive debate over Caxton's role in the formation of English literary culture surrounds his edition of Malory, *Le morte d'Arthur* (1485). This

text was the only version available until 1934 when the Winchester Malory manuscript was discovered. This discovery led Eugene Vinaver to argue that Caxton had corrupted Malory's text by altering the intended structure of the work. By changing the incipits and explicits found in the Winchester MS, Vinaver argued, Caxton recast Malory's series of tales as a single book. This highly influential argument has supported the characterization of Caxton as a business-man first and literary figure second (perpetuated by Blake and others). Two recent volumes of the journal *Arthuriana* have been devoted to the challenge to Vinaver's thesis prompted by arguments from the late William Mathews. For the present study, the most important conclusions to come from this debate are those stated by Robert Kindrick in his introduction to Mathews' essay on Caxton: "We are forced by [Mathews'] evidence to assume Caxton was serious in his interest in a good text and that he told the truth in his prologues. Caxton worked with editorial integrity" (Kindrick 18). See *Arthuriana* 7:1 (Spring 97), a special issue devoted to "William Mathews on Caxton and Malory," and *Arthuriana* 5:2 (Summer 95), a "Special issue on Editing Malory" guest edited by Michael N. Salda; in addition to Salda's introduction, see essays by Kevin Grimm, Shunichi Noguchi, Charles Mooreman, and P.J.C. Field.

22. Fisher is quoting from Blake, *Caxton His World*, 128.

23. Painter discusses the strictures of the Mercers' company on page 23 of his biography.

24. Prior lists such word pairs on page xxiv of his introduction. The notes to his edition include those places where Caxton's text differs significantly from the French MS. For a close comparison and side by side printing of Caxton's translation and the French version of the prologue, see Blake, *Caxton and His World*, 154-160. Blake's work on the character of Caxton's translations is very convincing. For example, his description of Caxton's translations as occupying a "middle position" in relation to the translations of his contemporaries seems right, as does his conclusion that "The faults and virtues of Caxton's trans-lations...are typical of most fifteenth-century translations" (*World* 149, 150). This assessment does not compromise the present argument. I would simply stress that more attention needs to be given to the impact of print on the way Caxton's translations were packaged as books. For in the move from manuscript to print, more than linguistic translation was at stake, as is witnessed by the debate over the Caxton and Winchester versions of Malory. The movement of even the most typical of fifteenth-century translations onto the printed page and into the more public space of the printed book market, itself constitutes an important development.

25. As Caxton retained the reference to the horned people of France, it is fairly clear that his motives were nationalistic. My point is simply that he consistently left himself room for a defense of his edition that would preserve the authority of the original: that he did not presume himself an author.

26. Prior notes that Caxton sometimes "translates word for word and sacrifices clearness to accuracy" (Prior xxiii). A good example of this is his

translation of the French "Ele repont ses faons es illes ou il n'a boz ne couluevres" (fol. 58^v) as "She fawneth her fawnes & hydeth them where is no woode" (f1^r). Prior points out that Caxton apparently mistook "boz" (toads) for "bois" (wood), but an examination of MS Roy. 19A IX reveals that this was an honest mistake, as the ligature between the "o" and the "z" could easily have been taken for an "i." Caxton's decision to choose the less likely "wood," forcing him to omit the reference to "couluevres" (adders), attests to his desire to follow his copy as closely as possible. He created a readable text, but one that was guided by what probably appeared to him to be an error in the original.

27. See Langlois, "Note Sur L'Illustration Du Volume," xxxi.

28. See essays by Tedeschi and Hindman in *Printing the Written Word*.

29. This illustration is reproduced in Hodnett, figure 1.

30. Such categories are simply the result of an attempt to organize the material for this study and are biased by my twentieth century perspective; it will become clear below that discussions of the particular illustrations often reveal idiosyncracies that offer a much better account of the role of the illustrations than could any broad category.

31. Blake's comparison of the two scenes highlights the similarities of the two compositions. See *First Publisher* 135-138.

32. This is the copy microfilmed by University Microfilms.

33. Though the diagram in Roy. 19A IX which corresponds to Caxton's weighted stones (figure 7) does not include representational features, its precursor in MS Fonds fr. 574 does. More importantly, though Caxton's illustrations abandon representational features for the remainder of the text, the Bruges MS does include human figures and other ornamental features in such schematic illustrations as the description of the order of bodies in the cosmos (diagrams which appear after this point in the text).

Works Cited

Belyea, Barbara. "Caxton's Reading Public." *English Language Notes* 19:1 (1981): 14-19.

Benjamin, Walter. "The Task of the Translator: An Introduction to the Translation of Baudelaire's Tableaux Parisiens." *Illuminations*. Ed. Hannah Arendt. Trans. Harry Zohn. New York: Schocken Books, 1968. 69-82.

Blake, Norman F. *Caxton: England's First Publisher*. New York: Barnes & Noble, 1976.

---. *Caxton and His World*. London: Andre Deutsch, 1969.

---. *William Caxton and English Literary Culture*. London: Hambledon, 1991.

Burnley, J. D. "Late Medieval English Translation: Types and Reflections." *The Medieval Translator: The Theory and Practice of Translation in the Middle Ages*. Ed. Roger Ellis. Cambridge: D. S. Brewer, 1989. 37-53.

Copeland, Rita. "The Fortunes of 'non verbum pro verbo': or why Jerome is not a Ciceronian." *The Medieval Translator: The Theory and Practice of Translation in the Middle Ages*. Ed. Roger Ellis. Cambridge: D.S. Brewer, 1989.

---. *Rhetoric, Hermeneutics, and Translation in the Middle Ages: Academic Traditions and Vernacular Texts*. Cambridge: Cambridge UP, 1991.

Crotch, W. J. B. *The Prologues and Epilogues of William Caxton*. Ed. Humphrey Milford. London: Oxford U P, 1928.

Ellis, Roger. "The Choices of the Translator in the Late Middle English Period." In *The Medieval Mystical Tradition in England*. Ed. Marion Glasscoe. Exeter: Short Run Press Ltd., 1982. 18-46.

Fisher, John H. "Caxton and Chancery English." *Fifteenth Century Studies: Recent Essays*. Ed. Robert F. Yeager. Hamden, CT: Archon, 1984. 161-185.

Hellinga, Lotte. "Importation of Books Printed on the Continent into England and Scotland before c. 1520." *Printing the Written Word: The Social History of Books, circa 1450-1520*. Ed. Sandra Hindman. Ithaca: Cornell, 1991. 205-224.

Hindman, Sandra L., ed. *Printing the Written Word: The Social History of Books, circa 1450-1520*. Ithaca: Cornell UP, 1991.

Hodnett, Edward. *English Woodcuts. 1480-1535*. Rev. ed. Oxford: Oxford UP, 1973.

Kindrick, Robert L. "Introduction: Caxton, Malory, and an Authentic Arthurian Text." *Arthuriana* 7:1 (Spring 1997). 6-21.

Langlois, Charles V. *La Vie en France au Moyen Age: La Connaissance de la Nature et du Monde*. 4 vols. Paris: Librairie Hachette, 1925-28.

Millet, Bella. "Chaucer, Lollius, and the Medieval Theory of Authorship." *Studies in the Age of Chaucer: Proceedings*, No. 1 (1984): 93-103.

Needham, Paul. *The Printer and the Pardoner: An Unrecorded Indulgence Printed by William Caxton for the Hospital of St. Mary Rounceval, Charing Cross*. Washington, D. C.: Library of Congress, 1986.

Painter, George Duncan. *William Caxton: A Biography*. New York: G.P. Putnam's Sons, 1977.

Pratt, Karen. "Medieval Attitudes to Translation and Adaptation: The Rhetorical Theory and the Poetic Practice." *The Medieval Translator II*. Ed. Roger Ellis. London: Centre for Medieval Studies, 1991. 1-27.

Prior, O. H. Introduction. *Caxton's Mirrour of the World*. London: Kegan Paul, Trench, Trübner, 1913. v-xxv.

Rutter, Russell. "William Caxton and Literary Patronage." *Studies in Philology* 84:4 (1987): 440-470.

Tedeschi, Martha. "Publish and Perish: The Career of Lienhart Holle in Ulm." *Printing the Written Word: The Social History of Books circa 1450-1520*. Ed. Sandra Hindman. Ithaca: Cornell UP, 1991. 41-67.

Venuti, Lawrence, ed. *Rethinking Translation: Discourse, Subjectivity, Ideology*. New York: Routledge, 1992.

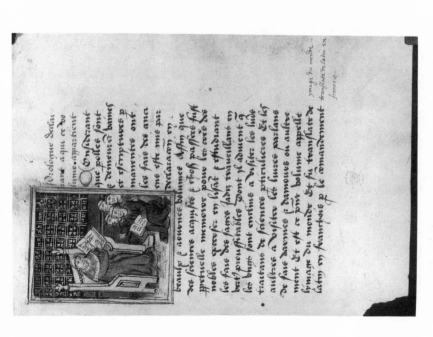

Figure 1. Master and Scholars, illumination from MS. Roy. 19A, XI fol. 4. (By permission of The British Library.)

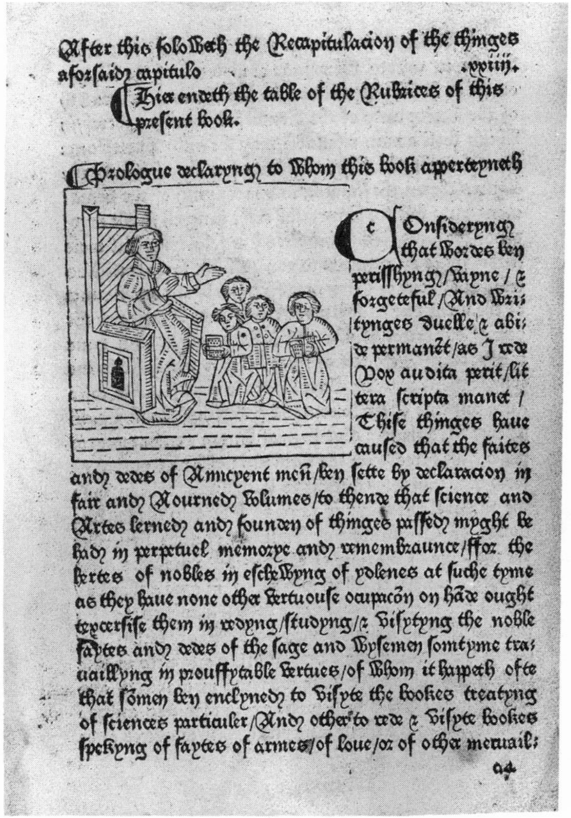

Figure 2. Master and Scholars, woodcut from Caxton's *Mirrour of the World.* (Pierpont Morgan Library, New York. PML 776. Sig. a4r.)

Be before ben / vnderstonde the
bettre / and more
clerely conceyue / þe
may vnderstande by
another ensample ,
yf the crosse were ve-
rayly right in the
mydole , in suche wyse that the heuen myght be seen
thurgh. And yf one threwe a stone or an hep promette
...

O̶f the firste
of the vij, sciences
is grāmaire /
of whiche for
the tyme that
is now, is
not knowen
the fourth pr
a / wythout
Whiche science / ʃikerly alle other sciences in especial ben
of lytel recommendacion, by cause wythout grāmaire the
may none prouffite / For grāmaire is the foundement and
the begynnyng of clergye / And it is the gate by the
Whiche in entraunce is begonne ʒ in contynuyng men

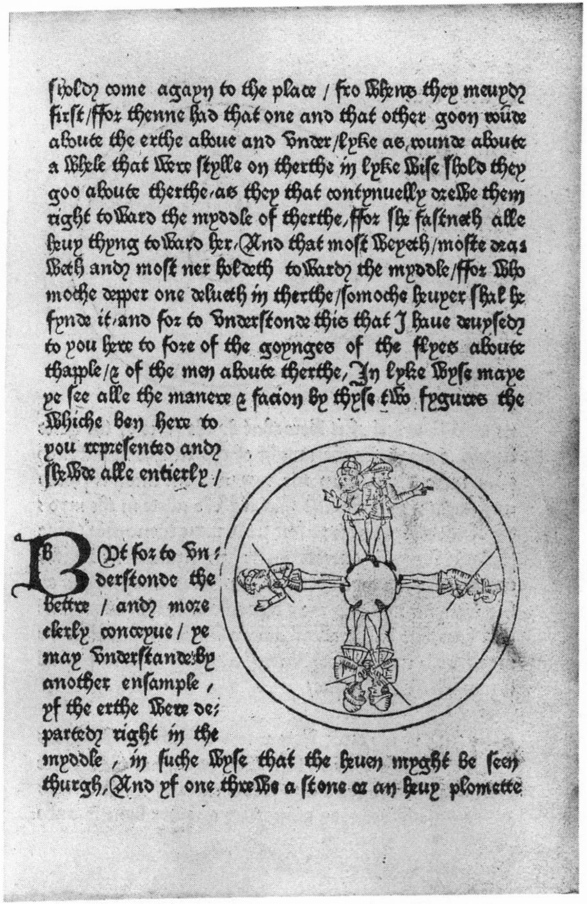

Figure 3. Instruction of Logic, woodcut from Caxton's *Mirrour of the World*. (Pierpont Morgan Library, New York. PML 776.

Figure 4. Theoretical journey to the antipodes, woodcut from Caxton's *Mirrour of the World*. (Pierpont Morgan Library, New York. PML 776. Sig. K4.)

Ilz seroient partiz Et puis reviendroient tous deux au lieu dont ilz meurent premierement Car lors avoit et luy et laut fait ung tour alentour de la terre par dessus et par dessoubz aussi comme entour une roe qui seroit toute quoye sur terre pareillement iroient ilz entour la terre comme ceulx qui continuellement se traveroient droit vers le milieu de la terre Car elle serre tous poins en vers elle et que plus poise tant plus attrait et le plus pres se tient du milieu Car de tant plus que on cave en terre en parfont et plus la treuve on pesante Et pour entendre ce que je

Figure 5. Journey to the antipodes, illumination from MS. Roy. 19A IX, fol. 42. (By permission of The British Library.)

in lyke wyse on bothe sides, and that eche of them threwe a stone in to the hole, whether it were grete or lytyl / eche stone shold come in to myddle of therthe, without ever to be remeued fro thens / But yf it were drawen away by force/ And they shold holden them one aboute another for to take place everiche in the myddle of therthe/ And yf the stones were of like weight, they shold come therto alle at one tyme, assone that one as that other/ For nature wold suffre it none other wise/ And that one shold come ayenst another as ye may playnly see by this fygure/

And yf their weyght and powers were not egall fro the place fro whens they shold falle / that whiche were most hevy/ that sholde sonnest come to the myddle of therthe/ And the other shold be al aboute her as this seconde figure sheweth playnly on that other side/

And so moche may be caste therin that the holes may be full, lyke as they were to fore/ As ye may

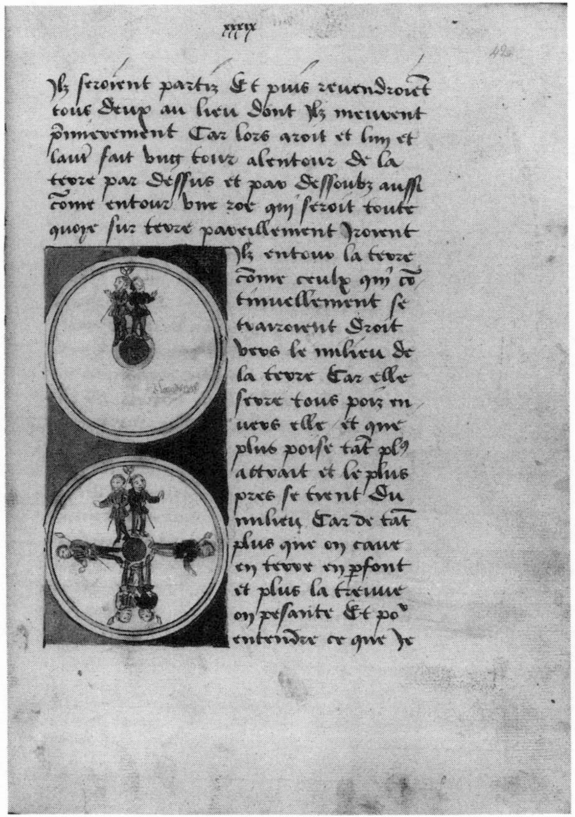

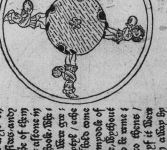

Figure 6. Men dropping stones to the center of the Earth, woodcut from Caxton's *Mirrour of the World*. (Pierpont Morgan Library, New York. PML 776. Sig. d7r.)

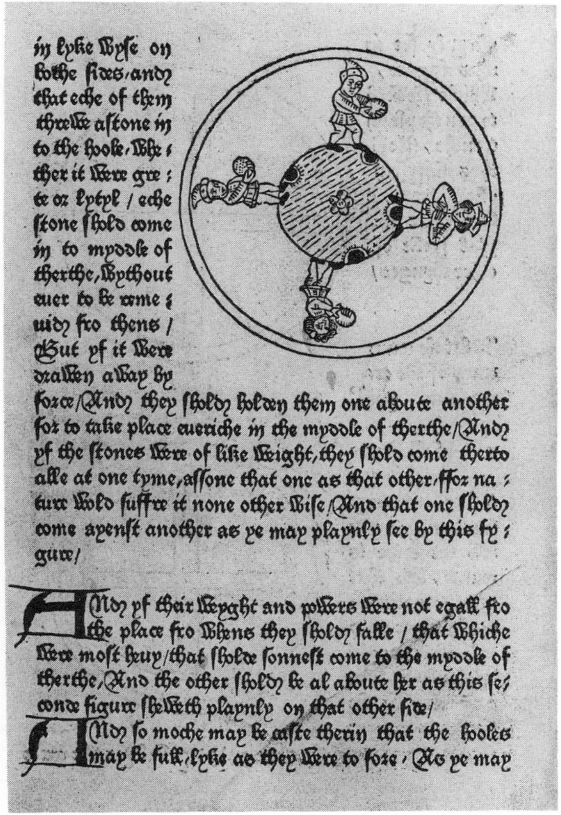

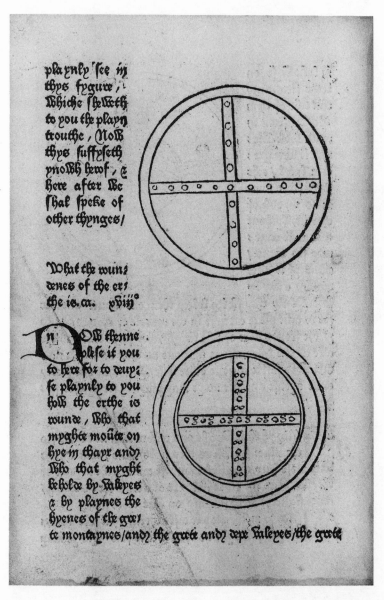

playnly see in thys fygure, Whiche sheweth to you the playn trouthe, Now thys suffyseth nowgh herof, & here after we shal speke of other thynges/

What the rundenes of the erthe is. ca. ×viij°

N NOW thenne olese if you to here for to wyse se playnly to you how the erthe is wunde, Who that myghte moute on hye in thayr and who that myght beholde by valeyes & by playnes the hyenes of the gret

te montaynes/and the gret and depe valeyes/the gret

Figure 7. Stones drawn to the center of the Earth, woodcut from Caxton's *Mirrour of the World*. (Pierpont Morgan Library, New York. PML 776. Sig. d7v.)

St. Catherine, Lacan, and The Problem of Psycho-History

David Metzger

Why should anyone assume that there is a rapport between history and psychoanalysis? Even if we grant that the transferential relation between analyst and analysand provokes or delineates something that might be known, what encourages us to find that something outside of the clinic? Certainly, no member of the psychoanalytic community would be surprised to discover a colleague's interest in mystical literature, since Freud himself suggests that the study of myth, literature, and philosophy are crucial to the analyst's training (*Question of Lay Analysis*, 200). But why would a student of religion, literature, or philosophy be, interested in psychoanalysis? Certainly, psychoanalytically-specific language can be reoriented in terms of solutions to ethical or epistemological problems that, in the clinic, emerge as nosological categories; Freud's work on neurosis/religion and Slavoj Zizek's recent popularizations of Lacanian thinking would provide the most accessible examples. But is "applicability" a guarantee of accuracy? Isn't analogy more a tool of explanation than a mode of demonstration -- as Freud himself admits in *Obsessive Actions and Religious Practices*?

The relationship between history and psychoanalysis must then be expressed so that the differences between the two are reasserted precisely when we are tempted to constrain what we know about the one in order to protect what we might know about the other. To say that we will not "protect" our knowledge of the one means that the evidentiary conditions for this inquiry cannot be satisfied when the one has provided a subject position for the other; quite the contrary, we will know when we've said something precisely when the one (history or psychoanalysis) offers up what cannot be held as a potential subject position for the other. In this way, we might see how both history and so-called psychoanalytic theory resist the construction of the analyst's position which Lacan saw as beyond satisfaction or dissatisfaction (Lacan, *Seminar XI*, 276).

So, where does this promise of something more than an analogy leave us with regard to the relationship of history and psychoanalysis?

Both history and psychoanalysis provide techniques by which the Other might be constructed -- but whereas history runs the risk of conflating the Other with the symbolic order, psychoanalysis runs the risk of conflating the Other with the Real. Understandably, such terms as the Other and the Real might be frustrating or seemingly irrelevant to a non-Lacanian audience. However, let us take this opportunity to see what of Lacan's technical knowledge concerning the analytic session might be reworked in light of the promise of a transdisciplinary inquiry. In order to make sense of such a Lacanian-specific statement, one must assume that "coherence, sense, meaning, knowledge" are produced through the perception of a body. What Aristotle identified as an "action" in his *Poetics*, a Lacanian would identify as "the movement of a body in space" (Metzger, *The Lost Cause*, 38-49). What Kenneth Burke called "identity" would be recognized as "the necessary construction of another body when our own bodies or the bodies of others fail to lend coherence/meaning/knowledge to our world." From a Lacanian point of view, Aristotle understood that narratives lend coherence/meaning/knowledge to the world precisely because they show how the modalities of experience (what is possible, necessary, or impossible) are expressed by distinguishable corporeal capacities; what can happen is delimited by what kind of body we're talking about. For example, if we were watching a movie in which a body was pushed from a cliff, then the narrative would take very different turns depending on whether or not that body could fly. It is also possible that, if a body were pushed from a cliff cannot fly, it might fall in such a way that is appears to be flight -- such as we see in Ridley Scott's film *Thelma and Louise*. At the end of the film, the two women drive into the Grand Canyon in their Thunderbird, but Scott freezes the car in flight, washes out the background, and leaves Thelma and Louise suspended on a white screen. Bringing Thelma and Louise back into the narrative would mean their deaths or the necessity for some intervention. Divine intervention is out of the question; Yoda's not in the trunk; and the car's name isn't Chitty-Chitty-Bang-Bang. So, the film maker intervenes, creating something akin to metaphor by forcing us to accept that what we've been watching is a "body of film" whose modalities are expressed/constrained by the medium and by the director's/editor's craft, not by the identification of our bodies with the images of bodies on the screen. Burke understood that metaphors lend coherence/meaning/knowledge to the world precisely because they show what happens when a distinguishable corporeal capacity fails to identify the modalities of experience (what is possible, necessary, or impossible): the presence of another body is invoked.

Furthermore, once this "another body" is invoked, the story ends or this "another body" becomes part of the narrative; there is no metaphor of metaphor. This another body (metaphor) can only become "another metaphor" once it has be realized as the continuation of a narration whose coherence was put in jeopardy by its reliance on one body (what a car can do, what a human can do, what my parents can do) rather than another body (what Ridley Scott can do).

Psychoanalysis and history enter into our discussion at this point, the point at which one might ask the question, "What could Thelma and Louise do if there were no Ridley Scott? ...that is, if there were no maker?" Who or what might Thelma and Louise be? In these terms, my previous statement regarding psychoanalysis and history would mean that history runs the risk of trying to save the maker/the Other by conflating it with the symbolic order (the author might be dead but the author doesn't know it) and that analysis risks saving the maker/the Other by conflating it with the Real (the author might be dead but the author nevertheless continues to function). The three orders that Lacan speaks about and we hear so much about (the Imaginary, Symbolic, and Real) might then be viewed as refuges for the Other/the maker. If the Other/maker can not secure itself in the Imaginary, then one tries to secure it in the Real; if it cannot be secured in the Real, one tries to secure it in the Symbolic.

Some readers will have already guessed that this discussion of the Other's flight is, in fact, an elaboration of Lacan's mirror stage essay.[1] In terms of the so-called "Mirror-stage," one might think of one's image in a mirror or in language as something Other, the maker of oneself. When one sees that image cannot support the existence of the Other (that the image cannot make a human subject), one assumes that one's body (the real of one's body and not the image) is the Other/Maker (for further discussion of this point, see Metzger, "Lacanian Psychoanalysis and the Neurotic Orientation of Religious Experience.") When one's body cannot account for one's existence, the Other or the Maker enters the symbolic order. It would seem that theology and psychoanalysis have the same jumping-off point (when the real of one's body cannot identify one's maker), but this is not quite so. For the theologian, we might associate this jump-start with mysticism. The analyst, however, must see that the association of the maker with the symbolic does not answer an important question: where does this presumption of the Other/maker come from?

As an analyst, Lacan associates the presumption of the Other/Maker with the unconscious -- which leads him to reduce Freud's *Moses and Monotheism* to the statement that God (the Other/Maker) is the unconscious, while gods are from the Real (Lacan, *Seminar XI*, 59; Regnault, 11).[2]

Understandably, these particular orientations of theology, psychoanalysis, and history may be difficult to understand without the help of a specific example or case. With this difficulty in mind, let us turn to the issue of St. Catherine's devotion to the eucharist. In the United States, Catherine of Siena has been discussed in two very popular books: Rudolph Bell's *Holy Anorexia* and Caroline Walker Bynum's *Holy Feast and Holy Fast*. Each book seeks to address the fact that, at the age of twenty-five, Catherine Beninacasa (1347-1380) said to her confessor, Raymond of Capua, "I eat nothing." I think part of the reason for the success of these books and the general interest Americans have in the subject is the fact that historical discussions of a symptom, such as anorexia, inevitably lead one to speak of nosology in terms of choice. Earlier, I suggested that we will know when we've said something precisely when the one (history or psychoanalysis) offers up what cannot be held as a potential subject position for the other. In this way, we might see how both history and theology resist the construction of the analyst's position (which Lacan saw as beyond satisfaction or dissatisfaction). Our task, then, will be to see how St. Catherine used her satisfaction with the eucharist to keep God in her life and out of the unconscious. We will also see how Christianity, which was the master discourse of 14th-century Europe, helped to produce a saint, something that analysis has as yet failed to do.

In her letters and in her book, which she herself titled *Il libro*, hereafter cited as *The Dialogue*), we find someone very much concerned about the moral condition of the Christian state.[3] She isn't concerned with the possibility of a Christian state (as we see in Augustine). St. Catherine, in the same century as Aquinas, wrestled with the question of how Christian a Christian state could be. If the deity's appointed ministers on earth are corrupt, impatient, and clever men, what guarantee might there be that the church represents something other than earthly concerns? How might the church be reformed? How might those who chose to rebel against the church learn patience?

Let us admit the temptation to relate St. Catherine's questions to a familiar set of philosophical problems: the relation of seeming and being, the question of whether existence is a predicate or no. But having admitted this temptation, let us avoid it, since St. Catherine's answer is always to contemplate the Christ and the eucharistic mystery. She inherited a variety of commonsensical questions regarding the body of Christ (how is it possible that Christ's body should be in more than one place at a time? how is it possible that Christ's body should not be diminished when eaten?). Her answers, however, do not depend upon the theologian or natural philosopher's distinction between the absolute power (potentia abstracta) and the ordered power (potentia ordinatia) of the deity (Duhem, 390). Her answers reintroduce the reader to the everyday. If one wonders how Christ's body might be undiminished, St. Catherine refers one to the sun's undiminished generosity with light. If one wonders how Christ's body might be in more than one place at a given time, she suggests that one contemplate the lighting of several candles from one candle. If these everyday occurrences are possible, St. Catherine tell us, then so are the miracles of this most holy sacrament.

The problem with such explanations is that they seem to suggest that miracles are all around us, that they are everywhere. What need is there, then, for a church or a clergy? For this reason, it is not difficult to see how church officials might consider this young woman from Tuscany to be more of a problem than a solution (Scott 107-109). Having been successful in establishing Christianity as the symbolic order (the rational language) of medieval Europe, the church finds it necessary to protect itself from "imposters," "heretics," and the rhetorical demands of mass culture (Bynum, *Jesus as Mother*, ; Rubin, 51).[4]

The church had established itself as Christ's body, and we encounter throughout St. Catherine's writing the phrase, "the mystic body of the holy church." This position, however, is not without its problems. In St. Thomas' *Summa* we can see that it is difficult enough to establish the contours of and the logical constraints for this mystical body when one need only respond to the dictates of reason. What logical course might one chart with regard to the affective dimension of this mystical body? For example, if one grants that there is such a thing as a vision, how is it possible to distinguish between false visions and real ones? If the body and blood of the Christ appear as bread and wine at the moment of consecration, how is it possible to distinguish between bread that has become the body, and the bread that has not?

We can see here the appearance of the unconscious. What is called "the problem of affect" by psychoanalytic theorists is in Lacanian terms the recognition that the unconscious might appear to some as Real. That is, this presumption of an Other/Maker, which I earlier associated with the unconscious, is no longer something to be charted in terms of the imaginary and symbolic. The Other takes possession of the first available body, the body of the true believer. Unfortunately, from the standpoint of Church officials, it is difficult to police the Real. The Real may be everywhere, but its secrets, like the secrets of another person's pain, are available only to those who experience and, therefore, already know the Real as such.

In these terms, the psycho-social function of communion would be to allow the symbolic order to bear the burden of the Other's existence. By promoting the eucharist as the symbol of Christian/Church authority, clergy (perhaps beginning in the early ninth century) effectively removed the Other from the Imaginary and the Real. In the following passage from the *Summa*, Aquinas clearly shows us how removing the Other from the imaginary is a crucial step in the creation of a Christian community:

> It is obvious to our senses that after consecration all the accidents of bread and wine remain. And, by divine providence, there is a good reason for this. First, because it is not normal for people to eat human flesh and to drink human blood; in fact, they are revolted by this idea. Therefore Christ's flesh and blood are set before us to be taken under the appearance of those things which are of frequent use, namely bread and wine. Secondly, if we ate our Lord under his proper appearance, this sacrament would be ridiculed by unbelievers. Thirdly, in order that, while we take the Lord's body and blood invisibly, this fact may avail toward the merit of faith. (llla, q.75, a5; p. 71)

This passage from the *Summa* also shows us how, when the Other is removed by the Imaginary, the Other attempts to situate itself in terms of the Real (eating human flesh and drinking human blood). But since this image is horrific -- rendering the possibility of community as the necessity for nourishment -- the eucharist must evoke the Other in the position of the symbolic. Notice that I do not say evoke the Other in terms of language, since the conversion of bread into body cannot be simply figural. The metaphor out of which the symbolic order emerges must itself be embodied; it must become a part of the narrative of Christian community. One can find here an invitation for discussions of Christ as the mark of an intersection between the eternal time of God and the finite history of man. Or, one can see the necessity for an embodied metaphor as an invitation for love:

For you know that Christ says, `Do not turn back to look at what you've plowed.' It is perseverance that is crowned. Turn in affectionate love, with the dear loving Magdalene, and embrace the sweet venerable cross. There you will find all the sweet solid virtues, since it is there we find the God-Man." (Letter 59)

The bottom line for St. Catherine is always "Can it be embodied" (Bynum, *Holy Feast and Holy Fast*, 179)? In the above example, we see that the story of human endeavor is simply the story of an extended absence, a nothing scratched into the earth's face -- while the Christian's story takes its form as a single image of an embrace. We know that there is a maker; we know that there is a god precisely because the miracle of the Christ's sacrifice (the making of the human divine and the divine human) occurs in the eucharistic ceremony. And we know that the Church is god's instrument because the church is the mystical body of Christ:

> So you see, in no way can the heat and color and brightness that are fused in this light be divided -- not by the scant desire the soul brings to this sacrament, nor by any fault in the soul who receives it or in the one who administers it. It is like the sun, which is not contaminated by the filth it shines on. Nothing can contaminate or divide the gentle light in this sacrament. (207)

When Saint Catherine teaches this way of knowledge to others in her writings she always indicates that there is something more to do than simply follow the routine; there is the necessity of haste. One must rush onto the feet of the crucified Jesus and there recognize one's "nothing-ness." One must rush into the wound at his side and there encounter the God-Man,

> seeing nothing but his blood, shed with such blazing love ... . Then aflame with desire, you get up and climb to the next stair, his mouth. There you find rest in quiet calm; there you taste the peace of obedience. A person who is completely drunk, good and full, falls asleep and in that sleep feels neither pleasure nor pain" (Letter 62).

Notice the change in person, here: you climb the stairs; you recognize you're nothing; you are aflame, then "A person who ... ." "A person who ... " introduces something that almost seems like an analogy -- as if this "neither pleasure nor pain" were not to be experienced in a body except that of the crucified. There appears to be no enjoyment beyond the body of Christ. Yet, because the subject has recognized her nothingness (the first step toward knowledge) "she finds herself conformed with Christ crucified, united with Him." Our joy in Christ, therefore, as St Catherine assures, is not "disproportionate." In other words, there is no compounding of pleasures in Christ: the joy of Christ + the joy of a lot of money + the joy of a small but comfortable home. In these circumstances, pleasure itself is a limit, its own limit, and it is equal to itself.

A Lacanian discussion of St. Catherine's fasting would translate this discussion of pleasure into the following question, "What would St. Catherine's fasting do with or for the Other?" After examining *The Dialogue*, we might say that she was trying to make herself the image and object of the Other which Aquinas -- in a previous example -- had embodied in the symbolic. As the image of the Other, she notices that her mouth becomes the "mouth of holy desire," and her upper and lower rows of teeth become "hate for herself" and "love for virtue in herself and others" (140). Her food, she tells us, is suffering: "every sort of assault -- derision, insult, slander, reproach, endless persecution" (141). Her heart becomes the stomach which accepts all this approbation, while the soul "delights in and chews it over and over in such a way that she lets go of her delicacy about her bodily life in order to be able to eat this food at the table of the cross, the table of the teaching of Christ crucified" (141). The soul, as the image of the Other, then becomes fat on the cross, so much so that the soul bursts out of its physical body leaving the "sensual will" dead where the body should be and depositing the "well ordered will" in God (the Other).

Using the mirror stage model presented earlier, we might suggest that St. Catherine takes the Other's position in the Imaginary by leaving there a small, albeit dead, part of herself. However, in order to move the Other into the Symbolic, something must take up the potential place for the Other in the Real. For this reason, St. Catherine chooses to suffer; she makes her home in the Real so that the Other might become the deity's namesake in the Symbolic: "She brings forth virtue for her neighbors without pain. Not that this is in itself painless, but the dead will feels no pain because it endures pain willingly for my [god's] namesake" (141). We can see here one reason for the Saint's asceticism: in order to make living in the Real bearable, her "sensual will" must be dead. What is more, supporting this Imaginary identification will require rigorous demonstrations, repetitions of the fact that some part of her is dead. The curious logic here is that physical pain brought on by fasting makes the Real bearable by supporting her imaginary identification with the death of sensual will. In sum, St. Catherine is able to situate the Other in the Symbolic by taking its place in both the Imaginary and the Real. If, however, the Other were to move into the unconscious or the Imaginary or the Real, then St. Catherine's choices would be to suffer in the Real while the dead Other/Maker takes over her (dead) place in the Imaginary, to be dead herself (altogether Imaginary), or to represent herself as God (altogether Symbolic). Given this choice, representing oneself as God (altogether Symbolic) does not seem to be such a bad idea. Of course, when St. Catherine presumed to speak on the deity's behalf, she was criticized for her vanity; she was even accused of being a witch and a false prophet. St. Catherine's responses to these accusation was quite simply: She would encourage God to confirm that she was, in fact, the deity's representative by allowing her to "grow fat" on the eucharist, the so-called "table of the cross." By situating the Other in the symbolic, communion gives St. Catherine access to the Imaginary from the Real place of her suffering. However, if the Other were to slip from its symbolic position into the Imaginary, then there would be no difference between consecrated and unconsecrated bread (the seeming of the one would equal the seeming of the other) (Bynum, *Holy Feast and Holy Fast*, 172). St. Catherine would then starve not from a lack of nourishment but because the Other would begin feed the part of her that suffers (the part of her that suffers would become the object of the Other's/the Maker's desire). St. Catherine can consume the sacramental wafer precisely because it would not feed that part of her which suffers.

We can easily see how this type of discussion cashes out in terms of psychoanalysis. St. Catherine's reliance on communion might be seen as a register for some such thing as the unconscious. If St. Catherine's visions did not take the Other's position in the unconscious, then the Other might just stay there, appearing only at the level of one's fantasies. If the deity (the Other/Maker) did not sometimes slip from its position in the Symbolic, falling into the unconscious, then communion would not be needed to reassert the deity's Symbolic position. And if the deity did not sometimes wander into the unconscious (supporting the supposition that God is more than, if not other than, a "god-term" or a necessary fiction), then communion would only be figural, a symbol rather than a reenactment of the deity's sacrifice as the Christ. St. Catherine's writing also allows the analyst to see why a client would fear losing an Imaginary identification with death or fear becoming his/her own "subject" by losing the Other as her/his representative. In more technical terms, the case of St. Catherine is important because it shows why in the treatment of psychotic patients (for whom the Other is Real) the analyst helps the client to construct a prosthetic Imaginary (something dead enough not to feel pain). This case also shows why the analyst's treatment of hysteric patients is quite different -- coaxing the client out of her/his imaginary identification into a Symbolic order position where he/she can assume the position of a subject rather making the Other speak on his/her behalf and being disappointed, angry, or depressed (Miller 90).

But how does the delineation of the eucharist's psycho-social function by way of St. Catherine contribute to the study of medieval history? Has this study fallen into the psycho-historical trap identified by Erich Fromm in his study "The Dogma of Christ"?

> [They do] not interpret the ideologies as produced by men; [they re-construct] the men from the ideologies. Consequently [their] method is re-levant for the history of dogma and not as a method for the study of relig-ious and social history. (87)

Fromm's bifurcation is not without merit: either history of dogma or me-thod for the study of religious/social theory. Following the mirror-stage model, the presumed object of the psycho-historian's inquiries would be that part of the human subject that we see parred away in the St. Cath-erine's writings: the unfeeling objects of the Other. The psycho-historian then presumes to speak on behalf of these unfeeling objects in one of two ways: (1) when the past takes on the position of the Symbolic Other (what Fromm calls "ideology") for this missing hysteric or (2) when the past assumes the subject position (what Fromm calls "the man") for this missing hysteric.

In order to situate this discussion in terms of more contemporary scholarship, let us compare the position of the psycho-historian within this scheme to the description of the contemporary historian provided in Lee Patterson's introduction to *Negotiating the Past*: "Like Freud's civil-ization, historicism both issues from and entails discontent: the insuf-ficiency of the present directs us to the past, but what we recover fails to satisfy. And so history continues to be written" (i). In fact, we might go so far as to suggest that what Patterson proposes here is the historian's mirror stage: the insufficiency of the present (the insufficiency of the im-aginary), directs us to the past (the real), but what we recover (the symbolic) fails to satisfy (at the level of the unconscious). Furthermore, Patterson's project seems to offer up the possibility that objects might find themselves to be subjects (of history) when the Other is identified with the Symbolic order: he seeks a "model of cultural activity" that is not "dialectical but symbolic, in which cultural products are seen as full participants in a historical world that is equivalently densely symbolized" (*Negotiating the Past*, xi). In other words, we might identify Patterson's description of the historian's plight with the hysteric's desire to keep the Other out of the unconscious by identifying the Other with the Symbolic order. And *Negotiating the Past* may find itself in the company of other new historiographies that (albeit more explicitly) explore the relationship between history and hysteria.

The apparent compatibility of Patterson' position with a Lacanian brand of (psycho)historicism is underscored by the fact that, in the analytic session, the hysteric is not missing -- leaving what Patterson calls "the past" (which takes the hysteric's position in the Real) to make a place for itself in either the Symbolic or the unconscious. By introducing the potential movement of the Other in the Real, and Symbolic, and Imaginary, analytic practice provides historians with a way to reconstruct the experience of medieval religious culture -- as I think I've shown in my discussion of St. Catherine. In addition, Lacan's delineation of the hysteric's discourse shows us the edges to these psycho-historical investigations of religious experiences: we imagine that we have said something Real about our subjects and their motivations when the historical materials we pick over are providing us -- importantly but only -- with a list of the objects to which a historical subject might have identified.[5]

Old Dominion University

Notes

1. "The Mirror Stage" is something more than a developmental stage in the infant's "psychological growth." Lacan makes this clear in *Seminar I*: "As I have often underlined, the mirror-stage is not simply a moment in development. It also has an exemplary function, because it reveals some of the subject's relations to his [sic] image, in so far as it is the *Urbild* of the ego" (74). My discussion of the "mirror-stage model" includes the elaborations and clarifications offered by Lacan as the "Che Vuoi?" graph in "Subversion of the Subject and The Dialectic of Desire."

2. This is not to say that the analytic scene does not encourage the analysand to conflate the Other and the symbolic because Lacan has asserted that such is indeed an analytic goal (*Seminar XX: Encore*, 153-54). However, analysis does not encourage this conflation of the symbolic and the Other in order to save the

Other (from the Real) but to save the analysand from the Real Other whose presence is felt in psychosis. Lacan's rereading of Freud might be pushed in *Moses and Monotheism* to the point where one says that without monotheism there would be no psychoanalysis. But we should be careful not to assume that psychoanalysis is a religion. Lacan's statement is that "It is not atheistic to assert that God is dead; the atheist asserts that God is the unconscious." We might then associate this position with the frustration Freud seems to have felt when trying to distinguish psychoanalysis from religious experience. This is not Lacan's problem, however. Lacan sees the one god, but in terms of the Real (the potential for an identity position, a signifier in the Real; *Seminar XVII: L'envers de la psychanalyse*, 158-159).

3. For the reader's convenience, all citations are from the Noffke translations of *The Dialogue* and *Letters*. I must thank my colleagues in the Early Modern Studies Program at Old Dominion University for their assistance in checking Noffke's translation against the Cavalenni edition of *The Dialogue* and the handsome volume of the *Letters* prepared for the Ediziones Editorali Instituti Etudii Santi Catherini.

4. This is not to say that discerning between the deceived and the inspired was not a concern before the 14th century. We find the following in the letters of Cyprian: on a sudden, a certain woman ... in a state of ecstacy announced herself as a prophetess, and acted as if filled with the Holy Ghost ... . [She] would walk in the keen winter with bare feet over frozen snow ... [and] deceived many ... [by pretending] that with a powerful invocation she could sanctify bread and celebrate the Eucharist ... and also to baptize many, making use of the usual and lawful words of the rite."

5. Lacan is quite explicit with regard to how far a neurotic analysand might be pushed: "Ce qui est appelé un symptome névrotique est simplement quelque chose qui leur permet devivre. Ils vivent une vie difficile et nous essayons d'alléger leur inconfort. Parfois nous leur donnons le sentiment qui'ils sont normaux. Dieu merci, nous ne les rendons pas assez normaux pour qui'ils finnissent psycotiques. C'est le point ou nous avons a etre tres prudents. Certains d'entre eux ont reellement la vocation de pousser les choses a leur limit ... . Une analyse n'a pas a etre poussee trop loin" (*Scilicet* 6/7, 15). For a specific discussion of the cultural criticism's dependence on the discourse of hysteria, see Metzger's "A Response to Patricia Gherovici's 'The Ghetto's Sublime Hysterics.'"

Works Cited

Bell, Rudolph. *Holy Anorexia*. Chicago: U of Chicago P, 1985.

Bynum, Caroline Walker. *Holy Feast and Holy Fast*. Berkeley: U of California P, 1987.

Duhem, Pierre. *Medieval Cosmology*. Roger Ariew, ed. and trans. Chicago: U of Chicago P, 1985.

Fradenburg, Louise. "'So That We May Speak of Them': Enjoying the Middle Ages." *New Literary History* 28(1997): 205-230.

Freud, Sigmund. *Moses and Monotheism. S.E.* 23. London: Hogarth P, 1964: 7-140.

---. *Obssessive Acts and Religious Practices. S.E.* 9. London: Hogarth Press, 1959: 115-128.

---. *Question of Lay Analysis. S.E.* 20. London: Hogarth P, 1959: 179-258.

Fromm, Erich. "The Dogma of Christ." *The Dogma of Christ and Other Essays on Religion, Psychology, and Culture.* Trans. James Luther Adams. Garden City, NY: Doubleday & Company, 1966. 3-95.

Lacan, Jacques. "Entretiens entre les universités américaines." *Scilicet* 6/7: 6-63.

---. *Seminar I: Freud's Papers on Technique.* New York: Norton, 1991.

---. *Le Séminaire XVII: l'envers de la psychanalyse.* Ed. Jacques-Alain Miller. Paris: Seuil, 1991.

---. *Le Séminaire XX: Encore.* Ed. Jacques-Alain Miller. Paris: Seuil, 1986.

Metzger, David. "A Response to Patricia Gherovici's 'The Ghetto's Sublime Hysterics." *Bien Dire* 2/3 (1995-96): 23-26.

---. "Freud's Jewish Science and Lacan's Sinthome." *American Imago* 54.2 (Summer 1997): 149-164.

---. "Lacanian Psychoanalysis and the Neurotic Orientation of Religious Experience." *Looking at Lacan.* Stephen Friedlander and Kareen Malone, eds. Albany: SUNY, forthcoming.

---. *The Lost Cause of Rhetoric: the relation of rhetoric and geometry in Aristotle and Lacan.* Carbondale: Southern Illinois UP, 1995.

Miller, Jacques-Alain. "The Analytic Experience: Means, Ends, and Results." *Lacan and The Subject of Language.* Ellie Ragland and Mark Bracher, eds. New York: Routledge, 1991, 83-99.

Patterson, Lee. *Negotiating the Past.* Madison: U of Wisconsin P, 1987.

Regnault, Francois. *Dieu est inconscient.* Paris: Navarin Editeur, 1985.

Rubin, Miri. "The Eucharist and the Construction of Medieval Identities." *Culture and History 1350-1600.* David Aers, ed. Detroit: Wayne State UP, 1992, 43-64.

Scott, Karen. "Urban Space, Women's Networks, and the Lay Apostolate in the Siena of Catherine Benincasa." *Creative Women in Medieval and Early Modern Italy.* E. Ann Matter and John Coakley, eds. Philadelphia: U of Pennsylvania P, 1994, 105-119.

St. Catherine. *The Letters of St. Catherine of Siena.* Vol. I. Trans. Suzanne Noffke. Binghamton, New York: Center for Medieval and Early Renaissance Studies, 1988.

St. Catherine. *The Dialogue.* Trans. Suzanne Noffke. New York: Paulist Press, 1980.

St. Thomas. *Summa Theologica.* New York: Blackfriars (McGraw-Hill), 1968.

Shapeshifting and Berserkergang

Stephan Grundy

Shapeshifting, in its various forms, is one of the more common minor literary motifs in Old Icelandic literature. The identification of a human with an animal provided a rich symbological vocabulary for the poets and saga-writers: knowledge out of the ordinary, most usually prophetic knowledge, could be quickly and artistically expressed by, for instance, the representation of hostile persons as wolves, bears, or eagles. This identification, however, was clearly, in its origins, more than a literary device. The common Germanic usage of animal-elements in personal names[1] indicates that the association between a human and a specific animal was deeply grounded in the Norse culture, a grounding which is reflected both in heroic-mythological tales of shape-shifting and in the more prosaic context of the family sagas in which elements of this association may survive. Likewise, iconographic evidence such as that provided by the Torslunda helm-plate matrices and certain of the figures on the Oseburg burial tapestries, among other examples, gives clear evidence of the deliberate identification between the human warrior and the animal whose characteristics he was thought to embody, expressed by masking and the wearing of the appropriate animal's skin. This identification is made clearest in the problematical figure of the *berserkr*, who at times, particularly in the earlier sources, was said to use the physical animal-hide in order to induce his fits, but could also "change his hide" (*hamask*) in fury, or even involuntarily, without the use of a physical skin, leading to the fascinating question of the relationship between the different forms of shapeshifting known to the saga-authors, the psychological transformation of the berserk, and the specific importance of an animal's skin in the process of shapechanging.

The shapeshifting of Norse literature takes two chief forms: the changing of the body and the changing of the disembodied spirit (or spiritual manifestation of the human in the form of an animal). Of the two, the latter is by far the most common within a human context: physical metamorphosis in the world of human beings occurs only rarely and in the more fantastic materials such as *Vǫlsunga saga* and *Hrólfs saga kraka,* which will be discussed in more detail later. While the practical Icelandic mind in general rejected the concept of actual physical metamorphosis in favour of the more nebulous, but also more believable, shapeshifting of the temporarily disembodied soul, the differentiation between the physical transformation practiced by gods and *jǫtnar* and the spiritual transformation of the Icelander who is *hamrammr,* can be made only in regards to their normal realm of operation: gods and *jǫtnar* naturally belong to that sphere of existence which is entered by the human when he (or she) leaves the physical body behind. Hence, we may expect to find a direct relationship between the shape-shifting mechanisms of deities and their associates, and those used by humans in their extracorporeal activities: it can be demonstrated that the same fundamental principles underly the process by which gods and *jǫtnar* transform themselves in the otherworldly realms, legendary heroes transform themselves (or are transformed) physically in the human realms, and saga-characters transform their spirits and carry out activities separately from their actual bodies.

The chief consistent element in accounts of otherworldly shapeshifting is the shapeshifter's use of a skin in order to transform -- a necessity suffered even by the gods. Þjóðólfr's *Haustlǫng* describes Loki as making his flight "hauks flugbjalfa aukinn", (increased by a hawk's flying-pelt)[2] regarding which Snorri clarifies that Loki must ask "ef Freyia vill lia honvm valshams, er hon a" (if Freyja will lend him (the) hawk's hide which she owns)[3] in order to fly to and from Jǫtunheimr -- a description perhaps influenced by Þórr's request to Freyja in *Þrymsqviða* 3, "Muntu mér, Freyia, fiaðrhams liá, / ef ec minn hamar mættac hitta?" (Will you, Freyja, lend me your feather-hide, if I am to be able to get my hammer?)[4] - a loan necessary so that Loki can fly to Jǫtunheimr and make enquiries. Similarly, when Þjazi comes after Loki, according to Snorri, "teckr hann arnar haminn" (he takes the eagle's hide).[5] Even in as late a work as *Sǫrla þáttr*, it is described how "Loke verdr þa at einne flo...Þa dregr Loki af ser floar haminn" (Loki then becomes a fly...then Loki takes off his fly's hide).[6] The source of all winds is described in *Vafþrúðnismál* 37 as "iǫtunn, í arnar ham" (a giant in eagle's hide). That the belief in the gods' need for the use of a hide for shapeshifting was firmly rooted in the native religion of the Viking Age is borne out by the Larbrö St. Hammars III picture stone (Gotland, ca. 700-800) which shows a peculiar figure, half-human, half-bird, with the eagle's beak arching over the man's head. He is receiving drink from a woman, behind whom stands a threatening male figure with a sword. This scene is usually interpreted as showing Óðinn's reception of the mead of poetry from Gunnlǫð, the eagle-shape referring to his subsequent escape in that form.[7] Even in the realm of myth, instances where a skin is not specified are rare, and usually imposed from without. In his description of the return of Iðunn, Snorri says only that "bra Loki henni ihnotar liki"(Loki drew her into a nut's likeness).[8] No details of this transformation are provided in the *Haustlǫng* text from which Snorri was apparently working, but it seems reasonable to accept Richard North's explanation that "the two elaborate wing-kennings in 12/4 and /6, which imply painted images of birds flying, may show that Þjóðólfr is here inferring Þjazi's pursuit of Loki from a picture of two birds above a fire", with Iðunn concealed in some manner consonant with Snorri's description,[9] though the suggestion that the term *ása leika* for Iðunn may be understood as "play-thing/doll of the Æsir" may refer to her transformation into an easily portable shape[10] is perhaps a stretch of interpretation. In *Hyndluljóð*, Freyja transforms her lover Óttarr into a boar, and again, no hide is explicitly mentioned. It is worth considering, however, that in the case of Iðunn, the concealment of the goddess is achieved under the physical cover of a shell; while Freyja's statement in stanza 7, "þar er gǫltr glóar, gullinbursti / Hildisvíni, er mér hagir gørðo, / dvergar tveir, Dáinn oc Nabbi" (this is the glowing boar, golden-bristled Hildisvíni, which the skillful dwarves Dáinn and Nabbi made for me), suggests that Óttarr has, in some manner, been given not an entirely new boar-shape, but one already existing - that he may be hidden beneath the dwarf-made hide of Hildisvíni.

The same motif of using a skin to completely change one's shape appears within the human context in the more fantastical materials, most notably *Vǫlundarkviða* and *Vǫlsunga saga*. In these texts, we see people who are nominally in the human world transformed by the use of an enchanted hide, without which they do not have the ability to shapeshift. The swan-maidens of *Vǫlundarkviða* are easily typed according to the Animal Bride folkloric motif:[11] they lay their swanskins aside, are captured and wedded by Vǫlundr and his brothers, but fly away after nine years of marriage. *Vǫlsunga saga* presents a more complete picture of the shapeshifting process. In chapter 7, Sigmundr and Sinfjǫtli find two men sleeping in the woods, regarding whom it is said that "Þeir hofdu ordit fyrir uskopum, þviat ulfahamir hengu *í* husinu yfir þeim. It tiunda hvert degr mattu þeir komazt or haumunum...Þeir Sigmundr foru i haminaa ok mattu eigi or komazi, ok fylgdi su nattura, sem adr var, letu ok vargsrodda" (A spell had been cast upon them, for which reason wolves' hides hung in the house over them. Every tenth day they were able to come out of the hides...Sigmundr (and Sinfjǫtli) put on the hides and were not able to come out of them, and the same power followed as before, and they also howled like wolves). The wolfskin's nature leads them first to fall upon bands of travellers in the woods, then causes Sigmundr to mortally wound his son. When Sinfjǫtli is healed via magical intervention, "fara þeir til iardhuss ok eru þar til þess, er þeir skylldu fara ur ulfhaumunum. Þa taka þeir ok brenna i elldi ok badu engum at meini verda" (they went to the cave and were there until they were able to come out of the wolf-hides. Then they took and burned them in the fire and said that no further harm should come [of them]).[12] H.R. Ellis-Davidson observes that "This tale contains some of the elements of folktales, but in the agreement about taking on enemies and the reference to warlike achievements in the wolfskins, there seems to be a hint of a different tradition, one associated with young heroes living like wolves in the forest and learning how to support themselves by robbery and killing."[13] The similarity between this apparently initiatory shapeshifting and the iconographically documented use of wolfskins, in particular, as a part of warrior-ritual is too close to be ignored.[14] Within the fictional context of the legend, the symbolic transformation of the heroes is expressed as an actual physical change, taking place by means of the animal skin; however, the degree to which earlier Norse culture would have distinguished between the symbolic-ritual and the physical shapeshifting is impossible to determine.

The further transformations taking place in *Vǫlsunga saga* are of particular interest in regards to the distinctions they offer between forms of shapeshifting. The transformation of Ottarr is a complete physical transformation, achieved, as Reginn describes, by the fact that he "hafde adra idn ok naturu" (had a second occupation and nature);[15] his death is immediately recognised when his characteristic otter-skin, the embodiment of his second nature, is shown to Hreiðmarr. Similarly, Fáfnir's transformation to a dragon is a physical change; though the means by which it takes place are not described. However, when Sigurðr and Gunnarr exchange forms in order that Sigurðr may cross the fire to woo Brynhildr in Gunnarr's place, the phrase used is "Skipta nu litum" (they now changed appearances)[16] - they merely carry out an illusionary change of appearance, which does not affect their abilities or natures in the same manner as a change of *hamr*. Grani is willing to carry the disguised Sigurðr, where he had refused to bear Gunnarr, and Sigurðr can thus carry out his task in the other man's shape. Such illusionary shapeshifting, or *sjónhverfing*, appears occasionally in the family sagas;[17] however, it is purely a matter of deluding the eye, unrelated to the other types of transformation practised in Norse literature.

The fullest range of human shapeshifting, however, is demonstrated in *Hrólfs saga kraka*. In the account of Bjǫrn the father of Bǫðvar-Bjarki, a full physical metamorphosis takes place, and here again the change is demonstrated to be effected by means of a skin. Although when Hvít curses Bjǫrn, she strikes him with a glove of wolfskin,[18] when he performs his metamorphosis as he is cursed to do every morning, he "steypiz síðan bjarnarhamrinn yfir hann, ok gengr bjǫrninn svá ut" (afterwards pulled the bear-hide over him, and the bear thus went out),[19] while his paramour Bera finds the ring he has asked her to take from his body only after "Konungsmenn hǫfðu þá flegit bjǫrninn mjǫk" (the king's men had then largely flayed the bear);[20] that is to say, the item of human identification lies under the transforming skin. Bjǫrn's first two sons bear marks of their father's curse in varying degrees -- Elgfróði is an elk from the waist down, and Þórir has dog's feet[21] -- but it is only Bǫðvarr, the chief object of this account, who is a shapeshifter. Unlike his father, however, his transformation follows the usual Icelandic pattern: in Hrólfr's final battle,

> Þat sjá þeir Hjǫrvarðr ok menn hans, at bjǫrn einn mikill ferr fyrir Hrólfs konungs mǫnnum ok jafnan þar næst, sem konungrinn var; hann drepr fleiri menn með sinum hrammi en fimm aðrir kappar konungs; hrjóta af honum hǫgg ok skotvápn, en hann brýtr undir sik bæði menn ok hesti af liði Hjǫrvarðr konungs ok alt þat, sem nánd er, mylr hann með sínum tǫnnum, svá at illr kurr kemr í lið Hjǫrvarðr konungs. (Hjǫrvarðr and his men saw that a great bear went before the men of King Hrólfr, nearest to where the king was; he slew more men with his paws than five other warriors of the king; hewing- and shot-weapons bounced off him, and he broke under him both men and horses of the host of King Hjǫrvarðr and all which neared him he crushed with his teeth, so that ill murmuring came into the host of King Hjǫrvarðr).[22]

Bǫðvarr, meanwhile, is sitting motionless, only stirring when Hjalti comes from the field to rouse him, and when he goes out, "er þá bjǫrninn horfinn burt úr liðinu, ok tekr ná bardaginn at þyngjaz fyrir" (then the bear vanished away from the host, and the battle grew very heavy).[23] Although more physical in effect than most Icelandic shapeshifters, Bǫðvarr's technique of immobilizing the body while the soul goes out is typical of the general method as described by Snorri in chapter 7 of *Ynglinga saga*:

> Óðinn skipti hǫmm. Lá þá búkrinn sem sofinn eða dauðr, en hann var þá fugl eða dýr, fiskr eða ormr ok fór á einni svipstund á fjarlæg lond at sinum ørendum eða annarra manna (Óðinn changed hides. His body lay then as if sleeping or dead, but he was

then a bird or animal, fish or snake, and traveled in a moment to faraway lands on his errands or those of other men).[24]

Snorri's attribution of this skill to Óðinn is understandable only in its context: that is, as a euhemeristic account of the god-as-sorceror. Nevertheless, his description of this, and the various other magics he attributes to Óðinn, must be understood as based on genuine beliefs about magical practice. Although the word *hamr* is never used in regards to Bǫðvarr's shapechanging in *Hrólfs saga*, it is not unreasonable to expect that the Icelandic mind would have made an immediate connection between the physical *bjarnarhamr* used by his father Bjǫrn and the spiritual form which Bǫðvarr is able to take at need: Bǫðvarr may, in fact, be seen as having inherited the paternal *hamr*, albeit in a non-physical form.

For confirmation of this interpretation, it is necessary to examine the phenomenon of shapeshifting as it appears in the family and kings' sagas. In contrast to the tales of gods and legendary heroes, the relatively realistic style of these works largely precludes accounts of actual physical transformation: shapeshifting must take place either as a simple illusion or by the shifting of the metamorphosis to a different plane of existence. While well-documented, the nature of the evidence in regards to the Icelandic view of shapeshifting is in some ways confusing, inasmuch as it is tangled closely with the concept of the *fylgja*, itself difficult to pin down to a single specific definition. Nevertheless, as with the physical transformations of legend and myth, the theme of making use of an existing shape or *hamr*, albeit a non-physical one, is not only present in the shapeshifting known to the Icelanders, but may indeed be demonstrated to be a fundamental element of metamorphosis, whether it is explicitly described or merely understood.

The classic example of an Icelandic shapeshifter is Egill Skalla-Grímsson's grandfather Kveld-Úlfr, of whom it is observed in the first chapter of *Egils saga* that,

> var þat siðr hans at rísa upp árdegis ok ganga þá um sýslur manna eða þar er smiðir váru...En dag hvern, er at kveldi leiða, þá gerðisk hann styggr, svá at fáir menn máttu orðum við hann koma; var hann kveldsvæfr. Þat var mál manna, at hann væri mjǫk hamrammr; hann var kallaðr Kveld-Úlfr (it was his custom to get up early and go about men's business or where there was smith-work...But every day when evening came, then he became peevish, so that few men could speak with him; he was prone to sleep in the evenings. That was said among folk, that he was greatly *hamrammr*, he was called Evening Wolf).[25]

The strong implication is that Kveld-Úlfr is believed, when he lies down in his deep evening sleep, to be prowling about at the same time in the form suggested by his name. A similar example appears in *Landnámabók*, chapter S 350/H 309:

> Dufþakr í Dufþaksholti...var hamrammr mjǫk, ok svá var Stórólfr Hœngsson...Þá skildi á um beitingar. Þat sá ófreskr maðr um kveld nær dagsetri, at bjǫrn mikill gekk frá Hváli, en griðungr frá Dufþaksholti, ok fundusk á Stórólfsvelli ok gengusk at reiðir, ok mátti bjǫrninn meira. Um morguninn var þat sét, at dalr var þar eptir, er þeir hǫfðu fundizk, sem um væri snúit jǫrðinni, ok heitir þar nú Ǫldugróf. Báðir váru þeir

meiddir (Dufþakr of Dufþaksholt...was greatly *hamrammr*, and so was Stórólfr Hœngsson..They quarreled over grazing rights. A man with second sight saw in the evening near sunset, that a great bear went from Hváll, but a boar from Dufþaksholt, and they met on Stórolfsvǫllr and began to struggle, and the bear got the better of it. In the morning it was seen that the dale in which they had met was as if the earth had been turned up, and that place is now called Ǫldugróf. Both were then injured).[26]

The theme of battling shapeshifters is also found in chapter 19 of *Svarfdœla saga*, in which a fight between men is accompanied by a boar and a white bear, who take part in the fight; when Karl, one of the principals, comes home, he is greeted by his father Þorsteinn svǫrfuðr, who says,

> 'Sezt niðr, frændi, ok seg frá tíðendum, ok þykkjumst ek eigi vita, hví erfiði þetta hefir á mik fengit sem ek hafa verit með yðr í bardaganum, ok eigi má ek heðan ganga.' Karl mælti, 'Vissa ek, faðir, at þú vart í bardagunum ok veittir oss lið' ("Sit down, kinsman, and tell me the news, for it seems to me that I do not know what hardship has gripped on me since I have been with you in the battle, and I am not able to go hence." Karl said, "I know, father, that you were in the battle and helped our host").[27]

Þorsteinn svǫrfuðr dies very shortly afterwards, possibly as a result of his exertions, just as the old Kveld-Úlfr is overcome by the aftereffects of a berserk-fit.[28]

These instances do not mention the use of an animal-skin, spiritual or physical, although the latter is strongly implied by the adjective *hamrammr* (hide-strong); they do beg the question of whether a person who was *hamrammr* was able to take on more than one shape, or whether they were normally restricted to a specific *hamr*, as in the mythological instances where a single *hamr*, though it can be loaned for special purposes, is decidedly the characteristic property of a single person. Instances do appear where the choice of shape is either stated or implied, but these are generally qualified by the identification of the person as being skilled in magic: Óðinn as sorceror in *Ynglinga saga*, chapter 7, and the account in *Sturlaugs saga Starfsama* chapter 12 of a young wizard engaging in a magical battle with a Finn in the forms of dogs, then eagles,[29] are the two most notable examples of explicit multiple shapeshifting. The magical transformations in *Óláfs saga Tryggvasonar*, chapter 7, and *Egils saga*, chapter 59, while appearing as singular instances of the sorceror's capabilities, also seem, by their peculiar appropriateness to the given task, to suggest that the shapes may be chosen by the shapeshifter rather than being as, for instance, Bǫðvarr's bear-form is, sole options. In the former case, "Haraldr konungr bauð kunngum manni at fara í hamfǫrum til Íslands ok freista, hvat hann kynni segja honum. Sá fór í hvalslíki." (King Haraldr bade a wise man to go in hide-faring to Iceland and find out what he could say to him. He went in whale-shape.[30] In *Egils saga*, a swallow sits outside the house where Egill is trying to compose the poem that will save his life, and when his friend Arinbjǫrn goes out to look, "hann sá, hvar hamhleypa nǫkkur fór annan veg af húsinu" (he saw, where some hide-leaper went in another direction off the house).[31] Although the saga does not explicitly state it, the implication is that the swallow is Queen Gunnhildr, who was reputed to have learned magic from the "Finns".[32] The term *hamhleypa*, "hide-leaper", is much rarer than the relatively common *hamrammr*, and specifically suggests a shapeshifting witch. It is worth noting that in two of these four accounts, there is a direct connection with the foreign magics of the "Finns", or Saami,[33] while in Óðinn's case, the multiple shape-shifting is part of a general catalogue of extraordinary magical skills. While the question of whether Icelandic shapeshifting and related practices might be classified as forming part of a Nordic shamanic complex[34] is outside the scope of this article, there seems to be a clear difference between being *hamrammr* and being a magician. In general, the animal form taken by the Icelandic shapeshifter seems to be one expressive of the nature of the human, if not indeed actually linked directly with his name, as in the cases of Kveld-Úlfr and Bǫðvarr bjarki, and implied by the pedigree from *Harðar saga* chapter 17, in which a hostile man introduces himself as "Bjǫrn blásíða...son Úlfheðins Úlfhamssonar, Úlfssonar, Úlfhams sonar ins hamrama"[35] -- a most threatening list of names, clearly intended to intimidate the heroes with the suggestion that they are about to face someone who is in some way *hamrammr*, whether he is a berserk or a shapeshifter; while the ability to shift into the animal form and/or go berserk also seems to be largely an inherited, rather than a learned, characteristic in the minds of the Icelandic saga-writers,[36] and hence in general to be distinguished from the practice of magic, although some magicians obviously include shapeshifting among their skills.

The identification of a human with a single animal-shape expressive of that person's nature leads inevitably to the consideration of the Icelandic belief in the *fylgja*, and the question of whether a direct relationship exists between *fylgja* and *hamr*. H. R. Ellis sums up the difference between the two neatly:

> The distinction between the animal *fylgia* and the animal form assumed by the spirit of the shape-changer lies of course in the fact that in the se-cond case the animal form is only active while the body of the owner lies in a state of unconsciousness; it is informed, apparently, by the whole conscious mind of the human owner. The *fylgia* however is the active, invisible companion which attends the owner in his waking state; it would usually appear, in spite of its name, to precede him.[37]

It can further be observed that, although being *hamrammr* is an unusual characteristic, implying the special power of the shapechanger, the possession of a *fylgja* appears to be a commonplace of human nature. While the *fylgja* can be seen only in dreams,[38] by someone with powers of supernatural perception,[39] or under unusual circumstances such as the owner's impending death,[40] it is, nevertheless, invisibly present for everyone, serving, for those who can see it, as a sort of psychic indicator of personal character and status. This is demonstrated most explicitly in *Þorsteins þáttr uxafóts*, in which the young Þorsteinn's polar-bear fetch reveals that, as the perceptive Gæitir tells the boy, Þorsteinn is not the son of the couple who raised him, but rather of a great family.[41]

Defining the character of the *fylgja* in Icelandic literature is sometimes difficult, being affected both by the demands of literary convention and by the apparent conflation of two different sorts of accompanying spirits, the animal and the (human) female. Regarding the problem, Else Mundal concludes that the two should be distinguished, and that it is likeliest that the original term *fylgja* was transferred from the animal-*fylgja* to the woman-*fylgja* through their chief point of similarity, the motif of the accompanying spirit,[42] evaluating them separately in her examination of the *fylgja* phenomenon. Literary convention offers a different type of problem, particularly when the *fylgja* is seen in the context of a significant dream, at which point it may pass entirely from the realm of folk-tradition (albeit folk-tradition used for literary purposes) to a simple symbolic effect. The most marked examples of this divergence occur particularly in the Eddic poems *Guðrúnarqviða ǫnnor* 41-42 and *Atlamál in grœnlenzco* 17-19, wherein Atli appears in dreams as both bear and eagle and his sons as hawks and whelps, and the instances in the sagas when a group of men are perceived collectively as a gathering of animals, usually wolves about to make an attack.[43] In the former case, Kelchner observes that the variant fetches all have in common a similar relationship to both the person they portray and the dream-er: they serve as a direct form of symbolic expression.[44] Likewise, the "group-fetches" are representative of attitude and position, rather than being meant to be taken literally as the actual *fylgjur* of the men involved (and, indeed, the word *hugr* is often used instead of *fylgja*, suggesting that what the dreamer is seeing is the personified intention of his enemies, rather than their actual animal-spirits); only the leaders of such groups have different animal-forms which makes it possible to recognise them. It is safe, therefore, to accept Mundal's firm conclusion that the animal-*fylgja* is a completely stable attribute, so that the same animal-shape will follow its person unchanging from cradle to grave.[45]

The similarity between the character of the *fylgja* and that of the *hamr* leads to the question of a relationship between the two. They overlap in both form and function, as expressions of the extra-physical force of the person to whom they are attached; one may compare, for instance, the description of the battle between Dufþakr and Stórólfr cited above with the dream described in *Søgubrot af nokkrum fornkongum í Dana ok Svía veldi*:

þar sá ek einn hjǫrt standa á vellinum; þá rann or skóginum einn hlébarðr, ok þótti mér fax hans sem gull, ok hjǫrtrinn stakk hornunum undir bóg dýrinu, en þat féll dauðt niðr; þar næst sá ek, kvar flaug flugdreki mikill, ok kom þar, sem hjǫrtrinn var, ok greip þegar í klór sér, ok sleit allan í sundr; þá sá ek bjarndýr eitt, ok fylgdi húnn úngr, ok vildi drekinn taka hann, en beran varði, ok vaknaða ek þá. Hún mælti: þetta er mikill draumr...þar hefir þú sét konúnga fylgjur, ok munu þeir eigast við orrostur ("There I saw a hart standing on the field; then a leopard ran out of the wood, and its mane seemed golden to me, and the hart stuck its horns under the shoulder of the animal, and it fell down dead; there next I saw where a great flying dragon flew and came where the hart was, and gripped it in its claws, and tore all apart; then I saw a bear, and her cub followed, and the dragon would take him, but the bear defended, and then I awoke." She said, "That is a great dream...there you have seen the *fylgjur* of kings, and they shall deal with each other in battle").[46]

Although the latter instance is a prophetic dream, while the former is an account of a contemporary battle of shapeshifters, it may be argued that the struggle of *fylgjur* in the dream could, in and of itself, be seen as an actual battle, with a comparison being made to Finni's analysis of the cause of Eyjólfr's misfortune in chapter 20 of *Ljósvetninga saga*:

> 'Þat mynda ek ætla, at þar myndir þú eigi hafa getat staðizk fylgjur þeira Þorvarðs ok frænda hans, er fjándskap leggja á þik.' Eyjólfr mælti: 'Ætlar þú, at þeira fylgjur sé meiri fyrir sér en mínar ok minna frænda?' Finni mælti: 'Ekki kveð ek at því; þó þat er reynt, ef vér spyrjum um fǫr Þorvarðs' ("I would expect that there you were not able to stand against the *fylgjur* of Þorvarðr and his kinsmen, who are your foes." Eyjólfr said, "Do you think that their *fylgjur* are greater than mine and my kinsmen's?" Finni said, "I did not say that; but that is proven, if we ask about Þorvarðr's journey").[47]

The belief expressed here is clearly that the conflict of *fylgjur* is the decisive element in the struggle, a belief also expressed by Þorsteinn frá Hofi in chapter 30 of *Vatnsdœla saga*, when he cautiously advises that the hostile brothers Jǫkull and Þórir be greeted well because, "hafa þeir brœðr rammar fylgjur" (the brothers have powerful *fylgjur*):[48] he is not concerned with their physical prowess, but with the question of their superior force on the spiritual plane, which is embodied in their *fylgjur*.

An etymological analysis of *fylgja* and *hamr* also suggests the possibility of an original association. The noun *fylgja* may be connected with the verb *fylgja*, "to accompany", which accords with and may have had some influence upon the Icelandic image of the *fylgja* as an animal-spirit attached to a human being. There also, however, exists the noun *fylgja* meaning "afterbirth" or "caul", regarding which Turville-Petre observes "This noun could also be derived from the verb, but is more likely to be related to Icelandic *fulga* (thin covering of hay) and Norwegian dialect *folga* (skin, covering) and with the verb *fela* (to hide)", commenting that *fylgja* (accompanying spirit) cannot be divorced completely from its homonym.[49] Mundal also accepts a connection between *fylgja* and afterbirth, though observing that the connection between an animal-shape and the afterbirth is not clear.[50] Further, the verb *fela* is also indicated as a possible origin for *fylgja* (spirit).[51]

The comparison of these interpretations with the etymology of *hamr* seems to suggest further the possibility of a close association of the two concepts. The word *hamr* indicates a covering or skin;[52] de Vries cites a Middle Low German *ham* for covering or afterbirth, suggesting a relationship with *hams* (fruit-rind, snakeskin),[53] a concept upon which he elaborates in his *Altgermanische Religionsgeschichte*,

> Die moderne Sprache kennt noch als Bedeutung für *hamr*, 'Nachgeburt', ursprünglich wohl 'die Haut, in welche die Frucht eingeschlossen ist'...Diese Eihaut des Embryo wurde in einer besonderen Beziehung zum Kinde gedacht; sie enhielt seine Seele, oder ein seelenartiges Wesen, das ihn als Schutzgeist begleitete.[54]

Both *fylgja* and *hamr*, then, seem to derive from the concept of the afterbirth as embodying a form of spiritual protection, expressed in the former case as a universally present semi-independent being in the shape of an animal, in the latter as a means of disembodied activity in animal-shape of which only specially talented persons can avail themselves, changing spiritually in the same manner in which gods and legendary heroes physically transform themselves. The connection between the use of the afterbirth and shape-shifting appears constant throughout later Scandinavian folklore: in Denmark, it was believed that if a woman crawled naked through the caul of a foal, she could give birth painlessly, but her firstborn would be a *mare* or werewolf;[55] while Norwegian belief included the afterbirth, rather than the pelt, of a wolf pulled over the head of the would-be shapeshifter.[56] Like the *fylgja*, the *hamr* appears in most cases, as mentioned above, to be a specific and single animal-form. Although the sole case in which *fylgja* and *hamr* are specifically shown together is a *fornaldarsaga*, and hence particularly likely to demonstrate literary-fantastic usage rather than folk belief, it is worth mentioning: in *Þorsteins saga Víkingssonar*, the wizard Ógautan takes the shape of a vixen in order to spy upon the heroes, and he also appears as a vixen in *fylgja*-form.[57] The implication here is that when Ógautan takes on his animal-shape, he is actually taking possession of his *fylgja*: he is able to use it as a *hamr*, in the same way in which the various otherworldly beings cited above use their respective animal-*hamir*. The assembled evidence suggests, indeed, that this assumption of an invisible, but nevertheless omnipresent, animal-hide may have been the normal process by which the Icelandic shapeshifter operated; that to be *hamrammr* was to have the ability to depart the body and cloak oneself in the skin of one's *fylgja*, as, for instance, when Kveld-Úlfr wandered about at night in the form of a wolf, or Bǫðvarr bjarki took on the shape of a bear in order to fight for his king.

The use of the metaphysical *hamr* or *fylgja* was paralleled in the Viking Age by the practice of animal-masking for the purpose of transforming a human's nature, most frequently seen in the induction of berserkergang, regarding which the physical animal skin and the spiritual power of *hamr*-use appear to have been not only fundamental, but even perhaps interchangeable.Berserkergang and *hamr*-use are paralleled in *Egils saga*, chapter 27:

> Svá er sagt, at þeim mǫnnum væri farit, er hamrammir eru, eða þeim, er berserksgangr var á, at meðan þat var framit, þá váru þeir svá sterkir, at ekki helzk við þeim, en fyrst, er af var gengit, þá váru þeir ómáttkari en at vanda (It is said thus, that for those men who were *hamrammir*, or those, whom berserkergang was on, while it was upon them, then they were so strong that no one could stand against them, but at first, when it had gone off, then they were very weak and in difficulty).[58]

A very similar description is given in *Eyrbyggja saga*, chapter 28, which emphasizes the identification between berserkergang and *hamr*-shifting:

> Berserkirnir gengu heim um kveldit ok váru móðir mjǫk, sem háttr er þeira manna, sem eigi eru einhama, at þeir verða máttlausir mjǫk, er af þeim gengr berserksgangrinn. (The berserks went home in the evening and were greatly exhausted, as was the case with those men, who were not of one *hamr*, that they became very weak when the berserkergang went off them).[59]

There is also an apparent connection, although not a necessary one, between ber-serkergang and the possession of a powerful *fylgja*: in *Vatnsdœla saga*, chapter 30, Þórsteinn frá Hofi's description of the brothers Jǫkull and Þórir as possessing "rammar fylgur" follows almost immediately upon the characterization, "Á Þóri kom stundum berserksgangr" (Berserkergang came on Þórir at times).[60]

In this regards, however, a notable peculiarity of berserkergang which appears to distinguish it in character, as well as effect, from the shape-shifting described above, is that, while an individual's *hamr* or *fylgja* might be of various sorts, only the bear and the wolf are directly associated with berserkergang, as in the cases of Kveld-Úlfr and the pedigree of Bjǫrn blásíða. In relationship to this animal-association, H. R. Ellis-Davidson also cites a description of a group of dedicated warriors, similar to the accounts of berserk-bands, who were "said to be brothers ... on an island in Denmark ... in Book VI of Saxo's *Danish History* ... it may be noted that members of the group have names formed from *bjǫrn* (bear)."[61] Significantly, although there are a considerable number of references not only associating warriors with boars in general (such as the *heiti* "jǫfurr", boar, for a ruler) but identifying individual men with boars,[62] and, as mentioned in the examples above from *Landnámabók* and *Svarfdœla saga*, showing the boar as a powerful form assumed by shapeshifters, as well the direct transformation of the human Óttarr into a boar by the goddess Freyja in *Hyndluljóð*, there survive no references to a boar-equivalent of the wolf- or bear-berserk. Násström argues that "(the enemy warrior's) hostile character was sym-bolized by the word 'bear' - a notion which probably embodies the solution to the problem of berserks, ulfhednar, and werewolves. In the same way, the warrior would employ a 'boar' for instance, as a symbol of himself"[63] and suggests that the boar in *Hyndluljóð* is merely Óttarr's totem or representative. However, Freyja's words in stanza 45,

'Ber þú minnisǫl mínom gelti,
svát hann ǫll muni orð at tína,
þessar rœðo á þriðia morni,
þá er þeir Angantýr ættir rekia'

(Bear thou remembrance-ale to my boar so that he remembers all words to say, these speeches, on the third morning, when he reckons clans with Angantýr) make it clear that Freyja's steed is, despite her initial denial, Óttarr himself, albeit concealed in the form of Freyja's boar Hildisvíni: the case is one of transformation, rather than sym-bolic totemism. Boar-masking and even ritual possession by means of a boar-mask may have taken place -- H.R. Ellis-Davidson suggests that, in the context of the cult of Freyr, "the king put on (a boar-mask helmet) in order to be possessed by the god"[64] -- but such a possession, if it took place, would, in purpose and nature if not in meth-od, have been a phenomenon significantly different from that of the berserk-fit. There seems no practical reason why the ferocious boar should not be associated with berserkergang in the same way as the bear and the wolf; the only obvious suggestion is that the boar, when identified as a cultic animal, is firmly within the Vanic cult, whereas the wolf is certainly, and the bear probably, connected with Óðinn. The appearance of the boar-mask on some of the female figures in the Oseberg tapestry, who are easily interpreted as worshippers of Freyja,[65] as well as a woman wearing a bird-of-prey costume, who may well represent a priestess of the goddess or Freyja herself,[66] while no corresponding wolf- or bear-women are known, indicate the likelihood of berserkergang as an original Óðinnic specialization, just as Snorri describes in *Ynglinga saga*, chapter 6 (quoted below),with its actual occurrence and the memory of the associated animal-forms outliving the cult: the berserk, as suggested in the examples given above, was a man who had a bear or wolf *hamr* to take on. As an originally cultic specialization, berserkergang may provide a somewhat slanted perspective on the more general subject of ritual/psychological transformation in Norse culture. However, whatever other forms of ritual masking-transformation may have existed in Norse spiritual activity, the nature of our surviving references which concentrate to a large degree on battle, and the peculiar character of berserkergang as the sole practice related to masking/shapeshifting which continued to occur spontaneously after the ritual use of animal skins had been largely discarded, has determined that berserkergang is the only one which is extensively and explicitly documented, with a vocabulary of terms which describes its relationship to the types of transformation discussed above and offers the opportunity of clarifying the fundamental character of Norse shapeshifting-beliefs.

The two words used to describe those susceptible to berserk-fits, *berserkr* and *úlfheðinn*, directly indicate the use of an animal-skin in the induction of berserkergang. The latter term is a transparent formation, 'wolf-coat'; the former has been the subject of some debate as to whether it indicates 'bear-shirt' or 'bare-shirt', referring to the berserk's ability to go without armour, as described in *Ynglinga saga*, chapter 6: "(Óðins) menn fóru brynjulausir...Þeir drápu mannfólkit, en hvártki eldr né járn orti á þá. Þat er kallaðr berserksgangr" (Óðinn's men went without armour...they slew men, but neither fire nor iron could touch them. That is called berserkergang).[67] Although not universally recognised,[68] the interpretation of "bear-shirt", complementary to "wolf-coat", is, however, the more generally accepted; Ásgeirr Magnússon dismisses the alternate interpretation as rather unlikely.[69] The terms *úlfheðinn* and *berserkr* are identified from an early literary period, in Þórbjǫrn hornklofi's *Haraldskvæði* 8: "grenjuðu berserkir...emjuðu ulfheðnar"(berserks roared...*úlfheðnar* howled).[70] The characteristic use of the wolf-pelt in fighting is also mentioned by Eyvindr skáldaspillir in *Háleygjatal* 8: "Ok sá halr / at Hǫars veðri / hǫsvan serk / hrísgrisnis bar" (and the man bore the gray sark of the wolf in battle).

The donning of animal-skins to bring on a berserk-fit is explicitly attested in the saga-literature regarding berserks, demonstrating that the saga-writers were aware of the practice. Chapter 9 of *Vatnsdœla saga* describes "þeir berserkir, er Úlfheðnar váru kallaðir; þeir hǫfðu vargstakka fyrir brynjur ok vǫrðu framstafn á konungs skipinu" (the berserks, who were called *úlfheðnar*, they had wolf-cloaks for byrnies and were at the front of the king's ship).[71] The similarity of this account of Haraldr hárfagri's elite troops to the description in *Haraldskvæði* is suspicious; nevertheless, the added description of the wolfskin coats indicates a direct consciousness of the relationship between putting on the hide and entering the berserk state.[72]

The ritual use of animal hides, in particular that of a wolf, is most significantly attested in the iconographic evidence of the Vendel and Viking Ages. The helm-plate press from Torslunda is the best-known of these, and the one which has received the most comment in its suggestive juxtaposition of the wolf-skinned warrior with the apparently one-eyed dancer in the bird-horned helm, which is generally interpreted as showing a scene indicative of the relationship between berserkergang, masking-ritual, and the god Óðinn.[73] Similar wolf-man figures appear in the south-west Germanic area: the sword-decoration from Gutenstein and the bronze piece from Obrigheim, both 7th century, provide iconographic evidence of the ritual practice behind the Úlfheðinn/Wolfhetan-related names, regarding which Müller observes, "Der dem Kampfgott geweihte Tier-Krieger wurde für den Mann zu einem Leitbild, das auf die Namengebung einwirkte."[74] The image appears to have survived into the Viking Age, as shown by a small figure from a cremation-grave in Kungsängen, Uppland (ca. 800 C.E.), which shows a man in a wolf-coat apparently biting the head of a large serpent.[75] One of the Oseberg tapestry fragments has been interpreted as showing the battle of Brávalla, with the armed female figures representing valkyries and the man in a wolf- or bear-skin as a berserk.[76]

This being so, it is interesting to note that there is a relative paucity of saga-period references to the use of hides in inducing berserkergang, in contrast to those presenting berserkergang as a spontaneous shift of consciousness. The berserk state is identified as a heathen practice in the "Kristinna laga þáttr" of the law-book Grágás, in which it is proscribed in the same chapter as offering to heathen wights, practicing magic, and similar activities, with the same penalty (lesser outlawry) applying. However, there is no description of the means involved in going berserk - there is, for instance, no clause forbidding the possession or wearing of an animal skin -- and the proscription includes the peculiar addition that those men who are present when another goes berserk are responsible for restraining him or suffering the same penalty.[77] This latter clause suggests, as Jesse Byock interprets it, a simple social responsibility of private individuals to restrain violent individuals, rather than an explicit indictment of heathen ritual.[78]

The saga-characters who are prone to berserkergang, whether they are presented as primary characters or simply as stock literary villains, appear to need no particular preparation to undergo a fit. This could possibly be explained by the connection of the masked animal-warriors with the native religion,[79] of which the saga-writers may have been chary; however, the saga descriptions of berserks give less indication of deliberate avoidance than of a simple lack of any sense of the animal-hide being necessary. Berserkergang, in fact, appears as an involuntary or only semi-voluntary response to stress, occasionally happening at undesired and inappropriate times. The classic example of the latter occurs in Egils saga, chapter 40, where Skalla-Grímr, becoming unduly excited in the course of a ball-game that has lasted past sundown, kills one young man and then turns to attack his son, whereupon Egill's nursemaid Þorgerðr brák, who is described as "fjǫlkunnig mjǫk" (greatly skilled in magic), exclaims, "Hamask þú nú, Skalla-Grímr, at syni þínum?" (Are you now changing hamr, Skalla-Grímr, against your son?),[80] whereupon he turns on her instead, chasing and eventually killing her. The undesirability of berserk-fits is also played up in *Vatnsdœla saga*, chapter 37, in which, when the sons of Ingimundr are comparing their respective worth, "Þórir kvazk minnstháttr af þeim, - 'fyrir þat, at á mik kemr berserksgangr jafnan, þá er ek vilda sízt, ok vilda ek, bróðir, at þú gerða at'" (Þórir said himself to be the worst of them -- "because the berserkergang comes on me at times when I would least wish it, and I wish, brother, that you could do something about it").[81] The immediate sequel to this self-revelation, in which Þórir is cured of berserkergang by adopting and bringing up the exposed infant Þorkell krafla, is a decidedly Christian message; nevertheless, the whole would be impossible in a context in which the use of a physical animal-hide was a prerequisite to the achievement of the berserk-state. Further, at least in the Iceland of the sagas, putting on a bearskin alone was not sufficient to make one a berserk: Gunnell cites the scene from *Kórmaks saga* in which Steinarr Qnundarson appears at the spring Þórsnessþing masked and wearing a bear-skin cloak,[82] observing that "the purpose of the disguise is totally unclear, sinceᵽthere is nothing in either *Kórmaks saga* or *Egils saga* to suggest that he was ever regarded as a *berserkr* or needed to hide his identity."[83] Steinarr's intention is to challenge Hólmganga-Bersi to a duel, which does suggest a connection between the bear-disguise and ritualized combat, but a direct identification with berserkergang is entirely absent.

This leaves the question of how the transition from the original *úlfheðinn* or *berserkr* (if the "bear-hide" etymology is accepted) to the saga-character who, sometimes unwillingly, undergoes berserk rages was conceptualized. A possible answer is provided by the vocabulary used: the descriptions "sem eigi eru einhama" (who were not of one *hamr*),[84] "þá hamaðisk (Kveld-Úlfr)" (then Kveld-Úlfr changed *hamr*),[85] and "Hamask þú nú...at syni þinum" (are you now changing *hamr*...against your son)[86] attest to a direct connection between *hamr* and berserkergang. Given the previously discussed function of the *hamr* in regards to extra-physical shapeshifting, it is not unreasonable to postulate that, in the Icelandic mind, the spiritual *hamr* had largely or entirely replaced the actual animal hide previously used by the berserk warrior: that is to say, instead of using the *hamr*, or skin of the *fylgja*, to go out of the body in an animal's shape, the Icelandic berserk was able to draw it into himself (or susceptible to being overcome by it) so as to enter the spiritually transformed state of berserkergang. The reasons for this shift must remain a matter of speculation, though it may perhaps be postulated that, given the probable Óðinnic cultic/initiatory character of the original bear- or wolf-masking, both the transition to Iceland, where the cult of Óðinn was apparently considerably less practised than in the Continental homelands,[87] and then the conversion to christianity would have had a significant effect in regards to redefining the phenomenon. However, if the underlying complex of beliefs regarding the nature of the animal-*fylgja* and its relationship to the human, including the possibility of two-way possession, had not already been firmly in place, the shift from the use of a physical animal-pelt to the metaphysical skin of the *fylgja* in inducing either extra-corporeal or psycho-spiritual transformation would not have been initially possible.

It can, hence, be concluded that, when the secondary magic of illusion is left out, the various instances of transformation in Icelandic literature, rather than forming distinct typological groupings, can be seen as a general spectrum governed by the same overall rules, altered only by the nature and circumstances of the shapeshifter. The assumed form exists, in some manner, separately from the being who is donning it: it embodies the foreign capabilities and nature which the shapeshifter wishes to assume. In the transition between worlds and literary genres, the complete metamorphosis of a deity or legendary character upon putting on an animal's hide becomes the spiritual metamorphosis of the Icelander with access to his personal animal-*hamr* or the magician who, like Óðinn, can "shift *hamr*" in order to transform into a number of different shapes outside of his physical body. Finally, these transformations find their reflection in the physical world in the frenzy of the psychologically transformed *berserkr*, brought on either voluntarily by use of an animal hide (physical or metaphysical), or involuntarily when he is overcome by his bear- or wolf-*hamr*. The fundamental technique in all cases is the same: only the manifestations differ.

Shinrone, Republic of Ireland

Notes

1. Cf. Gunter Müller, "Germanische Tiersymbolik und Namengebung." *Frühmittelalterliche Studien* 2 (1968), 202-17.

2. Richard North, ed. and trans., *The Haustlǫng of Þjóðólfr of* 6, stanza 12.

3. Snorri Sturluson, *Edda Snorra Sturlusonar*, ed. Finnur, 80.

4. Gustav Neckel, ed., *Edda: Die Lieder der Codex Regius nebst verwandten Denkmälern*, rev. Hans Kuhn, 3rd ed. (Heidelberg: Carl Winter, 1962). All further Eddic quotations are from this edition.

5. Snorri Sturluson, *Edda*, 80.

6. *Flateyjarbók*, 1: 276.

7. Sune Lindqvist, *Gotlands Bildsteine* 1: fig. 85, p. 95; Erik Nylén and Jan-Peder Lamm, *Bildstenar* 50-52.

8. Snorri Sturluson, *Edda* 80.

9. North 51.

10. *Ibid.*, 52.

11. Cf. the common North Atlantic story of the seal-woman whose sealskin is captured and who is forced to wed her captor, bearing him children, but eventually regains her skin and escapes. Jacqueline Simpson, ed. and trans., *Scandinavian Folktales*, 205-6.

12. Magnus Olsen, ed., *Vǫlsunga saga ok Ragnars saga loðbrókar* 15-17.

13. H.R. Ellis-Davidson, "Shape-Changing in the Old Norse Sagas," *Animals in Folklore*, ed. J.R. Porter and W.M.S. Russel (London: D.S. Brewer, Ltd., and Totowa: Rowman & Littlefield for the Folklore Society, 1978). Rpt. in *A Lycanthropy Reader: Werewolves in Western Culture*, ed. Charlotte F. Otten (Syracuse: Syracuse UP, 1986), 142.

14. Cf. the discussion of the ritual use of animal skins in Terry Gunnell, *The Origins of Drama in Scandinavia*, 64-76.

15. Olsen 34.

16. Ibid., 67.

17. Cf. Einar Ól. Sveinsson and Matthías Þórðarson, eds., *Eyrbyggja saga*, 51-3, in which Katla casts the illusionary disguises of distaff, goat, and pig on her son Oddr; and Þórhallur Vilmundarson and Bjarni Vilhjálmsson, eds., *Þorskfirðinga saga*, 200-1, in which Askmaðr and his wife attempt to escape from a burning house disguised as a boar and a sow, but when the boar is killed, it is seen to be Askmaðr himself.#18. Finnur Jónsson, ed., *Hrólfs saga kraka ok*, 50.

19. Finnur Jónsson, *Hrólfs saga kraka* 52.

20. Ibid., 53.

21. Ibid., 54.

22. Ibid., 100.

23. Ibid., 102.

24. Bjarni Aðalbjarnarson, ed., *Heimskringla I*, (1941, 18).

25. Sigurður Nordal, ed., *Egils saga*, (1941, 4).

26. Jakob Benediktsson, ed., *Landnámabók*, (1936, 355-56).

27. Jónas Kristjánsson, ed., *Svarfdœla saga* (1956, 181-2).

28. Sigurður Nordal. 70-71.

29. Valdimar Ásmundarsson, ed., *Fornaldarsögur Norðrlanda*, 3: 476-77.

30. Bjarni Aðalbjarnarson, *Heimskringla I*, 271.

31. Sigurður Nordal, 182-3.

32. Cf. chapter 32 of *Haralds saga ins hárfagra*, in Bjarni Aðalbjarnarson, *Heimskringla I*, 135-6.

33. See R.I. Page, "Lapland Sorcerers," 215-32.

34. As suggested, for instance, by Peter Buchholz, "Schamanistische Züge in der altisländische Überlieferung," diss., U of Münster, 1968, 56 ff.

35. Þórhallur Vilmundarson and Bjarni Vilhjálmsson, *Harðar saga*,, 46.

36. For instance, Kveld-Úlfr is the son of a man named Bjálfi ("pelt") and the nephew of one Hallbjǫrn Half-troll (*Egils saga*, 3), while Kveld-Úlfr's own son, Skalla-Grímr, is a berserk; cf. also the previous observations about Bǫðvarr bjarki's inheritance of the bearshape.

37. Hilda Roderick Ellis, *Road to Hel* (1943, 129).

38. Georgia Dunham Kelchner (1935, 17-30).

39. *Þorsteins þáttr uxafóts*, *Flateyjarbók* 1: 252-53.

40. Einar Ól. Sveinsson, ed., *Brennu-Njáls saga*, 106.

41. *Flateyjarbók* I: 253.

42. See Else Mundal (1974, 73).

43. A hostile flock of cattle led by a large red ox appears in chapter 16 of *Ljósvetninga saga*, ed. Björn Sigfússon, 65; Þorbjǫrg dreams of a pack of wolves led by a white bear in chapter 31 of *Harðar saga*, 77; a similar pack of wolves led by a vixen appears in chapter 20 of *Hávarðar saga ísfirðings*, ed. Björn K. Þórólfsson and Guðni Jónsson, 349.

44. Kelchner, 18.

45. Mundal, 38.

46. See C.C. Rafn, ed., *Fornaldar Sögur Norðrlanda* 1: 367.

47. Björn Sigfússon, *Ljósvetninga saga*, 100-1.

48. Einar Ól. Sveinsson, *Vatnsdœla saga*, 83.

49. E.O.G. Turville-Petre, *Myth and Religion of the North*, 228.

50. Mundal, 44-45.

51. Ásgeirr Blöndal Magnússon, *Íslenzk*, 218-9; Jan de Vries, *Altnordisches etymologisches Wörterbuch*, 2nd ed., 147-8.

120

52. Ásgeirr Blöndal Magnússon, *Orðsifjabók*, 304.
53. de Vries, *Wörterbuch*, 208.
54. Jan de Vries, *Altgermanische Religionsgeschichte*, 3rd ed: 224.
55. E.T. Kristensen, ed., *Danske Sagn som de har lydt i folkemunde*, 2: 231.
56. Knut Strompdal, "Gamalt frå Helgeland," 63.
57. Valdimar Ásmundarson, *Fornaldar sögur* 2: 80.
58. Sigurður Nordal, 70.
59. Einar Ól. Sveinsson and Matthias Þórðarson, *Eyrbyggja saga*, 74.
60. Einar Ól. Sveinsson, *Vatnsdæla saga*, 83.
61. H.R. Ellis-Davidson, *Myths and Symbols*, 80.
62. Britt-Marie Näsström, *Freyja - The Great Goddess of the North*,, 169-73.
63. Näsström, 172.
64. H.R. Ellis-Davidson, *The Lost Beliefs*, 106.
65. Gunnell, 62-3.
66. Anne Stine Ingstad, "Oseberg-dronningen - hvem var hun?" 246-8.
67. Bjarni Aðalbjarnarson, *Heimskringla I*, 17.
68. See Hans Kuhn's discussion of the word in "Kämpen und Berserker," 222.
69. Ásgeirr Magnússon, 52.
70. Finnur Jónsson, ed., *Den norsk-islandske Skjaldedigtning* B1, 23. All further skaldic quotations are from this edition and volume.
71. Einar Ól. Sveinsson, *Vatnsdæla saga*, 24-25.
72. Haraldr hárfagri's use of an elite berserk-troop is also mentioned in *Egils saga*, chapter 9; however, there it is only observed that "engi var ósárr á konungsskipinu fyrir framan siglu, nema þeir, er eigi bitu járn, en þat váru berserkir" (no one was unwounded on the king's ship before the first sail, except for those on whom iron did not bite, and that was the berserks). Sigurður Norðal, 23.
73. Heinrich Beck, "Die Stanzen von Torslunda und die literarische Über-lieferung,," 247-50; also Per-Olaf Ringquist, "Två vikingatida uppländska människofigurer i brons," 291-4.
74. Gunter Müller, "Zum Namen *Wolfhetan* und seinen Verwandten," 212.
75. Ringquist 287-89, figs. 2a-2b.
76. Ingstad, "Oseberg-dronningen", 245.
77. Vilhjálmur Finsen, ed. and trans., *Grágás:* 1: 22-23.
78. Jesse L. Byock, *Medieval Iceland* (1988, 26).
79. The issue has been extensively discussed; see, for instance, "Berserker," *Reallexikon der germanischen Altertumskunde*, Heinrich Beck and others, eds. (Berlin: de Gruyter 1973-) 2: 298-304; Otto Höfler, *Kultische Geheimbünde der Germanen* (Frankfurt: Diesterweg, 1934); de Vries, *Religionsgeschichte* 1: 492-99.
80. Sigurður Nordal, 101-02.
81. Einar Ól. Sveinsson, *Vatnsdæla saga*, 97.
82. Einar Ól. Sveinsson, *Kórmaks saga*, 247.
83. Gunnell, 81.
84. Einar Ól. Sveinsson and Matthías Þórðarson, *Eyrbyggja saga* 74.
85. Sigurður Nordal, 69.
86. Ibid., 101.
87. Turville-Petre, *Myth and Religion* 66-67; Turville-Petre, "The Cult of Óðinn in Iceland," *Nine Norse Studie* (London: Viking Society for Northern Research, 1972), 1-19.

121

Works Cited

Note: since Icelandic names are patronymics, all Icelandic authors have been alphabetized by first names.

Ásgeirr Blöndal Magnússon. *Íslenzk Orðsifjabók.* Reykjavík: Orðabók Háskolans, 1989.

Beck, Heinrich, et al., eds. *Reallexikon der germanischen Altertumskunde.* Berlin: de Gruyter, 1973-.

Beck, Heinrich. "Die Stanzen von Torslunda und die literarische Überlieferung." *Frühmittelalterliche Studien* 2 (1968): 237-50.

Bjarni Aðalbjarnarson, ed. *Heimskringla I.* Íslenzk fornrit 26. Reykjavík: Hið íslenzka fornritafélag, 1941.

Björn Sigfússon, ed. *Ljósvetninga saga.* Íslenzk fornrit 10. Reykjavík: Hið íslenzka fornritafélag, 1940.

Björn K. Þórólfsson and Guðni Jónsson, eds. *Hávarðar saga Ísfirðings.* Íslenzk fornrit 6. Reykjavík: Hið íslenzka fornritafélag, 1943.

Buchholz, Peter. "Schamanistische Züge in der altisländische Überlieferung." Diss. University of Münster, 1968.

Byock, Jesse L. *Medieval Iceland: Society, Sagas, and Power.* Berkeley: U of California P, 1988.

Christiansen, Arne Emil, Anne Stine Ingstad, and Bjørn Myhre. *Oseberg-dronningens Grav: Vår arkeologiske nasjonalskatt i nytt lys.* Oslo: Schibsted, 1992.

Davidson, Hilda Ellis. *Lost Beliefs of Northern Europe.* London: Routledge, 1993.

Davidson, H.R. Ellis. *Myths and Symbols in Pagan Europe.* Manchester: Manchester UP, 1988.

---. "Shapechanging in the Old Norse Sagas." *Animals in Folklore.* J.R. Porter and W. M. S. Russel, eds. London: D. S. Brewer; Totowa: Rowman & Littlefield for the Folklore Society, 1978. 126-42. (Rpt. in *A Lycanthropy Reader: Werewolves in Western Culture.* Ed. Charlotte F. Otten. Syracuse: Syracuse UP, 1986. 142-60.

Einar Ól. Sveinsson, ed. *Brennu-Njáls saga.* Íslenzk fornrit 12. Reykjavík: Hið íslenzka fornritafélag, 1954.

---., ed. *Kórmaks saga.* Íslenzk fornrit 8. Reykjavík: Hið íslenzka fornritafélag, 1939.

---., ed. *Vatnsdœla saga.* Íslenzk fornrit 8. Reykjavík: Hið íslenzka fornritafélag, 1939.

Einar Ól. Sveinsson and Matthías Þórðarsson, eds. *Eyrbyggja saga.* Íslenzk fornrit 4. Reykjavík: Hið íslenzka fornritafélag, 1935.

Ellis, Hilda Roderick. *Road to Hel.* Cambridge: Cambridge UP, 1943.

Finnur Jónsson, ed. *Hrólfs saga kraka ok Bjarkarímur.* København: Møller, 1904.

Finnur Jónsson, ed. *Den norsk-islandske Skjaldedigtning.* Vol. B 1. Leuterhausen: Strauss & Cramer 1912-15. 4 vols.

Finsen, Vilhjálmur, ed. and trans. *Grágás: Islændernes Lovbog i Fristaten Tid.* 4 vols. in 2. Kjøbenhaven: Brødrene Berlings Bogtrykkerei, 1852-70.

Flateyjarbók. 3 vols. Christiana: P.T. Malling, 1860-68.

Höfler, Otto. *Kultische Geheimbünde der Germanen.* Frankfurt: Diesterweg, 1934.

Gunnell, Terry. *The Origins of Drama in Scandinavia.* Cambridge: Brewer, 1995.

Ingstad, Anne Stine. "Oseberg-dronningen - hvem var hun?" *Oseberg-dronningens Grav: Vårarkeologiske nasjonalskatt i nytt lys.* Arne Emil Christensen, Anne Stine Ingstad, and Bjørn Myhre. Oslo: Schibsted 1992. 224-257.

Jakob Benediktsson, ed. *Landnámabók.* Íslenzk fornrit 1. Reykjavík: Hið íslenzka fornritafélag, 1936.

122

Jónas Kristjánsson, ed. *Svarfdœla saga.* Íslenzk fornrit 9. Reykjavík: Hið íslenzka fornritafélag, 1956.

Kelchner, Georgia Dunham. *Dreams in Old Norse Literature and their Affinities in Folklore.* Cambridge: Cambridge UP, 1935.

Kristensen, E.T., ed. *Danske Sagn som de har lydt i folkemunde.* 7 vols. Århus: 1892-1901.

Kuhn, Hans. "Kämpen und Berserker." *Frühmittelalterliche Studien* 2 (1968): 218-27.

Lindqvist, Sune. *Gotlands Bildsteine.* 2 vols. Uppsala: Almqvist & Wiksell, 1941-42.

Müller, Gunter. "Germanische Tiersymbolik und Namengebung." *Frühmittelalterliche Studien* 2 (1968): 202-17.

---. "Zum Namen *Wolfhetan* und seinen Verwandten." *Frühmittelalterliche Studien* 1 (1967): 200-12.

Mundal, Else. *Fylgjemotiva i norrøn Literatur.* Oslo: Universitetsforlaget, 1974.

Näsström, Britt-Marie. *Freyja - the Great Goddess of the North.* Lund: Dept. of History of Religions, 1995.

Neckel, Gustav, ed. *Die Lieder der Codex Regius nebst verwandten Denkmälern.* Rev. by Hans Kuhn. 3rd edn. Heidelberg: Winter, 1962.

Nordal, Sigurður, ed. *Egils saga.* Íslenzk fornrit 2. Reykjavík: Hið íslenzka fornritafélag, 1941.

North, Richard, ed. and trans. *The Haustlǫng of Þjóðólfr of Hvinir.* Middlesex: Hisarlik, 1997.

Nylén, Erik, and Jan Peder Lamm. *Bildstenar.* Stockholm: Gidlund, 1987.

Olsen, Magnus, ed. *Vǫlsunga saga ok Ragnars saga loðbrókar.* Copenhagen: Møller, 1906-08.

Page, R.I. "Lapland Sorcerers." *Saga-Book of the Viking Society* 16.2-3 (1963-64): 215-32.

Rafn, C.C., ed. *Fornaldarsögur Norðrlanda.* 3 vols. Copenhagen: 1829-30.

Ringquist, Per-Olaf. "Två vikingatida uppländska människofigurer i brons." *Fornvännen* (1969): 287-96.

Snorri Sturluson. *Edda Snorra Sturlusonar.* Ed. Finnur Jónsson. København: Nordisk Forlag, 1931.

Strompdal, Knut. "Gamalt frå Helgeland". *Norsk folkeminnelags skrifter* 44 (1939).

Turville-Petre, E.O.G. "The Cult of Óðinn in Iceland." *Nine Norse Studies*, London: Viking Society for Northern Research, 1972): 1-19.

---. *Myth and Religion of the North.* 1964. Connecticut: Greenwood P, 1975.

Valdimar Ásmundarson, ed. *Fornaldar sögur.* 3 vols. Vols. 1-2: Reykjavík, Sigm. Guðmundsson, 1885-86. Vol. 3: Sigf. Eymundsson, 1893.

de Vries, Jan. *Altgermanische Religionsgeschichte.* 2 vols. Berlin: de Gruyter, 1956.

---. *Altnordisches etymologisches Wörterbuch.* 2nd edn. Leiden: Brill, 1962.

Þórhallur Vilmundarson and Bjarni Vilhjálmsson, eds. *Harðar saga.* Íslenzk fornrit 13. Reykjavík: Hið íslenzka fornritafélag, 1991.

Variance and Late Medieval *Mouvance*:
Reading an Edition of Georges Chastellain's
"Louange à la tresglorieuse Vierge"

Cynthia J. Brown

The transformation of literary texts from their supposedly, but rarely verifiable, original state through their multiple reincarnations during subsequent decades and centuries, is a commonly discussed feature in medieval scholarship. It was Paul Zumthor who first labeled this phenomenon *mouvance*, a term coined initially to describe the oral creation and transmission of works, such as the Old French epic, but later adapted to depict the manuscript culture as well.[1] Text editors are perhaps most familiar with the transformations effected by the ever-changing medieval community of authors, scribes, compilers, and editors. But too often readers of critical editions focus exclusively on the edited text itself, implicitly according it the status of a fixed, finalized state. Scholars and students should take into account more often the process of *mouvance* that critical editions provide readers, for it is in this arena that the inherently dynamic nature of medieval works most clearly emerges and becomes alive. This textual dynamism, however, cannot always be easily accessed, like the edited text itself. It is unfortunate that only rare models, such as the edition of Jaufré Rudel by Rupert Pickens, for whom the idea of *mouvance* formed a conscious part of his editorial presentation, provide direct evidence of medieval textual dynamism.[2] Thanks to the adaptable nature of Rudel's writings -- a limited number of short poetic compositions -- and the unusual support of the Pontifical Institute of Mediaeval Studies for Pickens' editorial concept, all versions of Rudel's poems are given equal space and consideration in Pickens' edition. But in most instances, prohibitively high publication costs cannot support this particular format. Ideally, text editors should provide an analysis of *mouvance* at work in their critical editions, but too often this is not the case, since analysis generally pertains to the base text alone. At best, lists of variants appear at the bottom of the page of edited texts, so that readers who understand editorial shorthand can, depending on the conscientiousness of the editor, follow specific textual transformations as they advance in the text. However, this system may inhibit the discovery of the larger underlying patterns of change that might emerge from an overarching comparison of extant versions. More often than not (as in the very edition presented below), publishers relegate variants to an appendix, an arrangement that tends to discourage any active reconstruction of a work's textual dynamics.

With the goal of encouraging this very kind of engagement -- a focus on textual transformations through a more active "horizontal" reading of critical editions, in conjunction with the "vertical" study of the edited text itself --, I propose to examine late medieval *mouvance* at work in "La Louange à la tresglorieuse Vierge," composed around 1455 by Georges Chastellain (1415?-1475), official historiographer at the Burgundian court and one of the most prominent French writers during the third quarter of the 15th century. From alterations at the textual level that reveal a concern for linguistic or grammatical correction, modernization, greater logic of thought, and clearer expression, to a variation of titles, images and other so-called paratextual details, to the intensified focus of one manuscript of the work on authorial concerns, the modern reader of Georges Chastellain can, through a comparative study of the multiple extant versions of the "Louange," come to understand the very texture of late medieval composition.

Before providing an edition of Chastellain's "Louange," including the numerous variants of its multiple versions, I would like to discuss both microscopic aspects of the textual variation of this work and the more macroscopic shift that appears to have occurred over a period of some 45-50 years. But first some details concerning the six late medieval versions themselves are in order.

As far as I can determine, only one of the surviving versions of Chastellain's work was transcribed during the author's lifetime, sometime between 1450 and 1460: ms. 2355 (fols. 1-25^v) of the Bibliothèque Royale in Brussels, hereafter identified as B1. I have selected this oldest existing version as the base text of my critical edition. Three other extant manuscripts of the work date from a period of about 20 years after the author's death: ms. 3635 of the Bibliothèque de l'Arsenal in Paris (fols. 1-21^v), hereafter referred to as A, is dated 1493; a second manuscript at the Bibliothèque Royale in Brussels, II 6977 (fols. 6-22), hereafter cited as B2, was transcribed in 1495; and ms. nouv. acq. fr. 4061 in the Bibliothèque Nationale in Paris, hereafter referred to as P1, dates from 1498. A fifth manuscript, housed in Paris, B.N. f.fr. 2226, hereafter cited as P2, dates from after Chastellain's death in 1475, but has no other specific reference; codicologists have placed it in the early 16th century. A sixth version was printed by Jean de Liège in Valenciennes, sometime around 1500; only one known copy of this imprint is known and is housed in the Musée de Condé in Chantilly, France (IV.E.89). In 1865, Kervyn de Lettenhove edited all of Chastellain's works, but his version of the "Louange" in volume VIII of *Oeuvres de Georges Chastellain* (pp. 269-92) is a composite edition based only on manuscripts B1, A, and P2, because Lettenhove was unaware of the existence of versions B2, P1 and V. Moreover, his edition does not provide a complete list of variants, nor does he mention an important series of rubrics that are found in two of the three manuscripts he examined (AP2). Although it does not appear as if any of the five extant manuscripts or the one imprint of the "Louange" are direct copies of any other extant versions, B1, A, and P2 share a significant number of readings as do B2, P1, and V. Closer affiliations can be drawn between A and P2, on one hand, and P1 and

V, on the other. Thus, the critical edition of the "Louange à la tresglorieuse Vierge" I provide below, which takes into account the *six* known versions, offers a more thickly textured edition of Chastellain's poem than Lettenhove's 19th-century version and a more dramatic example of *mouvance* at work during the last half of the 15th century.[3]

Traditional editors, like Lettenhove himself, have considered many textual transformations to be scribal errors or unwarranted interventions, as the so-called "common error method" of determining affiliations among different versions suggests.[4] But recent theoreticians and practicians of text editing, drawing from Zumthor's discussions of *mouvance*, tend to view many of these changes more positively as an innate part of the system of medieval composition itself.[5] Some textual alterations can, of course, be ascribed to scribal or editorial oversights. Such examples surface in each version of Chastellain's "Louange" and range from misspellings or typos,[6] to a missing word[7] or two,[8] to an omitted verse[9] and even missing stanzas. In V, for example, eight of the fifty 14-verse stanzas (XXXIII-XXXVI, XLV-XLVIII), or 112 verses in all, are missing. As a careful material assessment of the imprint suggests, this oversight can likely be ascribed to the compiler or editor of version V, or its model, not to the copyist, since the eight omitted stanzas comprise the equivalent of a bifolium, which could well have been lost in the assemblage of folios.[10] In three versions, entire stanzas are out of place: stanzas XI and XII are reversed in P1, stanzas XLV and XLVI are reversed in B2, and stanza XII precedes stanza X in V. The fact that these differences tend to occur in one version alone and that there is often a resulting lack of logic or presence of hypo- and hypermetric lines all but confirm that they are indeed scribal or editorial errors.[11]

But most of the variance among the versions of Chastellain's "Louange" appears to consist of conscious modifications made by scribes in the later versions to update and upgrade their text and correct the one(s) from which they were copying. While these divergent readings can never be determined in a definite chronological sequence, since manuscripts that were transcribed at a later date than others may have been based on earlier models and vice-versa, certain patterns nevertheless emerge. These patterns can be most clearly identified in the case of B2, because its readings diverge most dramatically from all other versions, including those of the printed edition (V), and appear to be modifications consciously made at a later date by the B2 scribe or his model. The role of the scribe of manuscript B2, then, approaches most closely that of the so-called author, for, in comparison with the other extant versions, a large number of verses in B2 have been partially or completely reformulated. To a certain degree, the emphasis of the poem itself has been thereby altered, as we will see below.[12]

Whereas some studies of works composed and reproduced after the advent of print suggest that variants in printed editions often offer substantially different readings than those in manuscript versions,[13] the case of Chastellain's "Louange," authored by a writer unfamiliar with the print culture yet reproduced in print after his death, suggests otherwise. In fact, the readings of the one extant printed edition of the work (V) diverge far less from those of other versions than B2 does. Thus, no notable textual distinctions set the imprint apart, although, as I will discuss below, certain paratextual aspects do.[14]

One type of transformation that emerges from a careful study of the textual *mouvance* of the known versions of the "Louange" involves the correction of mistakes that occur in earlier versions being copied. In one example, a hypermetric line in B1 is corrected, but in three different ways, in the later versions of the work:[15]

v. 391   B1   Et tout benoit sein et giron qui sentoient (+1)

           AP2   Et tous benois saincts girons qui sentoient

           P1V   Et ton benoit saint geron qui sentoient

           B2   Et tout benoit qui son sainct corps sentoient.

The result is that an essential element in B1, the *sein* (breast), one of two physical details used metonymically to represent all blessed people, appears in no other version; instead one finds the adjective *saint*, essentially a homonym for *sein*, whether in singular or plural form. The singular form found in P1V closely resembles the earlier version B1, but, with the absence of the conjunction *et* (and), the P1V reading provides a correctly metered decasyllabic line. *Tout* (Every), however, has become *ton* (your), significantly altering the perspective of the speaker and audience: instead of referring in the third person to anonymous others, the narrator has shifted focus in P1V by directly addressing the Virgin about what has become *her* physical trait, "your blessed saintly bosom." Although using *tout* and the third-person perspective found in B1, version B2 provides an example of its closer affiliation with P1V than with AP2 by adopting a singular adjective (*sainct*), and, with the absence of *et*, maintaining a decasyllabic line. However, in a fashion characteristic of the more divergent version B2, a significant change was made by replacing the idea of *giron* (lap, bosom) found in all other versions with *corps* (body), personifying it with a personal adjective, (*son*=its), and shifting the beginning of the relative clause (*qui...* [which/who...]) to an earlier point in the verse. Both the P1V and the B2 "corrections," however, resulted in a grammatical error in subject-verb agreement: instead of the two subject-nouns (*sein, giron*) found in B1, the singular subject in B2P1V calls for a singular not a plural verb (*sentoient*); but *sentoit* would not have rhymed with the other words in the stanza (*prestoient, portoient, chantoient, allaittoyent*).[16] In the end, the most felicitous reading is found in AP2, which, like the other later versions, uses an adjective instead of a subject-noun (*saincts*) and maintains a decasyllabic verse without *et*; but, by making the indefinite adjective, descriptive adjective and noun plural, the AP2 scribes achieved agreement between subject and verb.[17] An examination of *mouvance* in this one verse, then, offers direct insight into what motivated the scribes and one printer copying Chastellain's "Louange" to employ, and in some cases, transform certain words and expressions found in their models.[18]

A second type of transformation involves the conscious modernization of vocabulary and grammar. For example, the B2 scribe goes to extremes on at least ten occasions, to avoid using the expression *droit cy* (right here), as the following sequence of verses and variants, in which each modification differs from the others, shows: [19]

v. 258-	B1AP1P2V	Venez *droit cy* aloes et seraines
60	B2	Venes ycy alouettes et seraynes
	B1P1V	Venez *droit cy* vos soefvetez espandre
	B2	Voz doulces voix et plaisans chants espandre
	B1AP1P2V	Venez *droit cy* armonies repletes...
	B2	Venez aussy armonyes impletes
v. 262	B1AP1P2V	Venez *droit cy* monstrer vos vertus pleines...
	B2	Venes y toutes monstrer vos vertus plaines
v. 264	B1AP1P2V	Venez *droit cy* les oeuvres Dieu completes
	B2	Venes avec les oeuvres Dieu completes[20]

Another example of the effort to modernize earlier versions involves the replacement of Old French adjectival forms, from the second class of adjectives that had the same form for the masculine and the feminine, with Middle French forms, which are gender-specific. For example *Vigne excellent* in B1AP1P2V reads *Vigne excellente* in B2 (v. 309) and *royal excellence* in B1AP1P2V reads *royale excellence* in B2 (v. 368).[21] For v. 146, B2 offers a more modern verbal and syntactical construction than the other versions:

| B1AP1P2V | Apres avoir commis Adam son vice |
| B2 | Apres qu'Adam si eut commis son vice[22] |

With an awareness of these modifications,[23] scholars are brought into direct contact with how the very transition from Old French to Middle French worked itself out, a process that took hundreds of years. By focusing on the edited text alone, modern readers miss these fascinating transformations which constitute the very texture of the work.

In one final example, the B2 scribe avoids reuse of the same word at the rhyme (*affaire*) in verses 484-86:

B1P1P2	Mais en visant en celui noble affaire
A	" " usant " " " "
B2	Mais meditant " " " "

> B1AP1P2   La ou note a bien dangereuse afaire
> B2   Que j'ay empris pour te service faire

> B1AP1P2   Pour un tel corps qui de sens a sobresse...
> B2   Considerant de mon sens la sobresse...

In most versions, the meaning of these lines remains vague and abstract: "But in aiming in this noble matter where ill report has a very dangerous charge (?) for such a body, which is sober in knowledge..." By contrast, the author-scribe of B2 adopted more concrete vocabulary, and in shifting from 3rd-person to 1st-person discourse, a move more consistent with the direct address mode of this stanza, made the passage much more accessible: "But meditating upon this noble matter that I have undertaken in order to serve you, considering the sobriety of my mind..."

Indeed, a third kind of transformation that characterizes the later versions of Chastellain's "Louange" emerges from this last example, namely an effort to provide a clearer, more concrete meaning. Whereas some transformations of this type emphasize the voice or actions of the author-narrator, as in verses 484-86 above, in the following example the writer's act of composing is highlighted by a shift from the metaphoric expressions in the first two readings ("I seek to serve you and offer you flowerings / nourishment") to the literal expression of B2 ("I seek to serve you through poetry and writing"):

> v. 124   B1AP2   Te quiers servir et offrir floriture
>   P1V   "   "   "   "   "   nourreture
>   B2   "   "   "   par dict et escripture

It is true that throughout Chastellain's homage to the Virgin Mary, the author-figure voices concern about whether he is worthy or capable enough of success-fully completing his literary task of composing a poem in her honor (see stanzas VIII-IX, XXXII, XXXVII-XXXIX, XLVIII, etc.). Yet, as the five following passages suggest, the later textual transformations, particularly in the B2 version, draw the reader's attention even more so to the artist's self-consciousness:

> v.165   B1   Yci descens, cy entour t'avironne
>   AP1P2V   "   "   et   "   "
>   B2   A toi me rendz ou tout a toy me donne

> v.166   B1A   Cy entour moi t'humblie et t'agironne
>   P1P2V   Et   "   "   "   "   "
>   B2   De toutes pars ma voix tramblant resonne

> v.167   B1AP1P2V   Qui par adjoust sur ton reluisant tronne
>   B2   Entor loant vers et dis je jargonne

v.168   B1AP1P2V   T'envoye ou ciel mon offre aromatique
          B2   Que je transmectz en moult simple praticque

The reading in most versions of this passage, which relates how the author-narrator receives divine inspiration to write, provides a confusing relationship between the narrator and the Virgin. With its particular use of personal pronouns, which includes the absence of subject pronouns, so common in Old French and Middle French, the verse is very difficult to understand: "Come down here, here I envelop you (around), here I humble myself before you and I pursue you (?), I who, by adding to your gleaming throne, send to you in the heavens my aromatic offering." By contrast, B2 offers a completely transformed text whose meaning is much clearer: "I yield myself to you, or I give you all of myself. From all sides my trembling voice resounds; praising everything around, I babble confusedly verses and poems, which I transmit in very simple form." In the following example, it is the versions P1V that make literary references in providing a more literal reading than B1AP2, while the verse in B2 is radically different:[24]

v. 304   B1AP2   Fleurs et verdeurs [P2: verdures] en toi se fructifient
          P1V   Rethoriques ta haulteur [V: tes haulteurs] magnifient
          B2   Tous bons devotz en t'amour s'ediffient

In the two following examples, the author-figure, in conventional self-deprecatory fashion, describes his failing talents. Again, the B2 version introduces more specific details about poetic composition:

v.515   B1AP1P2V   Et puis j'en voy la sentence petite
          B2   Voyant mon oeuvre et sentence petite

v.516   B1AP1P2V   Si povre en soi [V: foy] le sens qui y habite
          B2   En quoy nul sens ne science habite

v.517   B1AP1P2V   Je me pers tout et m'argue [P1V: argue] et despite
          B2   "   "   "   "   je m'argue   "   "   [25]

Or:

v.642   B1AP2   Ployant vers moi me voulsisses instruire
          B2   Courant "   "   "   "   "
          P1   Par ta doulceur   me   "   "

v.643   B1AP1P2   De ce qui duit et affiert pour déduire
          B2   "   "   "   "   pour mon oeuvre construyre

v.644	B1AP1P2	Ton corps ou est tel gloire contenue
	B2	Ou soit ton loz et gloire contenue

v. 645	B1AP1P2	Ainsi estaint par naturel foiblesse
	B2	" " " naturelle "

v.646	B1	Ceur contemplant, mes muet, je te lesse
	AP2	" " et " " " "
	P1	Mon povre cueur contemplant je te lesse
	B2	Mon coeur tremblant tout muet je te lesse[26]

In a final example, the general references in other versions are directly related to the literary enterprise in B2:

v. 686	AP2	Toute ma force y est enregistree
	B1P1V	J'y ai mis tout le beau de ma ventree
	B2	Car g'y ay mis ma science lettree[27]

The accumulation of these micro-textual changes results in a significant emphasis in B2 on the author-figure and his poetic enterprise. It is impossible to determine why this version, transcribed in 1495, displays such characteristics. However, the fact that the B2 version of the "Louange" is found in the same manuscript as another work by Chastellain about poetic creation, the *Douze Dames de Rhétorique*, may explain in part this increased emphasis on authorial details.[28]

In fact, three kinds of paratextual variants reaffirm the nature of the B2 textual transformations discussed above:[29] title announcements, the use of images, and the presence of rubrics. Although B1 bears no title whatsoever, those found in manuscripts A and P2 and the variation on that title in P1 acknowledge the Virgin as the subject of focus in the work:

AP2: Louenge a la tresglorieuse vierge.... (Praise to the most glorious Virgin)

P1:   S'ensuivent les nobles dictiers composez a l'onneur de la vierge marie...
      (Here follow noble verses composed in honor of the Virgin Mary...)

However, the B2 scribe, while referring to the Virgin, offers a significantly different title than AP1P2:

B2:   Cy finent les hympnes louanges et canticques ditz georgines.....en l'onneur
      de la glorieuse et sacree vierge et mere du doulx Jhesus marie...

      (Here end the hymns, praises and so-called Georgian cantiques...in honor
      of the glorious and sacred Virgin and mother of sweet Jesus, Mary)

The allusion to *canticques ditz georgines* (so-called Georgian canticles) is based on the last verse of Chastellain's poem, where the poet entitled his work *mes chansons georgines* (my Georgian songs) through a pun on his first name. In fact, version V bears this exact name on its title page (my emphasis): S'ensuivent les *chanchons georgines*... ("Here follow the Georgian songs.."). The absence of any verbal allusion to the poem's subject in version V is counter-balanced by a wood-cut image of the Virgin that figures centrally on the title page as well. But only in B2 does the title place equal emphasis on the subject while highlighting the title invented by Chastellain himself for his own work. In this sense, the title in B2 reinforces this manuscript's textual emphasis on the author and his poetic enterprise. Furthermore, a miniature in B2 depicts the author in his study (fol. 6). Looking up at an image of the Virgin and Child above, the author-figure, identified by Chastellain's name (Castelin), which is actually written across the illustration, sits at his desk and writes. No other version of the "Louange" draws the reader's attention to the author in such a dramatic manner. Although an image is also found on the title page of the printed edition (V), this is a worn woodcut, used previously in other contexts, which depicts the Virgin and the Archangel Gabriel during the Annunciation. By contrast, it is the direct relationship between the Virgin's divine inspiration and the poet's process of creation, the very subject of the "Louange," that is emphasized in B2.

While the earliest extant version, B1, which serves as the base manuscript for my edition, contains no rubrics, the two other versions most closely affiliated with it, A and P2, contain 45 rubrics. Whether the author himself originally devised these sub-titles -- that is, whether A and P2 were copied from versions closer to Chastellain's own manuscript than B1 -- is difficult to ascertain. The fact that the rubrics greatly facilitate an understanding of the sometimes abstract and difficult text by announcing five introductory sections[30] and each of the forty stanzas thereafter[31] suggests that scribes or editors may have added them at a later date. The rubrics essentially provide the general content of a particular stanza, as the following examples show:

XII: Loenge par figure des saincts peres (Praise through
         representation of the Holy Fathers)

XXVI: Loenge sur la grace que son sainct corps portoit
         (Praise about the grace which her saintly body carried)

XXXI: Loenge par recitacion de ses vertuz (Praise through
         recitation of her virtues)

XL: Explication de sa gloire par les diverses substances celestes
         droit cy specifiees (Explanation of her glory through
         the various celestial substances specified herein)

B2 is the only other version of the "Louange" in which rubrics are found (in this case 44 rubrics), a surprising fact since B2 textual variants rarely coincide with AP2. As one might expect, however, B2 provides a number of divergent readings. In several cases, the B2 version offers a correction of the AP2 reading. The rubric for stanza XXIII in AP2 mistakenly refers to the use of a metaphor of a saintly virgin (*Loenge par figure d'une saincte vierge*), while B2 alludes instead to a saintly *vine* (*vigne*), in keeping with the very subject of the stanza. In the rubric preceding stanza XLIX, B2's reading does not contain the grammatical error found in AP2, in which a noun (*saincteté*) instead of an adjective (*saincte*) modifies another noun (*integrité*), and, unlike the other versions, personalizes the Virgin:

> AP2: Loenge sur la virginité et *saincteté* integrité et dont les haulx et glorieux tiltres sont de vray et perpetuel effect et fruict (Praise of virginity and *saintliness* (?) integrity and of which the high and glorious titles are of a true and perpetual influence and fruitfulness)

> B2: Loange sur *sa* virginité et *saincte* integrité et dont les haultz et glorieux tiltres... (Praise of *her* virginity and *saintly* integrity and *whose* high and glorious titles...)

Moreover, reflecting its clearer focus on authorial concerns in the body of the work, B2, in two of the introductory rubrics, makes a reference to the author that is not found in the AP2 versions:

VII   AP2: Icy fine le proheme tourné a Dieu et Icy se conturne a glorieuse Vierge (Here ends the prologue directed to God and here one turns to the glorious Virgin)
           B2: Cy fine le proheme tourné a Dieu *et se retourne l'acteur a la Vierge* Marie (Here ends the prologue directed to God and *the author turns to the Virgin*)

VIII-IX AP2: Excusacion (Justification)
           B2: Excusation *par l'acteur* (Justification *by the author*)

Nevertheless, all three versions incorporate references to the author in a number of other rubrics.[32]

In the end, we can see how the paratextual formulations in version B2 reconfirm its textual transformations. Both kinds of modifications constitute a significant rewriting of the "Louange" in comparison with all the other extant versions and, through their use of more concrete references, direct much more attention to the author-narrator's voice and literary project than the other versions do. Given the conformity of most other versions and the fact that the B2 manuscript was transcribed 20 years after the author's death, it is highly unlikely that

Chastellain himself was responsible for the transformations found in B2. It appears, then, that the B2 scribe appropriated a certain authorial power in not only copying but in reworking his version, which he labelled the *Georgian Canticles*, furnishing the most significant dimension of the *mouvance* of Chastellain's work. Indeed, the B2 version is as important for an understanding of the history of the work as version B1, the manuscript I selected as the base text of my edition, because it was transcribed during the author's lifetime and was, as a result, likely the closest to Chastellain's own version. And yet readers following the conventional pattern of focusing exclusively on an edition's base text, thereby implicitly -- and perhaps unconsciously -- ascribing a superior, fixed status to it, are not likely to experience the richness of this work in particular and of late medieval composition in general. It is my hope that these introductory remarks will encourage scholars and students to read this and other editions in a more enlightened manner.

University of Santa Barbara

Notes

1. See, for example, his *Essai de poétique médiévale* (Paris, Seuil, 1972), 70-75, 507; "Le texte-fragment," *Langue française*, 40 (1978), 75-82; and "Intertextualité et mouvance," *Littérature* 41 (1981), 8-16.

2. See *The Songs of Jaufré Rudel* (Toronto: Pontifical Institute of Mediaeval Studies, 1978).

3. For more bibliographical details about these versions, see my article "De 'La Louange à la tresglorieuse Vierge' aux *Chansons georgines*: la transformation d'une oeuvre de Georges Chastellain" (hereafter cited as *Chansons georgines*), forthcoming in *Le Moyen Français*.

4. For a discussion of this and other terms and theories associated with the history of text editing, see Alfred Foulet and Mary Speer, *On Editing Old French Texts* (Lawrence, Kansas: Regents Press of Kansas, 1979).

5. See, for example, Bernard Cerquiglini's *Eloge de la variante: Histoire critique de la philologie* (Paris: Seuil, 1989).

6. Even though spelling in Old French and Middle French was open to a wide number of possibilities, certain formulations were obviously incorrect. See, for example, vv. 25 (P2), 32 (A), 55 (V), 318 (B1), 449 (B1), 696 (P2), etc.

7. A (cf. vv. 37, 76, 403, 465, 667); B2 (cf. vv. 36, 302, 343, 533, 553); P1 (cf. vv. 65, 77, 84, 245, 291, 500, 517, 641); P2 (cf. vv. 84, 283, 289, 403, 465, 543, 667); V (cf. vv. 291, 517).

8. B2 (v. 699), P1 (v. 639).

9. A (v. 653), P2 (v. 256)

10. Since two stanzas are printed per folio in V, the complete version, with fifty instead of forty-two 14-versed stanzas, would have yielded 12½ folios of text; instead text covers only 10½ folios, with the entire first folio serving as a

title page. The four missing stanzas XXXIII-XXXVI would have formed a folio that should have fallen after the 8th folio of text. If this 4-stanza omission occurred in a manuscript without title page that served as V's model, it could well have found its original place at the beginning of a new quire, if there were, as was often the case, 4 folios - or two bifolia - per quire. That being the case, the second group of omitted stanzas, XLV-XLVIII, would have formed the second half of the same bifolium containing stanzas XXXIII-XXXVI. The eight stanzas that come in between the missing stanzas (XXXVII-XLIV) would have likewise formed an entire bifolium in themselves and, together with the missing bifolium, a quire.

11. The same single words are missing in versions P1 and P2 (v. 84), P1 and V (vv. 291, 517) and A and P2 (vv. 403, 465, 667), but the absence of entire lines or stanzas is not repeated in any two versions.

12. For discussions of the overlapping of scribal and authorial roles, see Chapter 1 of David Hult, *Self-Fulfilling Prophecies: Readership and Authority in the First "Roman de la Rose"* (New York: Cambridge UP, 1987); Sylvia Huot, "The Scribe as Editor: Rubrication as Critical Apparatus in Two Manuscripts of the *Roman de la Rose*," *L'Esprit Créateur* 27 (Spring 1987), 67-78; and Kevin Brownlee, "Transformations of the *Charrete*: Godefroi de Leigni Rewrites Chrétien de Troyes," *Stanford French Review*, XIV, 1-2 (Spring-Fall 1990), 161-178.

13. See, for example, my critical edition of André de la Vigne's *Ressource de la Chrestienté* (Montreal: CERES, 1989).

14. For a discussion of works composed by pre-print authors that did undergo significant textual as well as paratextual transformations in print, see my articles on Christine de Pizan and François Villon: "The Reconstruction of an Author in Print: Christine de Pizan in the 15th and 16th Centuries," in *Christine de Pizan and the Categories of Difference*, ed. Marilynn Desmond (Minneapolis: U. of Minnesota Press, 1998) and "Author, Editor and the Use of Illustrations in the Early Imprints of Villon's Works: 'Ung chacun n'est maistre du scien'" forthcoming in *Chaucer's French Contemporaries*, ed. R. Barton Palmer (New York: AMS Press, 1998), 215-35.

15. In these and all other verses cited, as in the edition itself, abbreviations have been expanded, capital letters have been added to mark the beginning of a proper name or of a verse, the use of *i* and *j*, and *u* and *v* has been regularized, word separation has been modernized, apostrophes have been added to indicate elided vowels, ç has been used as in modern French, é serves to indicate both past participles in the masculine singular and in plurals ending in -*s* (but not those ending in -*ez*) and a final pronounced syllable (as in *aprés*). To facilitate syllable count, diereses have been indicated. Punctuation has been added when necessary.

16. For other problematic "corrections," see the variants for vv. 147, 338, 628, 629, 645, 664.

17. In point of fact, the verse in B1 may constitute a later error, while the versions AP2 may provide a reading closer to Chastellain's version.

18. For other kinds of corrections, see vv. 301, 311, 312, 313, 314, 318, 378, 423, 428, 439, 469, 475, 527, 677, etc.

19. For other similar modifications, see the following examples: in B2 *au rebours* replaces *en rebout* (11), *plaisir* replaces *delit* (39), *heure* becomes *chose* (79) [*heure* is replaced by *oeuvre* in P1], *druerie* becomes *industrie* (184), *destruict* replaces *occy* (325), *plaisans* replaces *tretis* (*traictifs*) (384), *demoura* replaces *parmaindra* (420), *quiert* becomes *tend* (474), *angels* becomes *anges* (554) [the same change appears in P1P2], *sens* replaces *engin* (637), *uns yeuls* becomes *mes yeulx* (647), *je m'essaray* replaces *j'attempteray* (669); in P1 *tomber* replaces *cheoir* (433). In an opposite, though less common, trend, the different readings suggest that later scribes sometimes rejected the use of neologisms in their model. For example, *formeuse* (beautiful) *ymage* (162) in versions AB1P1P2 is rendered *fermeuse ymage* in V and *tres doulce ymage* in B2. *Commixtion d'herbage* (213) in AB1P2 reads *quelque odeur [de] nature* in B2P1V. Cf. also vv. 132, 133, 210, 294, 564, 566, 574.

20. See also vv. 273, 280, 341, 571, 695.

21. See also vv. 340, 449, 561, 645. Why B2 reads *redolent lavende* like B1P1 and does not make a similar adjectival alteration in verse 449 is unclear. If it was consciously to avoid a hypermetric line, like AP2's reading, *redolente lavende*, one wonders why the B2 scribe made that very same error in modernizing the adjectival form of *imperial substance* to *imperiale substance* (v. 561) and *naturel foiblesse* to *naturelle foiblesse* (v. 645), both of which resulted in hypermetric verses.

22. The first version reads "After having committed Adam his sin..." and the B2 version reads "After Adam had committed his sin..."

23. The following transformations can be found as well: *En* is replaced by *a* (78) or *ou* by *en* (468), while the Old French pronoun form *cui* is replaced by *qui* (562). B2 repeatedly updates the use of pronominal verbs (see, for example, vv. 88, 90) and avoids the *ne...ne* sequence (see vv. 272, 294, 453, 475, 572).

24. B1AP2: Flowers and greenery within you bear fruit; P1V: Poets magnify your greatness (greatnesses); B2: All good devotees edify themselves in your love.

25. B1: And then I see the little thought in it, the meaning so poor in itself (V: in faith) there, I lose myself completely and chide myself (A: and dispute) and am angry with myself; B2: Seeing the smallness of my work and thought, in which no meaning or understanding is found, I lose myself completely, I chide myself and am angry with myself.

26. B1: Bending towards me (P1: By your sweetness) you wished to instruct me about what is customary and appropriate to discuss about your body, where such glory is contained; thus consumed by natural weakness, heart contemplating, but (A: and) silent (P1: My poor heart contemplating), I leave you... B2: Running towards me you wanted to teach me about what is appropriate to construct my work, wherein all your praise and glory will be. Thus, consumed by natural weakness, my poor heart trembling, completely silent, I leave you...

27. AP2: All my power is registered therein; B1P1V: I have put there all the beauty of my belly; B2: For I have placed there my knowledge of letters.

28. Ironically, the *Douze Dames* text, whose readings are, like those in the B2 version of the "Louange," radically different from all other versions, contains numerous abstract passages that are difficult to understand. For details on the relationship between the text of the *Douze Dames de Rhétorique* found in Bibliothèque Royale ms. II 6977 and the other versions of the work, which tend to offer more modern readings, see my articles "Du nouveau sur le 'mistere' des *Douze Dames de Rhétorique*: Le rôle de Georges Chastellain," *Bulletin de la Commission Royale d'Histoire*, CLIII (1987), 188-223 and "A Late Medieval Cultural Artifact: *The Twelve Ladies of Rhetoric* (*Les Douze Dames de Rhétorique*), Allegorica*, 16 (1995), 73-105.

29. See Gérard Genette's *Seuils* (Paris: Seuil, 1987), for a discussion of the paratext.

30. Prologue (I), Invocation for Divine Aid (II-VI), Address to the Glorious Virgin (VII), Justification (VIII-IX), Question Serving as Justification (X).

31. See the variants below for a listing of all of these rubrics.

32. See, for example, the rubrics preceding stanzas XXXII, XXXVII, XXXVIII, XLI, XLVII, XLVIII, L). In the rubric preceding stanza XLV, the B2 scribe used the work *facteur*, meaning writer, instead of *acteur* (author), the term found in AP2. For a discussion of the many meanings of *acteur* at this time, see Chapter 5 in my *Poets, Patrons and Printers: Crisis of Authority in Late Medieval France* (Ithaca: Cornell UP, 1995). For details about the various terms used to identify the author in the different authorship announcements in five of the versions of the "Louange," see my *Chansons georgines*.

La Louange à la tresglorieuse Vierge

I   Querant l'ung oeil envers les cieulx estendre, (fol. 1)
Dont le regard m'est trop foible et trop tendre
Pour y voler non enpenné de grace,
L'autre oeil donne a rude et gros entendre, 4
Sans enquerir trop avant ne contendre.
Craintif nientmoins soubs le divin attendre,
Je offre a la terre et lui flecis ma face;
Tendant au ray d'aveuglissant lumiere 8
Me vient l'object de terreste fumiere,
Qui mon arc fait descorder et destendre,
Et en rebout de ma joye sommiere,
De mon tresor et richesse fermiere, 12
Comme en tel cas nature est coustumiere,
Me fait faillir de mon ardant pretendre.

II   O le hault ray de lumiere eternelle,   (fol. 1ᵛ)
       Sourgon parfont de splendeur supernelle,   16
       Dont toute rien prent substance et essence,
       Droit cy m'eslieve et enpenne mon ele
       Tant qu'a ce vol que mon ceur quiert et cele,
       J'ataigne ung peu par clarté sensuele   20
       Desoubs ung net plumage d'innocence.
       Je n'en quier pas resplendir ma personne,
       N'aquerir bruit qu'en la terre on messonne
       Et dont la gloire est vaine et temporele,   24
       Mais esclarcir et deliter ton tronne,
       Perlifier ton ceptre et ta couronne,
       Et toute rien qui servant t'avironne
       Magnifier de ma voix corporele.   28

III   Eslargi m'as eloquence et faconde   (fol. 2)
       Pour servir, las, ce soullie, povre monde
       Dont j'ay amé la volupté et gloire.
       Mais, o ruisseau de clemence parfonde   32
       Sueffre et atten premier donc que je fonde,
       Qu'en ton hault ciel et en ta clarté monde
       Puisse en ton los tendre et getter mon loire.
       Je quiers mes yeuls de la terre distraire,   36
       Le ceur vers toi tramettre et la retraire,
       Comme en celui ou tout solas habonde,
       Et dont la gloire et le delit du traire
       Me donront feu et grace pour extraire   40
       Mos et beauls dis pour le corrage attraire
       De celle en qui tout mon espoir redonde.

IV   Purge mes sens, o bonté pardurable,   (fol. 2ᵛ)
       Retray mon oeil de ce siecle plorable,   44
       Le ceur m'enflambe et larme purifie,
       Me soit ta grace aidant et secourable
       Que de mon sain vicieux, miserable
       Fleur ou bourgon se puist traire honnorable   48
       Qui sente en terre et ou ciel fructifie.
       Veines et ceur et toutes mes entrailles
       S'euuvrent vers toi et se presentent trailles
       Pour y planter ta racyne ammirable,   52
       De quoi le clos de tes saintes orailles,
       Que je requier que droit cy m'apparailles
       Porront coeillir fleurs vives et parailles
       A ta haulteur et gloire inreferable.   56

V   Requis t'ay dont de grace et assistence,   (fol. 3)
Souverain bien, donnant toute existence
Et a rien toute estre ou entendre ou vivre;
Dont s'en espoir doy avoir persistence   60
Que humble vers moi fleciras advertence;
Je te pry donc sans faire desistence
Qu'en mon desir ta main secours me livre.
Amour fervent, faveur contemplative   64
M'ont eslevé ma virtu sensitive
En hault emprendre et en haulte sentence,
Dont du durant de ceste vie active
Ja ne porray par force intellective   68
Venir a chief, si non a main craintive,
Se de ton ray ne m'en vient la potence.

VI   Ame et desir, veines et ceur me tirent   (fol. 3ᵛ)
A prendre en moi ce que les cieulx amirent,   72
Et que n'ont peu circuir ne comprendre,
Et en quoi tous les clers qui oncq nasquirent
Et, ententis en cestui cas, escrirent;
Plume et papier a crainte en oeuvre y mirent   76
Pour la haulteur qui y est a emprendre:
C'est en loer ta glorieuse mere,
Dont le laissier me seroit heure amere
Et encor plus folie l'entreprendre;   80
Mais non obstant tel facteur et rimere
Qui ne suis pas Virgille ne Omere,
G'y assairay et compere et commere
Sur espoir plus d'y gaignier que mesprendre.   84

VII   O splendeur sainte en la court seraphine,   (fol. 4)
Subject haultain de science augustine,
Puisoer de joye a tous sains et prophetes,
En qui fermoer toute grace divine,   88
Toute vertu celeste se recline,
Tout y obombre et tout s'i attermine,
Tout y respant ses richesses secretes.
O saint miroer d'esmerveillable gloire,   92
De qui on list que humilité notoire
T'a fait monter, si excelse royne:
Toute humble, donc, ta doulceur meritoire,
Tourne envers moi dedens mon oratoire,   96

Et me permes faire une sobre histoire,
Parlant a toi du mesmes de ma mine.

VIII Non pas qu'en moi je prengne l'arrogance   (fol. 4^v)
    D'attaindre a toi en ta resplendissance,   100
    La ou tu siez ou ciel glorifiee,
    Mais ung petit selon povre puissance
    D'humain engin et de sa congnoissance
    Touchant ton estre ou monde et ta naissance: 104
    La je requiers grace fortifiee.
    Je suy l'oiseau qui vole emprez la terre
    Et n'ose pas haulte proye requerre
    Par jugement de propre insuffisance;   108
    Mais en gardant mon humble et mon bas erre,
    Je m'entretiens et vis de mon acquerre,
    S'il n'est que force ou ardant fain me serre
    De m'escoeillir en plus haultaine usance.   112

IX   Ainsi, o tressainte divine proie,   (fol. 5)
    Autour de qui tant de mistere ombroye
    Et tant de hauls et nobles oiseauls volent,
    Je ne quier pas et aussi ne vouldroye   116
    Te querir la, car je m'y decevroye;
    Ains en pensant a ce, je m'en effroye,
    Et tes splendeurs m'aveuglent et affolent.
    Je suis de terre et en telle nature   120
    Me prens a toi, o sainte creature;
    Ailleurs bien sçay que je m'abuseroye.
    Dont comme humaine et en telle estature,
    Te quiers servir et offrir floriture,   124
    Se aprez de grace et de bonne aventure,
    Ton hault monter plus hault vol ne m'octroye.

X   Clos virginal, cyboire precïeuse,   (fol. 5^v)
    Vergier flory de beaulté specïeuse   128
    Ou le soleil ne souffrit oncq umbrage,
    Flairant rosier, rose solacïeuse,
    Quels mos, quels dis, quel doulceur gracïeuse
    Metray je avant, Vierge sciencïeuse,   132
    Par quoi parer je puisse mon ouvrage?
    Je te voi tant et digne et delitable
    Qu'en moi ne croi la puissance habitable
    Pour mettre a chief telle oeuvre curïeuse,   136
    Se de toi propre en pité charitable,

En propre amour, n'envoies a ma table

Ce qui sera duisant et profitable
Pour illustrer ta face glorïeuse.   140

XI   Restoer d'Adam, d'Eve reparatrice,   (fol. 6)
       Du juste Abel le sainty sacrifice,
       Promise a Seth, vraye misericorde,
       L'aer zephirin du paradis felice,   144
       Dont tout le siecle et terreste edifice,
       Aprez avoir commis Adam son vice,
       Ont pris depuis la flaireur de concorde.
       Tu es et fus le saint abre de vie   148
       Sur qui Sathan congrea son envie,
       Voyant en toi le futur benefice
       Que de ta plante et racine plevie,
       De ton bourgon et fleur pure assovie   152
       Naistroit salut, verité, voye et vie,
       Qui mort vaincroit et le sien malefice.

XII   Foy d'Abraham, vision moysaÿque,   (fol. 6ᵛ)
       Harpe a David, palais salomonique   156
       Construit d'azur, de fin or et d'ivyere,
       Royal bourgon, lignie davitique,
       Sur qui s'espant la doulceur armonique
       Du Pere et Fils en leur mainte cantique,   160
       Comme en l'object preveu en leur lumiere;
       Formeuse ymage, o gente vingeronne
       Que Salomon invita a couronne
       Par tant de hault bel parler angelique: 164
       Yci descens, cy entour t'avironne,
       Cy entour moi t'humblie et t'agironne
       Qui par adjoust sur ton reluisant tronne
       T'envoye ou ciel mon offre aromatique.   168

XIII   Forte Judich, humble Hester figuree,   (fol. 7)
       De qui doulceur et beaulté decoree
       S'enamoura l'offensé roi celeste.
       Mille ans et plus prescrite et proferee,   172
       Premier jamés que fusses engendree
       Pour mettre paix et amour restoree,
       Seule entre Li et son peuple moleste;
       O voix mirable, o demonstrance sainte,   176
       Faitte a achas que jeusne vierge enchainte

Concevroit fruit en sa sale paree
Et ne seroit maternité ratainte
De riens qui feist virginité estainte,   180
Mes mere et vierge ensemble en une enchainte
Pardemorroit a tousjours a duree.

XIV Flairant espargne, effluant tresorie,   (fol. 7ᵛ)
      Dont Salomon par noble druerie   184
      Tira avant les precïeuses herbes,
      En quoi loant ta haulte seigneurie
      Te propina tant de doulceur cherie,
      Tant de nouvelle invencïon florie   188
      Que melodie en est d'oÿr les verbes.
      Te prefera sur or et perle fine,
      Te figura ymage cristaline,
      De l'air du ciel, non de terre, norrie;   192
      S'enamoura de ta doulceur cedrine,
      S'aveuglit tout en ta face angeline,
      Brief, tant li pleut ta beaulté saphirine,
      Que tout le monde en parle encore et crie.   196

XV Montaigne excelse en ferme rocq assise,   (fol. 8)
      La en qui Dieu restablist la francise
      De l'umain genre en merveilleux mistere,
      Toute alentour paree et circoncise   200
      Comme une fine esmeraude precise,
      Dedens, dehors, toute entiere et mascise,
      D'un mesmes estre et tout d'une matere,
      La en dedens et sur le hault d'icelle,   204
      O preeslite et sainte jouvencelle,
      Se vint descendre et prendre sa cointise
      Le Fils de Dieu entrant dedens ta celle
      Sans rompre riens, ne cloistre, ne courcelle,   208
      Lors que tu dis, veu ton humble ancelle:
      "De moi soit fait selon ta libertise."

XVI Qu'est emprez toi baulme ne cynamome,   (fol. 8ᵛ)
      Senteur d'encens, de mirre, ou d'aultre gomme,   212
      Commixtïon d'erbage ne conserve
      Qui as attrait Celui qui Trois se nomme
      A naistre en toi, vray Dieu et parfait homme,
      Compris ensemble ainsi qu'en une pomme,   216
      Deité pure en humanité serve?
      N'est riens pourtant de lis ou d'encolie,

N'est riens de riens que nature jolie
Cree et produit en Syon ne en Romme,   220
N'est rien d'or fin ne de perle pollie,
N'est rien de quoi je te voi enbellie,
S'il n'est qu'en toi ta doulceur s'umilie
De prendre en gré l'amour qui nous y somme.   224

XVII Tu es la seule et sainte creature   (fol. 9)
    A qui ne peut nulle oeuvre de nature
    Pour comparer proprement bien suffire,
    Quant ciel ne terre en dedens leur closture,   228
    Ne tout ce que est dedens leur norriture
    N'ont peu logier ne mettre en fermeture
    Ce que tu seule en ton sainty porphire.
    Si en as eu les gloires si extremmes   232
    Que tu en es benoite entre les femmes
    Et surpassant angelique faiture;
    Et sont benois en toi les hauls cieulx mesmes,
    Saintes et sains plus clers en dyademmes,   236
    Fleurs et verdeurs et precieuses gemmes
    Plus pleins de joye et de riche aventure.

XVIII Mais nonobstant si couvient il ton estre,   (fol. 9ᵛ)
    Ton sainty corps, ton dignité, ton nestre   240
    Affigurer a dignité aulcune
    Telle que Dieu et nature font estre,
    Pour persuader ta porte ou ta fenestre,
    Consideré que clerc ne archiprestre   244
    Aultrement point n'y voit ne qu'en la lune.
    Ainsi tendant d'impossible a possible;
    Et comme plus se peut trouver loisible
    Ciel, terre et mer et paradis terrestre,   248
    Je t'euvre tout visible et invisible,
    Substance pure et matere sensible,
    Car tout il fault aproprier paisible
    Pour ta haulteur umbroyer et repaistre.   252

XIX Venez dont fleurs, lauvendes, marjolaines,   (fol. 10)
    Venez rosiers, violiers, porcelaines,
    Venez palmiers, amandriers et amandre,
    Venez cyprés et soefves alaines   256
    Que les hauls cieulx produisent de leur vaines;
    Venez droit cy aloës et seraines,
    Venez droit cy vos soefvetez espandre,

Venez droit cy armonies repletes, 260
Venez beaultez de nature secretes,
Venez droit cy monstrer vos vertus pleines,
Venez soleil, estoilles, et planetes,
Venez droit cy les oeuvres Dieu completes, 264
Venez chacun en vos vertus discretes:
Rendre et offrir vos loenges haultaines.

XX Eslargissez vos vertus, lis et roses, (fol. 10ᵛ)
    Prestez vouloir, toutes exquises choses, 268
    D'icy venir jubiler et adjoindre;
    Ciel cristalin, enclinez vous par poses,
    Boutez dehors vos richesses recloses
    Et ne tardez ne heures ne reposes: 272
    Chantez droit cy, loer et vos mains joindre,
    Ouvrez vos ceurs, toutes nobles natures;
    Tous hauls engins, disposez vos clostures
    Pour faire yci ou sentences ou gloses, 276
    Offrez vos flairs, fleurs, herbes, et plantures,
    Riez de l'oeil de vos nobles paintures,
    Car en usant de vos vrayes droitures,
    Vous devez tous graces droit cy et proses. 280

XXI O comme eureuse et nee de bon enge, (fol. 11)
    Vierge annoncee en Gabriel l'archange,
    Le messagier des hauls mos salutaires,
    Quant toute rien creee, et homme et ange, 284
    S'emploie et tourne et tend en ta loenge:
    Tout se pourvoit d'onneur et de rendange
    Sougneusement comme a toi tributaires,
    Tout en ferveur se delite et contemple, 288
    Tout de ta grace et de ton amour s'emple,
    Tout devant toi chiet a tes piez en fange,
    Tout en tes meurs se norrist et s'exemple,
    Tout s'enrichist en l'ombre de ton temple, 292
    Tout en toi prent solas, vie et exemple
    Sans qu'a nul soit ne peine ne coustange.

XXII Les haultains cieulx clamans te glorifient, (fol. 11ᵛ)
    Trones, vertus, servans te clarifient, 296
    Tous elemens t'enclinent et honneurent,
    Les oiseles en l'aer te sacrifient;
    Ceurs virginaux loans te saintifient,
    Les sains docteurs ta haulteur verifient, 300

Ciel, terre et mer tout rient et faveurent,
Orgues et voix sonans en toi resonent,
Toutes vers toi musicques se foisonnent;
Fleurs et verdeurs en toi se fructifient,   304
Espices, fruis en ton pris se messonnent,
Humains engins s'aguisent et saisonnent;
Dont pour les biens qui en toi s'amaisonnent,
Les chiens mordans d'enfer se mortifient.   308

XXIII Vigne excellent entre aultres preeslite,   (fol. 12)
    Qui le hault ciel imperïal delite,
    Qui neuf ceurs perce et les abymes oeuvre,
    Qui part d'une humble ouverture petite   312
    Et tient la terre en rondeur circonscrite,
    Les vivans sauve et les mors ressuscite,
    Les bons umbroye et les mauvais receuvre:
    Vigne en ton fruit et en ton noble vivre   316
    L'umain engin se delite et enyvre,
    Devotion s'i explique et habite,
    Chascune fueille y est de vie ung livre,
    Chacun grumeau de fin or une livre,   320
    Et tant y a que fust un ceur de cuivre
    Si y prent il saveur qui l'abilite.

XXIV Tu es le vray paradis voluptaire,   (fol. 12^v)
    Tu es et fus la puisant sagitaire   324
    Qui as occy la serpent de ta vire;
    Tu es vergier sans porte solitaire,
    Des hauls divins consauls la secretaire,
    L'espoir du monde et reclaim salutaire,   328
    Ciel inmobile a fluctuant navire;
    Tu es jardin de deliteux umbrage,
    Cief oultrepas de tout divin ouvrage,
    Creee exempte en grace voluntaire;   332
    Tu es le port de vray et sceur ancrage,
    Tu es la sain et giron de suffrage,
    Le seul garant de povre humain naufrage
    Sur qui tout crie et n'en puet langue taire.   336

XXV Sainte, sainte, sainte, trois fois saintie,   (fol. 13)
    Qui as produit la trois fois Sainte Ostie,
    Ou Trinité se comprist toute entiere;
    Sainte excellent, benoite sacristie,   340
    Bien as mery droit cy qu'on te festie

Et c'on t'essaulse en loenge bastie:
Qui as esté d'un si hault fruit rentiere,
Tu as porté le forment et la paille,   344
De qui tu fus premier l'umble semaille,
Tu as esté du Facteur mere et fille,
Tu as emblé au ciel ceste espousaille,
De quoi nature, ignorant de la taille,   348
S'amire en soi, mais n'y voit riens qui faille;
Ains en l'enqueste elle se pert et sille.

XXVI Benoite face en qui oncq oeil laidure   (fol. 13^v)
    Ne suspica ne ne s'esprist d'ordure,   352
    Ne de feu nul de charnelle foiblesse;
    Tant a esté ta grace soude et dure
    Que oncq oeil n'y prist de pointe de roidure
    Par quoi pechié y entendist bordure,   356
    N'effacement de virginal noblesse.
    Pourquoi? Pour ce que tu, fleur virginale,
    Mesmes portas la plante originale
    De bonté toute en dedens ta soudure,   360
    A qui pechié ne ordure infernale
    N'eut oncq pooir n'agression finale.
    Ains propre estoit vertu moriginale,
    Qui pechié mist a mort et a froidure.   364

XXVII O tressaintie et benoite influence,   (fol. 14)
    Benoit preau, benoite corpulence,
    Benoit portail, benoit cloistre eviterne,
    Benoit fermoer de royal excellence,   368
    En cui oudeur et soefve redolence
    Ung si hault roy prist sa benivolence,
    Toi faisant mere et vierge sempiterne.
    Benoit ton ceur, benoit ton saint corps digne,   372
    Benoit ton oeil, benoit ton fons benigne,
    Benoit ton ventre en sa pure innocence,
    Benoit ton sens qui tel bien nous assigne,
    Benoit le doi qui nous garde et consigne   376
    Et nous preserve encontre le maligne
    Soubs la vertu de ta mainte effluence.

XXVIII Benoites mains qui tel fruit manyerent,   (fol. 14^v)
    Benois les dois doulces qui l'atoucherent,   380
    Benoite levre, et beneditte bouche
    Qui tant de fois par amours le baiserent.

146

Benois tes yeulx qui sougneux le garderent,
Benois tes bras tretis qui l'embracerent,   384
Levant, couchant, dedens sa digne couche;
Benois les ris que tes yeulx lui prestoient,
Benois les dons que tes mains lui portoient,
Benois les mots mignos qui l'aflaterent,   388
Benois les flans qui joyeux lui chantoient,
Benois tetins qui enfant l'allaittoyent,
Et tous benois saincts girons qui sentoient
Ce a quoi oncq les cieulx touchier n'oserent.   392

XXIX Pourprine fleur, violette azuree,   (fol. 15)
       Plus soef flairant que solsie doree
       Ne que lis blanc ou vignoble d'engade
       Desur la perle ou toppaize espuree,   396
       Mieuls que l'or fin en purge preparee,
       Belle en couleur sur beaulté naturee,
       Plus vive en l'oeil que pomme de grenade,
       Rayant ymage, o Vierge mignolette: 400
       Ton propret corps, ta fachon gentelette
       M'ont larme esprise et toute enamouree;
       Mais quant j'avise ou vol ou je volette
       Et que mon ele est foible et rudelette,   404
       J'entre en tristeur de povreté seulette,
       Et n'ay fors peur de faulte maleuree.

XXX Tu es l'or fin dont l'eglise se dore   (fol. 15ᵛ)
       Et dont la foi s'enrichist et decore,   408
       Tu es la nois dont l'uile vif procede,
       Tu es l'escrin que oncq nul n'a peu desclore
       Et dont l'entrer nature en soi ignore
       Quoi et comment, la maniere et tempore,   412
       Comme il y vint Celui qui le possede.
       Tu es la vive orïentale conce,
       La ou dedens la perle estoit absconsce,
       Qui oncq n'y prist entree par enfore,   416
       Dont y parust ne macule ne fronce
       Pour bien au vray y seoir sa responce,
       Mais remanoit entiere et non effonse,
       Et parmaindra sans fin et jusqu'a ore.   420

XXXI Tu es du ciel la sainte doulce pluie   (fol. 16)
       Qui tout l'amer de cestui monde et suye
       A lavé jus et debouté en soute.

Tu es ossy la potence et l'apuye   424
D'humain espoir, qui tout sur toi s'appuye,
Et comme en garde et maniere d'estuye
Met son salut et son attente toute.
Tu es la pluye ymbreuse aussi des ames,   428
Qui par randon les vicieuses flames
Noye et estaint quant trop on s'i engluie,
Et dont les pleurs par les divers royames
Font amolir des ceurs les dures lames   432
Et cheoïr jus le rongnes et les scames,
Pourveu que a toi on se traye et affuye.

XXXII O, que je sens mon ceur poindre et semondre   (fol. 16ᵛ)
Pour voler hault et pour beaucop espondre   436
Droit cy, o Vierge, en ta haulte matere,
S'en moi avoit sens pour y correspondre;
Mais sur ung oef n'a que prendre ou que tondre
Qui d'aulcun art ne le casse ou effondre   440
Pour agouster le fons de son mistere;
Pareillement, o Vierge debonnaire,
Qui partie es d'un sy noble et bon aire
Que le fenix en toi s'est venu pondre,   444
Moi qui sui rude et de science ygnaire
Pour atouchier a si hault luminaire,
Se de don frais ne me fais parchonnaire,
Je ne sçay mais que te respandre ou fondre.   448

XXXIII Preste moi dont, o redolent lavende,   (fol. 17)
Terre ou verdeurs et jolis biens je prende
Pour toi offrir a plaine grant brascee,
Et que premier que mon ceur plus s'esprende   452
Ne que plus hault m'escueille ne enprende,
Que plus parfont je m'enquiere et aprende
De ta haulteur que fol j'ay embrascee;
Car quant de grace et de ma joyeuse heure   456
Me pourverras d'un ris qui me seceure,
Et d'un terroir ou je semme et reprende,
J'ay soing tresgrant qui volentiers labeure
En ton vergier, o precieuse meure.   460
Pourvoi moi doncq du hault de ta demeure,
Et j'entendray songeux en ta legende.

XXXIV Je sui comme est l'aloette ramage   (fol. 17ᵛ)
Qui, par honneur a la divine ymage,   464

Chantant, loant, ou hault du ciel s'escueille,
La ou sentant l'ardeur sur son plumage,
Et que durer n'y porroit sans dammage
A cop descent et rechiet ou semmage,   468
La ou el scet sa pessure et sa fueille.
Et la pessant se degoise et pourmaine,
Son repos prent, se remet en alaine
Pour retourner arriere en son homage,   472
Dont qui premier monta a dure peine;
Arriere y quiert remonter plus haultaine,
Et n'a en lui jusier ne ceur ne vaine
Qui tout n'entende a cely estimage.   476

XXXV Ainsi m'est il, o sage entenderesse,   (fol. 18)
France emperris, des cieulx commanderesse,
Ainsi m'est il, ton humble servant lige:
J'ay ci tourné ma bouche pecheresse,   480
Cuidant la faire haultaine chanteresse
Jusqu'a l'attainte en ta haulte fortresse,
Par vraye ardeur d'amour qui m'y oblige;
Mais en visant en celui noble affaire,   484
La ou note a bien dangereuse afaire
Pour ung tel corps qui de sens a sobresse,
En my chemin contendant au parfaire,
Me voi si loings de pooir satiffaire   488
Que relenquir m'en couvient tout le faire
Et redescendre en basse secheresse.

XXXVI La tout quati je me pose et sommeille,   (fol. 18ᵛ)
Quant tout a cop nature me resveille   492
Et me regette en mon ardeur premiere;
Lors me resours et montant treille a treille,
Rebouté hors la voix de ma ventraille,
Dont chant, ne vol, ne riens ne me traveille   496
Par grant desir que j'ay a la lumiere,
Si m'esbas lors et me juc et degoise,
J'entens, j'enquiers, je maine doulce noise,
J'espars mon oeil, je labeure et je veille,   500
Mon ceur je sens eslargir d'une toise,
J'estens mon esle en mainte serventoise
Dont la fin toute, ou que je cerche et voise,
N'est que pour joindre a ta saintie oreille.   504

XXXVII Mais veci, las, la pité a l'issue,   (fol.19)
    En quoi d'annuy et de douleur je sue
    Et me tourmente en non commun mesaise.
    C'est qu'en visant sur mon oevre tissue   508
    Que j'ay cuidié tant belle et si houssue,
    Je la voi tant de foible engin cousue
    Qu'a paine y puis riens trouver qui me plaise;
    Car regardant sur la haultesse eslite   512
    Qu'en ceur parfont j'ay circuié et descrite
    Par amour grant, qui la s'est repaissue,
    Et puis j'en voi la sentence petite,
    Si povre en soi le sens qui y habite;   516
    Je me pers tout et m'argue et despite,
    Comme se corne avoye ou front bochue.

XXXVIII Ainsi, o sainte emperris souveraine,   (fol. 19ᵛ)
    Moi qui n'ay peu qu'en rudesse terraine   520
    Par aourner ton ympne et ton cantique,
    Et ay cuidié par noveauté puraine
    Surpasser tout Philomene et seraine,
    Si n'esse riens fors liqueur souterraine   524
    Emprez encens ou basme aromatique,
    Quant ta gloire est si haulte et amirable
    Et ton fait tant extremme, incomparable
    Emprez toute aultre espece temporaine,   528
    Qu'en regardant ton lieu insuperable,
    Dont la veue est bien doulce et souspirable
    Il n'y a point de voye aprez tirable,
    Tant est excelse en splendeur et foraine.   532

XXXIX C'est abus doncq a toute humaine entente   (fol. 20)
    De mettre en toi ne regard ne attente,
    Cuidant attaindre a ta haulteur sublime,
    Quant la splendeur de gloire omnipotente,   536
    De quoi ton Fils t'aministre et contente,
    Est tant en toi glorieuse et patente
    Que meismes l'oeil angelique s'y lime.
    Mesmes droit la les bras divins t'acolent,   540
    Les seraphins tout autour circonvolent,
    Cerubins sains t'aöurent en ta tente,
    Tronnes vertus te chantent et cymbolent,
    Tous esperis jubilans te karolent;   544
    Brief, tous les cieulx organisent, flagolent
    Ton los et gloire en ardeur persistence.

XL   Toute exultant milicie celeste,   (fol. 20)
    Toute angelique assistence modeste,   548
    Toute rien pure, invisible et visible,
    Lune et soleil par honneur manifeste,
    Tout te dit los, tout te fait gloire et feste,
    Tout envers toi agenoillant s'appreste,   552
    Comme a leur roine imperial paisible.
    Millïons mille angels vers toi aceurent,
    Vierges en tourbe innombrable y labeurent,
    Tout l'entier ciel service humble te prestent,   556
    Tous divers sains t'enclinent et honneurent,
    Tous contemplans te chantent et faveurent,
    Et telle grace et vie en toi saveurent
    Qu'aprez Dieu seul n'ont gloire aultre que ceste.   560

XLI   O donc excelse imperial substance,   (fol. 21)
    En cui la sainte inmuable constance
    De Dieu a mis telle beatitude
    Que tous les cieulx et toute leur prestance   564
    Rendent en toi service et humble instance,
    Et sont a toi subgez en aprestance,
    Comme a Lui propre en grative habitude;
    O, et moi doncq, aprez ung tel empire   568
    Soubs qui je tramble et fremissant souspire,
    Que la mon oeil ne puet prendre arrestance:
    Quels mos, helas, porray je droit cy dire,
    Quels vers ditter ne chanter ne escripre,   572
    Quant mille riens, bien sçay, n'y puet souffire,
    Pour sa treshault et merveilleuse obstance?

XLII   Melodieuse ymage glorieuse,   (fol. 21ᵛ)
    Bien te duist doncq d'estre victorieuse,   576
    Triumphant dame en royal siege assise,
    Quant tu seule as par vertu curieuse
    Paré le ciel de sa nieble envieuse,
    Que Lucifer, serpent malicieuse,   580
    Y relenqui maculee et incise,
    En quoi ensemble, o fleur des creatures,
    Tu reparas deux distinctes natures
    De l'ange et d'omme, ambedeux umbroieuse,   584
    Ce qu'oncq les cieulx en toutes leurs clostures,
    N'en la vertu de leurs substances pures,
    N'ont obtenu par milles aventures,
    Que seule en toi, sur tous eulx precïeuse.   588

XLIII Tu n'ez pas une avec Dieu en essence,   (fol. 22)
    Mais tu es une en grace et en licence,
    Conjointte o Lui en voloir sempiterne,
    Et est de Lui a toi celle adjacence   592
    De vraye amour en parfaitte innocence,
    Que riens a toi ne peut estre en absence
    Que est en pooir filial ou paterne.
    Grace et amour indivisibles lient   596
    Vos ceurs ensemble et telement allient
    En une estroite, ardant concupiscence
    Que les hauls cieulx joyeux s'en enjolient,
    Tous en vertu et gloire en multiplient;   600
    Car tant plus bas tes bontez s'umilient,
    Tant plus t'essourt hault en magnificence.

XLIV Ung ceur, ung veul, une charité clere   (fol. 22ᵛ)
    De toi a Lui sans aulcun refrigere,   604
    Sans entreget d'encombrance moyenne;
    Tu fille au Fils, vraye espeuse es du Pere,
    Et fille au pere arriere es du Fils mere,
    Par quoi amour si vous serre et adhere   608
    Que gloire a Lui si est la propre tienne.
    Lui qui crea et mist estre a nature
    S'est submis Dieu, subject a norriture;
    Purain, simple, estre en toi a pris matere 612
    Et creeur seul de toi, sa creature,
    S'est fait en toi sa serve geniture;
    Dont s'assise es sur toute sa facture:
    C'est bien raison qu'en toi sa gloire apere. 616

XLV O et com grande et glorieuse et mainte   (fol. 23)
    Doit estre en toi la gloire et clarté sainte
    Que tu, regnant ou ciel, possedes ore,
    Quant toi, estant mere en terre et enchainte, 620
    Tu fus de gloire et de joye surchainte,
    Dedens, dehors, partant, et telle attainte
    Que tous les cieulx s'i venoient desclore
    Baisiers divins, legions mille d'anges   624
    Pour l'eure alors, et princes et archanges
    Se tindrent prez de ta closture estrainte.
    Dont et se ja tu rechois les loenges
    Par cent fois double et par mille rendanges, 628
    Et par cent mille et milliers de rechanges,
    N'est pas mirable en ceur de bonne emprainte.

XLVI L'oeil m'atendrist et m'esblouist la veue,   (fol.23ᵛ)
Presumant prendre et querir repaissue   632
En toi, o sainte angelique formiere;
Car tant ay quis ta radieuse nue
Et la splendeur d'icelle maintenue
Qu'es bruy tout et ars jusqu'en char nue.   636
Me voi privé d'engin et de lumiere,
Si ne sçay mes du coffret quoi produire,
Qui peust servir ne proffiter ne duire
A ta haulteur, dont j'ay quis l'avenue,   640
Si non que toi de ton haultain reluire,
Ployant vers moi, me volsisses instruire
De ce qui duist et affiert pour deduire
Ton corps ou est tel gloire contenue.   644

XLVII Ainsi estaint par naturel foiblesse,   (fol. 24)
Ceur contemplant, mes muet, je te lesse;
Ensemble uns yeuls aveuglis je t'envoie,
Ausquels posé que ce a esté simplesse   648
D'exposer soing en si hault ray qui blesse,
Nientmoins pourtant demorra ta noblesse,
Painte en mon clos, se morir j'en devoie.
J'ay fait ung vol qui ma nature passe,   652
Cuidant attaindre a clarté oultre passe,
Dont l'attempter plus avant je delesse,
Et repaissant arriere en terre basse
A ma main triste et a ma plume lasse,   656
Repos j'ottroye et lui baille une espasse
Jusqu'au renvoy de ta grace et humblesse

XLVIII Quant millions de ceurs et autant de ames (fol. 24ᵛ)
Et autant de yeuls qu'en mez goutes et drames 660
En mon seul corps clervoyans logeroient,
Et aveuc ce le sens de dix royames,
Quant je regarde a tes gloires et fames,
Dont tant sont fait de notes et de games,   664
Si ne croy pas que tous y souffiroient;
Mais non obstant se je demeure en vivre
Et que de grace a ton epistre et livre
Mes esperis revocquez et reclamez,   668
J'attempteray de plus mettre a delivre
Mon ceur de toi dont le desir m'enyvre,

Et de novel feray graver en cuivre
Ton nom sainty ou en dorees lames.   672

XLIX Marteau d'enfer, de paradis l'entree,   (fol. 25)
   Fleur noble en qui le saint miel se congree,
   De quoi les ez celestiaulx se paissent,
   Vergier fremmé ou toute est obombree,   676
   La deité entiere et enventree,
   Sans riens soullier, ne porte, ne contree,
   Ne fleurs, ne fruis qui y croissent ou naissent,
   Bourgon sainty vers qui les cieulx descendent, 680
   Journal estoile en qui tous yeulx s'attendent
   Et en qui toute esperance est ancree:
   Se mes sens las ta haulteur ne comprendent
   Ne tes vertus ainsi que ou ciel resplendent,   684
   Pardonne a l'oeuvre et aux mos qui offendent;
   G'y ay mis tout le beau de ma ventree.

XL Rose en qui sont toutes graces divines,   (fol. 25^v)
  Toutes vertus et clartez cerubines,   688
  Toute infallible esperance de grace,
  Seule en ce siecle ou sont tes origines,
  Nette en croissance et pure en tes racines,
  Croissant nientmoins soubs ronces et espines,   692
  Ou oncq vil doi ne toucha par audace,
  Tresor du ciel, richesse de la terre:
  A toi me rens, droit cy te viens requerre
  Que humble envers moi tes oreilles enclines,   696
  Et metant tout le fruit de mon acquerre
  En ton franc vueil sans riens vouloir surquerre,
  Pour ung seul cas les mains te joing et serre
  De prendre en gré mes chansons georgines.   700

Variants and Rejected Readings

A Louenge a la tresglorieuse Vierge composee par messire George Chastellain chevallier trescler escripteur entre ceulx de son temps, *P1* S'ensuivent les nobles dictiers composez a l'onneur de la Vierge Marie par feu messire George Chastelain orateur du duc Phelippes de Bourgongne en son temps demourant en la ville de Vallenciennes, *P2* Louenge a la tresglorieuse Vierge Composee par messire George Chastellain chevalier trescler orateur entre ceulx de son temps, *V* S'ensuivent les Chansons georgines faittes par George Chastelain. Imprimés a Vallenchienes De par Jehan de Liege.

154

AP2 Prologue - 1 *AP2* ung o., *B2* en. le ciel - 4 *B2* gros et rude - 5 *P1* plus av. - 11 *B2* Et au rebours - 14a *AB2P2* Proheme par Invocacion de divine Ayde - 16 *AP1P2* S. parfait, *B2* S. profond et splen. - 20 *AP2* J'actainde - 23 *A* N'acquerit br. qui en terre fleuronne, *B2* br. qui en terre fleuronne, *P2* br. que en terre fleuronne (-1) - 24 *P1* sa gl. - 25 *B2* esc. la haulteur de t. t., *P2* trhonne - 30 *AB2* ce povre fraile m., *P2* ce povre raille m. - 32 *A* pafonde - 33 *B2* at. permet qu'en ta cité tant munde (+2), *V* preuir d. - 34 *B2* c. ou toute joye habonde - 35 *P1V* los prendre, *B2* P. en mon los - 36 *B2* yeulx *missing* - 37 *A* la *missing*, *B2P2* le ret. - 38 *B2* ou mon sol. se fonde - 39 *B2* le plaisir d. - 40 *AP2P2* Me donroit, *B2* d. grace et le sens p. ex. - 43 *AB2P2V* mon s. - 44 *P1* du siecle pardurable, *V* siecle durable - 45 *A* m'enfl. et mon corps pur., *B2* Mon c., *P2* m'enflamble et mon corps pur. - 46 *P1V* aidable et s. - 47 *AB2P2* mon pis v. - 49 *AP2* Qui vaille, *L* au c. - 52 *P1* ta rac. - 55 *AP2* P. trouver, *B2* P. mesler fl. blanches et vermeilles, *P1* P. mesler, *V* P. merler - 56 *AP2* A ta hault. qui m'est inref., *B2* A ta loange qui est inref. - 57 *B2* R. je t'ay de grace l'affluence - 58 *B2* t. assistence, *V* t. eloquence - 59 *AP2* et ent., *B2* A toute chose d'e. ent. et v. - 60 *B2* Car j'ay esp. en ta doulce clemence, *P1* D. en esp. d'y avoir, *V* d'y av. - 61 *B1* envers m. (+1), *P1* Et que hum. - 62 *AP2* prie (+1), *B2* Si te pr., *P1* te supply s. f. - 64 *P1* saveur con. - 65 *P1* M' *missing* - 66 *B2* haulte - 68 *AB2P1P2* Je - 70 *AP2* ne me v., *B2* n'en me v. - 71 *AP2* A. desire, *B1* Arme, *B2* A. desir nerfz et veines me t. - 73 *A* cycuir, *B2* qu'ilz n. p. c. ni com. - 74 *B2* qu'oncques n. - 75 *B2* Qui de ce cas tres ententif esc. - 76 *A* y *missing* - 77 *P1* y *missing* (-1) - 78 *B2* a louer, *L* la gl. - 79 *AB2P2* chose am., *P1* oeuvre am. - 80 *B2* pl. m'est folie - 81 *AP1P2* fac. ou rim., *B2* ob. soit honte ou impropere - 82 *B2* Q. pas ne suis V. - 83 *B2* Ma plume fraile touchera ce mistere (+1), *V* Sy as. - 84 *B2* plus gaignier que d'y m., *P1P2* plus *missing* (-1) - 84a *AP2* Icy fine le proheme tourné a Dieu Icy se conturne a la glorieuse Vierge, *B2* Cy fine le proheme tourn"e a Dieu et se retourne l'acteur a la Vierge Marie - 87 *B2* Solas et j. - 88 *B2* En qui remaint, *P1V* En qui se ferme - 89 *P1* s'i rec. - 90 *B2P1V* Tout s'i o. - 95 *B2* Ta grace donc - 96 *B2P1V* T. vers moi - 97 *B2V* parmes - 98 *B2* du metail de - 98a *AP2* Excusacion, *B2* Excusation par l'acteur - 99 *AP2* prende - 100 *B2* n'a ta r. - 101 *L* au - 103 *B2* eng. a simple con. - 104 *B2* Toucher - 105 *AP2* La requiers je, *B2* La quiers ta grace en moy f. - 112 *V* haultain - 113 *B2* A. tressaincte ou ciel d. p. - 114 *AP1P2V* Entour, *B2* Entour de qui l'air zephirin umb. - 115 *B2* Ou tant - 116 *B2* p. ne aus. - 117 *A* decepveroye (+1) - 123 *AP2* t. stature - 124 *B2* s. par dict et escripture, *P1V* off. nourreture - 125 *B2* Se apres grace et ta b. a. (-1) - 126 *P1* Ton doulx plaisir - 126a *AB2P2* Question servant a l'excuse - 127-140 *V Stanza XII replaces Stanza X* - 127 *B2* v. d'odeur delicīeuse - 131 *A* que ditz, *B2* oevre grac. - 132 *B2* Te puis je offrir v. tres precīeuse, *V* v. solacīeuse - 133 *AP1P2V* ton ouv., *B2* Dont embellit je p. - 135 *B2* ne voy - 136 *AP2* tel o. - 137 *P1* Et de t. - *B2* En saincte am. ne m'envoye en ma t. - 140a *AP2* Louenge par confirmacion sur Adam, *B2* Louange par conformacion sur Adam - 141-154 *V Stanza X replaces Stanza XI* - 141-168 *P1 Stanza XI and Stanza XII are reversed* - 141 *L* dūe - 142 *P2* sainctin sac. - 144 *B2* Air cristallin - 145 *A* s. est t. - 146 *B2* Ap. qu'Adam si eut commis s. v. - 147 *B2* Prindrent en eulx le fl. d'en concorde - 148 *AP2* f. l'abre qui ne devye - 149 *B2P1V* congera - 150 *AP2* Conjecturant le f. - 154a *AB2P2* Louenge par figure des saincts peres - 155-168 *V Stanza XI replaces Stanza XII* - 155 *L* Loy, *P1* Le oy - 157 *A* or et dyvine, *B2* or la matiere - 159 *A* s'espont - 160 *B2* De P. e. F. e. l. saincte c. - 162 *B2* Tres doulce ym., *V* Fermeuse ym. - 163 *B2* S. decora la c. - 164 *A* beau, *P1* biau - 165 *AP1P2V* d. et ent., *B2* A toi me rendz ou tout a toy me donne - 166 *B2* De toutes pars ma voix tramblant resonne, *P1P2V* Et ent. - 167 *B2* Entor loant vers et dis je jargonne - 168 *B2* Que je transmectz en moult simple praticque, *L* au - 168a *AB2P2* Louenge par figure des sainctes femmes - 169 *AB2P1* Judith - 171 *B2P1* S'en. l'essence Dieu c., *V* Dieu c. - 172 *B2* Mil, *P1* Mil a. e. p. p. e. preferee, *V* preferee - 173 *AP2* feussies eng., *B2* Et efleuré avant que feusse eng. (+1), *P1V* fussiez engenree - 175 *AP2* Seul, *B2* Entre luy seul et homme en sa mol. - 176 *AP2* mir. et dem., *B2* v. du ciel haulte visīon s. - 179 *B2* Et n'y s. - 180 *B2* En cas dont fut v. e., *V* fuist v. - 181 *B2P1V* emprainte - 182 *B2* P. par tous temps - 182a *AB2P2* Louenge par reduction sur les Cantiques -

183 *B2* F. e. doulce Vierge Marie (+1), *P2* espargne *missing* - 2 - 184 *B2* S. prudente industrie - 187 *A* porpina t. d. d. serie, *B2* T. p. loange tant serye, *P1P2V* d. serie - 189 *B2* m. si naist d. - 193 *B2* Il print clarté au ray de ta vitrine, *P1* d. benigne, *V* d. codine - 194 *A* S'av. tant, *B2* Et s'aveuglit en loant ta doctrine - 195 *B2* seraphine - 196 *B2* Q. saincte Esglise en chante parle e. c. - 196a *AB2P2* Louenge par Introduction de sa singuliere grace - 197 *P1* roche, *V* rose - 200 *B2* en l'ent., *P1P2* Tout - 202 *B2* Et ens et hors - 204 *B2* Depuis le bas jusques au hault d'icelle - 205 *B2* presesleute - 206 *B2* Ou v. asseoir - 208 *P1* croistre - 210 *B2* f. a ta saincte devise - 210a *A* Louenge par confutacion de toute chose precieuse emprés elle, *B2* Loange par confutation de toutes choses precieuses, *P2* Louenge par confirmacion de toute chose precieuse emprez elle - 212 *A* d'ences - 213 *B2P1V* Ne quelque odeur que nature con. - 214 *B2* at. le seul qui - 215 *B2* Pour n., *P1V* Par n. - 217 *B2* D. franche - 218 *AP1P2V* ne d'an., *B2* r. vers toy de l. ne d'en. - 219 *B2* riens de fleurs - 220 *B2* S. ou en R., *P1V* S. et en R. - 222 *B2* N. r. des biens dont terre est em. - 223 *AP2* Sy n., *B2* Vers la doulceur qu'en toy tant s'h. - 224a *A* Louenge par samblable confutacion encoire, *B2* Loange par samblable confutation, *P2* Louenge par samblable confirmacion encoire - 231 *B2* toy s. e. t. sainctif p., *P2* en tout s. - 232 *B2* Dont tu as e. l. g. tant e. - 234 *AP2* facture, *B2* Et excedant ang. nature, *P1V* ang. nature - 236 *AB2P2* cl. que d. - 237 *B2* Herbes ver. - 238 *B2* Tous pl. - 238a *AB2P2* Argument sur le possible de l'homme - 239 *AB2P1P2V* ton naistre - 240 *AP1P2V* ton estre, *B2* T. sainctyf c. t. d. t. estre - 243 *B2* Et que poons et entendre et congnoistre, *P1* p. et ta f., *V* Paur p. - 244 *B2* Pour ton sainct nom exaulser et accroistre - 245 *B2* Car la matiere a noz yeulx est trop brune, *P1* ne *missing* (-1) - 247 *B2* puist - 248 *AP2* C. terre mer - 249 *AP2* Je vueil tout prendre invisible et visible, *B2V* Je treuve t., *P1* Je y semons t. - 250 *P2* *the verse is missing* - 252a *AP2* Convocacion a tout ce qui est precieux et de noble nature a louer, *B2* Invocation a tout ce qui est precieux et de noble nature a la louer - 253 *B2* fl. et lavendes humaines - 254 *B2* v. marjolaines, *P1* lavendes por. - 255 *A* amandriers, *B2* amandries - 258 *B2* V. ycy alouettes - 259 *AP2* v. soestes e., *B2* Voz doulces voix et plaisans chants e., *P1* souriettes - 260 *B2* V. aussy a. impletes - 261 *AP1* V. b. de natures s. - 262 *B2* V. y toutes m. - 264 *B2* V. avec l. - 265 *B2* Lune et splendeurs e. v. clartés d. - 266a *AP2* Addicion encoires du mesmes, *B2* Addition encores de mesmes - 267 *B2* E. vous lyz et roses oudeurs - 268 *AP2* P. v. a toutes e. c.(+1) - 272 *B2* Ouvres voz portes trop vous les tenes closes - 273 *B2* C. loanges a haultes voix sans faindre - 274 *B2* Fendez v. c. - 276 *B2* P. f. cy texte s. - 278 *B2* par vos n. - 279 *P1* nobles d. - 280 *A* poses, *B2* Deves a Dieu graces en rime et pr., *P1* tous hympnes, *P2* grace - 280a *A* Louenge par recours a tout ce qui est ou ciel et qui la sert et honnoure, *B2* Loange par recours a tout ce qui est ou ciel qui le sert et honnoure, *P2* Louenge par recours a tout ce qui est ou ciel et qui le sert et honnoure - 282 *B2P1* a Gab. - 284 *AB2P1P2V* cree (-1) - 285 *AB2* a t. l. - 286 *A* Tant s., *B2* Soubz ton escuse conserve et se range - 288 *B2* se delecte - 289 *P2* et *missing* (-1) - 290 *B2* en tes p. - 291 *P1V* s' *missing*, *P2* s'emple - 294 *B2* soit grief dueil ne peine estrange - 294a *AB2P2* Louenge par specificacion des haulx honneurs qu'elle recoit - 296 *B2* v. anges te cl. - 298 *B2* oysillons - 301 *A* te rient, *B2* te servent, *P2* Ciel et terre m. te rient (+1), *V* tous rient - 302 *B2* sonnans *missing* (-2) - 303 *B2* T. instrumens mus., *P2* Toutes vertuz vers t. (+2) - 304 *B2* Tous bons devotz en t'amour s'edifient, P1 Rethoriques ta haulteur magnifient, *P2* verdures, *V* Rethoricquez tes haulteurs magnifyent - 305 *B2* en ton cloz se moyssonnent, *P1V* ton clos, *P2* Especes - 306 *ALP2* faisonnent, B2 raisonnent - 307 *AP2* se moisonnent - 308 *B2* d'enfer *missing* (-2) - 308a *AP2* Louenge par figure d'une saincte vierge, *B2* Louange par figure d'une saincte vigne - 309 *B1* Vinge, *B2* V. excellente e. a. eslite - 310 *B2* Ou l. h. c. triumphant se del. - 311 *B2* neuf cieulx, *P1* neuf cieulx p. e. l. a. oeuvres (+1), *V* oeuvres (+1) - 312 *P1* pars, *P2* d'un - 313 *P1* tiens - 315 *P1V* receuvres - 316 *B1* Vinge, *B2* V. en tout fr. fleur frappe vin et v. - 317 *B2* Dont l'humain gendre en la goustant s'en. - 318 *A* et subite, *B1* esplucque, *B2* D. si eslieve - 320 *AP2* C. gramyau, *B2* C. cepeau - 321 *B2* E. t. de grace et de biens aux bons livre - 322 *B2* Que rude cueur la sav. habilite, *P1* faveur - 322a *AP2* Louenge par atribucion de tous les haulx tiltres, *B2* Louange par attribution de tous haulx tiltres - 325 *B2* Qui destruict as - 327 *AB2P1P2* le sec.,

156

B1 consanls - 329 *B2* et effluant n., *P1* affluctuant nav. - 330 *B2* jar. refrigerant um. - 331 *B2*
C. l'outrepas - 332 *AV* Cree ex.(-1), *B2* Cree es cieulx (-1), *P2* Cree exemple (-1) - 336 *AP2* et
ne p. - 336a *AB2P2* Louenge sur la nature de sa dignité - 337 *AP2* saincte (-1), *V* saintys - 338
B2 trois foys la s. h., *P1V* as porté la - 339 *A* tuit e., *P2* comprent t. e. - 340 *AP2* S. excellence
(+1), *B2* S. excellente et digne s. - 341 *B2* m. qu'on te chante et f. - 343 *B2* esté *missing* (-2) -
347 *AB2P2* Et as - 348 *AP2* D. qui, *B2* ig. la fyansaille - 349 *B2V* vaille, *P1* n'y vault r. q.
vaille - 350 *AP1P2* en la queste, *B2* A. d'y muser se perit et exile - 350a *AB2P2* Loenge sur la
grace que son sainct corps portoit - 352 *B2* N. conspira n. n. s'es. d'ardure - 353 *B2* de nul feu -
355 *B2* oncq homme n. p. chault ne froidure, *P1V* de p. de r. - 356 *AP2* Pour quoi, *B2* ordure,
P1 pretendist - 360 *A* b. tuote, *B2* b. t. et sans d'homme s. - 361 *B2* A q. n'es ung de la secte in.,
P1 ny ord. - 364 *AP2* Que p., *B2* m. en totale fondure - 364a *AB2P2* Loenge par benediction de
toute chose qui est d'elle - 365 *AB2P2V* tressainte - 367 *P1* ben. cierge et lanterne - 368 *B2*
royale - 369 *B2* E. q. l'odeur feut de tel r., *P1* En cui, *P2V* soeuf (-1) - 370 *B2* Q'ung - 377 *B2*
pr. de tout effort m. - 378 *AP2* t. m. affluence, B2 S. ta v. en moult large affluence, *P1* ta
manutenence - 378a *AB2P2* Loenge par benediction de son maternel office - 380 *B2* dois
traictis, *L* doulcets - 381 *AB2P2* Benoites levres (+1), *P1* Benoites levres et benoitte la b. (+1) -
382 *P1* Q. par amours tant de fois le b. - 383 *B2* q. tant le regarderent - 384 *B2* br. plaisans, *V*
embracereut - 386 *B2* B. regars que ta vue l. p. (+1) - 387 *B2* l'y p. - 388 *AB2V* l'aflaterent, *P1*
q. le flaterent - 389 *B2* B. l. chantz que j. l'y ch., *P1V* B. l. chantz - 390 *P1V* q. soeuf l'al. - 391
B1 Et tout benoit sain et giron q. s. (+1), *B2* Et tout benoit qui son sainct corps sentoient, *P1V*
Et ton benoit saint geron q. s. - 392 *B2V* Et a q. - 392a *AB2P2* Louenge par affiguracion a toute
chose noble - 394 *B2* Pl. odourant que, *P1V* Pl. fort fl. - 395 *P1* d'engarde - 398 *B2* b. preparee
- 400 *P1P2* Riant - 403 *AP2* Mais *missing* (-1) - 406 *AP2* Je n'ay - 406a *AB2P2* Loenge par
exposicion de ses tiltres - 407 *V* s'adore - 410 *B2* n. ne peult d. - 411 *A* l'entier n. - 413 *B2*
Comment vint ens c., *P1* Comment y v. - 416 *B2* Et dont l'entrer n'est congneu jusqu'a ore -
417 *AP2* perut, *B2* Ou ne parut - 418 *B2* Ne tache nulle de virile semonce (+1), *P1V* la r. - 419
AP2 M. ramenoit, B2 M. demoura - 420 *AP2* jusques a ore (+1), *B2* Et demourra d'eternelle
memoire - 420a *AP2* Louenge par recitacion de ses vertuz, *B2* Louange par meditation de sa
vertu - 421 *P1* T. e. des cieulx l. s. et digne pl., *V* T. e. des cieulx l. s. digne pl. - 422 *B2* Q. mer
mondaine purgect si assuye, *P2* t. la mer, *V* essuye - 423 *B2* De tout pechié que tu as mis e. s.,
P2 As lavé - 426 *B2* g. affin que mieulx t'ensuye - 427 *B2* s. entente - 428 *AB2P2* T. e. le
fleuve eternel pour les a. - 430 *B2* trop en - 431 *AP2* donc, *P1* par mainte d. (+1) - 432 *P1V*
larmes - 433 *AP2* les ronces, *B2* rongeurs, *P1* Et tumber - 434 *V* Proveu - 434a *AB2P2*
Admiracion que fait l'acteur craintcif de son entreprise - 436 *AP1P2V* P. v. loing, *B2* P. loing
voler - 439 *A* oef puet on prendre ou t.(-1), *B2P1P2V* oef peult on peu prendre ou t. - 440 *A* ou
enfondre, *B2P2V* c. et e., *P1* Que d'auc. a. n. l. c. et e. - 441 *AP2* ag. plus parfait le m., *B2P1V*
ag. plus parfond en m. - 447 *P1* me sens p. - 448 *P2* responder - 448a *AB2P2* Imploracion de
grace pour mieulx parfaire - 449-462 *V Stanza XXXIII missing* - 449 *AP2* redolente (+1), *B1*
lavrende, *L* redolente lavende - 450 *B2* v. ou fleurs je puisse pr. (-1), *P1* verdeur ou j., *P2* T.
ou verdures ou joly bois je pr. (+1) - 452 *B2* Ains que - 453 *B2* Et q. p. h. m'es. ou entreprande,
P1 n'y emp. - 454 *B2* Ne p. p. j. n'enquiere et enprende - 456 *B2* g. a bien fortunee h. - 459 *B2*
J. desir grant que cultive et l. - 462 *B2* Et je seray - 462a *AP2* Figure que fait la devote ame de
foy par comparoison a la loe, *B2* Figure que faict l'ame devote par comparaison a l'alouette -
463-476 *V Stanza XXXIV missing* - 465 *AP2* du *missing* (-1), *L* au - 468 *AP1P2* en sem., *B2* A
c. rechiet et descend en sem. - 469 *AP2* Ou elle s. sa pasture, *B2* La ou mieulx scet pasture grain
ou feuille, *L* pressure - 472 *AB2* en s. h. - 473 *B2* Puis ou p., *P1* D. se p. - 474 *B2* De rechief
tend r. - 475 *B2* en elle j. oeil cueur (+1) - 476 *A* n'etende - 476a *AB2P2* Exposicion de la
figure par comparoison de l'un a l'autre - 477-490 *V Stanza XXXV missing* - 478 *B2* emperesse
(+1) - 480 *P1* ma plume - 482 *AP2* Jusque l'at. e. t. h. forteresse (+1), *P1* Jusques l'at. - 484 *A*
usant en c., B2 M. meditant en c., *L* a celui - 485 *B2* Que j'ay empris pour te service faire - 486
B2 Considerant de mon sens la sob. - 487 *B2* a parf., *P1* Emmy - 488 *L* vois s. l. du p. - 489

B2P1 t. l'affaire - 490a *AB2P2* Ampliacion sur le mesmes - 491-504 *V Stanza XXXVI missing* - 491 *B2* me repose (+1) - 494 *AP2* en montant - 495 *B2* v. que je recueille - 496 *B1* ch. ne riens ne vol ne me t., *B2* en rien - 498 *B1* Sis m'esb., *B2P1* me joue, *L* jue - 500 *P1* et *missing* (-1) - 501 *AP2* eslargi, *P1* esl. une t. - 502 *B2* e. jusqu'a la mer gregoise - 504 *AP1* saincte, *B2* N'est qu'a complaire - 504a *AP2* Desprisement que fait l'acteur de son edifier. Et de son noble propos qui riens n'est, *B2* Desprisement que faict l'acteur de sa matiere qui rien n'est - 506 *B2* doul. tressue, *V* d'envy - 508 *B2* qu'au regard de m., *P1* a mon o. - 509 *A* que je cuide, *B2* tant hous., *V* Qui j. c. - 510 *B2* Je l'apperçay tant simplement c. - 513 *A* c. parfait j. circui, *B2* j. touchee et d., *P1V* c. partout j. circuee - 514 *B2* Par grant amour - 515 *B2* Voyant mon oevre et s. p. - 516 *B2* En quoy nul sens ne science hab., *V* en foy - 517 *B2* t. je m'arg., *P1V* m' *missing* - 518 *AB2P1P2* au f. bossue - 518a *AB2P2* Probacion de la cause de sa peur - 520 *B2* n'ay sens qu'en r. - 521 *B2* Pour a. t. h. e. ta c., *V* aourer - 523 *B2* oultrepasse Ph. - 526 *B2* Car t. g. - 527 *B2* t. digne et inc., *V* ext. et comparable - 528 *AP2* tout - 529 *P1* reg. ta gloire in., *V* Quant reg. - 530 *B2* moult doulce, *P1* tant d. et desirable, *V* suparable - 532 *B2* seraine - 532a *A* Probacion sur le mesmes par argument de non possible, *B2P2* Probation sur le mesmes par argument du non possible - 533 *B2* donc *missing* (-1) - 534 *B2* reg. cure n'atente, *P1* toi ny reg. ny at. - 535 *L* en t. h. - 538 *B2* Est en toy tant gl. - 529 *B1* ang. y si l., *V* Que incisives l'o. ang. y sy l. (+1) - 541 *AP2* t. entour, *B2* ser. entour. toy c. - 542 *AP2* Les cherubins, *B2* Les cherubins t'adorent, *P1V* Cherubins saincts - 543 *B2* ch. et consolent, *P2* et *missing* (-1) - 544 *B2* cymbolent - 545 *P1V* organisent - 546 *B2* en lyesse excellente - 546a *AP2* Explicacion de sa gloire par les diverses substances celestes droit cy specifiees, *B2* Explication de sa gloire par les diverses substances celestes cy specifiees - 547 *AP2* Tout - 551 *AB2P1P2V* te dit gloire - 553 *B2* leur *missing* (-1) - 554 *B2P2* anges, *P1* mil anges - 557 *B2* Sainctes et sainct t'encl. - 560a *AP2* Exclamacion a elle en sa dignité dont l'acteur se repent l'avoir arroguee, *B2* Exclamation a elle en sa dignité dont L'acteur se reprent l'avoir arroguee - 561 *B2* imperiale (+1) - 562 *B2* A qui - 564 *A* c. en tout l, *B2* c. ou tu fais assistence - 565 *B2* Soffrent a toy en grande reverence, *P1* R. a toi - 566 *B2* Et si te rendent service en humble instance, *P1* Et s. subjectz trestous en circonstance - 567 *B2* a Dieu p. - 571 *B2* h. cy te pourray je dire - 572 *B2* dit. proferer ou esc., *P1* ny esc. - 573 *V* ne p. s. - 574 *AP1P2* treshaulte, *B2* ta treshaulte et digne preference, *L* ta tr. - 574a *AB2P2* Recours a elle par glorificacion de ce qu'elle est et vault - 576 *AP2* donc estre v. - 579 *B2* Ciel reparé de sa perte env., *L* Puré, *P1* Purgé - 581 *B2* Y conspira par sa macule inc. - 583 *B2* As reparé d. - 584 *B2* D'ange et d'h. royne tresglorieuse - 585 *AP2* Et qu'onc, *B2* Ce que l. c., *P1* les clostures - 586 *AP2* Ne en v. *B2* Ne la v. - 587 *B2* par quelques factures - 588 *AP2* Fors s., *B2* Que tu seule as sur toutes pr. - 588a *AB2P2* Loenge par conjonction qu'elle a avec la deité - 591 *B2* C. a l., *V* Conjoinct - 592 *AP2* tel ad., *P1* telle ad. - 593 *AB2P2* vray, *P1* et parf. in. - 595 AP2 Qui est en cueur f. o. p., *B2* au pooir, *V* en pour f. - 596 *AB2P1P2V* indivisible - 599 *B2* s'en ajolyent - 600 *AP2* vertuz et gloire mult. (-1), *B2* de gloire, - 602 AP2 pl. tressourt, B2 pl. te sourt haulte magnificience - 602a *AB2P2* Loenge par union de leurs volentez - 606 *AP1P2V* tu esp., *B2* tu espouse es au P. - 607 *B2* ar. et du F. - 608 *B2* vous joinct et - 612 *B2* Pur et s. e. - 613 *A* Et createur de t. - 614 *B2P1V* seule gen. - 615 *AB2* D. assise, *P2* tout sa f. - 616a *AP2* Retour que fait l'acteur de son hault vol dont le pouoir luy est clos, *B2* Retour que faict le facteur de son hault vol dont le pooir luy est cloz - 617-644 *B2 Stanzas XLV and XLVI are reversed* - 617-630 *V Stanza XLV missing* - 618 *B2* gl. clere et s. - 619 *L* au c., *P2* possede (-1) - 621 *AP1P2* de joye et de gloire - 622 *B2* par tout en telle at. - 623 *L* y ven. - 624 *B2* Coulors d. - 625 *B2* Trosnes vertues et p. - 628 *AP2* doubles, *B2* d. de privez et estranges - 629 *B2* par millïons de gens nud en langes, *P1* mil - 630 *AP2* Merveilles n'est en c., *B2* poinct mir. a c., *P1* point mir. - 630a *A* Loenge par comparacion de sa gloire en terre empres celle du present ou ciel, *B2* Loange par comparation de sa gloire en terre emprés celle de present ou ciel, *P2* Loenge par comparacion de sa gloire en terre emprez celle du present ciel - 631-644 *V Stanza XLVI missing* - 632 *B2* Parlant de toy a science impourveue - 633 *B2* Presumer crainctz ang. fervere, *P1* ang. formiere - 634 *A* a quiz - 636 *AP1P2* chair n.,

158

B2 a char n. - 637 B2 Privé me voy de sens et de l., P1 Me voy pr. de sens et d. l. - 638 AB2P1P2 que prod. - 639 P1 ne duire *missing* (-2) - 640 B2 donc - 641 P1 ton *missing* (-1) - 642 B2 Courant, P1 Par ta doulceur - 643 B2 duyt pour mon oeuvre construyre - 644 B2 Ou soit ton loz et gl. c. - 644a A Offre que luy fait l'acteur neantmoins de ce qui est remis en luy et tel qu'il est, B2 Offre que luy faict l'acteur neantmoins de ce qui est demouré en luy et tel qu'il est, P2 Offre que lui faict l'acteur neantmoins de ce qui est remes en luy tel qu'il est - 645-658 V *Stanza XLVII missing* - 645 B2 naturelle (+1) - 646 AP2 cont. et m., B2 Mon coeur tremblant tout m., P1 Mon povre cueur contemplant j. - 647 B2 Aussy mes y. aveuglés, P1P2 aveuglés - 648 B2 ce ait esté, P2 ça a esté - 651 AB2P2 mor. en d., P1 mor. y d. - 653 A *this verse missing*, B2 at. de cl. l'oultrepasse, P1 at. a lumiere o. - 658 B2 ta gloire - 658a AP2 Argument sur le non possible a l'acteur par desir de retourner cy aprés, B2 Argument sur non possible a l'acteur Par desir desir de retourner cy aprés - 659-672 V *Stanza XLVIII missing* - 662 B2 les sens - 664 B2 D. sont faictes tant de n. (+1) - 667 AP2 de *missing* (-1) - 669 B2 Je m'essaray - 671 B2 Et si metray se Dieu terme me livre - 672 AP2 et en dor., B2 Tes grans louanges en tableaux sur mes ames - 672a AP2 Loenge sur la virginité et saincteté integrité et dont les haulz et glorieux tiltres sont de vray et perpetuel effect et fruit, B2 Loange sur sa virginité et saincte integrité et dont les haultz et glorieux tiltres sont de vray et perpetuel effect et fruitct - 674 B2 concree - 675 AB2P1P2 epz - 676 B2 V. fermé, P1P2V V. fermé o. t. e. aumbree - 677 B2 d. de celeste contree, P1 d. de la char obumbree - 678 AP2 p. ne ventree, B2 soul. ni avoir porte n'entree - 679 AP2 fleur - 685 B2LV au c. - 686 AP2, Toute ma force y est enregistree, B2 Car g'y ay mis ma science lettree - 686a AP2 Sommiere fin de louenge sans demande faire fors de prendre en gré et la ou l'acteur baptise ses dictiers de son nom, B2 Sommiere fin de louange sans demande faire fors de prendre en gré et la ou l'acteur baptise ses dittiers en la denomination de son nom - 689 B2 inf. espoir a tous propice - 691 AB2P1P2 croissant - 693 B2 par malice - 695 B2 r. et si te v. - 696 P2 ourlles - 697 B2 En m. - 699 B2 les mains *missing* (-2) - 700 B2 Qu'en gré preignes

B2 Cy finent les hympnes louanges et canticques ditz georgines de George Castellin Acteur et composeur d'icelles en l'onneur de la glorieuse et sacree Vierge et mere du doulx Jhesus Marie Et feurent excriptes a Rethel 1495

Translation

I   Seeking to extend toward the heavens my one eye,
Whose view is too weak and too inconstant for me
To fly there un-feathered with grace,
My other eye offers ignorant and dull understanding,
Without inquiring too much beforehand or contesting (anything).
Fearful, nonetheless, under divine expectation,
I offer and bow my head to the earth;
Stretching out towards the ray of blinding light,
The object of earthly vapor, which makes my bow
Discordant and loose, comes toward me,
And in reaction to my summary joy,
To my treasure and rural richness,
As is often the case,
I fail in my fervent intent.

II O, the lofty ray of eternal light,
    Deep source of lofty splendor,
    From which all things take their substance and essence,
    Lift me from here and give me wing
    So that in this flight that my heart seeks and conceals,
    I might attain a little through sensorial clarity
    Beneath a spotless plumage of innocence.
    I do not seek to enhance my person,
    Nor to acquire the fame that one reaps on earth
    And whose glory is vain and temporal,
    But rather to display and provide delight in your throne,
    To decorate your scepter and your crown,
    And to magnify with my corporal voice,
    All things serving and surrounding you.

III You have bestowed upon me eloquence and linguistic facility
    To serve, alas, this poor, sullied world
    Whose pleasures and glory I have loved.
    Yet, o stream of profound mercy,
    Abide and wait for me to lay the foundation,
    So that in your lofty heaven and in your pure light
    I might spread your praise and throw out my lure.
    I seek to avert my eyes from the earth,
    To transmit my heart towards you and to draw it back,
    As in someone in whom all solace abounds,
    And whose glory and joy in drawing it in
    Will give me fire and grace to extract
    Words and beautiful verses to attract the heart
    Of her in whom all my hope redounds.

IV Purge my senses, o everlasting goodness,
    Take my eye from this lamentable world,
    May your heart enflame me and your tear purify me,
    Let your grace aid and assist me
    So that from my corrupt, miserable breast
    Any flower or bud that smells on earth or bears fruit in heaven
    Might be depicted as honorable.
    Let my veins and my heart and all my entrails
    Be opened to you and presented as arbors
    In which to plant your admirable roots,
    Of which the enclosure of your holy ears,
    Which I request to appear right here before me,
    Will be able to pick living and identical flowers
    In the name of your greatness and unrepeatable glory.

V   I have therefore asked for your grace and support,
Sovereign goodness, you who grant all existence,
Understanding or life to all beings;
Therefore, in hope I must have persistence
So that humbly you will advise me.
I beg of you, therefore, without ceasing
That your hand deliver help to me whenever I desire it.
Fervent love, contemplative favor
Have raised in me my excitement
For this lofty undertaking and for lofty order
Which, for the rest of my active life,
I will never be able to reach
Through intellectual force, unless with fearful hand,
If power does not come to me from your light.

VI   Soul and desire, veins and heart draw me
To take for myself what the heavens consider with astonishment in me,
And what they have been unable to encompass or understand,
And in which all the clerics who have ever lived
And, having considered your case, written;
In fear they put to work pen and paper
In the name of your greatness, which is to be described here:
It is to praise your glorious mother,
The abandon of which would be a bitter hour for me
And still greater folly to undertake it;
But even though I am not a poet or versifier
Such as Virgil or Homer,
I will try and prepare myself and execute
In the hopes of being more successful than not.

VII   O saintly splendor in the court of seraphim,
Lofty subject of Augustinian knowledge,
Well of joy for all saints and prophets,
In whom all divine grace is contained,
All celestial virtue is inclined (toward you),
Everything is overshadowed and everything ends (in you),
Everything expands in you its secret riches.
O holy mirror of miraculous glory,
About whom one reads that notorious humility
Made you rise, so highly elevated queen:
Very humbly, therefore, turn your worthy sweetness
Towards me in my oratory,
And allow me to write a measured story,
Speaking to you from my very mouth.

VIII   Not that I take from myself the arrogance
Of reaching you in your radiant splendor,
There where you sit glorified in heaven,
But, according to my lowly power, a little of my
Human spirit and my knowledge
Concerning your existence in the world and your birth:
There's where I seek strengthening grace.
I am the bird who flies near the earth
And does not dare to look for lofty prey
Because of his own incapacity;
But, in keeping my humble and lowly course,
I sustain myself and live from my acquisitions,
Unless force or ardent hunger press me
To soar to higher use.

IX   There, o very holy divine prey,
Around whom so much mystery hangs
And so many lofty and noble birds fly,
I do no seek and also would not wish
To seek you there, for I would disappoint myself;
But in thinking upon this matter, I become fearful,
And your splendor blinds me and drives me mad.
I am of the earth and with such a nature
I come to you, o holy creature;
Moreover, I know well that I would err.
Therefore, like a human and in such a state,
I ask to serve you and to offer you flowerings,
If, after grace and success
Your lofty mount does not grant me higher flight.

X   Virginal enclosure, precious ciborium,
Blossoming orchard of fair beauty,
Where the sun allows no shadow,
Sweet-smelling rose bush, delightful rose,
What words, what verses, what gracious sweetness
Will I put forward, wise Virgin,
With which I might decorate your work?
I consider you so worthy and lovely
That I do no believe I have in myself the innate power
To bring to completion such a refined work,
If you do not send to my table
Your own charitable pity and love,
Which will be appropriate and beneficial
For the illustration of your glorious face.

XI   Restoration of Adam, restitution of Eve,
The saintly sacrifice of the just Abel,
True mercy promised to Seth,
The sweet wind of joyful paradise,
From whom the entire world and terrestrial edifice,
After Adam had committed his sin,
Have since taken the scent of peace.
You are and were the holy tree of life
Against whom Satan gathered his envy,
Seeing in you the future good office
From whose plant and absolved roots,
From whose bud and purely contented flower
Salvation, truth, order and life would be born,
And would vanquish death and his evil.

XII   Faith of Abraham, vision of Moses,
Harp of David, palace of Solomon
Constructed with azure, pure gold and ivory,
Royal bud, descendant of David,
Upon whom the harmonious sweetness
Of the Father and the Son in their many canticles spreads,
As upon the object foreseen in their light;
Beautiful image, o handsome vineyard keeper
Whom Solomon invited to the crown
Because of so many lofty, beautiful, angelic words:
Come down here, so that I can envelop you,
So that I might humble myself before you and pursue you,
I who, by adding to your gleaming throne,
Send to you in heaven my aromatic offering.

XIII   Strong Judith, humble Hester portrayed,
Whose sweetness and decorous beauty
The offended, celestial king grew to love.
Ordained and pronounced for a thousand years and more
Before ever you were born
To bring peace and restore love,
You alone, between Him and his troubled people;
O admirable voice, o holy manifestation,
Created for the price that a young virgin with child
Would conceive fruit in this impure place
And whose maternity would not be touched
By anything that would stain virginity,
But would remain mother and virgin together in one body
Forever and ever.

XIV   Sweet-smelling grace, rich treasure,
From whom Solomon, through noble affection
Drew forth precious plants,
Which, praising your great majesty,
Furnished you with so much dear sweetness,
So much new, inspiring imagination
That hearing his words about it is music.
He preferred you to gold and pure pearl,
He portrayed you as a crystalline image,
Nourished by the heavenly, not earthy, air;
He grew to love your cedar-like sweetness,
He was completely blinded by your sapphire-like beauty,
Which the entire world still speaks about and proclaims.

XV   Lofty mountain seated on firm rock,
Where God re-established a sanctuary
Of humankind in marvelous mystery,
Decorated and cut around
Like a pure, perfect emerald,
Within, without, complete and solid,
Of one and the same being and all of one entire material,
There within and above it,
O pre-elected and holy maiden,
The Son of God came down and brought his form
Entering into your cell
Without breaking anything, neither cloister or courtyard,
When you said, given your humble servant,
"Do with me freely what you will."

XVI   What is balm or cinnamon,
The scent of incense, of myrrh or of other resin,
A mixture of herbage or a preserve, next to you
Who attracted Him, who is called Three,
To be born in you, true God and perfect man,
Conceived as one, like an apple,
A pure deity as guardian of humanity?
There is nothing indeed in the lily or the flower,
There is nothing which beautiful Nature
Creates and produces in Sion or Rome,
There is no pure gold or polished pearl,
There is nothing with which I see you embellished,
If not that in you your sweetness humbles itself
To accept the love which we are.

XVII You are the one and only holy creature
    To whom no work of Nature
    Can suffice for apt comparison,
    When heaven and earth in their firmament,
    And all things under their maintenance
    Have been unable to lodge or enclose
    What you alone in your holy porphyry (have).
    And you have had glories so extreme
    That you, among all women, are blessed through them
    And surpass angelic form;
    And through you the high heavens themselves are blessed,
    Female and male saints made more bright in crowns,
    Flowers and greenery and precious gems
    Made more full of joy and of rich experience.

XVIII Nevertheless, it is necessary to compare
    Your being, your holy body, your dignity, your birth
    To some dignity
    So that God and Nature are as one,
    In order to open your door or your window,
    Considering that neither cleric nor arch-priest
    See otherwise but in the moon.
    Therefore, striving for the possible from the impossible,
    And as heaven, earth and sea and terrestrial paradise,
    Can be found more accessible,
    I find you completely visible and invisible,
    Pure substance and palpable matter,
    For one must appropriate everything peaceful
    To protect and nourish your greatness.

XIX Come, therefore, flowers, lavenders, marjorams,
    Come, rose bushes, violets, purslanes,
    Come, palm trees, almond trees and almonds,
    Come, cypresses and sweet-smelling breezes
    Which the high heavens produce from their veins;
    Come right here, larks and canaries,
    Come right here to spread your sweetness,
    Come right here, full harmonies,
    Come, beauties with secret natures,
    Come right here to display your full virtues,
    Come, sun, stars, and planets,
    Come right here, God's complete works,
    Come, each one with your distinct virtues:
    Render and offer your lofty praises.

XX   Increase your virtues, lilies and roses,
Lend your will, all exquisite things,
To come exult and unite here;
Crystalline heaven, bow down for a time,
Throw out your locked-up riches
And do not wait even an hour or minute:
Sing right here, praise and join hands,
Open your hearts, all noble natures,
All lofty spirits, arrange your forms
To bring here either ideas or interpretations;
Offer your scents, flowers, herbs and plantings,
Laugh at the sight of your noble paintings,
For using your true reason,
You all ought to offer graces and writings here.

XXI   O happy one born of good breed,
Virgin announced by the arch-angel Gabriel,
The messenger of lofty, salutary words,
When all things created, both man and angel,
Strive to turn to you and are inclined toward your praise:
All things are furnished with honor and restitution
Carefully, as if your tributaries,
Everything delights in and fervently contemplates (you),
Everything is filled with your grace and your love,
Everything falls before you at your feet in the mire,
Everything is nourished in and imitates your ways,
Everything is enriched in the shadow of your temple,
Everything takes solace, life and example from you
Without enduring any pain or cost.

XXII The lofty heavens crying out glorify you,
Thrones, virtues, servants purify you,
All elements bow before you and honor you,
The birds in the air offer sacrifice to you;
Virginal hearts in praise sanctify you,
The holy fathers confirm your greatness,
Heaven, earth and sea all laugh and favor you,
Organs and ringing voices resound in you,
All music abounds in you;
Flowers and greenery flourish in you,
Spices, fruits are harvested to your glory,
Human minds sharpen and season;
Therefore, because of the good that is housed in you,
The biting dogs of hell are tamed.

XXIII Excellent vine pre-elected above all others,
    Who delights the high imperial heaven,
    Who pierces through nine hearts and open abysses,
    Who begins as a small, humble opening
    And holds the earth circumscribed in its circularity,
    (Who) saves the living and resuscitates the dead,
    (Who) protects the good and rescues the bad:
    The vine in your fruit and in your noble life,
    Delights and intoxicates the human spirit,
    Devotion is explained in it and inhabits it,
    Each leaf is a book of life,
    Each bunch (of grapes) a pound of pure gold,
    And there is so much that a heart of copper
    Would take from it the savor that gives it strength.

XXIV You are the true, earthly paradise,
    You are and were the powerful, heavenly archer
    Who killed the serpent with your arrow;
    You are the orchard without a solitary gate,
    The secretary of lofty, divine counsels,
    Hope of the world and salutary claim,
    Immobile heaven of (our) wavering ship;
    You are the garden of pleasant umbrage,
    Eminent chief of all divine work,
    Created free from voluntary grace;
    You are the port of true and secure anchorage,
    You are the breast and bosom of election,
    The only protector of poor human drowning
    About whom all cry out and cannot keep quiet.

XXV Holy, holy, holy, three times holy,
    You who produced the triply Holy Host,
    Where the Trinity is completely enclosed;
    Excellent saint, blessed sacristy,
    You have well merited our celebration of you right here
    And our exaltation of you in erected praise:
    You who have been caretaker of such noble fruit,
    You who have carried the wheat and the chaff,
    From which you were first the humble seed,
    You were mother and daughter of our Maker,
    You took from heaven this bridegroom,
    Based on whom Nature, ignorant of his greatness,
    Admires herself, without seeing anything offensive;
    Yet, in the examination she is lost and blinded.

XXVI Blessed face in whom your eye never suspected
    Deformity nor caught sight of impurity,
    Or of fire or of carnal weakness;
    Your grace has been so strong and solid
    That no eye ever perceived any violence at all (in you)
    By which sin could find a seam,
    Nor erasure of virginal nobility.
    Why? Because you, virginal flower,
    You yourself carried the original plant
    Of goodness entirely within your single being,
    Upon which neither sin nor infernal impurity
    Ever had power or mortal assault.
    But pure was (your) well-bred virtue,
    Which put sin to death and out in the cold.

XXVII O very holy and blessed influence,
    Blessed be your meadow, blessed be your body,
    Blessed be your portal, blessed be your everlasting cloister,
    Blessed be your clasp of royal excellence,
    In whose scent and sweet odor
    Such a noble king placed his good will,
    Making you mother and everlasting virgin.
    Blessed be your heart, blessed be your worthy, holy body,
    Blessed be your eye, blessed be your bountiful fountain,
    Blessed be your womb in its pure innocence,
    Blessed be your understanding, which grants us such goodness,
    Blessed be your finger, which protects and delivers us
    And preserves us from malice
    Through the virtue of your great affluence.

XXVIII Blessed be your hands, which handled such fruit,
    Blessed be your sweet fingers, which touched Him,
    Blessed be your lip and blessed be your mouth,
    Which kissed Him so many times with love.
    Blessed be your eyes, which carefully protected Him,
    Blessed be your long arms, which hugged Him,
    Arising from (and) lying down in your worthy bed,
    Blessed be the laughter that your eyes accorded Him,
    Blessed be the gifts that your hands carried to Him,
    Blessed be your gentle words that flattered Him,
    Blessed be your sides, which joyously sang to Him,
    Blessed be your breasts, which nourished Him as an infant,
    And all blessed holy bosoms that felt
    What the heavens never dared touch.

XXIX Purple flower, azure-colored violet,
      More sweetly smelling than a golden marigold
      Or a white lily or vineyard of flowers (?)
      Beneath the pearl or purified topaz,
      Better than pure gold prepared by cleaning,
      More beautiful in color than natural beauty,
      More alive in the eye than a pomegranate,
      Shining image, o gentle little Virgin:
      Your own body, your noble manner
      Brought tears to my eyes and completely enamored me;
      But when I consider the flight I take
      And that my wing is weak and unskilled,
      I enter into a sadness of singular lowliness,
      And I have fear only of an unfelicitous error.

XXX You are the pure gold that decorates the Church
      And enriches and adorns faith,
      You are the seed from which the oil of life comes forth,
      You are the little chest that no one could ever unlock
      And about whose entry Nature herself does not know
      What or how, the manner or time,
      Or how He who owns it came there.
      You are the living, oriental vessel,
      In which the pearl was concealed,
      Which never entered there from without,
      In which there never appeared either impurity or blemish
      That could firmly implant its mark,
      But remained complete and undiminished,
      And will remain so without end, forever and ever.

XXXI You are the sweet holy rain of heaven
      That washed out and expelled below
      All the bitterness and darkness of this world.
      You are also the crutch and the support
      Of human hope, which relies completely upon you,
      And puts all its salvation and expectations (in you),
      As in the protection and manner of a sheath.
      You are also the protective rain of souls,
      That swiftly drowns and extinguishes
      Vicious flames when they are too engulfing,
      Whose tears throughout history
      Make the hard tombstones of hearts soften
      And roughness and scales disappear,
      Provided that one is drawn to you and seeks your help.

XXXII O, how I feel my heart stir and get excited
    At the thought of flying on high and exposing here
    Much about your greatness, o Virgin,
    If I had the necessary understanding;
    But whatever artist does not break or beat it
    To taste the source of its mystery
    Is only taking or quarreling without a cause;
    Likewise, o gentle Virgin,
    You who are developed from such a noble and good air
    That the phoenix came to lay eggs in you,
    I who am (too) ignorant and unknowing
    To reach your lofty light,
    If you do not bequeath to me a fresh gift (of inspiration),
    I know only how to scatter or bring you down.

XXXIII Lend me (aid), therefore, o sweet-smelling lavender,
    Let me take earth and greenery and pretty things
    To offer you in a large, filled armful,
    And before my heart is sparked more
    Or is more strongly excited or inflamed,
    Let me search out and learn more deeply
    About your greatness which I have foolishly embraced;
    For when with grace and with my joyous happiness
    You furnish me with a laugh that helps me,
    And land where I might sow and reap,
    I take such great care and voluntarily work
    In your orchard, o precious mulberry.
    Provide for me, therefore, from your residence on high,
    And I will be very attentive to your legend.

XXXIV I am like the untamed lark
    Who, in honor of (your) divine image,
    Singing, praising takes flight on high,
    To the point where he feels the intense heat of his plumage,
    And can no longer endure without injury,
    Suddenly descends and falls back down onto sown field,
    Where his pasture and leaf are familiar.
    And there, after feeding himself, he warbles and stirs,
    Takes repose, regains his breath
    So he might return back to his homage,
    For which he first arose in great effort;
    He seeks to return to a loftier place,
    And there is not in him throat, heart or vein
    That does not focus entirely on this cause.

XXXV Such is it with me, o wise, all-knowing woman,
    Kind empress, commander of the heavens,
    Such is it with me, your humble vassal and servant:
    I have turned here my errant voice,
    Hoping to make it a great singer
    Until it reaches your lofty fortress,
    Through the true ardor of love that forces me there;
    But in aiming in this noble matter,
    For the place where ill report has a very dangerous charge
    For such a body, which is sober in knowledge,
    Midway, striving for perfection,
    I see myself so far from being able to perform satisfactorily
    That I must abandon doing anything at all
    And descend back down into lowly dryness.

XXXVI There, all curled up, I sit and nod off,
    When suddenly Nature awakens me
    And throws me back into my original ardor;
    Then I recover and rising bit by bit,
    Thrown outside, my inner voice,
    Whose song, flight, or any other aspect do not trouble me,
    Because of the great desire I have to reach (your) light,
    I flap (my wings) and perch and warble,
    I listen, I observe, I make sweet sounds,
    I cast my eye, I labor, I am vigilant,
    I feel my heart increase sixfold,
    I spread my wing in many a song to the Virgin
    Whose entire aim, wherever I search and go,
    Is only to reach your holy ear.

XXXVII But, alas, in the end, sweating from vexation and effort
    And tormented in an uncommon malaise,
    I (fine) there is (only) pity.
    It is in examining my creation
    That I see how it composed of such weak spirit
    That I can scarcely find anything in it that pleases me;
    For considering the elite greatness
    That deep in my heart, which has found nourishment in it,
    I have circumscribed and described with great love,
    I then see the little thought in it,
    Its meaning so poor in itself;
    I completely lose myself and chide myself and am angry with myself,
    As if I had a horn on my swollen forehead.

XXXVIII Therefore, o holy, sovereign empress,
    I who have little except earthly ignorance
    To adorn your hymn and canticle,
    And thought I could outdo every Philomene and mermaid
    Through a perfect new form,
    If there is only subterranean liquid
    Next to incense or an aromatic balm,
    When your glory is so lofty and admirable
    And your accomplishment so great (and) incomparable,
    Next to all other temporal deeds,
    In studying your invincible site,
    Whose view is so sweet and desirable,
    (I conclude) that there is no subsequent path that can be designed,
    So magnificent is your place in splendor and strange.

XXXIX It is a mistake, therefore, for all human understanding
    To put consideration and expectation in you,
    Thinking it can attain your sublime greatness,
    When the splendor of your omnipotent glory,
    With which your Son serves and supports you,
    Is so glorious and manifest in you
    That even the angelic eye is reflected in it.
    Even there divine arms welcome you,
    The seraphim encompass you all around,
    Saintly cherubs adore you in your pavilion,
    Thrones sing your virtues and play cymbals,
    All jubilant spirits sing carols in your name;
    In short, all the heavens play the organ and pipes
    In ardent perseverance, to praise and glorify you.

XL   The entire exultant host of heaven,
    All humble angelic support,
    Everything pure, invisible and visible,
    The moon and sun, manifest through honor,
    Everything praises you, everything glorifies and celebrates you,
    All prepare to kneel down before you,
    As before their imperial queen of peace.
    A thousand million angels race toward you,
    Virgins in countless multitudes work on your behalf,
    The entire heaven offers you humble service,
    All the various saints bow before you and honor you,
    All those contemplating sing in your name and favor you,
    And savor such grace and life in you
    That after God alone there is only this glory.

XLI O ever-wondrous, imperial substance,
In whom the steadfast, holy constancy
Of God has placed such beatitude
That all the heavens and all their greatness
Render unto you service and humble favor
And are subject to your care
As to Him himself, in a grateful manner;
O, and I, therefore, after such a power
Under which I tremble and, with fear, sigh,
Since my eye cannot fix itself there:
What words, alas, will I be able to speak here,
What verses will I be able to rhyme or sing or write,
When a thousand things, I know well, cannot be enough,
Because of its very great and marvelous difficulty?

XLII Glorious, melodious figure,
It is good for you to be victorious,
A triumphant lady seated on a royal throne,
When you alone have, through scrupulous virtue,
Decorated the heavens with their enviable mist,
Which Lucifer, malicious serpent,
Left blemished and incised,
In whose wholeness, o flower of creatures,
You restored two distinct natures
Of the angel and of man, both cast in shadow,
Which the heavens in their firmament
And in the virtue of their pure substances,
Never obtained through a thousand attempts
Except only in you, most precious above all of them.

XLIII You are not one with God in essence,
But you are one in grace and in power,
Conjoined with Him in everlasting will,
And there is between Him and you this interdependence
Of true love in perfect innocence,
From which nothing of yours can be absent
That is filial or paternal in power.
Indivisible grace and love link
Your hearts together and ally them so closely
In one narrow, ardent desire
That the joyous heavens are beautified by it,
All in virtue and glory multiply;
For the more your goodness is humbled
The more you soar up aloft in magnificence.

XLIV One heart, one desire, one pure love
　　　Between you and Him, without any coolness,
　　　Without the interjection of any mediating encumbrance;
　　　You, the Son's daughter are the true spouse of the Father,
　　　And, daughter of the former father, are mother of the Son,
　　　Whose love brings you together and binds you
　　　Such that His glory is your own.
　　　He who created and brought life to Nature
　　　Submitted himself to God, as subject of (your) nourishment;
　　　Pure, simple, the being took shape in you
　　　And sole Creator of you, His creature,
　　　Made Himself in you His Son as Savior;
　　　Therefore, you are seated above all his creation:
　　　It is understandable, therefore, that his glory appears in you.

XLV O and how great and glorious and plentiful
　　　In you must be the glory and holy light
　　　That you, reigning in heaven, now possess,
　　　When you, mother on earth and with child,
　　　Were surrounded with glory and joy,
　　　From within, from without, therefore, and such an event
　　　That all the heavens came there to offer
　　　Divine kisses (and) thousands of legions of angels
　　　At that time, and princes and archangels
　　　Guarded over your pressing body.
　　　Therefore and if ever you receive twice a hundred times
　　　And a thousand praises
　　　And one hundred thousand and thousands of exchanges,
　　　It is not such a wonder in such a well-imprinted heart.

XLVI My eye softens and my view is dazzled,
　　　Anticipating that it will search for and find nourishment
　　　In you, o holy angelic being;
　　　For I have sought your radiant vapor
　　　And the splendor of your being so much
　　　That you are all sound and art down to the naked body.
　　　I see myself deprived of spirit and light,
　　　And I never know what to produce from my little chest,
　　　Which might serve or illuminate or fashion
　　　Your greatness, whose path I have sought,
　　　Unless you, from your lofty radiance,
　　　Bending toward me, might wish to instruct me
　　　About what is necessary and appropriate for describing
　　　Your body, where such glory is contained.

XLVII Therefore, consumed by natural weakness,
     With contemplating heart, but silent, I leave you;
     I send you both of my blinded eyes,
     In which, even if it is folly
     To be preoccupied with such a lofty, penetrating ray,
     Nevertheless, your nobility will remain,
     Painted within my being, even if I were to die.
     I have made a flight that goes beyond my nature,
     Thinking I would reach beyond brightness,
     Any further attempt of which I (now) abandon,
     And, nourishing my sad hand and my weary pen
     Back on lowly earth,
     I grant them rest and space
     Until I am discharged from your grace and humility.

XLVIII When millions of hearts and as many souls
     And as many eyes as in my drops and drams
     Inhabit my very own clairvoyant body
     And with this, the understanding often kingdoms,
     Where I observe your glories and fame,
     Made up of so many notes and scales,
     I do not believe that all this will suffice;
     But, notwithstanding, if I continue to live
     And if with grace you recall and reclaim
     My spirits for your letter and book,
     I will try to put more at ease
     My heart, whose desire for you intoxicates me,
     And I will have engraved again in copper
     Or on golden metals your holy name.

XLIX Torment of hell, entry to Paradise,
     Noble flower in whom gathers the holy honey
     In which celestial wings find nourishment,
     Enclosed orchard where all is protected,
     Complete and full deity,
     Without blemishing anything, neither port, nor country,
     Nor flowers, nor fruits which grow and are born,
     Holy bud toward whom the heavens descend,
     Diurnal star on whom all eyes focus
     And in whom all hope is anchored:
     If my weary senses do not comprehend your greatness
     Or your virtues, when they shine in heaven,
     Excuse this work and any words that might offend;
     I have put into it all the best of my soul.

XL   Rose, in whom all divine graces are found,
All virtues and cherubic light,
All infallible hope of grace,
Alone in this world where your origins are,
Perfect in development and pure in your origins,
Growing nevertheless beneath brambles and thorns,
Where never an evil finger dared touch,
Heavenly treasure, earthly richness:
Come to me here (where) I seek you
So that humbly you might incline your ears towards me;
And placing all the fruit of my knowledge
In your bountiful will, without wishing to ask for too much,
For this one case, I fold my hands and pray that you
Will willingly accept my Georgian songs.

Entrancing "tra(u)ns/c": Some Metamorphoses of 'Transformation, Translation, and Transubstantiation'

Fritz Kemmler

'We instruct the computer to ignore what we call grammatical words -- articles, prepositions, pronouns, modal verbs, which have a high frequency rating in all discourse. Then we get to the real nitty-gritty, what we call the lexical words, the words that carry a distinctive semantic content. Words like love or dark or heart or God. Let's see.' So he taps away on the keyboard and instantly my favourite word appears on the screen. What do you think it was?

Pondus ibi, color, atque sapor, si queritur an sint, Sunt et forma simul, tantum substantia transit.

The forme is kept, bot the matiere Transformed is in other wise.

1. Introduction

Before I sat down in front of the screen to record some thoughts that might be of help in writing this paper, I was "tapping away on the keyboard" writing a few short program-scripts. In the process of writing the paper, I decided to include the mottoes[1] above. Whereas the first motto illustrates both method and techniques of research, the second and third refer to the main theme of this paper presented in Section 4. There, I shall present some of the changing perspectives on, and transformations of, the concept and doctrine of transubstantiation, one of the central themes of the very old and recurring debate on the "substance" and "accidents" of the Sacrament of the Eucharist. However, as we shall see, the concept of transubstantiation can also be found in a quite different thematic context.

The first of my programs is designed to copy, from my general index of words occurring in Middle English texts,[2] those entries that contain the character-string "trans", the main subject of this volume of *Disputatio*. The results of this electronic search are presented in alphabetical order in Table 1 below. In the script, I have, of course, taken into consideration "orthographic" variants for the character-string "trans"; figures between "[ ]" indicate the number of texts in which the pertinent word occurs. Using this numeric information, a second program yielded a total of 103 references and a third program, operating on the system of references (file names) contained in my general index of Middle English texts, produced the results presented in Table 2: the number of "trans"-formations contained in a file.[3]

Table 1

trance [1], *traunce* [4], *tranceth* [1]
transbeacion [1]
transcendyng [1]
transferred [1]
transfigure [1], *transfiguren* [1], *transfigurid* [4], *transfiguring* [1]
transformate [1]
transforme [1], *transformed* [4], *transformeth* [3], *transformit* [1]
transgressioun [3], *transgressores* [1], *transgressours* [1]
transitorie [2], *transytory* [1]
translacion [3], *translacions* [2], *translacioun* [4], *translacyon* [1], *translait* [2], *translat* [2], *transulat* [1], *translate* [4], *translated* [3], *translateden* [1], *translaten* [3], *translatid* [3], *translatide* [1], *translatiden* [1], *translating* [1], *translatioun* [1], *translatit* [1], *translatour* [1], *translatouris* [1], *translatud* [1], *translatyd* [1]
transmewe [1], *transmewed* [1], *transmewen* [1]
transmutacions [1], *transmutacioun* [2]
traunsom [1], *traunsomes* [1], *traunsouns* [1], *traunsounys* [1]
transporten [1], *transporteth* [1]
transpose [2], *transposed* [2], *transposiþ* [1], *transposid* [1], *transposude* [1]
transsubstansinge [1], *transubstanciacioun* [1]
transuertyd [1]
trauers [1], *trauerse* [1], *trauersed* [1], *trauerste* [1], *travers* [4], *traversed* [1]

Table 2

ASNETH [4]	ASTROLAB [1]	AWNART [2]
BOECE [8]	CARL [1]	CHANCERY [1]
CHAPOEMS [1]	CRESSEID [1]	CT [10]
EVERYMAN [1]	FRIARDAW [1]	GOWERCA [10]
GREENEK [2]	HENRYSON [4]	HENRYSPO [2]
HOF [1]	LABELDAM [3]	LANCEL [3]
LANTERNE [1]	LGW [3]	LOLLSERM [2]
MARY [1]	MYRKFEST [2]	ORPHEUS [1]
PASTON [5]	PIERS [2]	ROMROSE [2]
SPECSAC [2]	TREVISA [1]	TROILUS [6]
UPLAND [1]	WYCLBIB [10]	WYCLIF [1]
WYCLIFWR [1]	WYCLSERM [1]	YORKPL [2]

The entries in Table 1 represent 17 lemmata (compounds) containing the first element *trans/c;* these lemmata and their occurrences in my electronic corpus are presented in Table 3; figures in "[ ]" indicate orthographic and morphological variants of the pertinent lemma. In my entire electronic corpus of Middle English texts, words containing the prefix "trans" occur 183 times.

Although I will concentrate on only three "trans"-formations, I shall also discuss the remaining fourteen "trans"-lemmata, including some interesting thematic contexts in which the 17 lemmata listed in Table 3 occur in the Middle English texts contained in my corpus, with particular emphasis on the concept "transubstantiation".[4] It will be seen that some of the "trans"-formations in Middle English texts possess a certain property: semantic "transitivity".

Table 3

(1) *trance: CT* [1]; GOWERCA [3]; TROILUS [1]

(2) *transbeacion:* SPECSAC [1]

(3) *transcend:* MARY [1]

(4) *transfer:* BOECE [1]

(5) *transfigure:* BOECE [1]; *CT* [1]; FRIARDAW [1]; WYCLIFWR [1]; WYCLSERM [2]

(6) *transform(ate):* BOECE [2]; CARL [1]; *CT* [2]; GOWERCA [3]; HENRYSON [2]

(7) *transgress:* HENRYSON [1]; HENRYSPO [1]; PIERS [1]; YORKPL [2]

(8) *transitory:* BOECE [1]; EVERYMAN [1]; TROILUS [1]

(9) *translate/lation/lator:* ASNETH [2]; ASTROLAB [1]; BOECE [1]; CHANCERY [1]; CRESSEID [1]; *CT* [4]; GOWERCA [2]; HENRYSON [1]; HENRYSPO [1]; LANCEL [3]; LGW [3]; LOLLSERM [2]; MYRKFEST [2]; ORPHEUS [1]; ROMROSE [1]; WYCLBIB [10]

(10) *transmewe:* ROMROSE [1]; TROILUS [2]

(11) *transmutation:* CHAPOEMS [1]; *CT* [1]; HOF [1]

(12) *transom:* PASTON [4]

(13) *transport:* BOECE [2]

(14) *transpose:* ASNETH [1]; GOWERCA [1]; GREENEK [2]; LANTERNE [1]; UPLAND [1]; WYCLSERM [1]

(15) *transubstantiate/tion:* TREVISA [1]; WYCLIF [1]

(16) *transvert:* SPECSAC [1]

(17) *traverse:* ASNETH [1]; AWNART [2]; *CT* [1]; GOWERCA [1]; PASTON [1]; PIERS [1]; TROILUS [2]

2. The cause accidental was 'trans'"

With this slight modification of Dame Prudence's teaching (*CT,* VII.1398) serving as a header, this section covers those "trans"-lemmata (except *transbeacion,* for which see Section 4.4; and *transfer,* for which see Section 3)[5] which do not belong to the thematic frame of this volume of *Disputatio.*

2.1 Some 'Transes' in Disguise

The first of these concepts in disguise, the noun *transom* (probably based on the Latin "transtrum") occurs in my corpus, with quite a variety of spellings, only in PASTON and with a total of 11 occurrences: eight in text 64, two in 195, and one in 230. In every instance, *transom* occurs in the context "bed"; and these occurrences confirm the interpretation based on a will offered in the *OED*.[6]

The second concept, *traverse,* is used both nominally and verbally with a wide range of meanings. Thus, in ASNETH, 301–306, it is used as a noun:

> With this cloth into here chamber sche returned sone,
> And schytte the dore with barre and bolt at travers upon othir,
> And in haste dide of here robe, with ful moche mone,
> That riall was with bise and goold ful preciously bygone,
> And so sche did here ceynte of goold that riche was of valour,
> And did on here the blake robe, the vesture of dolour.

In the genre *romance,* represented by AWNART (B), the concept is associated with clothing. It is used as a past participle (352-355) and adjectivally (508-511). The clothing of both antagonist (354) and protagonist (510) display similar ornamental patterns:

> The mon in his mantell sittes at his mete,
> In pal pured with pane prodly pight,
> Trefolyte and trauerste with trewloues in trete;
> Þe tasselles were of topas þat wer þereto tiȝt.
> ...
> Gawyn was gaily graþed in grene,
> With his griffons of golde engreled full gay,
> Trifeled and trauersed with trueloues bitwene,
> On a startand stede he strikes on stray.

In the *CT,* "travers" (IV.1817: curtains, a concrete object) occurs in Januarie's famous speech to curtail the marriage merriments; in TROILUS, III.674, we encounter a similar context and an almost identical wording: "Ther nys no more, but hereafter soone,/ The voide dronke, and travers drawe anon." Chaucer's friend and contemporary, John Gower, uses the concept as a noun and metaphorically, GOWERCA, VIII.3157:

> And thus forthy my final leve
> I take now for evere more,
> Withoute makynge any more,
> Of love and of his dedly hele,
> For his nature is so divers,
> That it hath evere som travers

> Or of to moche or of to lite,
> That pleinly mai noman delite,
> Bot if him faile or that or this.

Yet another abstract and metaphorical use of the concept can be found in PASTON, text 55; there, the context is that of land-tenure and judicial documents: "And if my feodaryes whiche lye in þe tye of my gret cofyr may ought wisse therin, lete them se it. Item, I wolde that William Barker shulde send me a copye of þe olde trauerse of Tychewell and Beyton." Unfortunately, the context for *trauerse* is not precise; the noun could refer either to a court case (*OED,* sense 9; *MED,* s.v. "travers n. 3. (b)) or to an indenture stating the right of passage and the levying of a toll for it (*OED,* sense 1). Since the place names "Tychewell" and "Beyton" also occur in items 70, 173, 187, 216, and 249, we may conclude that "trauerse" refers to a lawsuit. In PIERS, XII.285, the concept, a finite verbal form (past tense), also occurs in a judicial context:

> 'Ac truthe that trespased nevere ne traversed ayeins his lawe,
> But lyveth as his lawe techeth and leveth ther be no bettre,
> (And if ther were, he wolde amende) and in swich wille deieth –
> Ne wolde nevere trewe God but trewe truthe were allowed.

As the pertinent contexts for the third concept, *trance,* clearly reveal, we must differentiate between nominal and verbal forms, especially in GOWERCA. In this text, the noun "tra(u)nce" has four occurrences, all of them unproblematic: I.1800, III.1457, VIII.1367, and VIII.2813. The verbal form, however, does present a problem (IV.2115–2117): "The ground he sporneth and he tranceth,/ Hise large hornes he avanceth/ And caste hem here and there aboute."In the *OED,* "tranceth" is glossed as "to move about actively or briskly" (with obscure etymology). Reading the text, I think that we can accomodate "tranceth" under "trans", the meaning approaching, perhaps, that of "traverse".[7]

Examining the Chaucer corpus, we find six occurrences of the noun "traunce" in *CT:* I.1572, III.2216, IV.1108, IV.1750, V.1081, and VII.2716. Of the three occurrences in TROILUS, however, two are used as a noun (II.1306; IV.343), and one represents an infinitive (III.690): "Ther was nomore to skippen nor to traunce", the meaning approaching that of the verbal form in GOWERCA, IV.2115. Finally, Sir Richard Ros' translation of Alain de Chartier's "La belle Dame sans Merci" file (LABELDAM) contains two instances of the noun "traunce": stanza 52, l. 407, rhyming with "plesaunce", and in stanza 101, l. 800, rhyming with "contynaunce" (cf. Furnivall (1866, 95 and 103).

Though not a "trans" in disguise, the adjective "transitory" occurs in two texts of the Chaucer corpus: in TROILUS, III.827, in the context of worldly joy; but in BOECE connected with the gifts of Fortune in Book II, Prosa 5; with worldly dignities in Book III, Prosa 4; with the beauty of man's body in Book III, Prosa 8; and, finally, with the flow of time in Book V, Prosa 6, "this moevable and transitorie moment". In the early modern play *Everyman* (see also Sections 4.3 and 4.4), the adjective "transitory" is connected with the life of man in l. 6: "The Somonynge of Eueryman called it is,/ That of our lyues and endynge shewes/ How transytory we be all daye." and again, in l. 721, pointing out the remedy:

> Here in this transytory lyfe, for the and me,
> The blessyd sacraments vii. there be:
> Baptym, confyrmacyon, with preesthode good,
> And the sacrament of Goddes precyous flesshe & blod,
> Maryage, the holy extreme vnccyon, and penaunce.

2.2 Transitive 'trans'

The first concept to be discussed in this section, *transcend*, occurs only once in my database in the file MARY. In stanza 2 of a poem by William Huchen, entitled "Hymn to the Virgin" (MS CCCXX, New College, Oxford; cf. Furnivall (1886, 291) the concept is used as a present participle: "So fayre, so good, was neuer non;/ Transcendyng is ther-for þi place/ Aungels alle and seyntis echone;/ Next vnto God, such is þi grace."

The second concept, *transvert*, in my file SPECSAC, refers to a quite concrete context connected with the feast of Shere Thursday:

> The secund [cause] is for this day the spouse of holy chirche was withdrawyn, for in this day he descendid to helle. The thridde cause is for the vayle of the temple this day is cutte, and the hornys of the auter ben transuertyd, and so we haue no place where that he [the body of Crist] schuld be made (EETS ed., 109–110).

This passage of the *Speculum Sacerdotale* is based on Iohannes Beleth's Summa de ecclesiasticis officiis, chapter 97, "Cur non conficiatur corpus Christi in Parasceue et de ratione eius officii".[8]

Transport occurs exclusively in BOECE. The infinitive "transporten" in Book I, Prosa 4, is used metaphorically with reference to "guilt", whereas the two instances of finite "transporteth" are associated in Book III, Prosa 4, with virtue and dignity; and in Book III, Prosa 9, with true and false goods.

Among the less ambiguous concepts, transgress appears especially in moral and judicial contexts. In HENRYSON, in the fable "The Fox and the Wolf", 715, the precise context is that of "sin, confession and satisfaction": "'Weill,' quod the volf, 'thow wantis pointis twa,Belangand to perfyte confessioun; To the thrid part off pennance let vs ga:Vill thow tak pane for thy transgressioun?'" The context is somewhat different in HENRYSPO, in the poem "Ane Prayer for the Pest", 57-64; there, the focus is on worldly power and its just administration by its representatives:

> Bot wald the heidismen, that suld keip the law,
> Pvnis the peple for thair transgressioun,
> Thair wald na deid the peple than ourthraw;
> Bot thay ar gevin sa plenly to oppressioun
> That God will nocht heir thair intercessioun,
> Bot all ar pvnist for inobediens
> Be swerd or deid, withouttin remissioun,
> And hes iust caus to send ws pestilens.

In PIERS,[9] we find a similar context in I.94-99, where "Holi Chirche" instructs the dreamer that only "Treuthe" will ultimately avail him in his quest "to save my soule":

> "Kynges and knyghtes sholde kepen it by reson –
> Riden and rappen doun in reaumes aboute,
> And taken transgressores and tyen hem faste
> Til treuthe hadde ytermyned hire trespas to the ende.
> For David in hise dayes dubbed knyghtes,
> And dide hem sweren on hir swerd to serven truthe evere.

In mediaeval drama, the concept occurs twice in YORKPL play 36, the Butchers' "The Death of Christ" (ll. 11 and 25), in the opening stanzas designed for Pilate's boastful self-characterization. Since YORKPL contains "The Last Supper" (play 27, performed by the Bakers), we might expect a reference to the Eucharist and the hotly debated concept and doctrine of "transubstantiation". However, at the relevant point in the text, a leaf is missing from the MS.[10]

As well as the semantically less problematic "trans"-concepts, there are "trans"-formations used mainly metaphorically and tending towards semantic "transitivity": in particular *transfigure*, *transform*, *transmute*, and *transpose*. As some of my texts clearly show, the concepts "transfigure" and "transform" were used almost synonymously and in both the active and the passive voice. Thus, in BOECE "transfigure" occurs in Book IV, Metrum 7:

> and Acheleous the flod, defowled in his forheed, dreynte his schamefast visage in his strondes (that is to seyn, that Achaleous coude transfiguren hymself into diverse liknesse, and, as he faughte with Hercules, at the laste he torned hym into a bole, and Hercules brak of oon of his hornes, and he for schame hidde hym in his ryver)

In his *Confessio Amantis*, IV.2111-2112, Gower describes the same incident in similar terms: "And efte, as he that feighte wole,/ He torneth him into a Bole." In both BOECE and GOWERCA, "transfigure" is also represented by native words: torned and torneth, based on the quite rare late OE tyrnan, and reinforced by the Old French loan "turner, torner". As we shall see in the subsequent sections, the basic locative concept "trans" is represented in Middle English texts by a limited number of words and phrases with rather high frequency ratings, eg. "change, to be made in(to), turn" etc. (see below, Section 2.3).

The anti-Lollard text FRIARDAW uses the concept "transfigure" with reference to Satan, master in the art and craft of "transformation" and "transfiguration". Used as a past participle in a hypothetical conditional clause, the concept occurs in l. 345-346: "If Sathanas were transfigurid in to his forme fairnesse,/ Trowist þou he were ouȝt ellis but a dampned aungel?" WYCLIFWR also employs it in reference to Satan; however, the comparison is used to point out the malpractices of "yvele prelatis", based on 2 Cor. 11:13–15 ("ipse enim Satanas transfigurat se in angelum lucis" and "si ministri eius transfigurentur velut ministri iustitiae"):

And for þei tellen not Cristis gospel bi word and holy lyuyng and for feruent loue of soulis, þey ben ded in hemsilf and sleeris of soulis bitakun to her cure; and þouȝ þey diden none oþere malices þey ben antecristis and satanas transfigurid into an aungel of liȝt, nyȝt þeuys and day þeuys, sleeris and distrieris of scheep, makinge þe hows of preier a denne of þeuys (cf. Hudson (1978), text 12, 109-114).

Yet in *CT*, Satan's "transfiguration" is represented by the concept "transformation" used in both the active and the passive voice in "The Parson's Tale", X.895-896:

Preestes been aungels, as by the dignitee of hir mysterye; but for sothe, Seint Paul seith that Sathanas transformeth hym in an aungel of light. / Soothly, the preest that haunteth deedly synne, he may be likned to the aungel of derk-nesse transformed in the aungel of light. He semeth aungel of light, but for sothe he is aungel of derknesse.

My file WYCLSERM contains the concept "transfigure" in a sermon, represented by two past participles, "transfigurid", and one non-finite verbal form used as a noun: "transfiguring"; and it is this last form that is worth looking at since it again demonstrates the parallel use of both loan-word and native construction:

And Crist was transfigurid bifore hem, and his face shoon as þe sunne, and his cloþis weren maad white as þe snow. And þus men seyen þat transfiguring is turnyng into glorious forme, þat men seen not wiþ þis eye bi figure þat þey seen nou, as Cristis face whanne it shyned as sone was not seyn figurid as ouris ben nou (cf. Gradon and Hudson, III, 84).

The uses of the verbal concept "transmewe" very closely approximate to "transfigure/transform". In my texts, the term occurs only in the Chaucer corpus and appears to be a mixed compound of Latin "trans" and Old French "moveir".

Thus, in ROMROSE, 2526, we find: " Wherewith thi colour wole transmewe," and the meaning is ascertained by the highly frequent "chaungen" in 2528: "Thyn hewe eke chaungen for hir sake." In TROILUS, there are two occurrences, both in connection with Pandarus and both occurring in direct speech: an infinitive in IV.467 "Thow moost me first transmewen in a ston"; and, more concrete and factitive, a past participle used by Criseyde in her "pleynte" in IV.830: "That now transmewed ben in cruel wo." As the contexts containing the concept "transpose" clearly demonstrate, the meaning sometimes approaches that of "transfer, translate". Thus, in ASNETH, 28-32, it is clearly "translate":

Gyde this werke, gracious Lord, and graunte it good endynge,
Utterali the Latyn in Englyshe to transpose;
Hit is nuyus, but the sentence I schal sue in trace,
And yf ye fynde fautes, grave hem with yowr glose,
I pray yow thus, my maystresse, of yowre good grace.

And it is the same case in GOWERCA, IV.2653-2656: "And after that out of Hebreu/ Jerom, which the langage kneu,/ The Bible, in which the lawe is closed,/ Into Latin he hath transposed..." A different shade of meaning can be found, however, in GREENEK, 52, 56, and 442, where it approaches that of "transfigure" "transform", and the modern "transvest":

Shee cold transpose knights and swaine
Like as in battaile they were slaine,
Wounded in lim and lightt.
Shee taught her sonne the knight alsoe
In transposed likenesse he shold goe
Both by fell and frythe.
…
The Greene Knight rode another way;
He transposed him in another array,
Before as it was greene.

The concept "transpose" shifting into "transform" can also be found in a number of texts representing the debate over Lollardism. Thus, in LANTERNE, chapter 5, an anonymous author comments on *Isa* 5:20, developing a comparison bearing on the hotly disputed theme "pilgrimage": "And þus doþ anticrist whanne he transposiþ vertues in to vicis, & vicis in to vertues, as pilgrimage in to outrage, & outrage in to pilgrimage. And for þis weywarde entent God dispisiþ anticrist wiþ alle hise blindfelt peple, & wlatiþ alle her mysdispendid goodis in her moost tribulaciouns." Attacking the friars and their practices, we find a similar context in the anonymous UPLAND:

and summe [i.e. of the common people] crepen into feyned ordris and clepen hem religious, to lyue idilli bi ipocrisie and disceive alle þe statis ordeyned bi God, and þus bi Anticrist and hise clerkis ben uertues transposid to vicis: as mekenes to cowardise, felnes and pride to wisdom and talnes, wraþþe to manhode, enuye to iustificacioun of wrong, slouþe to lordlynes, coueytis to wisdom & wise puruyaunce, glotonye to largynes, leccherie to kindeli solace, mildenes to schepisshenesse, holines to jpocrisie, heryse to pleyne sadnes of feyþ and oolde vsage, & holy chirche to synagoge of Satanas (cf. Heyworth 1968, 56).

A similar context for the concept "transpose" approaching that of "transform" can be found in WYCLSERM. Edited by Pamela Gradon under the title "Vae Octuplex" (II, 366-378), some parts of the exposition of the theme are directed against the malpractices of the established church (note the verbal parallel in UPLAND, quoted above):

> And þus þe chirche here is fowly deformed fro children of God to þe feen-dys lymes and herto vertewys ben transposude to vyces, as mekenesse is cowardyse and felnesse of pruyde is clepud riȝtwysnesse for to maynteine Godis riȝte, wraþþe is clepud manhede and myldenesse is schepnesse, and enuye is condicion of Godis child to vengen hym, and slowþe is lordlinesse, as God restuþ euermore, coueytise is prudence to be riche and myhty, glotorie is largesse and lechery is merye pley, Godis seruaunt is an ypocryte and heretyke is sad in feyþ; and þus alle vertewis ben transposude to vyces, and so hooly chirche to synagoge of Sathanas (II, 376).

A further "trans"-formation, "transmutation", occurs exclusively in my Chaucer corpus (CHAPOEMS). In Chaucer's Fortune, l. 1, it is used in a context similar to that of "transitory": "This wrecched worldes transmutacioun", and this context is also found in HOF, 1969: "Of dyvers transmutacions/ Of estats, and eke of regions." As discussed in Section 4, both the term and the concept "transmutation" also occur in a quite different context.

2.3 Transformation
The Chaucer corpus contributes a few further uses of the concept, cf. BOECE, Book IV, Prosa 3, "Than betidith it that, yif thou seest a wyght that be transformed into vices, thow ne mayst nat wene that he be a man." In Book IV, Prosa 6, we find: "Thilke ordenaunce moveth the hevene and the sterres, and atemprith the elementz togidre amonges hemself, and transformeth hem by entrechaungeable mutacioun." In the romance genre, the concept is used in CARL, 410 by the Carl himself after his release by Gawain:

> By nigromancé thus was I shapen
> Till a knight of the Round Table

> Had with a sword smitten of my head
> If he had grace to doe that deede.
> Itt is forty winters agoe
> Since I was transformed soe.

In HENRYSON, there are two occurrences of the concept: in the "Prologue", 56, and in the fable "The Trial of the Fox", 890. In the first instance, the tone is a moralizing one:

> Na meruell is, ane man be lyke ane beist,
> Quhilk lufis ay carnall and foull delyte,
> That schame can not him renȝe nor arreisst,
> Bot takis all the lust and appetyte,
> Quhilk throw custum and the daylie ryte
> Syne in the mynd sa fast is radicate
> That he in brutal beist is transformate.

The second use can be assigned to the narrative "I" of the fable, in its description of the company of beasts appearing before their lord, the lion:

> And quhat thay wer, to me as Lowrence leird,
> I sall reheirs ane part off euerilk kynd,
> Als fer as now occurris to my mynd.
> The minotaur, ane monster meruelous,
> Bellerophont that beist of bastardrie,
> The warwolff, and the pegase perillous,
> Transformit be assent of sorcerie,

GOWERCA offers a highly interesting variety of morphological types and tokens of the concept: "transforme" [6]: I.2971; IV.3049; V.941, 6675; VI.2200, and VII.3364; the context usually being "taking on the shape of an animal or an other person". In IV.3049, however, the verbal context is more interesting since the concept is taken up again by the Old French loan "change": "The thridde suiende after this/ Is Panthasas, which may transforme/ Of every thing the rihte forme,/ And change it in an other kinde." The past participle, "transformed", has a total of six occurrences: II.194; III.375, 809; IV.2946; V.1873, 6201. And, finally, we find the finite "transformeth" [2]: IV.501, and 2560.The most interesting use in GOWERCA, in the thematic context "alchemy", is provided by IV.2560, "transformeth", where the concept approaches that of "transubstantiate":

> The thridde Ston in special
> Be name is cleped Minerall,
> Which the metalls of every Mine
> Attempreth, til that thei ben fyne,

And pureth hem be such a weie,
That al the vice goth aweie
Of rust, of stink and of hardnesse:
And whan thei ben of such clennesse,
This Mineral, so as I finde,
Transformeth al the ferste kynde
And makth hem able to conceive
Thurgh his vertu, and to receive
Bothe in substance and in figure
Of gold and selver the nature.

Note in particular the use of "substance" in l. 2563. Where Gower's use of "transformeth" differs essentially from the theological use of the concept "transubstantiate" is in the "transformation" of both "substance" *and* "figure". Gower's use of the concept clearly foreshadows the singular use of "transubstantiation" listed in the *MED* in a non-theological context: Thomas Norton's *Ordinal of Alchemy*. Writing about a century after Gower, Norton[11] explains the virtues of "oure stone Microcosmos", 2510, by a whole series of "trans"-formations:

Wherbie of metallis is made transmutacion
Not only in colour, but transubstanciacion.
In which ye haue nede to knowe this thynge,
How all the virtues of the elemente transmutynge
Vpon the transmutide moste haue full dominacion
Bifore that the substance be in transmutacion;

Since Gower turns to the subject "Lollardy" in Book V of his *Confessio Amantis*,[12] we should also take a look at V.1873:

Thus stant this world fulfild of Mist,
That noman seth the rihte weie:
The wardes of the cherche keie
Thurgh mishandlinge ben myswreynt,
The worldes wawe hath welnyh dreynt
The Schip which Peter hath to stiere,
The forme is kept, bot the matiere
Transformed is in other wise.

Gower's reference to the unchanged "forme" and the changed "matiere" (substance) in V.1872 clearly points to the concept "transubstantiation" with its highly significant terms "form, substance" and "subject" (see below, Section 4, and my second motto above). This brief survey of the concept "transform" and its related concepts "transfigure" and "trans-mute" reveals a surprisingly wide range of contexts, meanings and uses in Middle English texts. And, as we shall see in

Section 4, these terms were also used in the context of the debate about the new doctrine of "transubstantiation".

3. Transfer – Translate

For morphological reasons, I shall treat the present stem, "transfer", first. The meaning of this type and its tokens can be both concrete and metaphorical, as in Modern English. In my corpus, the concept occurs as a past participle, "transferred", exclusively in BOECE, Book II, Prosa 5; and the same section also contains the single occurence of "translate" in this text:

> What is most worth of rychesses? Is it nat gold or myght of moneye assembled? Certes thilke gold and thilke moneye schyneth and yeveth bettre renoun to hem that dispenden it than to thilke folk that mokeren it; for avaryce maketh alwey mokereres to ben hated, and largesse maketh folk cleer of renoun. For, syn that swiche thyng as is transferred fro o man to an othir ne may nat duellen with no man, certes thanne is thilke moneye precyous whan it is translated into other folk and stynteth to ben had by usage of large yyvynge of hym that hath yeven it.

Among the other texts belonging to the Chaucer corpus are 4 occurrences in *CT*: IV.385; VIII.25: "translacioun", and X.1085: "translacions", 1088: "translacion" ("Retraction"). The use of the past participle, "translated", with reference to Griseldis in IV.385 is different and quite concrete: "Unnethe the peple hir knew for hire fairnesse/ Whan she translated was in swich richesse." Examining the LGW, we find the noun "translacioun" in l. 324; the past participle, "translated" in ll. 329 and 425; and, finally, in l. 370, the infinitive "translaten", all instances referring to textual translation. This use we also find in ROMROSE, where the infinitive "translaten" occurs in l.5666, with reference to "Boece of Consolacioun": "Where lewid men myght lere wit,/ Whoso that wolde translaten it." Finally, in ASTROLAB, the type occurs in the Prologue: "But considre wel that I ne usurpe not to have founden this werk of my labour or of myn engyn. I n'am but a lewd compilator of the labour of olde astrologiens, and have it translatid in myn Englissh oonly for thy doctrine. And with this swerd shal I sleen envie." In non-Chaucerian texts listed in Table 2, we find the infinitive "translate" twice in ASNETH (in ll. 3 and 26):

> AS I on hilly halkes logged me late,
> Biside ny of a Ladi sone was I war;
> La Bele me desired in Englysh to translate
> The Latyn of that lady, Asneth Putifar.
> ...
> Concluded thus with gentilnesse, I toke on to me the cure,
> Asneth storie to translate after my cunnynge,
> Fro Latyn into Englysh as God me sendeth oevre.

Before embarking on his lengthy moralization, (885 ff.) the author ends his story proper with a *captatio benivolentiae* (884): "Thus endeth the storie of Asneth to youre remembrance./ My rude translacion I pray you tak hit with plesance."

In the various types of documents contained in my file CHANCERY, there are 3 occurrences of the concept, the noun "translacion", in item 24, 88, and 147. In two instances, the context is that of a bishop's "translation" (items 24 and 88), whereas in item 147 the reference is to "the feste of translacion of seint Thomas the martir". In the Henryson corpus, in CRESSEID, 127-130, Henryson uses the type metaphorically, though not referring to the translation of a text: "'3e gaue me anis ane deuine responsaill,/ That I suld be the flour of luif in Troy;/ Now am I maid ane vnworthie outwaill,/ And all in cair translatit is my ioy." In HENRY-SON, 1. 32, the context is that of translating a text:

> Of this poete, my maisteris, with 3our leif,
> Submitting me to 3our correctioun,
> In mother toung, of Latyng, I wald preif
> To mak ane maner of translatioun –
> Nocht of my self, for vane presumptioun,
> Bot be requeist and precept of ane lord,
> Of quhome the name it neidis not record.

The single occurence in ORPHEUS, 1. 42, refers to the "translation" of Greek in-to Latin: "Tersicor, quhilk is gude instruction/ Of ewiry thing, the thrid sister, I wis,/ Thus out of Grewe in Latyne translate is;" However, Robert Henryson of-ers a third use of the concept. In HENRYSPO, where it occurs as a past partic-iple, in the poem "The Thre Deid Pollis", 33-40, the context is really that of "transformation":

> O wilfull pryd, the rute of all distres,
> With humill hairt vpoun our pollis pens;
> Man, for thy mis, ask mercy with meiknes;
> Aganis deid na man may mak defens:
> The empriour, for all his excellens,
> King and quene, and eik all erdly stait,
> Peure and riche, salbe but differens
> Turnit in as and thus in erd translait.

Moving backwards, from Henryson to Gower, we may note that in GOWERCA, the second occurence of the concept, IV.2260, refers to the translation of literary texts. More interesting, however, is the first occurrence in II.3044:

> And yit, als ferforth as I dar,
> I rede alle othre men be war,

> And that thei loke wel algate
> That non his oghne astat translate
> Of holi cherche in no degree
> Be fraude ne soubtilite:
> For thilke honour which Aaron tok
> chal non receive, as seith the bok,
> Bot he be cleped as he was.

My file LABELDAM also contributes to the uses of the concept: firstly, an infinitive, l. 8 (stanza 2): "My charge was þis, to translat by and by", and secondly a noun: l. 842 (stanza 106) (see Furnivall (1866, 80; 111): "And forþermor, byseche hem, of þair grace,/ By þair fauour and supportacioun,/ To take in gre þis Rude translacioun." Even the popular genre romance makes a few contributions to the uses of the concept. Thus, in LANCEL, we find both the metaphorical and the concrete use, 209-11; 502-508; 2203-2206:

> Bot for that story is so pasing larg,
> Oneto my wit it war so gret o charg
> For to translait the romans of that knycht.
> …
> The King, qwhois hart was al wyth dred ybownd,
> And askit at the clerkis if thei fynde
> By there clergy that stant in ony kynde
> Of possibilitee fore to reforme
> His desteny, that stud in such a forme,
> If in the hevyne is preordynat
> On such o wiss his honor to translat.

The final occurrence is in the context of direct speech: "And now yow thinkith mak me dissolat/ Of knychtis and my houss transulat/ To sek o knycht and it was never more/ Hard sich o semblé makith o before."

In my file MYRKFEST, a collection of sermons, two examples appear in sermon 66, "De Solempnitate St. Martini", both referring to the "translation" of the body of the saint, first: "The foure and fourty ȝere aftyr þer come a byschop þat translatud hym." and second, representing a noun: "Then for God schewet gret myracles for hym yche ȝere at þe day of his translacyon, moch pepul drogh þedyr, forto bere hys schryne aboute yn dyuers stretys of þe towne." As might be expected, those texts which can be assigned to the Lollard movement contain a broad variety of types and tokens. In LOLLSERM, the concept is not used for textual translation; based on John 3:13-14, "nolite mirari si odit uos mundus", the preacher says:

> þat is: 'Merueileþ noȝt, breþeren, þou þe world hate ȝou, for we knowen þat we ben translatid fro deþ to lyif for we loueþ (þat is, God and oure

breþeren), and þei þat loueþ no3t (þat is, noþer God, neþer breþeren as þese loueris of þis world dooþ), þei dwellen in deeþ,' as Seynt Johun seiþ. And lyif and deþ ben contrarious directli, þerfore moun þei neuer acorde (cf. Cigman 1989, 5).

The second context is quite similar and contains the native word "change" for the concept: "Of þis changyng spekeþ Seynt Poule, þere he seiþ: Translato saderdotio [*Hebr.* 7:12]. Þat is: 'When presthode was translatid or chaungid.'" (cf. Cigman (1989, 22). Yet another shade of meaning can be found in the sermon for the fourth Sunday in Advent, based on John 1:19:

> But heere we musten vndurstonde for þe declaringe of þis mater þat Crist and þese messyngeris vnderstoden in diuerse maneres. Crist vnderstood of John þat he was Helye in figure, for in manie þinges þei weren like, as it is seyd bifore, but specially for John was þe foregoer of Cristis firste comynge, as Helye schal be tofore his comynge to þe Doom. And þe messingeris vnderstooden þat he was Helye in persone þat was translatyd in a firi chare as Hooly Wryt telleþ. And þus John seide þat he was no3t Helie in persone, as messingeris vnderstooden; but he denied not þat he was Helye in figure aftur Cristis menynge, and so Baptist was in no wey contrarious to Crist. (cf. Cigman 1989, 46)

Note the Latin text, *Luke*, 12:37: "Precynget se, et faciet illos discumbere, et transiens ministrabit illis.", is translated by the preacher with a loan word (present participle): "Þat is: 'He shal girde hymself, and make hem sitt to mete, and he passing shal ministre to hem'" (cf. Cigman 1989, 194).

The last Lollard texts to be surveyed,, occur in my file WYCLBIB, with a total of 10 variants of the concept "textual tanslation": translacions [1]; translacioun [8]; translate [7]; translaten [1]; translatid [6]; translatide [5]; translatiden [3]; translating [5]; translatour [1]; and, finally, translatouris [6]. Some of these occurences treat a "theory of translation", while others are associated with the theme "lawful translation of the Bible". Yet a third group examines particular translations of the Bible and their respective qualities and weaknesses (cf. Hudson 1978, text 14).

4 Transubstantiation

Approaching the third thematic field of this volume of *Disputatio*, let me illustrate this traditional concept and, in the late fourteenth century and beyond, the hotly disputed comparatively recent doctrine of *transubstantiation* with three quotations: the first from Ælfric's *Sermo de Sacrificio in Die Pascae* and the second and third from Thomas Hobbes' *Leviathan* (1651), chapter 8 ("Of the Vertues Commonly Called Intellectual; and their Contrary Defects") and chapter 44 ("Of Spirituall Darknesse from Misinterpretation of Scripture"):

Nu smeadon gehwilce men oft, and gyt gelome smeagað, hu se hlaf, þe bið of corne gegearcod and ðurh fyres hætan abacen, mage beon awend to Cristes lichaman; oððe þæt win, ðe bið of manegum berium awrungen, weorðe awend þurh ænigre bletsunge to Drihtnes blode. Nu secge we swilcum mannum, þæt sume ðing sind gecwedene be Criste þurh getacnunge, sume ðurh gewissum ðinge....Soðlice se hlaf and þæt win, ðe beoð þurh sacerda mæssan gehalgode, oðer ðing hi æteowiað menniscum andgitum wiðutan and oðer ðing hi clypiað wiðinnan geleaffullum modum. Wiðutan hi beoð gesewene hlaf and win, ægðer ge on hiwe ge on swæcce; ac hi beoð soðlice æfter þære halgunge Cristes lichama and his blod þurh gastlicere gerynu....Micel is betwux þære ungesewenlican mihte þæs halgan husles and þam gesewenlican hiwe agenes gecyndes. Hit is on gecynde brosniendlic hlaf and brosniendlic win, and is æfter mihte godcundes wordes soðlice Cristes lichama and his blod, na swa ðeah lichamlice ac gastlice....Soðlice hit is, swa swa we ær cwædon, Cristes lichama and his blod, na lichamlice ac gastlice. Ne sceole ge smeagan hu hit gedon sy, ac healdan on eowrum geleafan þæt hit swa gedon sy.

When men write whole volumes of such stuffe, are they not Mad, or intend to make others so? And particularly, in the question of Transubstantiation; where after certain words spoken, they that say, the White*nesse,* Round*nesse,* Magni*tude,* Quali*ty,* Corruptibili*ty,* all which are incorporeall, &c. go out of the Wafer, into the Body of our blessed Saviour, do they not make those *Nesses, Tudes* and *Ties,* to be so many spirits possessing his body? For by Spirits, they mean alwayes things, that being incorporeall, are neverthelesse moveable from one place to another (147).

Nor did the Church of Rome ever establish this Transubstantiation, till the time of *Innocent* the third; which was not above 500. hundred years ago, when the Power of Popes was at the Highest, and the Darknesse of the time grown so great, as men discerned not the Bread that was given them to eat, especially when it was stamped with the figure of Christ upon the Crosse, as if they would have men beleeve it were Transubstantiated, not onely into the Body of Christ, but also into the Wood of his Crosse, and that they did eat both together in the Sacrament (635).

Since the *doctrine* of transubstantiation was instituted by the Fourth Lateran Council of 1215,[13] we would expect the new doctrine and the comparatively recent concept and its terms to figure prominently in the English Synodalia issued after 1215; however, we shall see that this is not the case, at least as far as the terms are concerned. Before examining this (as we shall see) important corpus of texts, let us briefly consider some of the pastoral manuals composed in the early thirteenth century and indebted to the teaching of William de Montibus at Lincoln and ultimately to the Paris schools of practical theology in the late twelfth century.[14]

4.1 Manuals and Summae

Perhaps one of the most influential pastoral manuals is Thomas Chobham's *Summa Confessorum*, also known under the title *Summa Cum miserationes* and composed before 1216.[15] Since Chobham had studied in Paris under Peter the Chanter, we would expect that the term "transubstantiation" figuring so prominently in the Chanter's *Summa*,[16] would also appear frequently in Chobham's *Summa*; however, this is not the case. Although Chobham provides a rather detailed account of the Sacrament of the Eucharist, it is only on page 122 of Broomfield's edition that we encounter the term "transubstantiation":

> Et est etiam sciendum quod ex pane non conficitur nisi solum corpus Christi, et tamen non est ibi corpus sine sanguine, sed nihil ibi transsubstantiatum [MSS variants: C/R: transsubstatum] est in sanguinem. Similiter in calice ex vino nihil conficitur nisi sanguis Christi, et tamen non est ibi sanguis sine corpore, sed nihil est in calice conversum in corpus.

These textual variants would seem to suggest that the recent verb "transubstantiari" was one of the "hard words" for a number of mediaeval scribes. A further influential *summa* composed in England in the early thirteenth century is Richard Wetheringsette's *Summa Qui bene presunt*.[17] Instructing his clerical audience in the elements of the Sacrament of the Eucharist, Wetheringsette says: "De hoc sacramento instruendi sunt specialiter laici quod firmiter credant corpus Christi et sanguinem de pane et uino transubstantiari cum a sacerdote in forma ecclesie proferuntur uerba transubstantialia, scilicet hoc est corpus meum et cetera, hic est calix et cetera (BL MS Harley 3244, fol. 166ra)."

Concluding this brief survey of manuals and *summae*, is one of the more influential fourteenth-century works, the *Fasciculus Morum* (FM).[18] Though the term "transubstantiation" does not occur in the FM, we find the concept and the most important elements of the recent doctrine in the rather detailed subsection, "De Virtute Misse et Panis et Aque Benedicte" (404-417) in part 5, devoted to the explanation of the sin of sloth (*accidia*) and its remedies:

> Circa autem materiam et formam istius sacramenti est sciendum quod materia est panis et vinum....Et nota quod consecrato Christi corpore plura mirabilia ibi considerantur.... Quorum mirabilium unum est quod ad verbum hominis una substancia in aliam *convertitur*....Tercium est quod illud quod fuit prius, postea non est, et tamen in nullo adnichilatur. Quartum est quod multe substancie *convertuntur* in aliquid et illud non augmentatur....Duodecimum est quod accidencia existant in actus suos sine subiecto (FM, 406, 408; emphasis mine).

After this brief look at three Latin treatises, let us now examine some texts which belong to a different corpus of pastoral literature.

4.2 Synodalia

Examining the extensive corpus of English *synodalia* issued during the thirteenth century,[19] we find that many topics connected with the concept and doctrine of "transubstantiation", eg. elevation and adoration of the host, pyx, wine and water, etc., are mentioned frequently in these texts -- the term, however, occurs but rarely. And, as we shall see, the term -- and, by inference, the concept -- appears to have been problematic in many respects.

Among the earliest diocesan statutes composed after the Fourth Lateran Council are those for the diocese of Salisbury, issued between 1217 and 1219 by Bishop Richard Poore, one of the students of Stephen Langton at Paris. In this rather detailed set of statutes[20] we find the rubric "De sacramento redemptionis":

> Sequitur de sacramento nostre redemptionis quod viaticum sive eucharistia dicitur. Nam sicut solent homines peregre profecturi amicos suos convocare atque convivium letitie eis preparare, sic dominus noster Iesus Christus peregre proficiscens, id est, de mundo transiturus ad patrem, discipulis suis convivium preparavit, corpore et sanguine suo eos veraciter reficiens sub speciebus panis et vini transubstantiatis, pane in corpus et vino in sanguinem, potestate divina (*C&S*, 77).

Bishop Poore also admonishes his clergy that special care and circumspection is required in explaining this sacrament to the laity: "In super debetis instruere laicos quotiens communicant quod de veritate corporis et sanguinis Christi nullo modo dubitent. Nam hoc accipiunt proculdubio sub panis specie quod pro nobis pependit in cruce, hoc accipiunt in calice quod effusum est de Christi latere (*C&S*, 77-78)." Note that Poore's rather general statement, "quod effusum est de Christi latere", appears to have been a problematic issue in the concept "transub-stantiation" as discussed in the Paris schools in the late twelfth century, as is evident from the Chanter's *Summa,* 161162: "Queritur de aqua illa que fluxit a latere Christi in passione, utrum sumatur in sacramento altaris, et si sumitur, quid in illam conuertatur".[21] In the statutes for an English diocese, issued between 1222 and 1225, the Sacrament of the Eucharist is also treated with special reference to the laity:

> Item, frequenter moneantur laici ut ubicumque viderint corpus domini defferri statim genua flectant tanquam domino creatori et redemptori suo et iunctis manibus quousque transierit orent humiliter, et hoc maxime fiat tempore consecrationis in elevatione ostie, quando panis in verum corpus Christi transsubstantiatur [MSS variants: B: transsummatur; H:

transformatur; S: transmutabitur] et id quod est in calice in verum sanguinem Christi mistica benedictione transformatur *(C&S,* 143).

These MSS variants suggest in my view that the term "transubstantiation" -- let alone the concept and doctrine -- appears to have posed a host of problems.[22] And it is not only in this set of statutes that we can encounter variant MSS readings. In a third (and final) set, the synodal statutes for the diocese of Exeter, issued by Bishop Peter Quinel on 16 April 1287,[23] we find a brief account of the concept "transubstantiation" under the rubric "De eucaristia":

Quia vero per hec verba: Hoc est enim corpus meum, et non per alia, panis transsubstantiatur [MSS variants: D: transsubitur; H: transsubitiatur; F/G: transuberatur; B/D: transmutatur; A: vertitur] in corpus, prius hostiam non levet sacerdos donec ipsa plene protulerit, ne pro creatore creatura a populo veneretur. Hostia autem ita levetur in altum ut a fidelibus circumstantibus valeat intueri (*C&S,* 990).

In the same section, Quinel recommends a special method for instructing the laity in the Sacrament of the Eucharist:

Unde ne instigante diabolo ulla solicita dubitatio de corpore Christi mentes occupet laycorum, priusquam communicent instruantur per sacerdotes quod illud accipiunt sub panis specie quod pro ipsorum salute pependit in cruce, hoc accipiunt in calice quod effusum est de Christi latere: et ad hoc inducantur per *exempla, rationes, et miracula* que hactenus evenerunt (*C&S,* 991; emphasis mine).

As we shall see below (Section 4.4), this method was adopted in quite a number of works of religious instruction composed for the laity.[24]

After this brief evaluation of the difficult concept and term *transu-stantiation* and its (sometimes quite ingenious) variants which, in my opinion, help to explain the rare occurrence of the term in Middle English writings of religious instruction (see Section 4.4), let us now examine the contexts of the occurrences of "transubstantiation" as listed in Table 3.

4.3 "Transubstantiation" in Middle English Texts

The earliest text in my corpus in which we can find both the concept and the doctrine[25] is contained in my file WYCLIF. Towards the end of the short *Nota de Confessione,* we find the term in a brief account of the authority and duties of the priest:

if þou be a prest of cristis secte, holde þe payde of his lawe to teche his puple cristis gospel, al if þou feyne þee no more power; for crist haþ ȝyue power I-nowe to his prestis to teche his churche; & enioyned hem siche office þat ȝyueþ hem not occasioun to synne. & þus power þat prestis han standeþ not in transsubstansinge of þe oste, ne in makyng of accidentis for to stonde bi hemsilf; for þis power graunted not god to crist ne to any apostle, and so crist haþ speciali power to do awey mennes synne; & þise miracles þat ben feyned þat no man may see ne knowe, as þei waxen without profit, so þei han no grounde in god (cf. Matthew 1880, 345).

Matthew ascribes this tract to Wyclif; however, in view of the absence of the term in the texts edited by Hudson (1978) and in the collection of Wycliffite sermons edited by Gradon and Hudson (some of which will be examined in Section 4.4) we might have some doubts about Matthew's judgment. However, looking at the spelling of the word, "transsubstansinge", and its morphological properties, a present participle used as a verbal noun,[26] we could indeed say that these features suggest a well adapted use in Middle English of the Latin term by (certain) Wycliffites[27] with a solid knowledge of the academic debate (in Latin) over "transubstantiation".

There is another important characteristic of this use of the verbal noun text: "*þus power þat prestis* han standeþ not in *transsubstansinge of þe oste*" (empasis mine): It is used in the *active voice,* whereas in the Latin texts considered in Sections 4.1 and 4.2, the *passive voice* is characteristic for the use of the verbal forms.[28] This grammatical "transition" from the earlier passive to the active voice, in my view, points to a shift of perspective and emphasis in the discussion of the concept, and, in particular, of the doctrine: a shift away from the "mystery" of the consecrated host as the central point of this Sacrament, towards a new emphasis on the authority and power of the priest who, as a representative of the Church entrusted with the keys, *handles* and indeed "transubstantiates" the host, cf. *Everyman,* 739: "And handeleth his Maker bytwene his handes". This change of perspective, I believe, should be examined somewhat further in the Latin texts dealing with "transubstantiation".[29]

In the *Fasciculus Morum,* this new perspective is evident in the second of the fifteen *mirabilia* enumerated: "Secundum est quod ad verbum unius sacerdotis et non alterius hominis hoc fieri potest" (FM, 406). A similar view appears in the much later *Friar Daw's Reply,* 863-864 (see below, Section 4.4): "It wole not be confect but oonli of a preest/ þat awfulli is ordeyned bi Holy Chirche keies." In Quinel's synodalia examined in Section 4.2, the emphasis is somewhat different: "Quia vero per hec verba: Hoc est enim corpus meum, et non per alia, panis transsubstantiatur". Wetheringsette's *Summa,* mentioned in Section 4.1, (already?) somewhat emphasizes the function of the priest and the form provided by the Church: "cum a sacerdote in forma ecclesie proferuntur uerba transubstantialia". A close reading of the Chanter's *Summa* reveals a few uses of the verbal form in the *active voice.* The Chanter explains the "words and conditions" of "transubstantiation":

Tertio modo respondent quidam quod Dominus uerba illa *hoc est corpus meum*, proferendo, non transsubstantiauit panem in corpus suum, immo iam ante transsubstantiauerat cum benedixit illud....Quibus autem uerbis usus fuerit in transsubstantiando corpus suum, nos nescimus, sed hoc dicendum quod, siue in prolatione istorum uerborum *hoc est corpus meum*, facta fuerit transsubstantiatio, siue non, proferendo tamen illa, dedit eis uim et efficatiam, ut cum prolatione ipsorum a ministro ad hoc constituto, fiat transsubstantiatio (*Summa*, 148).

Note, in particular, "in transsubstantiando corpus suum", an active gerund, similar to the use of the present participle as a noun followed by a prepositional object which we encountered in WYCLIF. Though in this passage the agent is clearly Christ and the (historical) situation is the Last Supper, we should note the Chanter's emphasis on the "ministro ad hoc constituto" in the situation of the mass.

The most explicit reference to the dignity, authority, and power of the priest based on the Sacrament of the Eucharist, and thus on transubstantiation, can be found in the immensely popular *Speculum humanae salvationis*, composed in the early fourteenth century.[30] The *Speculum*, probably composed by a member of the new religious orders, was translated under the title *The Mirour of Mans Saluacioune* into Middle English in the early fifteenth century and shows some decidedly Northern dialectal characteristics. Using the techniques of typology and prefiguration, the anonymous author bases his account of the dignity and power of the priest on *Gen.* 14:18, Melchizedek's reception of Abraham, offering him bread and wine.[31] And since Melchizedek was both *king and priest*, the argument put forward to extoll the dignity of the priest hinges on these attributes (*Mirour*, ch. 16, 105, 1883-1902):

> This forsaide Melchisedec was preest of Godde and kynge,
> And of Oure Lorde Jhesu Crist bare he prefiguryng,
> For Crist is King of kynges whas regne cesses nevre,
> And þerto verraiest preest and first þat sange messe evre.
> Melchisedec, king and prest, both brede and wyne offride,
> And Crist in lykenes of brede and wyne this sacrament ordenid.
> Thus was Crist callid preest after the ordre of Melchisedec king,
> For he this sacrament figured in this forsaide offring.
> Melchisedec was a preest and also a prince realle,I
> n whilk was faire figured the dignitee sacerdotalle,
> For preestis princes real with resoune callid may be,
> For alle princes imperial passe thai in dignitee,
> For patriarches and prophetes in poustee thai excede,
> And vertues aungelike taking, on some wise, hede:
> For preestis the sacrament makes, þat aungels may noght do,
> Nor patriarkes nor prophetes moght noght attigne þerto.

> Be Marie Jhesus Gods Soun was on tyme incarnate,
> And oft be the preest is brede to flesshe transsubstanciate.
> Preestis for the sacrament shuld we honour forthy,
> Whaym Crist thus has ordeigned to sacre his preciousse body.

Line 1900 contains one of the few instances of a passive-construction, "trans-substanciate", a past participle, *with* an explicit agent: the priest. As a consequence of this argument, the priest, surpassing in dignity the angels, both patriarchs and prophets, and even the Virgin Mary ("on tyme ... And oft"), is second only to the Trinity. Note further that there is a marginal gloss to line 1900, "transsubstanciate", "turned fro o kinde of substaunce to anothere", that contains the native form "turned" we have already encountered in Section 2 and shall encounter again in Section 4.4. Not being an expert on Wyclif's textual background, I do not know whether he knew the *Speculum Humanae Salvationis*, but a comparison of Wyclif's "þus power þat prestis han standeþ not in transsubstansinge of þe oste" with the *Mirour's* "in poustee thai excede"(l. 1895), and "Preestis for the sacrament shuld we honour forthy" (1901), is quite intriguing.[32]

Pursuing the theme "the dignity and power of the priest" somewhat further, we find an interesting account of it in LOLLSERM: sermon 4 for the fourth Sunday in Advent, based on John 1:19:

> But for as miche as Johun knew (by þe Hooli Goost) þe opinion of þe peple, and wyste wel for to take vpon him þe staat and name of Crist was moost perelous synne, for hit hadde be a gret pride and blasfeme in God, þerfore at þe bigynnynge he putte awey þes estimacions and worschepe, and knelechede þat he was not Crist.
>
> Heere moun prelatis and preestes lerne at þis hooli prophete, fro þe hieste degree doun to þe lowest, þat ȝyf þe peple suppose of hem þat þei haue bi her dignitie eni power whiche þei haue not, or more þan þei haue, or in oþure wyse in baptiȝinge, or sacringe, or asoylynge of synnes, or in any oþer sacrament whiche þat þei doon, þei schulden not take þis vpon hem bi no similacion for enhauncynge of her pride and leue þe peple in þis erroure, but voide it sone fro hem for fere of hyȝe blasfemie. And so dide Seint Poule, as he telleþ in his pistel, þat wanne þe peple of Corenthis weren brouȝt in þis erroure þat þei wende þat her baptem hadde vertu of her ministres, þerfore summe seiden þei weren of Poule, and summe seiden þei weren of Petre, and summe of Apollo, and so of oþure disciples. Þere as Poule miȝte haue take þis worschepe vpon him, he voidide hit, for he wolde not leue þe peple in erroure and, for fere of blasphemie, to receyue dyuyne worschepe and lassene in ani þyng þe honoure þat longede to God aboue (cf. Cigman 1989, 45-46).

In the context of the shift of emphasis on the priest and away from the Sacrament of the Eucharist, there is a further "transformation" in the debate on "transubstantiation", concerning the "forma verborum" used by the priest in the act of consecration. Examining the play *Everyman*, we find that it also contains a brief reference to the concept and doctrine of "transubstantiation" in ll. 731-739:

> God wyll you to saluacyon brynge,
> For preesthode excedeth all other thynge:
> To vs holy scrypture they do teche,
> And conuerteth man fro synne, heuen to reche;
> God hath to them more power gyuen
> Than to ony aungell that is in heuen.
> With v. wordes he may consecrate,
> Goddes body in flesshe and blode to make,
> And handeleth his Maker bytwene his handes.

Note in particular the emphasis on the dignity of priesthood (732) and the native construction for "transubstantiari": "to make" (738; see also below, Section 4.4). The "v. wordes" mentioned in l. 737 are "hoc est enim corpus meum", taken from the Roman missal (see also Section 4.4, *N-Town Play*). Looking at the earlier tradition, represented in this study by the Chanter and Wetheringsette,[33] we note that only *four* "uerba transsubstantialia" are mentioned, the words found in the gospels of Matthew, Mark, and Luke. However, as early as 1287, in Bishop Quinel's statutes for the diocese of Exeter, we find *five* "uerba": "Quia vero per hec verba: Hoc est *enim* corpus meum, *et non per alia*" (emphasis mine), the "forma verborum" of the Roman missal, based on *Matt.* 26:26-28, *Mark* 14:22-24, and *Luke* 22:19-20.[34] This addition of *enim*, an affirmative and causal conjunction, I take as indicative of a rhetorical strategy chosen to affirm the new *doctrine* of "transubstantiation" since the Fourth Lateran Council.[35] The consecration formula with *enim* we find, for example, in the York ordinary of the mass, transmitted in an early fifteenth-century MS:[36]

> Qui pridie quam pateretur, accepit panem in sanctas et venerabiles manus suas, *Hic elevet oculos* et elevatis oculis suis in cœlum, ad te Deum Patrem suum omnipotentem, tibi gratias agens, benedixit, ac *Hic tangat hostiam* fregit deditque discipulis suis dicens: Accipite et manducate ex hoc omnes, Hoc est enim corpus meum.

Concerning this "new" consecration formula, we might refer to *Matt.* 26:28: "hic est *enim* sanguis meus novi testamenti" (emphasis mine). Nevertheless, as the quotations from Wetheringsette, Gerald, and the Chanter clearly show, in the earlier discussions there was no *enim* in the passages referring to the consecration of the host. A further investigation of the passive and active uses of the verbal forms of the concept "transubstantiation", as well as that of "enim"[37] finding its way into the consecration-formula of the Missal (note that some revisions of the missal are due to Innocent III and to the new religious orders) might lead to new insights into the history of both the concept and the doctrine and, indeed, into Wyclif's attack against the abuses of the doctrine.[38]

The second occurrence of the term "transubstantiation" in my corpus is in Book 9, chapter 31, "De pascha" of John Trevisa's *On the Properties of Things*.

> Þe ferthe priuylege [of Cene Day] is in presentinge of þe maundement of oure lord, and þat is done in waisschinge of feet and in fedinge of pore men and in vnhilinge and waisschinge of auters. Þanne þe Cene Day is day of reconciliacion, of transubstanciacioun, of consacracioun and of sacringe, of halewinge of oynement, day of fedinge and of waisschinge. Also to oure ester longiþ Goode Fryday, for þat day oure lord soffrid deþ; bycause of his passioun alle Frydayes ben in reuerence and worschipe (cf. *On the Properties,* 548).

This quotation from John Trevisa's translation of Bartholomæus Anglicus' *De Proprietatibus Rerum*[39] also shows, by the spelling of the term, that, in the late fourteenth century, "transubstantiation" had been well assimilated into the English language, at least that of certain classes with a solid academic background. Trevisa's text also contains other important verbal elements, "day ... of consacracioun and of sacringe", and these elements allow us to accomodate the single occurrence of *transbeacion,* in my file SPECSAC, under the term and concept *transubstantiation* (see Section 4.4).

Given that, in both Chaucer (cf. *CT*, VI.539: "And turnen substaunce into accident") and Gower, we find a number of references to the concept "transubstantiation" but not the term itself, let us modify the parameter specifications for an extended electronic search in the corpus. The new specifications are based on those terms we have encountered so far in the passages dealing with both the concept and the doctrine in the thematic context of the Sacrament of the Eucharist: "body, bread, host, wine; substance, subject, accident; consecration, sacrament" and the Middle English 'sacringe' and related forms.

4.4 Some Transformations and Translations of "Transubstantiation"

After the issue of Decree 21 of the Fourth Lateran Council, "Omnis utriusque sexus" and its treatment in the diocesan statutes, the Sacrament of the Eucharist occupied a prominent place in works of religious instruction.[40] Let us therefore examine three manuals of religious instruction, one composed for the laity and two for the clergy, and their treatment of the new doctrine of *transubstantiation.*

Among the early Middle English works of religious instruction, Robert Mannyng's *Handlyng Synne*[41] contains a detailed section on the sacrament of the altar (9891-10810). Explaining this difficult sacrament to his lay audience, Mannyng opens this section with a prayer for divine assistance (9891-9902). In his account of both the concept and doctrine of *transubstantiation,* Mannyng refers his audience to God's omnipotence (9961-9974):

Yn þe olde lawe, þus ys wryte,
Boþe Iewes and crysten weyl hyt wete
"God seyd, and hyt was wroȝt;
He commaunded alle þyng of noȝt."
Þese wurdes are verry and clere;
Dauyd hem seyth yn þe sautere;
Syn he made alle þat noȝt er was,
Lesse maystry were hyt þan yn kas,
For to chaunge þe lekenes
Yn-to an ouþer þyng þat es;
Þe lykenes of bred and wyne,
Yn flesshe and blode to turne hyt ynne;
Yn flessh and blode þe brede be broȝt,
Syn he made alle of noȝt.

This section contains the necessary elements of the concept transubstantiation: bread, wine, words, and "lekenes/lykenes"; the term, however, Mannyng "translates" for his audience of laymen into the less difficult and, as yet, unproblematic terms *chaunge, yn ... be broȝt,* and *turne.*[42] To confirm the "miraculous" process of transubstantiation, Mannyng uses the popular *exemplum* from the *Vitas Patrum* (cf. Migne, *PL*, 73, cols. 978D-980A): the miraculous[43] transformation of the host into a child's body (9999-10072; quotation: 10061-10070):

Þan gan he cry, with loude steuene,
"Mercy! Goddys sone of heuene!
Þe brede þat y sagh on þe auter lye,
Hyt ys þy body, y se hyt with ye.
Of þe brede, þurgh sacrament,
To flesshe and blode hyt ys alle went;
Þys y beleue, and euer y shal;
For verryly we se hyt alle."
Whan he and þey were alle certeyn,
Yn forme of brede hyt turned aȝeyn;

Note again Mannyng's "translations" "To...went" and, in particular, "Yn *forme* ... hyt turned aȝeyn."[44] In John Myrk's *Instructions for Parish Priests*, the Sacrament of the Eucharist is frequently mentioned, though indirectly, by phrases like "Goddes body, Goddes blode", with a total of seven occurrences. In his first treatment of this sacrament, 244-263, Myrk[45] also uses a "translation" of the term "transubstaniation", l. 261, "ys ... made", and again we find the noun "forme":

Teche hem þenne wyth gode entent,
To be-leue on that sacrament;

> That þey receyue in forme of bred,
> Hyt ys Goddes body þat soffered ded
> Vp on the holy rode tre,
> To bye owre synnes & make vs fre.
> Teche hem þenne, neuer þe later,
> Þat in þe chalys ys but wyn & water
> That þey receyueth for to drynke
> After that holy hoselynge;
>
> …
>
> But teche hem alle to leue sadde,
> Þat hyt þat ys in þe awter made,
> Hyt ys verre Goddes blode
> That he schedde on þe rode.

Myrk returns to the Sacrament of the Eucharist in ll. 1769-1804, and in his section "Adhuc alia necessaria capellano scire" (1839-1912).

The new search parameters reveal two passages in PIERS, XII.82-87 and XIX.386-394, dealing with both the concept and the doctrine. In the section on grace, "Ac grace is a gifte of God, and of greet love spryngeth" (XII.68), based on the exposition of John 8:3–9, the woman taken in adultery, we read:

> Holy Kirke knoweth this – that Cristes writyng saved;
> So clergie is confort to creatures that repenten,
> And to mansede men meschief at hire ende.
> 'For Goddes body myghte noght ben of breed withouten clergie,
> The which body is bothe boote to the rightfulle,
> And deeth and dampnacion to hem that deyeth yvele;

In XIX.386-394, in the long section on Confession, the perspective is somewhat different since the emphasis is clearly on the gift of Christ (Grace):

> Cometh,' quod Conscience, 'ye Cristene, and dyneth,
> That han laboured lelly al this Lenten tyme.
> Here is breed yblessed, and Goddes body therunder.
> Grace, thorugh Goddes word, gaf Piers power,
> Myght to maken it, and men to ete it after
> In helpe of hir heele ones in a monthe,
> Or as ofte as thei hadde nede, tho that hadde ypaied
> To Piers pardon the Plowman, *redde quod debes.*'

Before looking at some later Middle English sermons and Wycliffite texts and their treatment of the concept and, in particular, the doctrine, of "transubstantiation", let us examine the type "transbeacion" contained in Tables 1 and 3 above. In the sermon for Good Friday the anonymous author of this section of the SPECSAC states:

> There ben two causes why the body of Crist is reseruyd and kept in the day of Cena Domini. The first cause is for that there schuld noon dye withoute þei reseyuyd of the body of God. And þat ordeynede Innocent þe pope. The secund cause is for in tho two dayes oweþ al men for to reseyue Godis body and specially men of religion. But it is noȝt lawefull þat day for to halowe and make the blode of Crist for to be kept for wyne is moyste and may noȝt wele be kept and may of necligence be lykkyd and þerfore it is noȝt reseruyd.... This day is noȝt þe wyne consecrate by the body immyttid and put to, but it is made sanctificat. Consecracion is transbeacion and ouerblissyng. And þat is sanctificatyd þat is made holy by holy wordes (EETS ed., 111).

As the editor of the *Speculum Sacerdotale,* Edward H. Weatherly, has pointed out, this portion of the text is based on John Beleth's *Summa de ecclesiasticis officiis,* chap. 99 "Quare corpus Christi reseruetur in die cene et non sanguis":

> Si autem queratur, utrum uinum, quod ea die sumitur in communione, adtactu dominici corporis consecretur, licet plurimorum scripta hoc uideantur astruere, nos magis ueritatem sequentes et sanctorum patrum traditiones dicimus illud uinum non esse consecratum adtactu illo, sed sanctificatum. Est enim differentia inter consecratum et sanctificatum. Consecratum est, quod in consecratione transsubstantiatur, sanctificatum, quod per uerborum sanctificationem efficitur sanctum sine transsubstantiatione ut aqua benedicta (Beleth, *Summa,* 183).

Migne's text of Beleth's *Summa* contains slightly different version of the first use of the verbal form: "Consecratum dicitur quod in consecratione, ut ita dicam, transubstantiatur."[46] Note that in one of the early discussions of the new concept "transubstantiation", the phrase "ut ita dicam" occurring in a similar context ("In hac autem consecratione nullius qualitatis fit transformatio, set huius substantie in illam, ut ita dicam, transubstantio uel transmutatio") has been interpreted by Goering (1991), 150, to imply "a conscious novelty or innovation on the part of the author". Since Migne's text is based on Cornelius Laurimanus' edition (1553) who, as Douteil, CCCM XLI, 35*, briefly points out, "das Werk Bel-eths in seinem Geist stilistisch umformte und bearbeitete", it is difficult to deter-mine -- in the absence of textual variants *ad loc.* in Douteil's edition -- whether the subjunctive-formula in Migne's text is based on a particular MS of Beleth's *Summa* used by Laurimanus, or, perhaps more likely, should be taken as Lauri-manus' carefully and cautiously formulated "re-introduction" and affirmation of the concept, and, particularly, doctrine, in the days of the counter reformation.

Whereas in the three manuals examined so far, and especially in Mannyng and Myrk, the instruction on the Sacrament of the Eucharist can be said to be performed with a tone of benevolence and real concern for both the laity and fellow curates, we encounter a very different mode of presentation in later texts which originated during and after the Wycliffite- and Lollard-debate (see Section 4.5). However, as in Mannyng and Myrk, in these texts the concept and doctrine of "transubstantiation" is also presented without the use of the term itself. Texts printed by Hudson (1978), and especially text 1, "Wyclif's Confession on the Eucharist" (17-18), do not use the term "transubstantiation" but the concept is present and is represented by the terms "bread, wine; sacrament; body; accident, subject, and substance":[47]

> But þe most heresie þat God sufferide come tyl his kirke is to trowe þat þis sacrament is an accident wiþouten a substance, and may on no wyse be Goddus body. ...Owe! howe grete diuersite is betwene vs þat trowes þat þis sacrament is verray brede in his kynde, and betuene heretykus þat tellus þat þis is an accident wiþouten a subiecte. For before þat þe fende, fader of lesyngus, was lowside, was neuer þis gabbyng contryuede.

In the three volumes of *English Wycliffe Sermons* edited by Gradon and Hudson, I have not encountered the term "transubstantiation", but the concept and the attack on the doctrine, signalled by the terms noted above, can be found in several sermons. Thus, in sermon 46 (for Easter Sunday, based on Mark 16:1-7) there is a detailed reference to the concept "transubstantiation":

> Her aftur þis wyt men may large þis gospel, and trete what matere þat þei wenon schulde profiʒte to þe puple. But hit is comunly teld of þe sacrament of þe auter, and how men schal disposon hem now to take þis sacrament. And hit is seid comunly þat, as þese hooly wymmen hadden left þer formere synne and take þeir fresch deuocion, so men schulden come to þe chirche to take þis hooly sacrament, and þus come wiþ þese wymmen wiþ lyʒt of þe sonne. And þus men schulden cloþen hem wiþ þese þre vertewys: byleue, hope and charite to receyue þis sacrament. Byleue is furst nedful, and algatis of þis breed, how hit is Godis body by uertew of Cristis wordis. And so hit is kyndely breed, as Powle seiþ, but hit is sacramentally verrey Godis body. And herfore seiþ Austyn þat þat þing is breed þat þine eyʒen tellon þe and þat þow seest wiþ hem. For hit was not trowed byfore þe feend was loosyd þat þis worþi sacrament was accident wiþowte suget; and ʒeet dwellon trewe men in þe oolde byleue, and laten frerus fowle hemsylf in þer newe heresye. For we trowen þat þer is betture þing þan Godis body, syþ þe holy Trinnyte is in eche place. But owre byleue is set upon þis poynt: what is þis sacrede host, and not what þing is þere (cf. Gradon and Hudson, I, 431-432).

A similar exposition of the concept "transubstantiation" can be found in the sermon entitled "Of Mynystris In Þe Chirche" (cf. II, 328-365):

> And, as anentis sacramentis, wiþ tellyngus of doutis in Godus lawe, þe world haþ mad þis court vnable to knowon owt of þis mater; for where Crist telluþ in his gospel þat þe hoost, wenne it is sacrud, is Cristus body in figure and verey breed in his kynde, freris seyn now þat it is nowt, or accident wiþowte suget. And, as þei sclaundren, þe court seiþ þus, and oþur ground han þei noon. But it was seyd in oold tyme, byfore þat þe frerus comen in, þat as Crist is God and mon, so þis hoost is bred and Godis body; but on dyuerse maner as Baptist was Hely, and not Hely. Ny Godus body is þe beste þing þat is in place of þis hoost, for þere is þe Trinnyte þat is betture þen Godus body. And cristene men axe not what is þere, but what ys þat as Crist spekuþ. And þus bytwene þe pope and freris feiþ of þe gospel is put obac and a new þing is feyned, boþe aȝen resoun and feiþ and monnys wyt wiþ al pref; and vnneþis dremys may meyntene it. Þus wul þe pope declare Goddes lawe and susteyne pes (cf. Gradon and Hudson, II, 363-364).

Sometimes, the tone of the preacher is quite angry, as in sermon 206 (III, 247-248), based on *John* 6:55-58, "Caro mea uere est cibus":

> But Goddis lawe biddiþ þat we shulden not speke fals of oure neyebore, and it is myche more synne to speke fals of Crist, boþe God and man. Þes ben to ruyde heretikis þat seyen þey etyn Crist bodily, and seyen þey parten eche membre of hym, necke and bac, hed and foot. And alle siche heresies spryngen for þey witen not what þis oost is: þis oost is bred in his kynde, as ben oþere oostis vnsacrid, and sacramentaliche Goddis body, for Crist seiþ so þat may not lye. And so, ȝif þis sacrament be foulid in þat þat it is bred or wyn, it may not þus be defoulid in þingis whiche it figuriþ. And so a man brekiþ not Goddis body ne drynkiþ his blood wiþ his mouþ, al ȝif he ete and drynke þe bred and þe wyn þat is þes; for þey ben not þes in kynde, as Baptist was not in kynde Hely. And þus a mous etiþ not Cristis body, al ȝif he ete þis sacrament, for þe mous fayliþ gostly witt to chewe in hym þis bileue.

For the last part of the argument, see the teaching concerning the keeping of the host, as stated, for example, in Myrk's *Instructions for Parish Priests,* 1. 1893 ff.[48] Before turning to a different genre, let us examine a further sermon in the edition by Gradon and Hudson,[49] sermon 67 (II, 65-70), based on *Luke* 21:14-19, "ponite in cordibus uestris":

> It was takon as byleue, longe byfore þat frerys cam in, þat þe sacryd hoost þat men seen at yȝe is verreyly Godus body, by vertew of his wordys.

Frerys seyn þat þis is false, but it is an accident wiþowton any suget; and þus þei gylon þe puple....And herfore, but ȝif þe frere brynge vndir his comun seel, what is þe sacred hoost, þei wole not comune wiþ hym. For, as seyn Iohn seiþ, whoeuere gretuþ an heretyke schal haue of his synne, what man euere he be, and þus ȝif a trew man loue more Crist þan þe worldus fame, he may liȝtly wiþ worschipe auoyde suche false frerus. And certis þis dede were vnsuspecte boþe to God and man. For ȝif þei han a ryȝt byleue, þei schulden tellon it for charyte, and ȝif þer byleue were false, þei schuldon wylle þat it were destruyed. And algatis þei wyton wel, þat þei varyon in byleue fro þe gospel and comun puple, and monye weyes disseyue men, for þei telle not what is þat, but þat þere is Godys body. But þese ydiotis schilden wyte, þat boþe þere and euerywhere is betture þing þan Godys body, for þe Hooly Trinnyte is in ech place. And so men axen what is þat, þat þe preest sacreþ, and aftur he brekuþ, and þat men worschipon as Godys body, but not accident wiþowton suget. And þus defaute of ryȝt byleue, practisud among þese freris, schulde dampne hem as heretykes, and take hem in þer owne falshede (II, 69-70).

In some further Lollard texts, the term "transubstantiation" also is avoided, but both the concept and the doctrine are discussed in detail. Thus, in my file UPLAND, the doctrine is taken up by the terms noted at the end of Section 4.3:

Frere, whi sclaundre ȝe trewe preestis & othere trewe meke men of þe sacrament of Goddis bodi, for þei seien þat þe holi breed duli sacrid is Goddis bodi in foorme of breed, & ȝe seien þat it is an accident wiþ outen subiect, & not Goddis bodi. Frere, who ben eritikis here & fer fro Cristis wordis, þat took þe breed & blissid it & brak it & seide, þis is my bodi; & Seint Poul seiþ, þe breed þat we breken is Goddis bodi; and Seynt Austin seiþ, þat not eche breed is Goddis bodi but þat breed þat reseyueth blissynge is Goddis bodi. & to þis acordiþ þe oold doctouris & comoun bileue bifor þat freris camen in ouer þe walle a þousande ȝeer & more (cf. Heyworth 1968, 71).

In "Friar Daw's Reply", we find the following exposition (cf. Heyworth 1968, 98-99). Note that a new term is introduced into the debate: "figure", a term we have already encountered in GOWERCA, IV.2563 (see Section 2.3, above).

Anoþer mater þou mouest, Iak, moost to be chargid,
Of þe solempne sacrament of Cristis owne bodye,
Conteyned in figure of brede, sacrifise for synne.
Þou drawist a þorn out of þin hele & puttist it in oure,
Þou berist vs on honde þat we seien þer is not Cristis bodye,
But roundnesse & whitenesse, and accident wiþouten suget.
Iak, we seie wiþ Holy Chirche þat þer is Cristis body

& not material breed with Wiclyf ȝour maistir
Þe whiche put þer but as a signe & not verre Cristis bodi,
Aftir a manere spekyng þat Holy Chirche vsiþ –
As we clepen Crist a stoon, a lomb, & a lioun,
& noon of þese is Crist but oonli in figure.
Þis heresie holde not we but ȝe his false folowers,
Priuyly as ȝe doren & openli ȝe wolden
Ne were þe sharp ponishinge of ȝour former fadirs.
And now I wil þee telle þe freris confiteor
Touching to þis sacrament how þat þei bileuen.
Þei seie breed is turned in to fleish, & wyne in to blood,
Þourȝ þe myȝt of oure God & vertue of his wordis:
Þe fleish is mete, þe blood is drynke, & Crist dwelliþ,
No þing rasyd, no þing diuidid, but oonli broken in signe,
& as moche is in oo partie as is al þe hole.
Þer leeueþ not of þe breed but oonli þe licnesse,
Which þat abidiþ þerinne noon substeyned substans;
It is deþ to yuel, lyf to good, encresing of oure grace.
It wole not be confect but oonly of a preest
Þat lawfulli is ordeyned bi Holy Chirche keies.
And so carpenters ne sowters, card makers ne powchers,
Drapers ne cutellers, girdelers, coferers, ne coruysers,
Ne no manere of artificeris þis sacrament mowe treten
But þe priuite of preesthode wer prickid in her soulis.
& ȝit ȝour sect susteynes wommen to seie massis,
Shewyng to trete a sacrament as preestes þat þei were,
Reuersynge holy doctours & decree of Holy Chirche.

Again, we encounter a native construction for "transubstantiari": *is turned in to*.
In addition, note the emphasis on the power of the priest, "It wole not be confect
but oonly of a preest", pointed out in Section 4.3 in connection with the
Fasciculus Morum. In the text known under the title "Upland's Rejoinder" we
find the layman's reply to the friar's accusations and denouncements (cf.
Heyworth 1968, 113):

Þou saist, Dawe, as þou felist, þat þere is Cristis body;
Bot I afferme faiþfully þat þat is Cristis body.
Daw, aske þi capped maisters as if þai were heritikes,
What is þe sacred host – & grounde hem in scripture –
To whiche we knele & doffe our hodes & don alle þis wirchip.
And I bileue þat sacred whiche is boþe whit & rounde,
Is verrei Cristes body, as men shuld bileue,
& did to þe tyme þat Sathanas was vnbounde.
Þe wittnesse of þis reson is Crist & his apostles,

With many holi doctoures of þe thousande ȝere;
Bot þis ȝe falsely forsake, with alle ȝour secte or many,
& blynden þe puple with heresie, & leuen Goddis lawe,
For ȝe sayen þer is Cristis body & nouȝt þat sacred host.

Leaving the debate between Lollards and Friars and examining some of the reactions to this debate that can be found in sermons composed and preached by beneficed priests, we also find that the concept and doctrine of "transubstantiation" is referred to indirectly by the terms noted at the end of Section 4.3.

In some the sermons edited by W. O. Ross,[50] when expounding the Sacrament of the Eucharist, the tone of the preacher becomes quite angry, since an attack on the doctrine of "transubstantiation", constituting, as we have seen above, the dignity of the priest, also meant an attack on his authority and power (see Section 4.5). Thus, in the sermon (No. 22) based on John, 6:59, "Qui manducat hunc panem, vivet in eternum" are a series of angry addresses and an emphasis on the traditional teaching of the church and the authority of the priest:

And ryght þe same body þat died on þe Crosse and þis day rose verry God and man, þe same bodie is on þe Sacrament on þe awtur in forme of brede....And anoþur, me þenkeþ þou þat arte a lewde men, þou shudest not fardere entermett þe þan holychurche techeþ þe. And þat may þou see by ensampull of þe Hoste, in þe whiche Hoste is Goddes bodie in þe forme of brede....Also in þe savour in þi mouthe it semeþ brede, and it is not so; for-why certeynly it is þe same flessh þat was borne of Oure Ladye Seynt Mary on Cristemasse day. So I sey, ȝiff þou shuldest deme aftur þe sight of þin eye, þan þou shuldest erre aȝeyns þe feythe. And þer-fore þou þat arte a lewd man, it suffice to þe to beleue as holychurche techeþ þe....By þis feeste þat Crist made I vndirstond þe grett feest þat oure Lorde makeþ to euery Cristen man with v loves and ij fisshes. Crist with oo loffe þis day, þat is ys owen precious body in þe forme of brede, fediþ many hundreþ þousaundes of men. But I prey þe, what is þe releue of þis brede? For-sothe þei be þe argvmentes and þe skill þat may be of þe Sacramente, and þat longeþ not to þe, shewynge well Crist, þat he wold lat no man geþur þe releue but is disciples, shewynge to þe þat arte a lewd man þat it is inowȝþ to þe to beleven as holychurche techeþ þe and lat þe clerkes alone with þe argumentes. For þe more þat þou disputes þer-of, þe farþur þou shall be þer-fro (Ross, 126-128).

After this indirect presentation of the issues connected with the doctrine of "transubstantiation", the anonymous author, like Mannyng, uses an exemplum to convince his audience of the truth of the sacrament of the altar and of "transubstantiation":

"ʒe," seid þe Iewe, "ʒe wene þat be þe vertew of þe wordes þat þe preest seis at þe masse, þat þe bred turneþ in-to Goddes fleshe and is blode." "ʒe, for-sothe," seid þe Cristen man, "and in þat feythe will I liff and die." "ʒe, ʒe," seid þe Iewe, "þou and oþur are fowle deseyved. For I dare ley to þe xxᵗⁱ li. þat myn hounde shall eten hym, þat I haue at home. And ʒiff þat he were God, certen, I am ryght sikere þat he shuld not mow eten hym."....Þan anoon þe Cristen man ranne to þe preeste þe whiche þat houseled hym, and told hym how it was and of þe dogge, suche an vnresonable beeste, how þat he did is dewe reuerence to Goddes bodie in þe forme of brede (Ross, 129-130).

This translation of "transubstantiation" by "turneþ" and the reference to "forma" we find not only in this sermon; another sermon (No. 39) in the collection also provides a further illustration of the "translation" of "transubstantiari". In this sermon, based on Matth. 2:2, "Natus est rex", the preacher says:

Also it is full wondurfull how þat oure modur Eve was made of a ribbe of Adam, as scripture wittnesse, Genesis 2ᵈᵒ. It is also a full gret wondur how þat in þe Sacrament of the awtur of brede and wynne is made verry Cristes fleshe and is blode, as scripture wittenesseth, Iohanis 6ᵗᵒ. And also it is a gret merveyll oþur miracle þat a maide is a childis modur. All þise beþ gret myracles and mervelous to mans witt, and all must be beleved vp-pon peyn of euer lastyng dampnacion. And þer-fore we þat beleve þus, lat vs not be to inquisitiff in oure own wittis, for God forbedeþ it and seyþ to euerych of vs þise wordes, "Com þou no nere hidurward. For þo þinges," seyþ oure Lord, "þat beþ a-boven kynde, seche not to knowe hem naturally, but raþur," seyþ God, "doþ of þi shoes of þi feete" – þat is to sey, þe sotell coueryngus of þin affeccion for þis erthe þat þin affeccion stondeþ on in þis – "dowtynge it is an holy grounde: Solue calciamenta pedum tuorum quia locus in quo stas terra sancta est" (Ross, 223).

Again, we encounter a native passive construction, "is made", and a similar authoritative tone, reinforced by the threat "and all must be beleved vppon peyn of euer lastyng dampnacion". The tone and mode of argumentation used in the anti-Lollard campaign are also evident in a sermon (transmitted in an early fifteenth-century MS) printed by Owst (1926, 137-138):

ffor aristotel teches, as kindely resoun acordes, thᵗ the accidentes of brede or wyne, thᵗ is (to) say the colour, the savour, and so forth of other, mowe not be bot in substance of brede or wyne after ther kinde. Bot the doctrine of holy chirch is thᵗ in this blessed sacrament, be special miracle of god above kinde, the colour, the savour, and other accidentes of brede and wyne bene ther wᵗ out the kindely subjecte, thᵗ is to say wᵗ out the substance of brede and wyne thᵗ was before the consecracioun. And for als mich as this doctrine of holy chirch is aȝeyns the principlas of philosophi th^t is naturele science, therfore the forsaide maister of lollardes repreved it, and so he erred himself, and many other made to erre touching the bileve of this holiest sacrament, the whech ȝiven more credence to him for the opinion of his gret clergy than to the trew doctrine of holy chirch.

To conclude this eclectic survey of some Middle English "translations and transformations of transubstantiation", let us return to the genre "mediaeval drama" (see also Section 4.3, above).[51] Our new search parameters reveal that the file TOWNELEY (*The Towneley Plays*) in my corpus contains a short reference to "transubstantiation", in play 26, "The Resurrection" (339-350; emphasis mine; cf. EETS ed., I,345-346):

> For I am veray prynce of peasse,
> And synnes seyr I may releasse,
> And whoso will of synnes seasse
> And mercy cry,I grauntt theym here a measse
> In brede, myn awne body.
> That ilk veray brede of lyfe
> *Becommys* my fleshe in wordys fyfe:
> Whoso it resaues in syn or stryfe
> Bese dede foreuer,
> And whoso it takys in rightwys lyfe
> Dy shall he neuer.

Concerning the sacramental formula in l. 346, "in wordys fyfe", note the similar presentation in *Everyman*, l. 737, quoted in Section 4.3 above. As Stevens and Cawley (II, 607, *add* 346) point out, this formula is is based on the Roman missal (see the discussion in Section 4.3, above). A further reference to both the concept and the doctrine can be found in the *N-Town Play*, play 27, "The Last Supper", 361-380 (EETS ed., 277-228, emphasis mine):

> Þis fygure xal sesse; anothyr xal folwe þerby,
> Weche xal be of my body, þat am ȝoure hed,
> Weche xal be schewyd to ȝow be a *mystery*
> Of my flesch and blood in *forme* of bred....
> Wherfore to þe, Fadyr of Hefne þat art eternall,
> Thankyng and honor I ȝeld onto þe,
> To whom be þe Godhed I am eqwall,
> But be my manhod I am of lesse degré.
> Wherefore I as man worchep þe Deyté,
> Thankyng þe, fadyr, þat þu wylt shew þis *mystery;*
> And þus þurwe þi myth, fadyr, and blyssyng of me,
> Of þis þat was bred *is mad* my body.

Whereas in the mediaeval plays examined so far, the doctrine of "transubstantiation" is treated in well established and rather traditional terms, "consecrate, miracle, to be made" and so on, *The Chester Mystery Cycle* offers a quite different account of the doctrine in play 18, "The Resurrection", 170-177, performed by the skinners (cf. EETS ed., I, 345; emphasis mine):

> I am verey bread of liffe.
> From heaven I light and am send.
> Whoe eateth that bread, man or wiffe,
> Shall lyve with me withowt end.
> And that bread that I you give,
> Your wicked life to amend,
> *Becomes* my fleshe through your *beleeffe*
> And doth release your synfull band.

In the commentary to their edition, Lumiansky and Mills (EETS SS 9, 282-283, *ad* 154-85) note that l. 176-177 "are difficult and perhaps wilfully obscure, they appear to suggest that an act of faith on the part of the recipient effects transubstantiation, a view partially but not wholly fulfilling Roman Catholic and Anglican criteria." Worth noting in the collection of *English Wycliffite Sermons,* in the tract "Vae Octuplex" (see Section 2.10) is a similar concept (cf. Gradon and Hudson, II, 375-376; Hudson (1978, 81; 178, notes to 238 ff.):

> And þe þrydde cawtel of þe fend, in whiche he traueyluþ most, is to uarye þe byleue þat God hymself haþ ordeynot, as we may see oponly of þe sacred hoost, þat is, þe whyte þing and rownd þat þe preest haþ sacred, and is parceyued monye weyes wiþ bodily wyttis, þat cristen men seyn is Godus body in forme of breed, as trewe clerkis and lewede men han byleued siþ God wente to heuene. But þe feend, siþ he was lowsud, haþ mouyd frerus to reuerse þis, and as þei seyn, þer newe seyntus and newe doctoures þat þei han, techen þat þis sacrament is an accident wiþowte suget, or ellis noȝt; for hit is quantite and qualite. Þis knewe not Ierom, ne Austyn, ne Ambrose, siþ Ierom seiþ þus aftur tretyng of þis mater, 'Here we þat þat bred þat Crist took in his hondis and blessyd it, and brac it, and ȝaf hise disciples for to eton it, is þe body of owre Lord, sauyour of mankynde siþ he seiþ and may not lyȝe þat þis þing is his body.' Seynt Austyn seiþ þus, and reson acordeþ þerwiþ, þat þat þing þat men seen wiþ þer yȝen is verrey breed, but þat þat *byleue* axiþ, þe breed is Godus body. And herfore seiþ Ambrose þat þat þing þat byfore was bred ys now maad Godus body by vertwe of Cristus wordis. Sich wytnesse of hooly wryt is not charged of þese frerus, but wytnesse of þer owne felowes þat þei holden more þan Crist. And, al ȝif þei knowon wel þat comunes byleuon as we

seyn, ꝫeet þei pursewon trewe men, and disseyuon comunes by false wordis, whois religioun is veyn (emphasis mine).

It appears that some of the views on the Sacrament of the Eucharist[52] propagated and entertained by Wyclif and his adherents have influenced this new presentation of "transubstantiation" in play 18 of *The Chester Mystery Cycle*.

4.5 Transubstantiation: The Seeds and Grapes of Wrath

At the end of Section 4.3, I noted that neither in Chaucer nor Gower do we find the term "transubstantiation", though the concept is clearly present in their work. I believe that Chaucer's allusion to the concept in the *CT*, VI.538, through the *figura* of the Pardoner, should put us on alert. In my view, Chaucer's allusion is more than a playful echo of the facetious uses of the concept in his time;[53] rather, I take it as a hint at the very real and concrete social implications of the doctrine with its inherent possibilities of the abuse and perversion of authority and power -- be it on the part of the Church and its representatives or on that of Wyclif and his followers.

In his stimulating essay, Maurice Keen argues: "I believe... that Wyclif attacked transubstantiation rather from the point of view of abuse"; and "What horrified Wyclif most of all about the doctrine of transubstantiation was just this, its carnality. The priests who followed that teaching sold the host.... A shoddy claim for physical, sacerdotal magic, that was what Wyclif thought of transubstantiation" (Keen 1986, 11 and 13). Keen's argument put forward in the last sentence[54] appears to be confirmed by a passage in part 5, chapter 15, of Reginald Pecock's *Repressor* (1455) lamenting some of the consequences of the debate over "transubstantiation":[55]

> The ix^e. principal gouernaunce for which summe of the lay peple vnwijsly and vnreuerentli blamen the clergie is this: That in the chirche ben had grete signes and sacramentis, and her vsis; as ben baptem, confermyng, hosil of Cristis bodi and blood, and othere mo; whiche sacramentis and her vsis summe of the lay peple holden *to be pointis of wicche craft and blindingis,* brouꝫt into Cristen men bi the feend and the anticrist and hise lymes. And in special thei abhorren aboue alle othere the hiꝫest and worthiest signe and sacrament of alle othere, the sacrament of the auter, the preciose bodi and blood of Crist for us hangid in the cros and for us out sched; in so miche that thei not oonli scornen it, but thei haaten it, mys callen it bi foule names, and wolen not come her thankis into the bodili chirche, whilis thilk sacrament is halewid, tretid, and vsid in the masse (III, 563; emphasis mine).

But to return to Chaucer: Is it a mere coincidence that Chaucer, through the *figura* of the Host arguing with the Parson (II.1172-1177) – and note the terms of abuse aimed at *both* parties concerned in the debate"

Oure Host answerde, "O Jankin, be ye there?
I smelle a Lollere in the wynd," quod he.
"Now! goode men," quod oure Hoste, "herkeneth me;
Abydeth, for Goddes digne passioun,
For we schal han a predicacioun;
This Lollere heer wil prechen us somwhat."

introduces the theme "Lollardism" from a decidedly negative point of view? The Host's "I smelle", I believe, can only be taken as a stigmatization: 'those stinking Lollards'. In his lecture, Paul Strohm, arguing from a different theoretical perspective, has pointed out some of the very real and concrete social consequences of the debate over "transubstan-tiation"[56] resulting from the stigmatization of both factions concerned in this debate of the doctrine. And, as we have seen above, in Section 4.4, both parties used the strategy of invective to denounce their respective opponents. We should not forget that these texts, to borrow a phrase coined by Hermann Gunkel[57] and used in recent studies on the theory of literary genres, had a very concrete "Sitz im Leben" ("place in life") and were addressed to a very real audience in a very real social and political situation. And the invective found in some of these texts, the "seeds of wrath", brought forth the "grapes of wrath", some of which have been pointed out by Strohm (1995).

As the quotations from Ælfric and Hobbes at the beginning of Section 4, as well as the *exemplum* in the *Vitas Patrum* (cf. *PL*, 73, col. 0979A: "et errabat pro eo quod erat idiota, et dicebat, non esse naturaliter corpus Christi panem quem sumimus, sed figuram ejus esse"), clearly show, the debate of the traditional concept of "transubstantiation" (cf. Ælfric's subjunctives "mage beon awend" and "weorðe awend") was a *recurring* debate in connection with one of the *central* sacraments: the Sacrament of the Eucharist. After the institution of the *doctrine* of transubstantiation, it was also a highly *political* debat -- and *not* just an abstract, academic debate of some (not infrequently rather vaguely defined) philosophical concepts during the thirteenth, fourteenth, and fifteenth centuries concentrating on the (fairly recent) term and the recent doctrine of "transubstantiation". That this debate and its social and political consequences -- the grapes of wrath -- has to be seen in a larger historical context becomes apparent in a most pessimistic passage in which Dean Swift's *figura*, Lemuel Gulliver, reflects on some of the causes of the Thirty Years' War. In one of his discussions with his Houyhnhnm master, Lemuel Gulliver refers to these *very real* consequences resulting from the hotly disputed *doctrine* of "transubstantiation" and from the abuse of authority, custom and power by *both* parties:[58]

He asked me what were the usual causes or motives that made one country go to war with another. I answered they were innumerable, but I should only mention a few of the chief. Sometimes the ambition of princes, who never think they have land or people enough to govern: sometimes the corruption of ministers, who engage their master in a war in order to stifle or divert the clamour of the subjects against their evil administration. Difference in opinions hath cost many millions of lives: for instance, whether *flesh* be *bread,* or *bread* be *flesh;* whether the juice of a certain *berry* be *blood* or *wine;* whether *whistling* be a vice or a virtue; whether it be better to *kiss a post,* or throw it into the fire; what is the best colour for a *coat,* whether *black, white, red* or *grey;* and whether it should be *long* or *short, narrow* or *wide, dirty* or *clean,* with many more. Neither are any wars so furious and bloody, or of so long continuance, as those occasioned by difference in opinion, especially if it be in things indifferent (*Gulliver's Travels,* Pt. IV: 5, 292).

5. Conclusion

This "factophile" and "factographic" study of seventeen "trans"-formations in some Middle English texts, concludes by offering as a possible explanation for the rare occurrence of the term "transubstantiation" in the well documented and lively debate of both the concept and the doctrine in Middle English texts a passage in sermon 59 edited by Gradon and Hudson,[59] based on *John* 12:24-26, "nisi granum frumenti":

> In þis schorte gospel ben dowtus boþe of o science and oþur. Furst philosophres dowton wher seed lesuþ his forme whan it is maad a new þing, as þe gospel spekuþ here. And somme men þenkon nay, siþ þe same quantite or qualyte, or vertew, þat was furst in seed, leueþ aftur in þe fruyt, ...and siþ alle þese ben accidentis, þat may not dwelle wiþowten sughet, it semeþ þat þe same body is furst seed and aftur fruyt, and þus it may ofte chawngen fro seed to fruyt aȝen. *Here mony clepyde philosophres glaueron dyuersely;* but in þis mater Godis lawe spekuþ þus, as dyden oolde clerkis, þat þe substanunce of a body is byfore þat it be seed, and now fruyt and now seed, and now qwyc and now deed. And þus monye formes may be togydre in o þing and specially whan þe partis of þat þing ben medled togydre; and þus þe substaunce of o bodi is now of o kynde and now of oþur. And so boþe þese accidentis, quantite and qualite, may dwellon in þe same substaunce, al ȝif it be chawnghed in kyndys, and þus þis same þing, þat is now a whete corn, schal be deed and turne to gras, and afturward to monye cornys. *But variaunce in wordis in þis mater falluþ to clerkys, and schewyng of equiuocacion, þe whiche is more redy in Latyn.* II, 21-25; emphasis mine).

Eberhard-Karls-Universität Tübingen

Notes

1. The mottoes are taken from (1) David Lodge, *Small World*, Bk. 3, Ch. 1; (2) William de Montibus, *Tractatus metricus de septem sacramentis ecclesie;* and (3) John Gower, *Confessio Amantis*, V.1872-1873.

2. My "general index" is based on a total of 140 "electronic" texts, ranging from the early Middle English *Peterborough Chronicle* to the early modern play *Everyman*. This "electronic" corpus, with 2.291 million words, includes all the major literary genres. Note that this study could not have been undertaken without the fairly recent "trans"-invention: the "trans(res)istor".

3. The Appendix provides details on the electronic texts used in this study and cited by file names.

4. Note that this corpus-based survey is far from complete. The *MED* main entry "trans-" states that there are "more than seventy words from L or OF" and that "the prefix appears not to have been active in ME." All texts containing "transubstantiation" mentioned by the *MED* are considered in this study.

5. While the treatment of "transbeacion" under "transubstantiation" is based on its context and meaning, that of "transfer" is based on its etymology.

6. See *OED*, s.v. "transom", sense 6; and *MED*, s.v. "traunsom n. (c)".

7. See *MED*, s.v. "trauncen v. (2)".

8. See Beleth, *Summa*, 175: "Secunda est, quia sublatus est sponsus ecclesie tali die. Descendit enim ad inferos. Tertia est, quoniam ea die uelum templi scissum est et cornua altaris transuersa [var.: uersa] sunt, et ita non haberemus, ubi corpus Christi conficitur."

9. Note that PIERS contains a second "trans"-item: "With half a laumpe lyne in Latyn, *Ex vi transicionis,*" in XIII.151.

10. See Beadle (1982, 230-231); Stevens and Cawley (1994, II.607, *ad* 345-50) and Section 4.4.

11. Cf. EETS ed. 78.

12. The term can be found in the Prologue, 349, and in Book V.1807, 1811, and 1819.

13. For the invention of the concept and the early uses of the terms "transubstant(iat)io" and "transubstantiari" see Goering (1991).

14. See Baldwin (1970, I.42-43); Goering (1992, 11f.; 83-9).

15. See Chobham, *Summa*, LXI; see also Goering (1992, 83-86).

16. See *Summa de Sacramentis*, I,133-182.

17. The most recent account of Wetheringsette and his *Summa* (ca. 1215) can be found in Goering (1995).

18. On the background of this Franciscan manual, see Wenzel (1978, 28; 41).

19. All quotations are taken from Powicke and Cheney (1984), cited as *C&S*.

20. "These statutes are some of the most important diocesan legislation of medieval England ... and remarkably comprehensive for their time", *C&S*, 57.

21. See also William de Montibus, *De septem sacramentis*, "Item queritur utrum aqua que exiuit de latere Christi cum sanguine sit sacramentum", Goering

(1995, 492 [44]); and Gerald of Wales, *Gemma Ecclesiastica,* D.I, cap. VII, 27. Gerald of Wales was also among the students of Peter the Chanter and, perhaps, of William de Montibus; see Baldwin 1970, I, 41-43.

22. For a variety of terms used to explain the new concept "transubstantiation" see Goering (1991), esp. 165, Appendix B (6), and 170, Appendix C.

23. On these statutes see also Goering and Taylor (1992).

24. See the long list of "exempla et miracula" illustrating both the concept and the doctrine of "transubstantiation" in Tubach (1969). See also the fifteenth-century "The (Croxton) Play of the Sacrament", ed. Norman Davies, for an "enacted" transubstantiation miracle. See also Rubin (1991, 108-129).

25. For Wyclif's attack of the concept and doctrine of "transubstantiation" and its abuses, see Keen (1986).

26. Unfortunately, the new *Anglo-Norman Dictionary* does not contain an entry for the term; see Fascicle 7: T-Z (London: Modern Humanities Research Association, 1992); I think we can thus almost rule out the influence of (late) Anglo-Norman texts.

27. For a succinct and stimulating account of the degree of "literacy" among the followers of Wyclif see Hudson (1994), especially 228 ff.

28. Other Latin sources dealing with the concept use either agent-less passive constructions or impersonal passive "fi(a)t+nominative"-formulas.

29. See the argument in Rubin (1991), esp. 49-50, concerning the new definition of the power and authority of the priest in connection with the Eucharist (transubstantiation).

30. Cf. *The Mirour of Mans Saluacioune,* 10, and the literature cited there.

31. Further references to Melchizedek can be found in *Ps.* 110:4; *Hebr.* 5:6, 10; *Hebr.* 6:20; and especially in *Hebr.* 7:1-21. A brief reference to Melchizedek in the context of "transubstantiation" can also be found in Gerald's *Gemma,* 28, and in the York Ordinal, 108. See also Rubin (1991, 129-131).

32. For a later and more moderate view on the power of the priest see Reginald Pecock's *The Reule of Crysten Religioun,* Treatise 3, chap. 15, esp. 313-14.

33. See also Gerald's *Gemma,* 27: "Forma verborum quam Dominus in cœna tradidit, dicens: 'Hoc est corpus meum,' 'Hoc est sanguis meus,' hæc sunt de substantia sacramenti, cætera solemnitatis ad laudandum vel orandum. Sed quæritur si verbis istis tantum prolatis a presbytero cum intentione consecrandi fiat transubstantiatum. Respondendum ita, quia nec Dominus solemnitates apposuit; vehementer tamen esset puniendus qui ecclesiæ statuta mutaret et contraveniret."

34. Note that Chobham, *Summa,* 101, points to the different forms in the Gospels: "Verba etiam sacra constituta a domino in evangelio ad hoc necessaria sunt, quia sine illis non consecratur eucharistia. Verumtamen quia alia est forma illorum verborum in uno evangelista et alia in alio, non credimus quod possit confici corpus Christi nisi tantum illis verbis evangelicis que approbata sunt in ecclesia, quia magna est auctoritas ecclesie.

35. I thank my colleagues Peter Godman and Dirk Kottke for suggestions concerning the conjunction *enim* and the *active* use of "transubstantiate".

36. Quoted from *The Lay Folks Massbook*, 106; bold face altered into italics. Simmons translates the conjunction *enim* with *for*, the English *for*, however, has much more causal force than the Latin *enim*.

37. Cf. Innocent's *Mysteria evangelicae legis et sacramenti eucharistiae*, in *PL*, 217, cols. 770A and 833C, 868B, and 874B: "hoc est enim corpus meum". An electronic search in the *Patrologia Latina Database* reveals some further texts containing this phrase, with a total of 71 occurrences.

38. This investigation could be carried out following the account in Rubin (1991, 49-82). Rubin also refers to Quinel's formula (57); however in her translation of Quinel's text, the crucial *enim* has been left out. Note that the York Ordinal contains some further 'transformations' of the texts of the Gospels reporting Christ's words during the Last Supper. In the passage dealing with the presentation of the chalice, we read, after the present participle "dicens" referring to Christ: "*Acccipite et* bibite ex *eo* omnes, Hic est enim *calix sanguinis mei*, novi *et æterni* testamenti, *mysterium fidei*, qui *pro vobis et* pro multis effundetur in remissionem peccatorum" (108; emphasis mine). The phrase "mysterium fidei" is probably based on 1 *Tim.* 3:9. On the contrast between the text of the Ordinal, "bibite ex eo *omnes*" (emphasis mine), and the "removal of the chalice" in the fifteenth century see Rubin (1991, 71-73).

39. Bartholomew's text is based on Beleth's *Summa*, chapter 95, CCCM XLI A, 167-170. For Bartholomew's text see the edition printed in Frankfurt (1601), Lib. 9, ca. 30, 464.

40. For a more comprehensive account see Rubin (1991, 83-129).

41. All quotations taken from the EETS edition. Note that Mannyng uses a native word for "translate": "In þat tyme turnede y þys / On englyssh tunge out of frankys" (77-78).

42. In Mannyng's source, the *Manuel des Pechiez*, 7297-7302, the corresponding section is: "Bien sauum, qe, de un estreim,/ Purreit Deu fere un blanc pain;/ Dunc, poet il le pain *muer*/ En char, & en sun cors tres cher,/ E le vin vermail ou blanc/ En sun precius sanc;" (emphasis mine).

43. Cf. Chanter, *Summa*, 179-180, on "transubstantiation" miracles: "Accidit quandoque non solum temporibus antiquorum sed et nostris, quod uel propter roborandam infirmitatem conficientis, uel alia aliqua causa quam ignoramus, rubicunda quedam et quasi carnea species apparuerit in sacramento, et solet queri in eo casu quid ibi apparuerit ... Quicquid autem super hoc queratur, certum est quod talia miraculose facta communem legem non obseruant."

44. Cf. *Manuel des Pechiez*, 7381-7382: "Quant le simple home out granté,/ En semblance de pain est turné;" where *semblance* covers both "form" and "substance".

45. All quotations taken from the EETS edition.

46. Migne, *PL*, 202, col. 104B.

47. The same holds true for the other texts printed by Hudson, even for text 21a, edited under the title "The Eucharist" (110-112).

48. See also *C&S*, index, *s.v.* host.

49. For further discussions of the concept and doctrine of "transubstantiation" see also sermon no. 151 and 162.

50. All quotations are from this edition. For the date and background of these sermons, see Ross, xxxiv-xlii, and lxv-lxi.

51. A rather detailed account of the doctrine of "transubstantiation" can be found in the *Myrour of Lewed Men*, ll. 727-770, in the section "Of the sacrament of the auter"; see Kari Sajavaara's 1967 edition, *The Middle English Translations*, 339-340.

52. See also the quotation from sermon 46 (I, 431-432), above.

53. Cf. *The Riverside Chaucer*, 908, *ad* 538-539. See also Strohm (1995).

54. For an earlier view concerning the "sacerdotal magic" see Hobbes, *Leviathan*, chapter 44: "A second generall abuse of Scripture, is the turning of Consecration into Conjuration, or Enchantment." 633-635.

55. See also "The Testimony of William Thorpe" in Hudson (1993, 52), ll. 936-946: the congregation running away from the priest after the ringing of "a sacringe belle".

56. See Strohm (1995, 32 ff.)

57. Cf. Gunkel (1913, 33): "Jede alte literarische Gattung hat ursprünglich ihren Sitz im Volksleben Israels an ganz bestimmter Stelle. ... Wer die Gattung verstehen will, muß sich jedesmal die ganze Situation deutlich machen und fragen: wer ist es, der redet? wer sind die Zuhörer? welche Stimmung beherrscht die Situation? welche Wirkung wird erstrebt?"

58. The other "differences in opinions" taken up by Swift can also be found in the Lollard debate. Thus, Swift's "whistling" refers to the issue of *church music* (cf. Matthew 1880, 191ff.; Hudson 1993, 66); "to kiss a post" to *images in worship* (cf. Gradon and Hudson, III, 247-248; Hudson 1978, 83-88, text 15), and, finally, "coat" to *church vestments* (cf. Hudson 1978, 83-88, text 16).

59. See also Hudson (1993, 119), note to ll. 1030-38.

Appendix

Electronic texts used in this study; "[S]" indicates selections.

(1) ASNETH: [S] *The Storie of Asneth*, ed. Russell Peck; originally published in *Heroic Women from the Old Testament in Middle English Verse* Kalamazoo, Michigan: Western Michigan University for TEAMS, 1991

(2) ASTROLAB: Chaucer, *A Treatise on the Astrolabe* (Oxford Electronic Texts)

(3) AWNART: *The Awntyrs off Arthure at the Terne Wathelyn*

(4) BOECE: Chaucer, *Boece* (Oxford Electronic Texts)

(5) CARL: *The Carle of Carlisle*, ed. Thomas Hahn; originally published in *Sir Gawain: Eleven Romances and Tales* Kalamazoo, Michigan: Western Michigan University for TEAMS, 1995

(6) CHANCERY: *An Anthology of Chancery English* (electronic text at the University of Virginia)

(7) CHAPOEMS: Chaucer's minor poems (Oxford Electronic Texts)

(8) CRESSEID: Robert Henryson, *The Testament of Cresseid* (electronic text at the University of Virginia)

(9) *CT*: Chaucer, *Canterbury Tales* (Oxford Electronic Texts)

(10) EVERYMAN: (electronic text at the University of Virginia)

(11) FRIARDAW: *Friar Daw's Reply*

(12) GOWERCA: John Gower, *Confessio Amantis* (electronic text at the University of Virginia)

(13) GREENEK: *The Greene Knight,* ed. Thomas Hahn; originally published in *Sir Gawain: Eleven Romances and Tales* Kalamazoo, Michigan: Western Michigan University for TEAMS, 1995

(14) HENRYSON: Robert Henryson, *The morall fabillis of Esope the Phrygian* (electronic text at the University of Virginia)

(15) HENRYSPO: Robert Henryson, *Minor Poems* (electronic text at the University of Virginia)

(16) HOF: Chaucer, *The House of Fame* (Oxford Electronic Texts)

(17) LABELDAM: *La Belle Dame sans Merci*

(18) LANCEL: *Lancelot of the Laik,* ed. Alan Lupack originally published in *Lancelot of the Laik and Sir Tristrem* Kalamazoo, Michigan: Western Michigan University for TEAMS, 1994

(19) LANTERNE: [S] *The Lanterne of Li3t*

(20) LGW: Chaucer, *The Legend of Good Women* (Oxford Electronic Texts)

(21) LOLLSERM: [S]: *Lollard Sermons*

(22) MARY: [S] Collection of texts relating to the BVM

(23) MYRKFEST: [S] *Mirk's Festial*

(24) ORPHEUS: Robert Henryson, *Orpheus and Eurydice* (electronic text at the University of Virginia)

(25) PASTON: [S] *Paston Letters and Papers* (electronic text at the University of Virginia)

(26) PIERS: *Piers Plowman* (electronic text at the University of Virginia)

(27) ROMROSE: Chaucer, *The Romaunt of the Rose* (Oxford Electronic Texts)

(28) SPECSAC: [S] *Speculum Sacerdotale*

(29) TREVISA: [S] John Trevisa, *On the Properties of Things*

(30) TROILUS: Chaucer, *Troilus and Criseyde* (Oxford Electronic Texts and electronic text (Whetherbee) at the University of Virginia)

(31) UPLAND: *Jack Upland*

(32) WYCLBIB: [S] *The Wyclif Bible*

(33) WYCLIF: [S] *The English Works of John Wyclif*

(34) WYCLIFWR: [S] Wycliffite Writings in English

(35) WYCLSERM: [S] *English Wycliffite Sermons*

(36) YORKPL: *The York Plays* (electronic text at the University of Virginia)

Works Cited

Baldwin, John W. *Masters Princes and Merchants. The Social Views of Peter the Chanter and his Circle.* 2 vols. Princeton, NJ, Princeton UP, 1970.

Bartholomæi Anglici De Genvinis Rervm Coelestivm, Terrestrivm et Inferarvm Proprietatibus, Libri XVIII. Frankfurt, 1601; rpt. Frankfurt: Minerva, 1964.

Iohannes Beleth. *Summa de ecclesiasticis officis.* Ed. Herbert Douteil. 2 vols. CCCM, XLI, XLI A [Text]. Turnhout: Brepols, 1976.

Pierre le Chantre. *Summa de Sacramentis et Animae Consiliis.* Ed. Jean-Albert Dugauquier. Pt. I. Analecta Mediaevalia Namurcensia, 4. Louvain: Editions Nauwelaerts; Lille: Librairie Giard, 1954.

The Riverside Chaucer. Ed. Larry D. Benson. 3rd ed. Boston, MA: Houghton Mifflin Company, 1987.

The Chester Mystery Cycle. Ed. R. M. Lumiansky and David Mills. 2 vols. EETS SS 3, 9. London: Oxford UP, 1974; 1986.

Thomae de Chobham Summa Confessorum. Ed. F. Broomfield. Analecta Mediaevalia Namurcensia, 25. Paris: Béatrice-Nauwelaerts, 1968.

Councils and Synods With Other Documents Relating to the English Church, pt. II: *A.D. 1205–1313.* Ed. F. M. Powicke and Cristopher R. Cheney. 2 vols. Oxford: Clarendon Press, 1964.

The English Works of Wyclif Hitherto Unprinted. Ed. F. D. Matthew. EETS OS 74. London: Oxford UP, 1880.

English Wycliffite Sermons. Ed. Anne Hudson and Pamela Gradon. 3 vols. Oxford: Clarendon Press, 1983-1990.

Fasciculus Morum. A Fourteenth-Century Preacher's Handbook. Ed. and trans. Siegfried Wenzel. University Park PA, Pennsylvania State UP, 1989.

Giraldus Cambrensis. *Gemma Ecclesiastica.* Ed. J. S. Brewer. Rolls Series, 21. London, 1862. Rpt. Kraus Reprint Ltd., 1964.

Goering, Joseph and Daniel S. Taylor. "The *Summulae* of Bishops Walter de Cantilupe (1240) and Peter Quinel (1287)." *Speculum,* 67 (1992): 576-594.

Goering, Joseph. "The Invention of Transubtantiation." *Traditio* 46 (1991): 147-170.

Goering, Joseph. *William de Montibus (c. 1140-1213). The Schools and the Literature of Pastoral Care.* Studies and Texts, 108. Toronto: Pontifical Institute of Mediaeval Studies, 1992.

Goering, Joseph. "The Summa 'Qui bene presunt' and Its Author." In *Literature and Religion In the Later Middle Ages. Philological Studies in Honor of Siegfried Wenzel.* Ed. Richard G. Newhauser and John A. Alford. Medieval & Renaissance Texts & Studies, 118. Binghamton, NY: Medieval & Renaissance Texts & Studies, 1995, 143-159.

Gunkel, Hermann. "Die Grundprobleme der israelitischen Literaturgeschichte" (1906). In *Reden und Aufsätze.* Göttingen: Vandenhoeck & Ruprecht, 1913, 29-38.

Hobbes, Thomas. *Leviathan.* Ed. with an Introduction by C. B. Macpherson. Pelican Classics. Harmondsworth: Penguin, 1968.

Hudson, Anne. "'Laicus litteratus': the paradox of Lollardy." In *Heresy and Literacy, 1000-1530.* Ed. Beter Biller and Anne Hudson. Cambridge: Cambridge UP, 1994, 222-236.

Jack Upland Friar Daw's Reply and Upland's Rejoinder. Ed. P. L. Heyworth. Oxford: Oxford UP, 1968.

Keen, Maurice. "Wyclif, the Bible, and Transubstantiation." In *Wyclif in his Times.* Ed. Anthony Kenny. Oxford: Clarendon Press, 1986, 1-16.

Kenny, Anthony. *Wyclif.* Oxford, New York: Oxford UP, 1985.

The Lay Folks Mass Book. Ed. Thomas Frederick Simmons. EETS OS 71 (1879). Rpt. London: Oxford UP, 1968.

Lollard Sermons. Ed. Gloria Cigman. EETS OS 294. Oxford: The Early English Text Society, 1984.

Mannyng, Robert. *Handlyng Synne.* Ed. Frederick J. Furnivall. EETS OS 119; 123. London, 1901-1903; rpt. Millwood: Kraus, 1978.

Middle English Sermons. Ed. Woodburn O. Ross. EETS OS 209. London, 1940; rpt. London: Oxford UP, 1960.

The Middle English Translations of Robert Grosseteste's Chateau d'Amour. Ed. Kari Sajavaara. Mémoires de la Société Néophilologique de Helsinki, 32. Helsinki: Société Néophilologique, 1967.

The Mirour of Mans Saluacioune. A Middle English translation of Speculum Humanae Salvationis. Ed. Avril Henry. Aldershot: Scolar Press, 1986.

Myrk, John. *Instructions for Parish Priests.* Ed. Edward Peacock. 2nd rev. edn. EETS OS 31. London, 1902; rpt. Millwood: Kraus, 1975.

The N-Town Play. Cotton MS Vespasian D.8 Ed. Stephen Spector. 2 vols. EETS SS 11, 12. Oxford: Oxford UP, 1991.

Non-Cycle Plays and Fragments. Ed. Norman Davis. EETS SS 1. London: Oxford UP, 1970.

Norton, Thomas. *Ordinal of Alchemy.* Ed. John Reidy. EETS OS 272. London: Oxford UP, 1975.

On the Properties of Things. John Trevisa's Translation of Bartholomæus Anglicus De Proprietatibus Rerum. A Critical Text. General Editor M. C. Seymour. 3 vols. Oxford: Clarendon Press, 1975-1988.

Owst G. R. *Preaching in Medieval England. An Introduction to Sermon Manuscripts of the Period c. 1350-1450.* Cambridge, 1926. Reissued New York: Russell & Russel, 1965.

Owst, G. R. *Literature and Pulpit in Medieval England. A Neglected Chapter in the History of English Letters & of the English People.* 2nd. ed. Oxford: Blackwell, 1966.

Pecock, Reginald. *The Repressor of Over Much Blaming of the Clergy.* Ed. Churchill Babington. 2 vols. Rolls Series, 19. London: Longman, 1860.

Pecock, Reginald. *The Reule of Crysten Religioun.* Ed. William Cabell Greet. EETS OS 171. London: Oxford UP, 1927.

Political, Religious, and Love Poems. Ed. Frederick J. Furnivall. EETS OS 15. London, 1866. Re-edited 1903. Rpt. London: Oxford UP, 1965.

Rubin, Miri. *Corpus Christi. The Eucharist in Late Medieval Culture.* Cambridge: Cambridge UP, 1991.

Selections from English Wycliffite Writings. Ed. Anne Hudson. Cambridge: Cambridge UP, 1978.

Speculum Sacerdotale. Ed. Edward H. Weatherly. EETS OS 200. London: Oxford UP, 1936.

Strohm, Paul. "Chaucer's Lollard Joke: History and the Textual Unconscious." *Studies in the Age of Chaucer,* 17 (1995): 23-42.

Swift, Jonathan. *Gulliver's Travels.* Ed. Peter Dixon and John Chalker. Intro. Michael Foot. Harmondsworth: Penguin, 1967; rpt. 1972.

The Towneley Plays. Ed. Martin Stevens and A. C. Cawley. 2 vols. EETS SS 13, 14. Oxford: Oxford UP, 1994.

Tubach, Frederic C. *Index Exemplorum. A Handbook of Medieval Religious Tales.* FF Communications No. 204. Helsinki: Suomalainen Tiedeakatemia, 1969.

Two Wycliffite Texts. Ed. Anne Hudson. EETS OS 301. Oxford: Oxford UP, 1993.

Wenzel, Siegfried. *Verses in Sermons.* Fasciculus Morum *and its Middle English Poems.* The Mediaeval Academy of America Publication No. 87. Cambridge, MA: The Mediaeval Academy of America, 1978.

The York Plays. Ed. Richard Beadle. London: Edward Arnold, 1982.

Transsubstantiation in Medieval and Early Modern Culture and Literature: An Introductory Bibliography of Critical Studies

Richard J. Utz and Christine Baatz

The titles of this bibliography have been compiled to complement the specialized scholarly contributions to this volume by providing those interested in 'trans-substantiation' with a solid introductory list of references. As Fritz Kemmler demonstrates in his essay to this volume, "Entrancing 'tra(u)ns/c'" the history of the term 'transsubstantiation' is a contested one. To do justice to this problematic reception history of the term, the bibliography unites ciritical studies on the semantic fields of 'transsubstantiation', 'real presence', and 'eucharist'. As a consequence of this broader focus, the following listings reflect the interdisciplinary and transnational nature of the topic as they include -- in addition to the expected entries in theology and philosophy -- entries from the realms of musicology, literature, history, sociology, law studies, manuscript studies, etc. For assistance in compiling and/or proofreading the bibliography, we would like to acknowledge the expert support we received from Axel Müller (International Medieval Bibliography, U of Leeds), Nadia Margolis (*Christine de Pisan Newletter*), and Anne-Françoise Le Lostec (Tübingen).

General Studies
This section contains investigations of the genesis and development of 'trans-substantiation' not restricted to the medieval and early modern periods.

Adam, Adolf. *Die Eucharistiefeier: Quelle und Gipfel des Glaubens.* Freiburg: Herder, 1991.

Adam, Karl. *Die Eucharistielehre des heiligen Augustin.* Paderborn: Schöningh, 1908.

Ahlers, Reinhild. *Communio eucharistica: Eine kirchenrechtliche Untersuchung zur Eucharistielehre im Codex iuris canonici.* Regensburg: Pustet, 1990.

Bacciocchi, J. de. "Présence eucharistique et Transsubstantiation." *Irenikon* 32 (1959): 139–61.

Bader, Günter. *Die Abendmahlsfeier. Liturgik, Ökonomik, Symbolik.* Tübingen: Mohr, 1993.

Betz, Johannes. *Eucharistie in der Schrift und Patristik.* Freiburg: Herder, 1979.

—. *Die Eucharistie in der Zeit der griechischen Väter.* 2 vols. Freiburg: Herder, 1955.

Bourassa, François, S.J. "Présence réelle – transsubstantiatión." *Science et Esprit* 22 (1970): 263–313.

Bouyer, Louis. *Eucharist. Theology and Spirituality of the Eucharistic Prayer.* Trsl. by Charles Underhill Quinn. Notre Dame and London: U of Notre Dame P, 1968.

Bridgett, T.E. *History of the Holy Eucharist in Great Britain.* London: Burns & Oates, 1908.

Buchel, W. "Quantenphysik und naturphilosophischer Substanzbegriff." *Scholastik* 33 (1958): 161–65.

Buxton, Richard F. *Eucharist and Institution Narrative: A Study in the Roman and Anglican Traditions of the Consecration of the Eucharist from the Eighth to the Twentieth Centuries.* Great Wakering: Publ. for the Alcuin Club by Mayhew-McCrimmon, 1976.

Chilton, Bruce. "The Eucharist -- Exploring its Origins." *Bible Review* 10.6 (1994): 36–43.

Coraluppi Tonzig, Luisa T. "The Teaching of St. Ambrose on Real Presence, Its Misunderstanding in Later Tradition, and the Significance of Its Recovery for Contemporary Eucharistic Theology." Diss. Duquesne U, 1988.

Crockett, William R. *Eucharist: Symbol of Transformation.* New York: Pueblo Publ., 1989.

Detisch, Scott-P. "Paul VI's 'Mysterium Fidei': Bridging the Objective and the Subjective Dimensions of Eucharistic Real Presence." Diss. Duquesne U, 1996.

Dix, Gregory. *The Shape of the Liturgy.* New York: Seabury Press, 1982.

Donegan, Augustine Francis. *Saint Augustine and the Real Presence.* Washington: Catholic U of America P, 1952.

Doueihi, Milad. "Traps of Representation." *Diacritics* 14.1 (1984): 66–77.

Dufort, Jean-Marc. *Le Symbolisme Eucharistique aux origines de l'Eglise.* Brussels and Paris: Desclee de Brouwer, 1969.

Echlin, Edward P. *The Anglican Eucharist in Ecumenical Perspective: Doctrine and Rite from Cranmer to Seabury.* New York: Seabury P, 1968.

Faber, Irene, Monique Van Rompay-Daniels, and Jeroen Westerman, eds. *"Neemt en eet": Avondmaal en eucharistie in kunst- en kerkhistorisch perspectief.* Zoetermeer: Boekencentrum, 1994.

Feeley-Harnik, Gillian. *The Lord's Table: Eucharist and Passover in Early Christianity.* Philadelphia: U of Pennsylvania P, 1981.

FitzPatrick, P. J. *In Breaking of Bread: The Eucharist and Ritual.* Cambridge: Cambridge UP, 1993.

Frank, Karl Suso, et al. "Eucharistie, Eucharistiefeier." *Lexikon für Theologie und Kirche.* 3., völlig neu bearbeitete Auflage. Freiburg; Basel; Wien: Herder, 1993ff., vol. 3: cols. 944–968.

Frankovich, Lawrence F. "Augustine's Theory of Eucharistic Sacrifice." Diss. Marquette U, 1976.

225

Gamber, Klaus. *Sacrificium vespertinum: Lucernarium und eucharistisches Opfer am Abend und ihre Abhängigkeit von den Riten der Juden.* Regensburg: Pustet, 1983.

—. *Eucharistiegebet und Eucharistiefeier in der Urkirche.* Regensburg: Pustet, 1986.

Gerken, Alexander. *Theologie der Eucharistie.* München: Kösel, 1973.

Gerrish, Brian A. *Grace and Gratitude: The Eucharistic Theology of John.* Minneapolis: Fortress P, 1993.

Gerwing, M. "Transsubstantiation." *Lexikon des Mittelalters.* Vol. 8. Eds. Robert Auty, et al. München: LexMa, 1997.

Gutwenger, E. "Substanz und Akzidens in der Eucharistielehre." *Zeitschrift für Katholische Theologie* 83 (1961): 257–306.

—. "Transsubstantiation." *Sacramentum Mundi* 4 (1968): 970–75.

Hoffmann, G. "The 'real presence' of Christ in the Eucharist According to Roman Catholic Theology." *Canadian Journal of Theology* 9 (1963): 263–70.

Holböck, Ferdinand. *Der eucharistische und der mystische Leib Christi.* Rom: Officium libri Catholici, 1941.

—. *Das Allerheiligste und die Heiligen: eucharistische Heilige aus allen Jahrhunderten der Kirchengeschichte.* Stein am Rhein: Christiana-Verlag, 1979.

Jones, Paul H. *Christ's Eucharistic Presence: A History of the Doctrine.* New York: Lang, 1993.

Kannengiesser, Charles. "Le symbolisme eucharistique dans l'eglise ancienne." *Laval Theologique et Philosophique* 29 (1973): 307–12.

Kelleher, Margaret-Mary, O.S.U. "The Communion Rite: A Study of Roman Catholic Liturgical Performance." *Journal of Ritual Studies* 5.2 (1991): 99–122.

Keller, Erwin. *Eucharistie und Parusie: liturgie- und theologiegeschichtliche Untersuchungen zur eschatologischen Dimension der Eucharistie anhand ausgewählter Zeugnisse aus frühchristlicher und patristischer Zeit.* Fribourg, Switzerland: Universitätsverlag, 1989.

Kilgour, Maggie. *From Communion to Cannibalism: An Anatomy of Metaphors of Incorporation.* Princeton: Princeton UP, 1990.

Kollmann, Bernd. *Ursprung und Gestalten der frühchristlichen Mahlfeier.* Göttingen: Vandenhoeck & Ruprecht, 1990.

Macy, Gary. *The Banquet's Wisdom: A Short History of the Theologies of the Lord's Supper.* New York: Paulist P, 1992.

Manders, H. "Sacrament van geloof. Enige recente publicaties over de euchar- istie." *Tijdscrift voor Theologie* 5 (1965): 442–50.

Marxsen, Willi. *Das Abendmahl als christologisches Problem.* Gütersloh: Mohn, 1963.

Mascall, Eric L. *Corpus Christi. Essays on the Church and the Eucharist.* 2nd ed. London: Longmans, 1965.

Masi, R. "Teologia eucaristica e fisica contemporanea." *Doctor Communis* 8 (1955): 31–51.

226

—. "La sostenza materiale e i suois accidenti." *Studia Patavina* 4 (1957): 125–42.

Mazza, Enrico. *The Origins of the Eucharistic Prayer*. Collegeville, MN: Liturgical P, 1995.

McCabe, H. "The Real Presence." *Clergy Review* 49 (1964): 749–59.

Megivern, James J. *Concomitance and Communion. A Study in Eucharistic Doctrine and Practice*. Fribourg, Switzerland: Universitätsverlag, 1963.

Mehl, Roger "Structure philosophique de la notion de présence." *Revue d'Histoire et de philosophie religieuses* 38 (1958): 171–76.

Mihailescu, Calin. "Corpus Epochalis. Mysticism, Body, History." *Surfaces* 1 (1991): http://tornade.ere.umontreal.ca/~guedon/Surfaces/vol1/mihaile.html

Moloney, Raymond. *The Eucharist*. London: Chapman, 1995.

Naegle, August. *Ratramnus und die heilige Eucharistie. Zugleich eine dogmatisch-historische Würdigung des ersten Abendmahlsstreites*. Wien: Meyer, 1903.

—. *Die Eucharistielehre des heiligen Johannes Chrysostomus, des Doctor Eucharistiae*. Straßburg: Herder, 1900.

Neunheuser, Burckhardt. "Transsubstantiation." *Lexikon für Theologie und Kirche*. Eds. Josef Höfer and Karl Rahner. 2., völlig neu bearbeitete Auflage. Freiburg: Herder , 1957–68, vol. 10: cols. 311–14.

Paprocki, Henryk. *Le mystère de l'eucharistie: genèse et interprétation de la liturgie eucharistique byzantine*. Paris: Editions du Cerf, 1993.

Pfaff, K. "Beiträge zur Geschichte der Abendmahlsbulle vom 16. bis 18. Jahrhundert." *Römische Quartalschrift für christliche Altertumskunde und für Kirchengeschichte* 38 (1930): 23–76.

Piolanti, Antonio. *Eucaristia*. Roma: Desclée, 1957.

Pousset, E. "L'Eucharistie: Présence réelle et transsubstantiation." *Recherches de science religieuse* 54 (1966): 177–212.

Ratzinger, Joseph. "Das Problem der Transsubstantiation und die Frage nach dem Sinn der Eucharistie." *Tübinger Theologische Quartalschrift* 147 (1967): 129–58.

Rayburn, Carole A. "Ritual as Acceptance/Empowerment and Rejection/Disenfranchisement." *Women and Religious Ritual*. Ed. Lesley A. Northrup. Washington, DC: Pastoral, 1993. 87–101.

Sala, G. B. "Transsubstantiation oder Transsignifikation? Gedanken zu einem Dilemma." *Zeitschrift für katholische Theologie* 92 (1970): 1–34.

Sayes, José A. *Presencia real de Cristo y transustanciación: La teología eucarística ante la física y filosofía modernas*. Burgos: Aldecoa, 1974.

Scheffczyk, Leo. *Die Heilszeichen von Brot und Wein*. München: Don Bosco, 1973.

Schillebeeckx, E. "Transsubstantiation, Transfinalisation, Transsignification." *Rivista di pastororale liturgica* 4 (1966): 227–48.

Schoonenberg, P. "Dans quelle mesure la doctrine de la transsubstantionation a-t-elle été déterminée par l'histoire?" *Concilium* 3.24 (1967): 77–90.

—. "The Real Presence in Contemporary Discussion." *Theology Digest* 15.1 (1967): 3–11.

Schrey, H. H. "Die Gegenwart Christi in reformatorischer Sicht." *Neue Zeitschrift für systematische Theologie* 9 (1967): 247–61.

Schützeichel, Harald, ed. *Die Messe: Ein kirchenmusikalisches Handbuch*. Düsseldorf: Patmos, 1991.

Semmelroth, Otto. *Eucharistische Wandlung: Transsubstantiation, Transfinalisation, Transsignifikation*. Kevelaer: Butzon & Bercker, 1967.

Slenczka, Notger. *Realpräsenz und Ontologie: Untersuchung der ontologischen Grundlagen der Transsignifikationslehre*. Göttingen: Vandenhoeck & Ruprecht, 1993.

Sokolowski, Robert. *Eucharistic Presence: A Study in the Theology of Disclosure*. Washington, DC: Catholic U of America P, 1994.

Sonnen, R. "Transsubstantiatie." *Verbum* 32 (1965): 82–94; 122–29.

Stone, Darwell. *A History of the Doctrine of the Holy Eucharist*. London: Longmans, Green & Co., 1909.

Tartre, Raymond A., ed. *The Eucharist Today. Essays on the Theology and Worship of the Real Presence*. New York: Kenedy, 1967.

Ternus, J. "'Dogmatische Physik' in der Lehre vom Altsakrament." *Stimmen der Zeit* 132 (1937): 220–30.

Thaler, Anton. *Das Testament des Abendmahls: Ein Blick auf die Geschichte und Zukunft der Eucharistie*. Freiburg, Switzerland: Paulusverlag, 1996.

Thorey, Lionel. *Histoire de la messe de Grégoire le Grand à nos jours*. Paris: Perrin, 1994.

Trooster, S. "Transsubstantie." *Streven* 18 (1965): 737–44.

Vloberg, Maurice. *L'Eucharistie dans l'art*. 2 vols. Grenoble: Arthaud, 1946.

Vogüé, A. de. "Eucharistie et vie monastique." *Collectanea cisterciensia* 48 (1986): 120–30.

Vollert, C. "The Eucharist: Controversy on Transsubstantiation." *Theological Studies* 22 (1961): 391–425.

Williams, Drid. *The Latin High Mass: The Dominican Tridentine Rite*. Sydney: Williams, 1994.

Williams, Rowan. *Eucharistic Sacrifice: The Roots of a Metaphor*. Bramcote, Notts.: Grove, 1982.

Wohlmuth, J. "Noch einmal: Transsubstantiation oder Transsignifikation? *Zeitschrift für katholische Theologie* 97 (1975): 430–440.

Wybrew, Hugh. *The Orthodox Liturgy: The Development of the Eucharistic Liturgy in the Byzantine Rite*. Crestwood, NY: St. Vladimirs Seminary P, 1990.

Transsubstantiation in Medieval and Early Modern Culture

In addition to the terminological fields indicated in the introduction, the following sections on Medieval and Early Modern Culture and Literature also include several titles on the history of accusations against the Jews (desecration of the host, ritual murder) which evolved together with Christian doubts about the dogma of transsubstantiation. Ample bibliographic information on this specific topic is provided by The Felix Posen Bibliographic Project which is working on establishing a comprehensive database of all published writings about antisemitism and the Holocaust. The database lists books, articles, dissertations, and MA theses published in a variety of countries and languages. At present it contains ca. 15,000 items. The database is part of the Israel Universities Library Network (ALEPH) and can be accessed via telnet://sicsa@ har2.huji.ac.il; har2.huji.ac.il. An excellent recent bibliography of primary and secondary sources on 'transsubstantiation' is available in Miri Rubin's *Corpus Christi. The Eucharist in Late Medieval Culture*, 1991, 369–419.

Accati, Luisa. "La cronologica differita dei simboli: intorno a un libro di Caroline Walker Bynum." *Studi medievali* ser. 3, 31.2 (1990): 821–36.

Acklin Zimmermann, Béatrice W. *Gott im Denken berühren: die theologischen Implikationen der Nonnenviten*. Fribourg, Switzerland: Universitätsverlag, 1993.

Adolf, Franz. *Die Messe im deutschen Mittelalter. Beiträge zur Geschichte der Liturgie und des religiösen Volkslebens*. 1902; repr. Darmstadt: Wissenschaftliche Buchgesellschaft, 1963.

Andrachuk, Gregory Peter. "Berceo's *Sacrificio de la Misa* and the *Clérigos ignorantes*." *Hispanic Studies in Honor of Alan D. Deyermond. A North American Tribute*. Ed. John S. Miletich. Madison, WI: Hispanic Seminary of Medieval Studies, 1986. 15–30.

Andrieu, M. "Aux origines du culte du saint-sacrement. Reliquaires et monstrances eucharistiques." *Analecta Bollandiana* 68 (1950): 397–418.

Angenendt, Arnold. *Geschichte der Religiosität im Mittelalter*. Darmstadt: Primus, 1997.

Anselm, Sigrun. "Angst und Angstprojektion in der Phantasie vom jüdischen Ritualmord." *Die Legende vom Ritualmord. Zur Geschichte der Blutbeschuldigung gegen Juden*. Ed. Rainer Erb. Berlin: Metropol, 1993. 253–265.

Arranz, Miguel. "Circonstances et conséquences liturgiques du Concile de Ferrare-Florence." *Christian Unity. The Council of Ferrara-Florence 1438/39–1989*. Ed. Giuseppe Alberigo. Leuven: Leuven UP, 1991. 407–27.

Atkinson, Charles. "Text, Music and the Persistence of Memory in 'Dulcis est cantica'." *Recherches nouvelles sur les tropes liturgiques*. Eds. Wulf Arlt and Gunilla Bjorkvall. Stockholm: Almqvist & Wiksell, 1993. 95–117.

—. "Further Thoughts on the Origin of the *missa graeca*." *De Musica et cantu: Studien zur Geschichte der Kirchenmusik und der Oper. Helmut Hucke zum 60. Geburtstag*. Eds. Peter Cahn and Ann-Katrin Heimer. Hildesheim: Olms, 1993. 75–93.

Avril, Joseph. "Remarques sur un aspect de la vie religieuse paroissiale: la pratique de la confession et de la communion du Xe au XIVe siècle." *L'Encadrement religieux des fidèles au Moyen Age et jusqu'au Concile de*

Trente. Actes du 109ᵉ Congrès national des sociétés savants, Dijon, 1984: Section d'histoire médiévale et de philologie, tome 1. Paris: Comité des Travaux historiques et scientifiques, 1985. 345–63.

Backhaus, Fritz. "Judenfeindschaft und Judenvertreibung im Mittelalter: Zur Ausweisung der Juden aus dem Mittelmeerraum im 15. Jahrhundert." *Jahrbuch für die Geschichte Mittel- und Ostdeutschlands* 36 (1987): 275–332.

Baix, François. "La Première célébration de la Fête-Dieu à Fosses en 1246." *Annales de la société archéologique de Namur* 44 (1947): 157–80.

— and C. Lambot. *La Dévotion à l'eucharistie et la VIIᵉ centenaire de la Fête-Dieu*. Gembloux: Duculot, 1946.

Barber, Charles. "From Transformation to Desire: Art and Worship after Byzantine Iconoclasm." *Art Bulletin* 75.1 (1993): 7–16.

Barnai, Jacob. "'Blood Libels' in the Ottoman Empire of the Fifteenth to Nineteenth Centuries." *Antisemitism Through the Ages*. Ed. Shmuel Almog. Trans. Nathan H. Reisner. London: Pergamon, for the Vidal Sassoon International Center for the Study of Antisemitism, 1988. 189–94.

Bastiaensen, A. "Un formulaire de messe du sacramentaire de Vérone et la fin du siège de Rome par les Goths (537–8)." *Revue bénédictine* 95.1–2 (1985): 39–43.

Battenberg, J. Friedrich. "Die Ritualmordprozesse gegen Juden in Spätmittelalter und Frühneuzeit – Verfahren und Rechtsschutz." *Die Legende vom Ritualmord. Zur Geschichte der Blutbeschuldigung gegen Juden*. Ed. Rainer Erb. Berlin: Metropol, 1993. 95–132.

—. *Das Europäische Zeitalter der Juden*. 2 vols. Darmstadt: Wissenschaftliche Buchgesellschaft, 1990.

Bell, David N. "Baldwin of Ford and the Sacrament of the Altar. Erudition at God's Service." *Studies in Medieval Cistercian History, XI. Papers from the 1985 and 1986 Cistercian Studies Conferences, organized by the Institute of Cistercian Studies of Western Michigan University, and held in conjunction with the 20th and 21st International Congress of Medieval Studies in Kalamazoo, Michigan, on May 9–12, 1985 and May 8–11, 1986*. Ed. John R. Sommerfeldt. Kalamazoo, MI: Cistercian Publications, 1987. 217–42.

Berg, Klaus. "Der Traktat des Gerhard von Köln über das kostbarste Blut Christi aus dem Jahre 1280." *900 Jahre Heilig-Blut-Verehrung in Weingarten 1094–1994: Festschrift zum Heilig-Blut-Jubiläum am 12. März 1994*. Eds. Norbert Kruse and Hans Ulrich Rudolf. 2 vols. Sigmaringen: Thorbecke, 1994. I: 435–84.

Bergeron, Richard. "La doctrine eucharistique de l'Enarr. in Ps. XXXIII d'Augustin." *Revue des Etudes Augustiniennes* 19 (1973): 101–20.

Bezer, Ernst. *Studien zur Geschichte des Abendmahlsstreits im 16. Jahrhundert*. Gütersloh: Bertelsmann, 1940.

Biale, David. "Blood Libels and Blood Vengeance." *Tikkun* 9.4 (1994): 39–40, 75.

Blaauw, Sible de. "Het ideaal van de stad als kerk. Verval en herleving van de

Romeinse statieliturgie." *Bouwkunst. Studies in vriendschap voor Kees Peeters*. Eds. Wim Denslagen, et al. Amsterdam: Architectura & Natura P, 1993. 77–86.

Blastic, Michael W. "Clare of Assisi, the Eucharist and John 13." *Clare of Assisi: Investigations*. Ed. Mary Francis Hone. St. Bonaventure, NY: Franciscan Institute Publications, 1993. 21–45.

Boehl, Felix. "Die hebräischen Handschriften zur Verfolgung der Juden Nordhausens und ihrem Tanz zum Tode im Jahre 1349." *Tanz und Tod in Kunst und Literatur*. Ed. Franz Link. Berlin: Duncker & Humblot, 1993. 127–38.

Bonano, Salvatore. *The Concept of Substance and the Development of Eucharistic Theology to the Thirteenth Century*. Washington: Catholic U of America P, 1960.

Boom, G. de. "La Culte de l'eucharistie d'après la miniature du moyen-âge." [Stephanus Axters et al.] *Studia eucharistica. DCC^i anni a condito festo sanctissimi corporis Christi 1246–1946*. Bussum: Brand; Antwerpen: De nederlandsche Boekhandel, 1946. 326–32.

Bosshard, Stefan Niklaus. *Zwingli, Erasmus, Cajetan: Die Eucharistie als Zeichen der Einheit*. Wiesbaden: Steiner, 1978.

Bossong, Georg. "Die Isotopie von Blut und Glaube: Zum Wortschatz des Antisemitismus im Spanischen des Inquisitionszeitalters." *Ketzerei und Ketzerbekämpfung in Wort und Text: Studien zur sprachlichen Verarbeitung religiöser Konflikte in der westlichen Romania*. Eds. Peter Blumenthal and Johannes Kramer. Wiesbaden: Franz Steiner, 1989. 99–110.

Boureau, Alain. "Le Calice de Saint Donat. Légende, autorité et argument dans la controverse hussite (1414/1415)." *Médiévales: langue, textes, histoire* 16–17 (1989): 209–15.

Boyle, Leonard E. "Robert Grosseteste and Transsubstantiation." *Journal of Theological Studies* n.s. 30.2 (1979): 512–15.

Braga, Gabriella. "La fortuna di un errore: la *Definitio brevis de Eucharistia*." *Bullettino dell'Istituto italiano per il Medio Evo e Archivio Muratoriano* 89 for 1980–1981 (1982): 393–412.

Brink, J. R. "'Fortres of Fathers': An Unpublished Sixteenth-Century Manuscript Relating to Patristic Writing on the Eucharist." *The Sixteenth-Century Journal* 10.1 (1979): 83–88.

Brooks, N. C. "An Ingolstadt Corpus Christi Procession and the *Biblia Pauperum*." *Journal of English and Germanic Philology* 35 (1936): 1–16.

Brooks, Peter N. *Thomas Cranmer's Doctrine of the Eucharist: An Essay in Historical Development*. London: Macmillan, 1965.

—. "Processional Drama and Dramatic Procession in Germany in the High Middle Ages." *Journal of English and Germanic Philology* 32 (1933): 141–71.

Browe, Peter. *Die Pflichtkommunion im Mittelalter*. Münster: Regensbergsche Verlagsbuchhandlung, 1940.

231

—. *Die Eucharistischen Wunder des Mittelalters*. Breslau: Müller & Seifert, 1938.

—. *Die Verehrung der Eucharistie im Mittelalter*. München: Hueber, 1933.

—. "Die Eucharistie als Zaubermittel im Mittelalter." *Archiv für Kulturgeschichte* 20 (1930): 134–54.

—. "Die Ausbreitung des Fronleichnamsfestes." *Jahrbuch für Liturgiewissenschaft* 7 (1927): 83–103.

—. "Die scholastische Theorie der eucharistischen Verwandlungswunder." *Theologische Quartalschrift* 110 (1926): 305–32.

—. "Die Hostienschändungen der Juden im Mittelalter." *Römische Quartalschrift für christliche Altertumskunde und für Kirchengeschichte* 34 (1926): 167–97.

Buescher, Gabriel Norbert. *The Eucharistic Theology of William Ockham. A Dissertation*. Washington, DC: Catholic U of America P, 1950.

Burr, David. "Eucharistic Presence and Conversion in Late Thirteenth-Century Franciscan Thought." *Transactions of the American Philosophical Society* 74.3 (1984) i–vi, 1–113.

—. "Scotus and Transsubstantiation." *Mediaeval Studies* 34 (1972): 336–50.

Bynum, Carolyn Walker. "The Female Body and Religious Practice in the Later Middle Ages." *Fragments for a History of the Human Body*. 3 vols. Ed. Michel Feher, Ramona Naddaff, and Nadia Tazi. New York: Zone, 1989. I: 162–88.

—. *Holy Feast and Holy Fast: The Religious Signification of Food to Medieval Women*. Berkeley: U of California P, 1987.

—. "The Body of Christ in the Later Middle Ages: A Reply to Leo Steinberg." *Renaissance Quarterly* 39 (1986): 394–439.

—. "Fast, Feast, and Flesh: The Religious Significance of Food to Medieval Women." *Representations* 11 (1985): 1–25.

—. "Women Mystics and Eucharistic Devotion in the Thirteenth Century." *Women's Studies* 11.1–2 (1984): 179–214.

—. *Jesus as Mother: Studies in the Spirituality of the High Middle Ages*. Berkeley: U of California P, 1983.

Byron, Brian F. "From Essence to Presence: A Shift in Eucharistic Expression Illustrated from the Apologetic of St. Thomas More." *Miscellanea Moreana: Essays for Germain Marc'hadour*. Eds. Clare M. Murphy, Henri Gibaud, and Mario DiCesare. Binghamton, NY: Medieval and Renaissance Texts and Studies, 1989. 429–41.

Callaey, F. "Documentazione eucaristica liegese, del vescovo de Liegi Roberto di Torote al papa Urbano IV (1240–1264)." *Eucaristia: il mistero dell'altare nel pensiero e nella vita della Chiesa*. Ed. Antonio Piolanti. Rome: Desclée, 1957. 907–33.

Camporesi, Piero. "The Consecrated Host: A Wondrous Excess." *Fragments for a History of the Human Body*. 3 vols. Eds. Michel Feher and Ramona Naddaff. New York: Zone, 1989. I, 220–37.

Cantin, Andre. "Ratio et auctoritas dans la premiere phase de la controverse eucharistique entre Berenger et Lanfranc." *Revue des Etudes Augustiniennes* 20 (1974): 155–86.

Caraza, I. "La doctrine eucharistique de S. Cyrille d'Alexandrie." *Studii Teologice* 20 (1968): 528–42.

Caspari, Hans. *Das Sakramentstabernakel in Italien bis zum Konzil von Trient. Gestalt, Ikonographie und Symbolik, kultische Funktion.* München: Uni-Druck, 1965.

Caspers, Charles. *De eucharistische vroomheid en het feest van Sacramentsdag in de Nederlanden tijdens de Late Middeleeuwen.* Leuven: Peeters, 1992.

Catto, J. I. "John Wyclif and the Cult of the Eucharist." *The Bible in the Medieval World: Essays in Memory of Beryl Smalley.* Eds. Katherine Walsh and Diana Wood. Oxford: Blackwell, for the Ecclesiastical History Society, 1985. 269–86.

Chadwick, Henry. "Symbol and Reality: Berengar and the Appeal to the Fathers." *Auctoritas und Ratio. Studien zu Berengar von Tours.* Eds. Peter Ganz, R. B. C. Huygens, and Friedrich Niewöhner. Wiesbaden: Harrassowitz, 1990. 25–45.

—. "Ego Berengarius." *Journal of Theological Studies* n.s. 40.2 (1989): 414–45.

Chavannes, H. "La présence réelle chez saint Thomas et chez Calvin." *Verbum Caro* 40 (1959): 157–70.

Chavasse, Antoine. "Le sacramentaire, dit Léonien, conservé dans le Veronensis LXXXV (80)." *Sacris Erudiri: Jaarboek voor Godsdienstwetenschappen* 27 (1984): 151–90.

Chiffoleau, Jacques. "Dels ritus a les creences. La pràctica de la missa a l'Edat Mitjana." *L'Avenç: Història del Països Catalans* 111 (1988): 38–49.

—. "Sur l'usage obsessionnel de la messe pour les morts à la fin du Moyen Age." *Faire croire: Modalités de la diffusion et de la réception des messages religieux du XII*e *au XV*e *siècle. Table ronde organisé par l'Ecole française de Rome (Rome, 22–23 juin, 1979).* Ed. André Vauchez. Roma: Ecole française de Rome, 1981. 235–56.

Chupungco, Anscar J. "Toward a Ferial Order of Mass." *Ecclesia orans* 10.1 (1993): 11–32.

Claire, Jean. "La musique de l'office de l'Avent." *Grégoire le Grand. Chantilly, Centre culturel Les Fontaines, 15–19 septembre, 1982. Actes.* Eds. Jacques Fontaine, Robert Gillet, Stan Pellistrandi. Paris: Éditions du Centre national de la recherche scientifique, 1986. 649–59.

Clark, Francis. *Eucharistic Sacrifice and the Reformation.* Oxford: Blackwell, 1967.

Clemons, Cheryl. "The Relationship between Devotion to the Eucharist and Devotion to the Humanity of Jesus in the Writings of St. Gertrude of Helfta." Diss. Catholic U of America, 1996.

Cohen, Jeremy, ed. *Essential Papers on Judaism and Christianity in Conflict: From Late Antiquity to the Reformation.* New York: New York UP, 1991.

Colette, Marie-Noël. "Jubilus et trope dans le *Gloria in excelsis Deo.*" *Recherches nouvelles sur les tropes liturgiques.* Eds. Wulf Arlt and Gunilla Björkvall. Stockholm: Almqvist & Wiksell, 1993. 175–91.

Congar, Yves. "Doctrines christologiques et théologie de l'Eucharistie (simples notes)." *Revue des sciences philosophiques et théologiques* 66.2 (1982): 233–44.

Costa, Francesco. "Simbolismo della celebrazione eucaristica in S. Bonaventura." *Miscellanea Francescana* 74 (1974): 161–215.

Cowdrey, Herbert Edward John. "The Papacy and the Berengarian Controversy." *Auctoritas und Ratio. Studien zu Berengar von Tours.* Eds. Peter Ganz, R. B. C. Huygens, and Friedrich Niewöhner. Wiesbaden: Harrassowitz, 1990. 109–38.

Cramer, P. J. "Ernulf of Rochester and the Problem of Remembrance." *Anselm Studies* 2 (1988): 143–63.

Cristiani, M. "La Controversia eucaristica nella cultura del secolo XI." *Studi Medievali* 3rd ser. 9 (1968): 167–233.

Crocker, Richard L. "Chants of the Roman Mass." *New Oxford History of Music,* vol. II: *The Early Middle Ages to 1300.* Eds. Richard Crocker and David Hiley. Oxford: Oxford UP, 1990. 174–222.

Croken, Robert C. *Luther's First Front: The Eucharist as Sacrifice.* Ottawa: U of Ottawa P, 1990.

Crowley, James P. "Liturgy, Sung Prayer and Quest in the Middle English *Saint Erkenwald.*" *Neuphilologische Mitteilungen* 93.3–4 (1992): 313–23.

Damerau, Rudolf. *Die Abendmahlslehre des Nominalismus, insbesondere die des Gabriel Biel.* Giessen: Schmitz, 1963.

Dauphine, James. "Une Lecture allegorique privilegiée au XVIᵉ siecle: Le Zodiaque eucharistique." *Bulletin de l'Association Guillaume Bude* 2 (1983): 206–16.

David, Zdenek V. "Jews in Sixteenth-Century Czech Historiography: The 'Czech Chronicle' of Vaclav Hajek of Libocany." *East European Jewish Affairs* 25.1 (1995): 25–42.

Davis, Thomas J. *The Clearest Promises of God: The Development of Calvin's Eucharistic Teaching.* New York: AMS Press, 1995.

Delaissé, L. M. J. "A la recherche des origines de l'office du Corpus Christi dans les manuscrits liturgiques." *Scriptorium* 4 (1950): 220–39.

Devereux, E. J. "Tudor Uses of Erasmus on the Eucharist." *Archiv für Reformationsgeschichte* 62 (1971): 38-52.

Devlin, D. "Corpus Christi: A Study in Medieval Eucharistic Theory, Development and Practice." Diss. U of Chicago, 1975.

Didier, Jean-Charles. "Aux débuts de la controverse eucharistique du XIᵉ siècle: Hugues de Breteuil, évêque de Langres et Bérenger de Tours." *Mélanges de science religieuse* 34 (1977): 82–97.

— and Philippe Delhaye. "Hugues de Breteuil, évêque de Langres (*ob.* 1050)." *Recherches augustiniennes: Supplément à la Revue des Etudes Augustiniennes* 16 (1981): 289–331.

Dimitrijevic, D. "Die Christologie des hl. Athanasius und ihre Bedeutung für die Auffassung der Eucharistie." *Kyrios* 14 (1974): 61–84.

Dobszay, László. "Local Compositions in the Office Temporale." *Max Lütolf zum 60. Geburtstag: Festschrift.* Eds. Bernhard Hangartner and Urs Fischer. Basel: Wiese, 1994. 65–74.

Dougherty, Therese M., S.S.N.D. "John Fisher and the Sixteenth-Century Eucharistic Controversy." *Moreana: Bulletin Thomas More* 21 (1968): 31–38.

Duffy, Eamon. *The Stripping of the Altars: Traditional Religion in England, c.1400 – c.1580.* New Haven, CT: Yale UP, 1992.

Dumoutet, E. "La Théologie de l'eucharistie à la fin du XIIe siècle: le témoignage de Pierre le Chantre d'après la 'Summa de sacramentis'." *Archives d'histoire doctrinale et littéraire du moyen âge* 18–20 (1943–45): 181–262.

—. *Corpus Domini. Aux sources de la piété eucharistique médiévale.* Paris: Beauchesne, 1942.

—. *Le désir de voir l'hostie et les origines de la dévotion au saint-sacrement.* Paris: Beauchesne, 1926.

—. Les Origines de la fête et de la procession du Saint-Sacrement." *La Vie et les arts liturgiques* 11 (1925): 343–8.

Dundes, Alan, ed. *The Blood Libel Legend. A Casebook in Anti-Semitic Folklore.* Madison, WI: U of Wisconsin P, 1991.

—. "The Ritual Murder or Blood Libel Legend: A Study of Anti-Semitic Victimization through Projective Inversion." *Temenos* 25 (1989): 7–32.

Dutton, Marsha L. "Eat, Drink, and Be Merry: The Eucharistic Spirituality of the Cistercian Fathers. Erudition at God's Service." *Studies in Medieval Cistercian History, XI. Papers from the 1985 and 1986 Cistercian Studies Conferences, organized by the Institute of Cistercian Studies of Western Michigan University, and held in conjunction with the 20th and 21st International Congress of Medieval Studies in Kalamazoo, Michigan, on May 9–12, 1985 and May 8–11, 1986.* Ed. John R. Sommerfeldt. Kalamazoo, MI: Cistercian Publications, 1987. 1–31.

Eder, Manfred. *Die "Deggendorfer Gnad": Entstehung und Entwicklung einer Hostienwallfahrt im Kontext von Theologie und Geschichte.* Passau: Passavia-Universitätsverlag, 1992.

Egger, Christoph. "Papst Innocenz III. als Theologe. Beiträge zur Kenntnis seines Denkens im Rahmen der Frühscholastik." *Archivum Historiae Pontificiae* 30 (1992): 55–123.

Engels, P. *De eucharistieleer van Berengarius van Tours.* Leuven: Katholieke U Leuven, 1965.

Erb, Rainer, ed. *Die Legende vom Ritualmord. Zur Geschichte der Blutbeschuldigung gegen Juden.* Berlin: Metropol, 1993.

Evans, Gillian R. "Gilbert Crispin on the Eucharist: A Monastic Postscript to Lanfrac and Berengar." *Journal of Theological Studies* n.s. 31.1 (1980): 28–43.

Fahey, J.-H. *The Eucharistic Teaching of Ratramn of Corbie*. Mundelein, IL: Seminarium Sanctae Mariae ad Lacum, 1951.

Ferretto, Bernardino. "La Messa di Pasqua nell'antica liturgia musicale beneventana." *Benedictina* 37.2 (1990): 461–82.

Foley-Beining, Kathleen. *Physicality and Women's Eucharistic Devotion in Catharina Regina von Greiffenberg's 'Andächtige Betrachtungen': 'Von Marien Schwanger-gehen' and the 'Abendmahls-Andachten'*. Diss. UCLA, Dissertations Abstracts International, Ann Arbor, MI. (DAI) 1992, Sept. 53:3, 823A.

Foucart-Borville, Jacques. "Les tabernacles eucharistiques de la France du Moyen Age." *Bulletin monumental* 148.4 (1990): 349–81.

—. "Essai sur les suspenses eucharistiques comme mode d'adoration privilégié du Saint-Sacrement." *Bulletin monumental* 145.3 (1987): 267–89.

Frank, Robert Worth. "Miracles of the Virgin, Medieval Anti-Semitism, and the Prioress's Tale." *The Wisdom of Poetry: Essays in Early English Literature in Honor of Morton W. Bloomfield*. Eds. Larry D. Benson and Siegfried Wenzel. Kalamazoo: Medieval Institute Publications, 1982. 177–88.

Frey, Winfried. "Ritualmordlüge und Judenhaß in der Volkskultur des Spätmittelalters." *Volkskultur des europäischen Spätmittelalters. Beiträge der Internationalen Tagung vom 24.–26. VI. 1986, veranstaltet vom Kulturamt der Stadt Böblingen in Verbindung mit der Oswald-von-Wolkenstein-Gesellschaft*. Ed. Peter Dinzelbacher and Hans-Dieter Mück. Stuttgart: Kröner, 1987. 177–97.

Fries, Albert. "Der Albertschüler Ambrosius da Siena und der Doppeltraktat *Über die Eucharistie* unter dem Namen des Albertus Magnus." *Die Kölner Universität im Mittelalter: Geistige Wurzeln und soziale Wirklichkeit*. Ed. Albert Zimmermann. Berlin: de Gruyter, 1989. 77–96.

—. *Der Doppeltraktat über die Eucharistie unter dem Namen des Albertus Magnus*. Münster: Aschendorff, 1984.

Fürstenberg, P. "Zur Geschichte der Fronleichnamsfeier in der alten Diözese Paderborn." *Theologie und Glaube* 9 (1917): 314–25.

Gahbauer, Ferdinand. "Theodoros von Mopsuestia und Ps.-Dionysios Areiopagites: Zwei Marksteine auf dem Weg zum Verständnis der Eucharistiefeier." *Studia Anselmiana* 105 (1992): 81–110.

Gavin, Charles D. "Luther's Use of 'The Humanity of Jesus' in the Eucharistic Controversy of the 1520's." Diss. Luther Northwestern Theological Seminary, 1993.

Gebhart, Alfons. *Das Bruderschaftsbuch des Zisterzienserklosters Worschweiler (15.–16. Jahrhundert)*. Speyer: Pilger 1992.

Geiselmann, Josef Rupert. *Zur frühmittelalterlichen Lehre vom Sakrament der Eucharistie*. Rottenburg a.N.: Bader, 1935.

—. *Die Abendmahlslehre an der Wende der christlichen Spätantike zum Frühmittelalter. Isidor von Sevilla und das Sakrament der Eucharistie.* München: Hueber, 1933.

—. *Die Eucharistielehre der Vorscholastik.* Paderborn: Schönigh, 1926.

Gerhards, Albert. "Der Stellenwert der Anaphora in den Liturgiekommentaren des Orients." *Ephemerides liturgicae* 107.3 (1993): 209–23.

Ghellinck, de, J. "Eucharistie au XII⁰ siècle en Occident." *Dictionnaire de Théologie catholique.* Paris: Librairie Letouzey et Ané, 1923–1972, vol. 5, cols. 1233-1302.

Gilbert, C. E. "Last Suppers and Their Refectories." *The Pursuit of Holiness in Late Medieval and Renaissance Religion.* Eds. Charles Trinkaus and Heiko A. Oberman. Leiden: Brill, 1974. 371–402.

Giniewski, Paul. "Old and New – The Mystery of the Bleeding Hosts." *Midstream* 41.3 (1995): 14–16.

Girgensohn, Dieter. *Peter von Pulkau und die Wiedereinführung des Laienkelchs. Leben und Wirken eines Wiener Theologen in der Zeit des großen Schismas.* Göttingen: Vandenhoeck & Ruprecht, 1964.

Glauche, Günter. "Neue Beobachtungen zur Überlieferung von *Exaggeratio, Dicta Herigeri* und verwandten Eucharistietexten." *Tradition und Wertung. Festschrift für Franz Brunhölzl zum 65. Geburtstag.* Eds. Günter Berndt, Fidel Rädle, and Gabriel Silagi. Sigmaringen: Thorbecke, 1989. 231–44.

Goering, Joseph and Mantello, Frank A.C. "Two 'opuscula' of Robert Grosseteste: *De Universi Complecione* and *Exposicio Canonis Misse.*" *Mediaeval Studies* 53 (1991): 89–123.

Goering, Joseph. "The Invention of Transsubstantiation." *Traditio* 46 (1991): 147–70.

Gollwitzer, Helmut. *Coena Domini: Die altlutherische Abendmahlslehre in ihrer Auseinandersetzung mit dem Calvinismus, dargestellt an der lutherischen Frühorthodoxie.* München: Kaiser, 1988.

Gordon, Briar. "Two Versions of a Middle English Exemplum of the Eucharist." *Neuphilologische Mitteilungen* 82:2 (1981): 204–10.

Göttler, Christine and Peter Jezler. "Doktor Thüring Frickers 'Geistermesse'. Die Seelgerätkomposition eines spätmittelalterlichen Juristen." *Materielle Kultur und religiöse Stiftung im Spätmittelalter. Internationales Round-Table-Gespräch Krems an der Donau, 26. September 1988.* Ed. Gerhard Jaritz. Wien: Verlag der österreichischen Akademie der Wissenschaften, 1990. 187–231.

Grant, G. G. "The Elevation of the Host: A Reaction to the Twelfth-Century Heresy." *Theological Studies* 1 (1940): 228–50.

Grasso, Giacomo. "Validità, oggi, del trattato sull'Eucaristia di san Tommaso d'Aquino." *Angelicum: Periodicum trimestre pontificae studiorum* 69.1 (1992): 55–68.

Graus, Frantisek. *Pest, Geissler, Judenmorde: Das 14. Jahrhundert als Krisenzeit.* Göttingen: Vandenhoeck & Ruprecht, 1987.

Grundy, Lynne. "Ælfric's *Sermo de sacrificio in die pascæ*: *figura* and *veritas*." *Notes and Queries* n.s. 37.3 (1990): 265–69.

Gy, Pierre-Marie. "Liturgy and Spirituality, II: Sacraments and Liturgy in Latin Christianity." *Christian Spirituality. Origins to the Twelfth Century*. Eds. Bernard McGinn and John Meyendorff. London: SCM P, 1989. 365–81.

—. "L'office du Corpus Christi et la théologie des accidents eucharistiques." *Revue des sciences philosophiques et théologiques* 66.1 (1982): 81–86.

—. "Le texte original de la *Tertia Pars* de la *Somme théologique* de S. Thomas d'Aquin dans l'apparat critique de l'édition léonine: le cas de l'Eucharistie." *Revue des sciences philosophiques et théologiques* 65.4 (1981): 608–16.

—. "L'office du Corpus Christi et S. Thomas d'Aquin: Etat d'une recherche." *Revue des sciences philosophiques et theologiques* 64 (1980): 491–507.

—. "Les paroles de la consécration et l'unité de la prière eucharistique selon les théologiens de Pierre Lombard à S. Thomas d'Aquin." *Studia Anselmiana* 79 (1980): 221–33.

Haacke, Rhaban, O.S.B. "Zur Eucharistielehre des Rupert von Deutz." *Recherches de théologie ancienne et médiévale* 32 (1965): 20–42.

Habig-Bappert, Inge. *Eucharistie im Spätbarock. Eine kirchliche Bild-Allegorese im deutschsprachigen Raum*. Münster: Regensberg, 1983.

—. "Eucharistische Allegorie im Spätbarock nördlich der Alpen: Phänomenologie der dogmatischen, apologetischen, katechetischen und devotionalen Bildelemente einer kirchlichen Allegorese." Diss. U of Münster, 1973.

Hamman, Adalbert. "Le symbole eucharistique des 'Grains nombreux du pain unique' chez Bonaventure: Origine et histoire de theme." *S. Bonaventura 1274–1974*. 4 vols. Eds. Jacques Guy Bougerol and Etienne Gilson. Roma: Collegio S. Bonaventura, 1974. 71–78.

Härdelin, Alf. *Aquae et vini mysterium. Geheimnis der Erlösung und Geheimnis der Kirche im Spiegel mittelalterlicher Auslegung des gemischten Kelches*. Münster: Aschendorff, 1973.

Hardt, Tom G. *Venerabilis et adorabilis eucharistia: En studie i den lutherska nattvardsläran under 1500-talet*. Uppsala: Alqvist & Wiksell, 1971.

Häring, N. M. "Berengar's Definitions of *Sacramentum* and Their Influence on Mediaeval Sacramentology." *Medieval Studies* 10 (1948): 109–46.

Häussling, A. "Literaturbericht zum Fronleichnamsfest." *Jahrbuch für Volkskunde*, n.s. 9 (1986): 228–40.

—. "Motives for Frequency of the Eucharist." *Concilium* 152 (1982): 25–30.

Henning, E. M. "The Architectonics of Faith: Metalogic and Metaphor in Zwingli's Doctrine of the Eucharist." *Renaissance and Reformation/ Renaissance et Reforme* 10.4 (1986): 315–65.

Heurtevent, R. "Durand de Troarn et les Origines de l'Hérésie bérengarienne." *Etudes de théologie historique* 5 (1912): 182–99.

Heywood, Thomas, J. "Logic and Metaphysics in Luther's Eucharistic Theology." *Renaissance and Modern Studies* 23 (1979): 147–59.

Hiley, David. "Ordinary of Mass Chants in English, North French and Sicilian Manuscripts." *Journal of the Plainsong and Mediaeval Music Society* (1986): 1–128.

Hödl, Ludwig. "Die theologische Auseinandersetzung mit Berengar von Tours im frühscholastischen Eucharistietraktat." *De corpore Domini. Auctoritas und Ratio. Studien zu Berengar von Tours.* Eds. Peter Ganz, R. B. C. Huygens, and Friedrich Niewöhner. Wiesbaden: Harrassowitz, 1990. 70–88.

—. "Abendmahl, Abendmahlsstreit." *Lexikon des Mittelalters.* München and Zürich: Artemis, 1980ff., vol. I, cols. 22–7.

—. "Der Transsubstantiationsbegriff in der scholastischen Theologie des 12. Jahrhunderts." *Recherches de théologie ancienne et médiévale* 31 (1964): 230–59.

Hoffmann, Philippe. "Une lettre de Drosos d'Aradeo sur la fraction du pain (Athous Iviron 190, A.D. 1297/1298)." *Rivista di studi bizantini e neoellenici* n.s. 22–3 for 1985–6 (1986): 245–84.

Holeton, David R. "The Communion of Infants and Hussitism." *Communio Viatorum: A Theological Quarterly* 27.4 (1984): 207–25.

Holopainen, Toivo J. *Dialectic and Theology in the Eleventh Century.* Leiden: Brill, 1996.

Hontoir, C. "La dévotion au saint sacrement chez les premiers cisterciens (XIIe–XIIIe siècles)." [Stephanus Axters et. al.]. *Studia eucharistica: DCC^i anni a condito festo sanctissimi corporis Christi, 1246–1946.* Bussum: Brand; Antwerpen: De nederlandsche Boekhandel, 1946. 132–56.

Houssieau, Albert. "Les rites de l'initiation chrétienne." *Les Rites d'initiation. Actes du Colloque de Liège et de Louvain-la-Neuve, 20–21 novembre 1984.* Eds. Julien Ries and Henri Limet. Louvain-la-Neuve: Centre d'histoire des religions, 1986. 415–29.

Houston, Julia. "Transsubstantiation and the Sign: Cranmer's Drama of the Lord's Supper." *Journal of Medieval and Renaissance Studies* 24.1 (1994): 113–30.

Hsia, Ronnie Po-chia. *The Myth of Ritual Murder: Jews and Magic in Reformation Germany.* New Haven, CT: Yale UP, 1988.

Hudson, Anne. "A Wycliffite Scholar of the Early Fifteenth Century." *The Bible in the Medieval World: Essays in Memory of Beryl Smalley.* Eds. Katherine Walsh and Diana Wood. Oxford: Blackwell, for the Ecclesiastical History Society, 1985. 301–15.

Hughes, Andrew. *Medieval Manuscripts for Mass and Office: A Guide to Their Organization and Terminology.* Toronto: U of Toronto P, 1982.

Huglo, Michel. "Le Répons-Graduel de la Messe. Evolution de la forme. Permanence de la fonction." *Schweizer Jahrbuch für Musikwissenschaft/ Annales suisses de musicologie* n.s. 2 (1982): 53–73.

Iserloh, Erwin. *Gnade und Eucharistie in der philosophischen Lehre des Wilhelm von Ockham.* Wiesbaden: Steiner, 1956.

Iversen, Gunilla. "On the Iconography of Praise in the Sanctus and in Its Tropes." *De Musica et cantu: Studien zur Geschichte der Kirchenmusik und der Oper. Helmut Hucke zum 60. Geburtstag.* Eds. Peter Cahn and Ann-Katrin Heimer. Hildesheim: Olms, 1993. 275–308.

—. "Tropen als liturgische Poesie und poetische Liturgie." *Zusammenhänge, Einflüsse, Wirkungen. Kongressakten zum ersten Symposium des Mediävistenverbandes in Tübingen, 1984.* Eds. Joerg O. Fichte, Karl Heinz Göller, and Bernhard Schimmelpfennig. Berlin: de Gruyter, 1986. 383–402.

Jacob, André. "Un opuscule didactique otrantais sur la liturgie eucharistique. L'adaptation en vers, faussement attribuée à Psellos, de la *Protheoria* de Nicolas d'Andida." *Rivista di studi bizantini e neoellenici* n.s. 14–16.24–26 (1977–79): 161–78.

James, M. "Ritual, Drama and Social Body in the Late Medieval Town." *Past and Present* 98 (1983): 3–29.

Jelenits, I. "Cena Agni – Mensa Christi: Contribution aux rapports de la terminologie eucharistique du moyen âge et de quelques phrases importantes de la Passio et de la Legenda Sancti Gerhardi." *Acta Antiqua Academiae Scientiarum Hungaricae* 23 (1975): 345–53.

Jesi, Furio. *L'accusa del sangue: Mitologie dell'antisemitismo.* Brescia: Morcelliana, 1993.

Jorissen, Hans. "Zum Verhältnis von Bild und Sakrament. Wandlungen des philosophischen Kontextes als Hintergrund der frühmittelalterlichen Eucharistiestreitigkeiten." *Streit um das Bild. Das Zweite Konzil von Nizäa (787) in ökumenischer Perspektive.* Ed. Josef Wohlmuth. Bonn: Bouvier, 1989. 97–111.

—. *Die Entfaltung der Transsubstantiationslehre bis zum Beginn der Hochscholastik.* Münster: Aschendorff, 1965.

Kandler, Karl Hermann. "Luther und die Frage nach dem 'Hausabendmahl'." *Luther: Zeitschrift der Luther Gesellschaft* 62.1 (1991): 21–27.

Kaufmann, Thomas. *Die Abendmahlstheologie der Straßburger Reformatoren bis 1528.* Tübingen: Mohr, 1992.

Keen, Maurice. "Wyclif, the Bible, and Transsubstantiation." *Wyclif in His Times.* Ed. Anthony Kenny. Oxford: Clarendon P, 1986. 1–16.

Kieckhefer, Richard. "Major Currents in Late Medieval Devotion." *Christian Spirituality: High Middle Ages and Reformation.* Eds. Jill Raitt, Bernard McGinn, and John Meyendorff. London: Routledge & Kegan Paul, 1987. 75–108.

—. *Unquiet Souls: Fourteenth-Century Saints and Their Religious Milieu.* Chicago: U of Chicago P, 1984.

Kinn, James W. "The Pre-Eminence of the Eucharist Among the Sacraments According to Alexander of Hales, St. Albert the Great, St. Bonaventure and St. Thomas Aquinas." Diss. Saint Mary of the Lake Seminary, 1960.

Kirkman, Andrew. "The Transmission of English Mass Cycles in the Mid to Late Fifteenth Century: A Case Study in Context." *Music and Letters* 75.2 (1994): 180–99.

Klingenberg, Heinz. "Eucharistischer Runenlöffel aus alemannischer Frühzeit." *Zeitschrift für Deutsches Altertum und Deutsche Literatur* 103 (1974): 81–94.

Kloft, Matthias Theodor. "Die Meßfeier und ihre Kodifizierung." *794 – Karl der Große in Frankfurt am Main: Ein König bei der Arbeit. Ausstellung zum 1200-Jahre-Jubiläum der Stadt Frankfurt am Main veranstaltet vom Magistrat der Stadt Frankfurt am Main, Amt für Wissenschaft und Kunst, Historisches Museum, in Kooperation mit der Frankfurter Projekte GmbH.* Ed. Johannes Fried. Sigmaringen: Thorbecke, 1994. 158–64.

Kolve, V. A. *The Play Called Corpus Christi.* Stanford: Stanford UP, 1966.

Kotter, Franz Josef. *Die Eucharistielehre in den katholischen Katechismen des 16. Jahrhunderts bis zum Erscheinen des Catechismus Romanus (1566).* Münster: Aschendorff, 1969.

Kruse, Norbert, ed. *900 Jahre Heilig-Blut-Verehrung in Weingarten, 1094 – 1994.* 2 vols. Sigmaringen: Thorbecke. 1994.

Kunzler, Michael. *Die Eucharistietheologie des Hadamarer Pfarrers und Humanisten Gerhard Lorich: Eine Untersuchung der Frage nach einer erasmischen Mess- u. Eucharistietheologie im Deutschland des 16. Jahrhunderts.* Münster: Aschendorff, 1981.

Ladner, Pascal. "Narrentum und Liturgie. Religiöse Parodie im Mittelalter." *Der Narr: Beiträge zu einem interdisziplinären Gespräch.* Ed. Hugo Huber. Freiburg, Schweiz: Universitätsverlag, 1991. 29–40.

Langmuir, Gavin I. "Thomas of Monmouth. Detector of Ritual Murder." *Speculum* 59 (1984): 820–64.

Laporte, Jean. *La doctrine eucharistique chez Philon d'Alexandrie.* Paris: Beauchesne, 1972.

Laurance, John D. "Eucharistic Leader According to Cyprian of Carthage: A New Study." *Studia liturgica* 15.2 (1982–1983): 66–75.

Leff, Gordon. "Ockham and Wyclif on the Eucharist." *Reading Medieval Studies* 2 (1976): 1–13.

Leinbaugh, Theodore H. "The Sources for Aelfric's Easter Sermon: The History of the Controversy and a New Source." *Notes and Queries* 33.3 (1986): 294–311.

Lewis, Keith D. "Unica Oblatio Christi: Eucharistic Sacrifice and the First Zurich Disputation." *Renaissance and Reformation/Renaissance et Reforme* 17.3 (1993): 19–42.

Libera, Alain de. "L'instant du changement selon saint Thomas d'Aquin." *Métaphysique. Histoire de la Philosophie: Recueil d'études offert à Fernand Brunner.* Neuchâtel: Editions de la Baconnière for the Université de Neuchâtel, Faculté des Lettres, 1981. 99–109.

Linage Conde, Antonio. "La liturgia de la misa en el sínodo del obispo de

Segovia Pedro de Cuéllar, 1325." *Anuario de Estudios Medievales* 16 (1986): 127–45.

Lindgren, Mereth. "Eukaristiska allegorier i uppländskt kalmåleri." *Kristus-fremstillinger. Foredrag holdt ved det 5. nordiske symposium for ikono-grafiske studier på Fuglsang, 29. aug. – 3. sept. 1976.* Ed. Ulla Haastrup. København: Gads, for the Institut for Kirkehistorie, Københavns Universitet, 1980. 183–202.

Lohrmann, Klaus. "Die Judenverfolgungen zwischen 1290 und 1420 als theologisches und soziales Problem." *Wellen der Verfolgung in der österreichischen Geschichte.* Ed. Erich Zöllner. Wien: Österreichischer Bundesverlag, 1986. 40–51.

Lossky, Nicolas. "Climat théologique au Concile de Florence." *Christian Unity. The Council of Ferrara-Florence 1438/39–1989.* Ed. Giuseppe Alberigo. Leuven: Leuven UP, 1991. 241–50.

Lotter, Friedrich. "Hostienfrevelvorwurf und Blutwunderfälschung bei den Judenverfolgungen von 1298 ("Rintfleisch") und 1336–1338 ("Armleder")." *Fälschungen im Mittelalter: Internationaler Kongress der Monumenta Germaniae Historica, München, September 1986,* Teil V. Hannover: Hahnsche Buchhandlung, 1988. 533–83.

Lubac, Henri de. *Corpus Mysticum. L'Eucharistie et l'église au moyen âge. Etude historique.* 2nd ed. Paris: Montaigne, 1942.

Mac Donnell, Kilian. *John Calvin, the Church, and the Eucharist.* Princeton: Princeton UP, 1967.

Macdonald, A. J. *Berengar and the Reform of Sacramental Doctrine.* London; New York: Longmans; Green, 1930.

MacGinty, Mary P. "Berengarius' Notion of Body as It Affected His Doctrine of Eucharistic Presence." Diss. Marquette U, 1967.

Macy, Gary. "The Dogma of Transsubstantiation in the Middle Ages." *Journal of Ecclesiastical History* 45.1 (1994): 11–41.

—. "Of Mice and Manna: 'Quid mus sumit' as a Pastoral Question." *Recherches de théologie ancienne et médiévale* 58 (1991): 157–66.

—. "Berengar's Legacy as a Heresiarch." *Auctoritas und Ratio. Studien zu Berengar von Tours.* Eds. Peter Ganz, R. B. C. Huygens and Friedrich Niewöhner. Wiesbaden: Harrassowitz 1990. 47–67.

—. "Some Examples of the Influence of Exegesis on the Theology of the Eucharist in the Eleventh and Twelfth Centuries." *Recherches de théologie ancienne et médiévale* 52 (1985): 64–77.

—. *The Theologies of the Eucharist in the Early Scholastic Period: A Study of the Salvific Function of the Sacrament According to the Theologians c. 1080 – c. 1220.* Oxford: Clarendon P, 1984.

Mangenot, E. "Eucharistie au XIIIe au XVe siècle." *Dictionnaire de Théologie catholique.* Paris: Librairie Letouzey et Ané, 1923–1972. vol. 5: cols. 1302–1326.

242

Marceau, William. "Théodore de Bèze et François de Sales: Deux spiritualités de l'eucharistie." *Dix-Septieme-Siècle* 170 (1991): 5–13.

Marcus, Ivan G. "Jews and Christians Imagining the Other in Medieval Europe." *Prooftexts* 15.3 (1995): 209–26.

Marin, Louis. "Un Chapitre dans l'histoire de la théorie semiotique: La Théologie eucharistique dans La Logique de Port-Royal (1683)." *History of Semiotics*. Eds. Achim Eschbach and Jürgen Trabant. Amsterdam: Benjamins, 1983. 127–44.

Martin, J. H. "The Eucharistic Treatise of John Quidort of Paris." *Viator* 6 (1975): 195–240.

Masi, R. "De notione transsubstantiationis disputatio scholastica." *Divinitas* 7 (1963): 285–332.

Mattern, G. *Zur Vorgeschichte und Geschichte der Fronleichnamsfeier besonders in Spanien: Studien zur Volksfrömmigkeit des Mittelalters und der beginnenden Neuzeit.* Münster: Aschendorff, 1962.

Mayer, A. L. "Die heilbringende Schau in Sitte und Kult." *Heilige Überlieferung: Ausschnitte aus der Geschichte des Mönchtums und des Heiligen Kultes.* Ed. Odo Casel. Münster: Aschendorff, 1938. 234–62.

McCue, James F. "Liturgy and Eucharist, II: West." *Christian Spirituality: High Middle Ages and Reformation.* Eds. Jill Raitt, Bernard McGinn, and John Meyendorff. London: Routledge and Kegan Paul, 1987. 427–38.

McInnis, Judy B. "Eucharistic and Conjugal Symbolism in The Spiritual Canticle of Saint John of the Cross." *Renascence Essays on Value in Literature* 36.3 (1984): 118–38.

McKinnon, James W. "The Roman Post-Pentecostal Communion Series." *Cantus Planus: International Musicological Society Study Group: Papers Read at the Fourth Meeting, Pécs, Hungary, 3–8 September 1990.* Eds. László Dobszay, Agnes Papp and Ferenc Sebö. Budapest: Hungarian Academy of Sciences, Institute for Musicology, 1992. 175–86.

McLaughlin, Megan. "On Communion with the Dead." *Journal of Medieval History* 17.1 (1991): 23–34.

McLaughlin, R. Emmet. "Schwenckfeld and the South German Eucharistic Controversy, 1526–1529." *Schwenckfeld and Early Schwenkfeldianism.* Ed. Peter C. Erb. Pennsburg, PA: Schwenkfelder Lib., 1986. 181–210.

McLelland, J. C. "Meta-Zwingli or Anti-Zwingli? Bullinger and Calvin in Eucharistic Concord." *Huldrych Zwingli, 1484–1531: A Legacy of Radical Reform.* Ed. E. J. Furcha. Montreal: Faculty of Religious Studies, McGill U, 1985. 179–95.

McNamara, Martin. "The Inverted Eucharistic Formula 'Conversio corporis Christi in panem et sanguinem in vinum': The Exegetical and Liturgical Background in Irish Usage." *Proceedings of the Royal Irish Academy. Section C. – Archaeology, Celtic Studies, History, Linguistics, Literature* 87.10 (1987): 573–93.

Merz, Hilde. "Die mittelalterliche jüdische Gemeinde in Rothenburg o.d.T." *Zur Geschichte der mittelalterlichen jüdischen Gemeinde in Rothenburg ob der Tauber.* Ed. Hilde Merz. Rothenburg o.d.T.: Verein Alt-Rothenburg, 1993. 9–28.

Meseguer Fernández, Juan. "El culto y la eucaristía en el monasterio de Pedralbes. Siglos XIV y XVI." *Archivo Ibero-Americano* 40.157 (1980): 115–22.

Messner, Reinhard. *Die Messreform Martin Luthers und die Eucharistie der Alten Kirche: Ein Beitrag zu einer systematischen Liturgiewissenschaft.* Innsbruck: Tyrolia, 1989.

Meyendorff, Paul. "Liturgy and Spirituality, I: Eastern Liturgical Theology." *Christian Spirituality. Origins to the Twelfth Century.* Eds. Bernard McGinn and John Meyendorff. London: SCM P, 1989. 350–63.

Miskuly, Jason M. *Thomas Murner and the Eucharist: The Defense of Catholic Eucharistic Theology in the Anti-Reformation Writings of Thomas Murner, "vnder Hürt, Hieter vnd Vorfechter der Christlichen Schefflin", 1520 – 1529.* St. Bonaventure, NY: Franciscan Institute of St. Bonaventure University, 1990.

Mitterwieser, Alois. *Geschichte der Fronleichnamsprozession in Bayern.* München: Knorr & Hirth, 1930.

Molinaro, A. "Sulla nozione de transsustanziazione. Saggio d'interpretatione tomistica." *Miscellanea Antonio Piolanti.* Rome: Fac. Theol. Pont. Univ. Lateranensis, 1964. 253–70.

Montcheuil, Yves de. "La raison de la permanence du Christ sous les espèces eucharistiques d'après Bonaventure et Thomas." *Mélanges Théologiques* 146 (1993): 71–82.

Montclos, J. de. *Lanfranc et Bérengar: la controverse eucharistique du XIe siècle.* Louvain: Spicilegium sacrum Lovaniense, 1971.

Morin, G. "Les 'Dicta' d'Heriger sur l'Eucharistie." *Revue Bénédictine* 25 (1908): 1–18.

Murphy, Gerard. "Eleventh- or Twelfth-Century Irish Doctrine Concerning the Real Presence." *Medieval Studies Presented to Aubrey Gwynn, S.J.* Eds. J. A. Watt, J.-B. Morrall, and F.-X. Martin. Dublin: Three Candles, 1963. 19–28.

Nau, Paul. *Le mystère du corps et du sang du Seigneur: la messe d'après saint Thomas d'Aquin, son rite d'après l'histoire.* Solesmes: Abbaye Saint-Pierre de Solesmes, 1976.

Neunheuser, Burkhard. "Wandel der Akzentsetzungen in eucharistischer Theologie, Praxis und Spiritualität." *Studia Anselmiana* 79 (1980): 191–220.

—. *Eucharistie in Mittelalter und Neuzeit.* Freiburg i.B.; Basel; Wien: Herder, 1963. (*Handbuch der Dogmengeschichte*, vol. 4, fasc. 4b).

Neuser, Wilhelm Heinrich. *Die Abendmahlslehre Melanchthons in ihrer geschichtlichen Entwicklung 1519–1530.* Neukirchen-Vluyn: Neunkirchener Verlag des Erziehungsvereins, 1968.

Niedermeyer, H. "Über die Sakramentsprozession im Mittelalter. Ein Beitrag zur Geschichte der kirchlichen Umgänge." *Sacris Erudiri* 22 (1974–75): 401–36.

244

—. *Eucharistie in Mittelalter und Neuzeit.* Freiburg: Herder, 1963.

Niscoveanu, M. "La Théologie de S. Basile le Grand dans les prières eucharistiques." *Studii Teologice* 19 (1967): 290–301.

Norn, Otto. "Det gotiske krucifix og den gotiske messe." *Kristusfremstillinger. Foredrag holdt ved det 5. nordiske symposium for ikonografiske studier på Fuglsang, 29. aug. – 3. sept. 1976.* Ed. Ulla Haastrup. København: Gads, for the Institut for Kirkenhistorie, Københavns Universitet, 1980. 227–39.

O'Meara, Carra Ferguson. "Eucharistic Theology and the House of God in Late Medieval and Early Renaissance Painting." *Classica et Mediaevalia. Studies in honour of Joseph Szövérffy.* Eds. Irene Vaslef and Helmut Buschhausen. Leiden and Washington: E.J. Brill and Classical Folia Editions, 1986. 125–37.

Parker, David A.. "The Act of Supremacy and The Corpus Christi Carol." *English Language Notes* 30.2 (1992): 5–10.

Pasquato, Ottorino. "Eucaristia e Chiesa in Giovanni Crisostomo." *Ephemerides Liturgicae* 102.3 (1988): 240–52.

—. "Eucaristia e Chiesa in Agostino." *Ephemerides Liturgicae* 102.1 (1988): 46–63.

Pastan, Elizabeth Carson. "'Tam haereticos quam Judaeos': Shifting Symbols in the Glazing of Troyes Cathedral." *Word and Image* 10.1 (1994): 66–83.

Pfleger, L. "Besondere eucharistische Devotionsformen des späteren Mittelalters." *Archiv für elsässische Kirchengeschichte* 8 (1933): 457–61.

Phillips, Heather. "John Wyclif and the Optics of the Eucharist." *From Ockham to Wyclif.* Eds. Anne Hudson and Michael Wilks. Oxford: Blackwell, for the Ecclesiastical History Society, 1987. 245–58.

Pipkin, H. Wayne. "The Positive Religious Values of Zwingli's Eucharistic Values." *Huldrych Zwingli, 1484–1531: A Legacy of Radical Reform.* Ed. E. J. Furcha. Montreal: Faculty of Religious Studies, McGill U, 1985. 107–43.

Planchart, Alejandro Enrique. "An Aquitainian Sequentia in Italian Sources." *Recherches nouvelles sur les tropes liturgiques.* Eds. Wulf Arlt and Gunilla Björkvall. Stockholm: Almqvist & Wiksell, 1993. 371–93.

Plotnik, Kenneth. *Hervaeus Natalis OP and the Controversies over the Real Presence and Transsubstantiation.* München: Schönigh, 1970.

Polc, Jaroslav V. "Il miracolo di Bolsena e Pietro di Praga. Un'ipotesi." *Rivista di storia della Chiesa in Italia* 45.2 (1991): 437–49.

Ponader, Ralph. "Die Abendmahlslehre des Andreas Bodenstein von Karlstadt in den Jahren 1521 – 1524: Die Kritik an der Realpräsenz durch Karlstadt untersucht vor dem Hintergrund der Chorismos-Problematik." Diss. Greifswald U, 1993.

Pouchelle, M.-C. "Mots, fluides et vertiges: les fêtes orales de la mystique chez Gautier de Coinci." *Annales* 42.1 (1987): 209–39.

Pratzner, Ferdinand. *Messe und Kreuzesopfer: Die Krise der sakramentalen Idee bei Luther und in der mittelalterlichen Scholastik.* Wien: Herder, 1970.

Pruett, Gordon E. *Thomas Cranmer and the Eucharistic Controversy in the Reformation.* Diss. Princeton U., 1968.

Purday, Keven M. "The Diffinicio Eucaristie of Robert Grosseteste." *Journal of Theological Studies* 27 (1976): 381–90.

Quere, Ralph W. "Changes and Constants: Structure in Luther's Understanding of the Real Presence in the 1520's." *The Sixteenth-Century Journal* 16.1 (1985): 45–78.

—. *Melanchthon's Christum cognoscere: Christ's Efficacious Presence in the Eucharistic Theology of Melanchthon.* Nieuwkoop: de Graaf, 1977.

Ramis Miquel, Gabriel. "La anámnesis en la liturgia eucarística hispánica." *I congreso internacional de estudios mozárabes, Toledo, 1975. Ponencias y comunicaciones presentadas. Serie D, 1: Liturgia y música mozárabes.* Toledo: Instituto de Estudios visigótico-mozárabes de San Eugenio, 1978. 65–86.

Rathey, Markus. "Eucharistische Ethik in Luthers Abendmahlssermon von 1519." *Luther: Zeitschrift der Luther-Gesellschaft* 63.2 (1992): 66–73.

Reynolds, Roger E. "A South Italian Liturgico-Canonical Mass Commentary." *Mediaeval Studies* 50 (1988): 626–70.

—. "Image and Text: A Carolingian Illustration of Modifications in the Early Roman Eucharistic *ordines.*" *Viator* 14 (1983): 59–75.

—. "A Visual Epitome of the Eucharistic *ordo* from the Era of Charles the Bald: The Ivory Mass Cover of the *Drogo Sacramentary.*" *Charles the Bald: Court and Kingdom. Papers Based on a Colloquium Held in London in April 1979.* Eds. Margaret Gibson, Janet Nelson, and David Ganz. Oxford: British Archaeological Reports, 1981. 265–89.

Riehle, Wolfgang. *The Middle English Mystics.* Trans. Bernard Standring. London: Routledge & Kegan Paul, 1981.

Ries, Rotraud. "Juden: Zwischen Schutz und Verteufelung." *Randgruppen der spätmittelalterlichen Gesellschaft: Ein Hand- und Studienbuch.* Ed. Bernd-Ulrich Hergemöller. Warendorf: Fahlbusch, 1990. 232–76.

Rohrbacher, Stefan and Michael Schmidt. *Judenbilder: Kulturgeschichte anti-jüdischer Mythen und antisemitischer Vorurteile.* Reinbek b. Hamburg: Rowohlt, 1991.

Rothkrug, Lionel. "Holy Shrines, Religious Dissonance and Satan in the Origins of the German Reformation." *Historical Reflections/Réflexions historiques* 14.2 (1987): 143–286.

Rubin, Miri. "Ein neuer Feiertag im liturgischen Buch. Das Fronleichnamsfest." *Der Codex im Gebrauch. Akten des Internationalen Colloquiums 11.–13. Juni, Münster 1992.* Eds. Christel Meier, Dagmar Hupper, and Hagen Keller. München: Fink, 1996. 31–40.

—. "Corpus Christi: Inventing a Feast." *History Today* 40.7 (1990): 15–21.

—. "Der Körper der Eucharistie im Mittelalter." *Gepeinigt, begehrt, vergessen: Symbolik und Sozialbezug des Körpers im späten Mittelalter und in der frühen Neuzeit.* Eds. Klaus Schreiner and Norbert Schnitzler. München: Fink,

1992. 25–40.

—. "Desecration of the Host: The Birth of an Accusation." *Studies in Church History* 29 (1992): 169–85.

—. "The Eucharist and the Construction of Medieval Identities." *Culture and History, 1350–1600: Essays on English Communities, Identities and Writing.* Ed. David Aers. Hemel Hempstead: Harvester Wheatsheaf, 1992. 43–63.

—. "What Did the Eucharist Mean to Thirteenth-Century Villagers?" *Thirteenth Century England, IV: Proceedings of the Newcastle upon Tyne Conference, 1991.* Ed. P. R. Coss and S. D. Lloyd. Woodbridge, Suffolk: Boydell & Brewer, 1992. 47–55.

—. *Corpus Christi: The Eucharist in Late Medieval Culture.* Cambridge: Cambridge UP, 1991.

Rückert, L. J. "Der Abendmahlsstreit des Mittelalters." *Zeitschrift für wissenschaftliche Theologie* 1 (1858), 22–53; 321–376; 489–561.

Rudolph, Hartmut. "Viehischer und himmlischer Leib: Zur Bedeutung von 1. Korinther 15 fur die Zwei-Leiber-Spekulation des Paracelsus." *Carleton Germanic Papers* 22 (1994): 106–20.

Sancho Andreu, Jaime. "Ritos de la infancia y la adolescencia en el antiguo rito hispánico." *Studia Anselmiana* 105 (1992): 207–45.

—. "Los formularios eucarísticos de los domingos *de quotidiano* en el rito hispánico." *I congreso internacional de estudios mozárabes, Toledo, 1975. Ponencias y comunicaciones presentadas. Serie D, 1: Liturgia y música mozárabes.* Toledo: Instituto de Estudios visigótico-mozárabes de San Eugenio, 1978. 87–104.

Scarry, Elaine. *The Body in Pain: The Making and Unmaking of the World.* Oxford: Oxford UP, 1985.

Schaefer, Mary Martina. "Twelfth-Century Latin Commentaries on the Mass: The Relationship of the Priest to Christ and to the People." *Studia liturgica* 15.2 (1982–1983): 76–86.

Schillebeeckx, Edward. "The Christian Community and Its Office-Bearers." *Concilium* 133 (1980): 95–133.

Schlette, Heinz R. *Die Lehre von der geistlichen Kommunion bei Bonaventura, Albert dem Grossen und Thomas von Aquin.* München: Hueber, 1959.

Schmid, Franz. "Die eucharistischen Wundererscheinungen im Lichte der Dogmatik." *Zeitschrift für katholische Theologie* 26 (1902), 492–517.

Schnitzler, Th. "Die erste Fronleichnamsprozession. Datum und Charakter." *Münchener theologische Zeitschrift* 24 (1973): 352–62.

Schrader, Charles R. "The Surviving Manuscripts of the Eucharistic Treatises of Heriger of Lobbes." *Manuscripta* 24.1 (1980): 10–11.

Schroubek, Georg-R. "Andreas von Rinn. Der Kult eines 'heiligen Ritualmordopfers' im historischen Wandel." *Österreichische Zeitschrift für Volkskunde* 49.4 (1995): 371–96.

Schulte, Raphael. *Die Messe als Opfer. Die Lehre frühmittelalterlicher Autoren über das eucharistische Opfer.* Münster: Aschendorff, 1959.

Schwarz, Reinhard. "Abendmahlsgemeinschaft durch das Evangelium, obwohl der Tisch des Herrn 'durch menschliche Irrung versperrt ist': Texte aus der Frühzeit der Reformation." *Lutherjahrbuch* 59 (1992): 38–78.

Sicilone, Ildebrando. "La memoria dell'instituzione dell'eucaristia." *Studia Anselmiana* 102 (1990): 55–69.

Scribner, Charles. *The Triumph of the Eucharist Tapestries Designed by Rubens.* Diss. Princeton U, 1977. Ann Arbor, MI: UMI Research P, 1982.

Sheedy, Charles E. *The Eucharistic Controversy of the Eleventh Century against the Background of Prescholastic Theology.* Washington, DC: Catholic U of America P, 1947.

Sheerin, Daniel J. "Gilbert of Airvau's Verses on the Holy Eucharist." *Revue des Etudes Augustiniennes* 20 (1974): 187–96.

Shrader, Charles-R. "The False Attribution of an Eucharistic Tract to Gerbert of Aurillac." *Mediaeval Studies* 35 (1973): 178–204.

Smith, R. U. "The Eucharistic Meditations of Arnold of Bonneval. A Reassessment." *Recherches de théologie ancienne et médiévale* 61 (1994): 115–35.

Snoek, Godefridus J.C. *Medieval Piety from Relics to the Eucharist: A Process of Mutual Interaction.* Trans. Michael J. Collins. Leiden: Brill, 1995.

Snow-Smith, Joanne. "Masaccio's Fresco in Santa Maria Novella: A Symbolic Representation of the Eucharistic Sacrifice." *Arte lombarda: Rivista di storia dell'arte* n.s. 84–85.1–2 (1988): 47–60.

Sprandel, Rolf. "Der Sakramentskult des Spätmittelalters im Spiegel der zeitgenössischen Chronistik." *Das Mittelalter – Unsere fremde Vergangenheit. Beiträge der Stuttgarter Tagung vom 17. bis 19. September 1987.* Eds. Joachim Kuolt, Harald Kleinschmidt, and Peter Dinzelbacher. Stuttgart: Helfant-Edition, 1990. 299–314.

Steiner, Ruth. "The Canticle of the Three Children as a chant of the Roman Mass." *Schweizer Jahrbuch für Musikwissenschaft/Annales suisses de musicologie* n.s.2 (1982): 81–90.

Stocker, Bärbel. "Die Opfergeräte der hl. Wiborada von St. Gallen – Eine Frau als Zelebrantin der Eucharistie." *Freiburger Diözesan-Archiv* 111 (1991): 405–19.

Stump, Eleonore. "Theology and Physics in *De sacramento altaris*: Ockham's Theory of Indivisibles." *Infinity and Continuity in Ancient and Medieval Thought.* Ed. Norman Kretzmann. Ithaca: Cornell UP, 1982. 207–30.

Suntrup, Rudolf. "Präfigurationen des Messopfers in Text und Bild." *Frühmittelalterliche Studien* 18 (1984): 468–528.

Sylla, Edith Dudley and John Emery Murdoch. "Autonomous and Handmaiden Science: St. Thomas Aquinas and William of Ockham on the Physics of the Eucharist." *The Cultural Context of Medieval Learning.* Eds. John Emery Murdoch and Edith Dudley Sylla. Dordrecht: Reidel, 1975. 349–90.

Taft, Robert F. "The Fruits of Communion in the Anaphora of St. John Chrysostom." *Studia Anselmiana* 105 (1992), 275–302.

—. "Melismos and Comminution: The Fraction and Its Symbolism in the Byzantine Tradition." *Studia Anselmiana* 95 (1988): 531–52.

—. "Mount Athos: A Late Chapter in the History of the Byzantine Rite." *Dumbarton Oaks Papers* 42 (1988): 179–94.

—. "Liturgy and Eucharist, I: East." *Christian Spirituality: High Middle Ages and Reformation.* Eds. Jill Raitt, Bernard McGinn, and John Meyendorff. London: Routledge and Kegan Paul, 1987. 415–26.

—. "Water into Wine. The Twice-Mixed Chalice in the Byzantine Eucharist." *Le Muséon: Revue d'études orientales/Tijdschrift voor oriëntalisme* 100.1–4 (1987): 323–42.

—. "The Frequency of the Eucharist throughout History." *Concilium* 152 (1982): 13–24.

Tavard, George H. "The Church as Eucharistic Communion in Medieval Theology." *Continuity and Discontinuity in Church History. Essays Presented to George Huntston Williams on the Occasion of His 65th Birthday.* Eds. F. Forrester Church and Timothy George. Leiden: Brill, 1979. 92–103.

Thorey, Lionel de. "Histoire de la Messe, de Grégoire le Grand à Vatican II." *Avatars du rit grégorien. Information historique* 49.3 (1987): 93–101.

Thurn, Hans and Claudia Wiener. "Eine illuminierte Handschrift von Hildeberts von Lavardin *De mysterio missae.*" *Würzburger Diözesan-Geschichtsblätter* 55 (1993): 13–35.

Towey, Anthony. "'Amicitia' as the Philosophical Foundation and the Principal Analogy of the Eucharistic Theology of Thomas Aquinas." Diss. Pontificia Universitas Gregoriana, 1995.

Treue, Wolfgang. "Schlechte und gute Christen: Zur Rolle von Christen in antijüdischen Ritualmord- und Hostienschändigungslegenden." *Aschkenas* 2 (1992): 95–116.

Tumbocon y Santamaria, Alberto C. "The Necessity of Means of the Eucharist According to St. Albert the Great." Diss. Pontificia Studiorum Universitas a S. Thoma Aquin Urbe, 1982.

Unterkirchner, F. "Eine alte Fronleichnamsmesse." *Archiv für Liturgiewissenschaft* 29 (1987): 47–9.

Van der Lof, L.-J. "Eucharistie et présence réelle selon Saint Augustin (à propos d'un commentaire sur De civitate Dei x,vi)." *Revue des études augustiniennes* 10 (1964): 295–394.

Vauchez, André. *Le laïcs au Moyen Age: Pratiques et expériences religieuses.* Paris: Editions du Cerf, 1987.

—. "Dévotion eucharistique et union mystique chez les saintes de la fin du Moyen Age." *Atti del simposio internazionale Cateriniano-Bernardiniano, Siena, 17–20 aprile 1980.* Eds. Domenico Maffei and Paolo Nardi. Siena, Accademia Senese degli Intronati, 1982. 295–300.

Veroli, Cristiano. "La revisione musicale bernardina e il graduale cistercense (II)." *Analecta Cisterciensia* 48.12 (1992): 3–104.

Veuthey, L. "Duns Scot et le mystère de la transsubstantiation." *De doctrina Ioannis Duns Scoti: Acta Congressus Scotistici Internationalis Oxonii et Edinburghi, 11–17 sept. 1966.* 4 vols. Rome: Cura Commissionis Scotisticae, 1968. III: 461–71.

Vogel, Cyrille. "Deux conséquences de l'eschatologie grégorienne: la multiplication des messes privées et les moinesprêtres." *Grégoire le Grand. Chantilly, Centre culturel Les Fontaines, 15–19 septembre, 1982. Actes.* Eds. Jacques Fontaine, Robert Gillet, Stan Pellistrandi. Paris: Éditions du Centre national de la recherche scientifique, 1986. 267–76.

——. "Anaphores eucharistiques preconstantiniennes." *Augustinianum* 20 (1980): 401–10.

——. "Une mutation cultuelle inexpliquée: le passage de l'Eucharistie communautaire à la messe privée." *Revue des sciences religieuses de l'Université de Strasbourg* 54.3 (1980): 231–50.

Vogüé, Adalbert de. "Monastic Life and Times of Prayer in Common." *Concilium* 142 (1988): 72–77.

Wamers, Egon. "Frühes liturgisches Gerät." *794 – Karl der Große in Frankfurt am Main: Ein König bei der Arbeit. Ausstellung zum 1200-Jahre-Jubiläum der Stadt Frankfurt am Main veranstaltet vom Magistrat der Stadt Frankfurt am Main, Amt für Wissenschaft und Kunst, Historisches Museum, in Kooperation mit der Frankfurter Projekte GmbH.* Ed. Johannes Fried. Sigmaringen: Thorbecke. 1994. 165–70.

Wappelshammer, Elisabeth. *Jüdische Geschichte – jüdische Kultur in Niederösterreich: Erinnerungen ans Mittelalter und seine Folgen.* Wien: Verein Kultur im Alltag, 1990.

Wiederanders, Gerlinde. "Die Hostienfrevellegende von Kloster Heiligengrabe: Ausdruck des mittelalterlichen Antijudaismus in der Mark Brandenburg." *Kairos* 29.1–2 (1987): 99–103.

Wohlmuth, J. *Realpräsenz und Transsubstantiation im Konzil von Trient: Eine historische-kritische Analyse der Canones 1–4 der Sessio XIII.* 2 vols. Frankfurt: Hubert Lang, Bern: Peter Lang, 1975.

Wolfe, Robert: "'The Lord's Supper': The Sources of Jew-Hatred in the Christian Ceremony of Cannibalism." *Nativ* 4.4 (1991): 44–48.

Woodhall, J. A. "The Eucharistic Theology of Ignatius of Antioch." *Communio* 5 (1972): 5–21.

Yuval, Israel Jacob. "Vengeance and Damnation, Blood and Defamation: From Jewish Martyrdom to Blood Libel Accusations." *Zion* 58.1 (1993): 33–90. [in Hebrew].

Zawilla, R. J. "The Biblical Sources of the Historia Corporis Christi Attributed to Thomas Aquinas: A Theological Study to Determine Their Authenticity." Diss. U of Toronto, 1985.

Zika, C. "Hosts, Processions and Pilgrimages in Fifteenth-Century Germany." *Past and Present* 118 (1988): 25–64.

Zinsmaier, P. "Die Einführung des Fronleichnamsfestes in Stadt und Diözese Konstanz." *Zeitschrift für die Geschichte des Oberrheins* 10 (1953): 265–8.

Transsubstantiation and Medieval and Early Modern Literature

Aronstein, Susan. "Rewriting Perceval's Sister: Eucharistic Vision and Typological Destiny in the *Queste del San Graal.*" *Women's Studies* 21.2 (1992): 211–30.

Baschera, Marco. "Transsubstantiation und Theater." *Colloquium-Helveticum: Cahiers Suisses de Litterature Comparée/Schweizer Hefte für Allgemeine und Vergleichende Literatur* 17 (1993): 89–103.

Beckwith, Sarah. "Ritual, Church and Theatre: Medieval Dramas of the Sacramental Body." *Culture and History, 1350–1600: Essays on English Communities, Identities and Writing.* Ed. David Aers. Hemel Hempstead: Harvester Wheatsheaf, 1992. 65–89.

Bischoff, Guntram G. *The Eucharistic Controversy between Rupert of Deutz and his Anonymous Adversary: Studies in the Theology and Chronology of Rupert of Deutz (c. 1076 – c. 1129) and His Earlier Literary Work.* Diss. Princeton University, 1965. Ann Arbor, MI: Univ. Microfilms, 1981.

Blair, L. "A Note on the Relation of the Corpus Christi Procession to the Corpus Christi Play in England." *Modern Language Notes* 55 (1940): 83–95.

Boenig, Robert E. "*Andreas*, the Eucharist and Vercelli." *Journal of English and Germanic Philology* 79.3 (1980): 313–31.

Bonnell, William. "Anamnesis: The Power of Memory in Herbert's Sacramental Vision." *George Herbert Journal* 15.1 (1991): 33–48.

Booty, John E. "Hooker's Understanding of the Presence of Christ in the Eucharist." *The Divine Drama in History and Liturgy: Essays Presented to Horton Davies on His Retirement from Princeton University.* Ed. John E. Booty. Allison Park, PA: Pickwick, 1984. 131–48.

Bowman, F. P. "Michelet et les métamorphoses de Christ." *Revue d'histoire littéraire de la France* 74 (1974): 824–51.

Breuer, Wilhelm. *Die lateinische Eucharistiedichtung des Mittelalters von ihren Anfängen bis zum Ende des 13. Jahrhunderts.* Wuppertal: Henn, 1970.

Bruce, J. D. *The Evolution of Arthurian Romance. From the Beginnings down to the Year 1300.* Göttingen: Vandenhoeck & Ruprecht; Baltimore: Johns Hopkins UP, 1923.

Bunte, Wolfgang. *Juden und Judentum in der Mittelniederländischen Literatur (1100–1600).* Frankfurt a.M.: Lang, 1989.

Carpenter, Dwayne Eugene. "Social Perception and Literary Portrayal: Jews and Muslims in Medieval Spanish Literature." *Convivencia: Jews, Muslims, and Christians in Medieval Spain.* Eds. Vivian B. Mann et al. New York: George Braziller, in association with the Jewish Museum, 1992. 61–81.

Coletti, Theresa. "Sacrament and Sacrifice in the N-Town Passion." *Mediaevalia* 7 (1981): 239–64.

Craig, H. "The Corpus Christi Procession and the Corpus Christi play." *Journal of English and Germanic Philology* 13 (1914): 589–602.

Crépin, André. "Aelfric et les controverses sur l'euchariste: Etude de vocabulaire." *Vivante tradition, sources et racines: Evolution de quelques formes et forces en littérature et civilisation anglaises.* Eds. Olivier Luduad, Marie-Madeleine Martinet, and Roger Lejosne. Paris: Centre d'Histoire des Idees dans les Iles Britanniques, 1982. 62–72.

Dachslager, Earl-L. "'Hateful to Crist and to His Compaignye': Theological Murder in 'The Prioress's Tale' and 'The Fixer'." *Lamar Journal of the Humanities* 11.2 (1985): 43–50.

Despres, Denise L. "Cultic Anti-Judaism and Chaucer's Litel Clergeon." *Modern Philology* 91.4 (1994): 413–27.

Dickson, Donald-R. "Between Transsubstantiation and Memorialism: Herbert's Eucharistic Celebration." *George Herbert Journal* 11.1 (1987): 1–14.

Diekstra, F. N. M. "Chaucer's Way with His Sources: Accident into Substance and Substance into Accident." *English Studies* 62 (1981): 215–36.

Dietz, Donald T. "Liturgical and Allegorical Drama: The Uniqueness of Calderon's Auto Sacramental." *Calderon de la Barca at the Tercentenary: Comparative Views.* Eds. Wendell M. Aycock and Sydney P. Cravens. Lubbock: Texas Tech P, 1982. 71–88.

DiPasquale, Theresa-M. "Receiving a Sexual Sacrament: 'The Flea' as Profane Eucharist." *John Donne's Religious Imagination: Essays in Honor of John T. Shawcross.* Eds. Jean Raymond Frontain and Frances M. Malpezzi. Conway, AR: UCA, 1995. 81–95.

Dunn, E. C. "Popular Devotion in the Vernacular Drama of Medieval England." *Mediaevalia et Humanistica* 4 (1973): 55–68.

Elsky, Martin. "The Sacramental Frame of George Herbert's 'The Church' and the Shape of Spiritual Autobiography." *Journal of English and Germanic Philology* 83.3 (1984): 313–29.

Erler, Mary C. "Spectacle and Sacrament: A London Parish Play in the 1530s." *Modern Philology* 91.4 (1994): 449–54.

Feistner, Edith. "Heilsgeschichte und Antisemitismus: Der Thüringer Helwig und sein 'Maere vom heiligen Kreuz'". *Zeitschrift für Deutsche Philologie* 110.3 (1991): 337–348.

Fisher, Lizette A. *Mystic Vision in the Grail Legend and in the Divine Comedy.* New York: Columbia UP, 1917.

Fjågesund, Peter. "Joyce's 'The Dead': Carnival, Eucharist and Medieval Visions." *English Studies* 78.2 (1997): 139–148.

Frey, Winfried. "Das Bild des Judentums in der deutschen Literatur des Mittelalters." *Judentum im deutschen Sprachraum.* Ed. Karl E. Groezinger. Frankfurt a.M.: Suhrkamp, 1991. 36–59.

Garber, Marjorie, "'Here's Nothing Writ': Scribe, Script, and Circumspection in Marlowe's Plays." *Theatre Journal* 36.3 (1984): 301–20.

Gardiner, Anne Barbeau. "Donne and the Real Presence of the Absent Lover." *John Donne Journal: Studies in the Age of Donne* 9.2 (1990): 113–24.

Guerreau, Jalabert. "Anita Aliments symboliques et symbolique de la table dans les romans arthuriens (XIIe–XIIIe siècles)." *Annales – Histoire, Sciences Sociales* 47.3 (1992): 561–94.

Hardison, O. B. *Christian Rite and Christian Drama in the Middle Ages.* Baltimore, MD: Johns Hopkins UP, 1965.

Helms, Chad. "The Desert Altar: Eucharistic Imagery in Selected Literary Works of Fenelon." *Seventeenth-Century French Studies 15* (1993): 269–78.

Hoy, J. F. "On the Relationship of the Corpus Christi Plays to the Corpus Christi Procession at York." *Modern Philology* 71 (193–74): 166–8.

Hunter, Jeanne Clayton. "'With Winges of Faith': Herbert's Communion Poems." *Journal of Religion* 62.1 (1982): 57–71.

Insolera, Manuel. "Robert de Boron, lo pseudo-germano e Onorio Augusto-dunense: Il Graal e il mistero della transustanziazione." *Romania* 108.2–3 (1987): 268–87.

Johnston, A. F. "The Guild of Corpus Christi and the Procession of Corpus Christi in York." *Mediaeval Studies* 38 (1976): 372–84.

—. "The Procession and Play of Corpus Christi in York after 1426." *Leeds Studies in English* n.s. 7 (1973–74): 55–62.

Jung, Emma and Marie-Louise von Franz. *Die Gralslegende in psychologischer Sicht.* Zürich: Rascher, 1960.

Keenan, Hugh T. "The 'General Prologue' to the 'Canterbury Tales,' Lines 345–346: The Franklin's Feast and Eucharistic Shadows." *Neuphilologische Mitteilungen* 79 (1978): 36–40.

Kerrigan, William. "Ritual Man: On the Outside of Herbert's Poetry." *Psychiatry: Interpersonal and Biological Processes* 48.1 (1985): 68–82.

Knight, R. C. "Ritual Murder at Versailles: Racine's Iphigenie." *Myth and Its Making in the French Theatre*. Eds. E. Freeman et al. Cambridge: Cambridge UP, 1988. 71–80.

Knoch-Mund, Gaby. "Das Judenbild in der erzählenden Literatur des Mittelalters." *Berliner Theologische Zeitschrift* 8.1 (1991): 31–50.

Koppitz, Hans-Joachim. *Wolframs Religiosität. Beobachtungen über das Verhältnis Wolframs zur religiösen Tradition des Mittelalters.* Bonn: Bouvier, 1959.

Kratz, Henry. *Wolfram von Eschenbach's Parzival. An Attempt at a Total Evaluation.* Bern: Francke, 1973. [esp. 574–89].

Kretzmann, P. E. *The Liturgical Element in the Earliest Forms of Medieval Drama, With Special Reference to the English and German Plays.* Minneapolis, MN: U of Minnesota, 1916.

Lepow, Lauren Ethel. *Enacting the Sacrament: Counter-Lollardy in the Towneley Cycle.* Rutherford, N.J. : Fairleigh Dickinson UP, 1990.

—. "Drama of Communion: The Life of Christ in the Towneley Cycle." *Philological Quarterly* 62.3 (1983): 403–13.

Lochrie, Karma. "The Language of Transgression: Body, Flesh, and Word in Mystical Discourse." *Speaking Two Languages: Traditional Disciplines and Contemporary Theory in Medieval Studies.* Ed. Allen J. Frantzen. Albany, NY: SUNY P, 1991. 115–40.

Loney, Glenn. "Oberammergau, 1634–1990: The Play and the Passions." *New Theatre Quarterly* 7 [27] (1991): 203–16.

Loomis, Roger Sherman. *The Grail. From Celtic Myth to Christian Symbol.* Cardiff: U of Wales P, 1963.

Lotter, Friedrich. "Das Judenbild im volkstümlichen Erzählgut dominikanischer Exempelliteratur um 1300: Die 'Historiae memorabiles' des Rudolf von Schlettstadt." *Herrschaft, Kirche, Kultur: Beiträge zur Geschichte des Mittelalters. Festschrift für Friedrich Prinz.* Ed. Georg Jenal. Stuttgart: Hiersemann, 1993. 431–45.

MacGarry, Loretta. *The Holy Eucharist in Middle English Homiletic and Devotional Verse. A Dissertation.* Washington, DC: The Catholic U of America, 1936.

Mancinelli, Laura. (Trsl.by Evelyn Bradshaw and Yvette Marchand). "Tristan versus Parzifal: The 'Prologue' to Gottfried von Straßburg's *Tristan.* J. A. W. Bennett Memorial Lecture, Perugia, 1982–1983." *Medieval and Pseudo-Medieval Literature.* Eds. Piero Boitani and Anna Torti. Tübingen: Narr; Cambridge: Brewer, 1984. 11–17.

Mann, Jill. "Eating and Drinking in *Piers Plowman.*" *Essays and Studies* n.s. 32 (1979): 26–43.

Manuszak, David. "Milton's Apology against a Pamphlet and the Communion Liturgy." *English Language Notes* 22.3 (1985): 39–41.

Marti, Kevin Douglas. *Minor Mundus: The Figurative Use of the Body in Pearl.* Dissertation-Abstracts-International, Ann Arbor, MI (DAI). 1988 June, 48:12, 3107A.

Matar, Nabil I. "George Herbert, Henry Vaughan, and the Conversion of the Jews." *Studies in English Literature, 1500–1900* 30.1 (1990): 79–92.

McGill, Jr., William J. "George Herbert's View of the Eucharist." *Lock Haven Review* 8 (1966): 16–24.

McNees, Eleanor J. *Eucharistic Poetry: The Search for Presence in the Writings of John Donne, Gerard Manley Hopkins, Dylan Thomas, and Geoffrey Hill.* Lewisburg: Bucknell UP, 1992.

McNeir, W. F. "The Corpus Christi Passion Plays as Dramatic Art." *Studia Philologica* 48 (1951): 601–28.

Muir, Lynette R. "The Mass on the Medieval Stage." *Comparative Drama* 23.4 (1989–1990): 314–30.

Nichols, Ann-Eljenholm. "Lollard Language in the Croxton Play of the Sacrament." *Notes and Queries* 36 (1989): 23–25.

O'Donnell, Mary. "Quam Oblationem: The Act of Sacrifice in the Poetry of Saint Robert Southwell." Diss. U of North Carolina, Greensboro, 1994.

O'Gorman, Richard. "Ecclesiastical Tradition and the Holy Grail." *Australian Journal of French Studies* 6 (1969), 3–8.

Ortuno, Manuel J. "Religious Ritual in the Poetry of Francisco de Quevedo." *Revista de Estudios Hispanicos* 15.2 (1981): 251–64.

Phillips, Heather. "The Eucharistic Allusions of *Pearl*." *Mediaeval Studies* 47 (1985): 474–86.

Pickens, Rupert T. "Villon on the Road to Paris: Contexts and Intertexts of *huitain* XIII of the *Testament*." *Conjunctures: Medieval Studies in Honor of Douglas Kelly*. Eds. Keith Busby and Norris J. Lacy. Amsterdam: Rodopi, 1994. 425–53.

Pickering, O. S. "A Middle English Poem on the Eucharist and Other Poems by the Same Author." *Archiv für das Studium der Neueren Sprachen und Literaturen* 215 (1978): 281–310.

Pierson, M. "The Relation of the Corpus Christi Procession to the Corpus Christi Play in England." *Transactions of the Wisconsin Academy of Sciences, Arts and Letters* 18 (1915): 110–65.

Plummer, John F. "The Logomachy of the N-Town Passion Play I." *Journal of English and Germanic Philology* 88.3 (1989): 311–31.

Priscandaro, Michele Theresa. *Middle English Eucharistic Verse: Its Imagery, Symbolism, and Typology*. Dissertation-Abstracts-International, Ann Arbor, MI 1976, 36, 5275A.

Prosser, Eleanor. *Drama and Religion in the English Mystery Plays: A Reevaluation*. Stanford, CA: Stanford UP, 1961.

Reid-Schwartz, Alexandra. "Economies of Salvation: Commerce and the Eucharist in *The Profanation of the Host* and the Croxton *Play of the Sacrament*." *Comitatus: A Journal of Medieval and Renaissance Studies* 25 (1994): 1–20.

Renn III, George A. "Chaucer's 'Canterbury Tales'." *Explicator* 43 (1985): 8–9.

Roach, William. "Eucharistic Tradition in the *Perlesvaus*." *Zeitschrift für Romanische Philologie* 54 (1939): 10–56.

Ross, Malcom Mackenzie. *Poetry and Dogma: The Transfiguration of Eucharistic Symbols in Seventeenth-Century English Poetry*. New York: Oktagon Books, 1969.

Schröder, W. J. *Der Ritter zwischen Gott und Welt. Idee und Problem des Parzivalromans Wolframs von Eschenbach*. Weimar: Böhlau, 1952.

Schuetz, Hans J. *Juden in der deutschen Literatur: Eine deutsch- jüdische Literaturgeschichte im Überblick*. München: Piper, 1992.

Shullenberger, William. "The Word of Reform and the Poetics of the Eucharist." *George Herbert Journal* 13.1–2 (1989–90): 19–36.

Solterer, Helen. "Dismembering, Remembering the Chatelain de Couci." *Romance Philology* 45.2 (1992): 102–24.

Staley, Grant B. "Pagan Mythology as Eucharistic Vehicle in an Auto Sacramental of Lope." *Selected Proceedings of the Thirty-Ninth Annual Mountain*

Interstate Foreign Language Conference. Eds. E. Torres Sixto and Carl S. King. Clemson: Clemson UP, 1991. 83–89.

—. *The Eucharist in Its Symbolic Manifestations in Selected Autos Sacramentales of Lope de Vega.* Dissertation-Abstracts-International, Ann Arbor, MI 1980, 41, 2632A–33A.

Stemmler, Theo. *Liturgische Formen und geistliche Spiele. Studien zu Erscheinungsformen des Dramatischen im Mittelalter.* Tübingen: Niemeyer, 1970.

Stevens, Martin. "The York Cycle: From Procession to Play." *Leeds Studies in English* n.s. 6 (1970): 37–61.

Sticca, Sandro. "Drama and Spirituality in the Middle Ages." *Mediaevalia et Humanistica* n.s. 4 (1973): 69–87.

—. *The Latin Passion Play: Its Origins and Development.* Albany, NY: SUNY, 1970.

Strohm, Paul. "Chaucer's Lollard Joke: History and Textual Unconscious." *Studies in the Age of Chaucer* 17 (1995): 23–42.

Toldo, Peter. "Leben und Wunder der Heiligen im Mittelalter, XII: Umgestaltungen. Verwandlungen." *Studien zur vergleichenden Literaturgeschichte* 5 (1905), 343–53.

Travis, Peter W. "The Social Body of the Dramatic Christ in Medieval England." *Early Drama to 1600.* Eds. Albert H. Ticomi and Martin Stevens. Binghamton: Center for Medieval and Early Renaissance Studies, SUNY, 1987. 17–36.

Ulreich, Jr., John C. "Milton on the Eucharist: Some Second Thoughts about Sacramentalism." *Milton and the Middle Ages.* Ed. John Mulryan. Lewisburg; London: Bucknell UP; Associated UP, 1982. 32–56.

Utz, Richard J. "Hugh von Lincoln und der Mythos vom jüdischen Ritualmord." *Herrscher – Helden – Heilige* (Mittelalter-Mythen, 1). Eds. Werner Wunderlich and Ulrich Müller. Konstanz: Universitätsverlag, 1996. 681–92.

—. *Literarischer Nominalismus im Spätmittelalter. Eine Untersuchung zu Sprache, Charakterzeichnung und Struktur in Geoffrey Chaucers* Troilus and Criseyde. Frankfurt a.M.: Lang, 1990. [esp. 157–92].

Very, F.G. *The Spanish Corpus Christi Procession: A Literary and Folkloric Study.* Valencia: Tipografia Moderna, 1962.

Waite, Arthur Edward. *The Holy Grail. The Galahad Quest in the Arthurian Literature.* New Hyde Park, NY: University Books, 1961.

Wenzel, Edith. "Synagoga und Ecclesia: Zum Antijudaismus im deutschsprachigen Spiel des späten Mittelalters." *Internationales Archiv für Sozialgeschichte der Deutschen Literatur* 12 (1987): 57–81.

Wessels, Paulus B. "Wolfram zwischen Dogma und Legende." *Beiträge zur Geschichte der deutschen Sprache und Literatur* 77 (1955): 112–35.

Willms, Eva. "'Der lebenden brôt': Zu Gottfried von Straßburg *Tristan* 238 (240)." *Zeitschrift für deutsches Altertum und deutsche Literatur* 123.1 (1994): 19–44.

256

Wirtjes, Hanneke. *"Piers Plowman* B. XVIII.364–73: The Cups That Cheer But Not Inebriate." *Sentences for Alan Ward. Essays Presented to Alan Ward on the Occasion of His Retirement from Wadham College, Oxford.* Ed. D.M. Reeks. Southampton: Bosphorus, 1988. 63–73.

Young, R. V. "Herbert and the Real Presence." *Renascence: Essays on Value in Literature* 45.3 (1993): 179–96.

Zoeller, Sonja. "Judenfeindschaft in den Schwänken des 16. Jahrhunderts." *Daphnis* 23.2–3 (1994): 345–69.

Editorial Policy

Disputatio is an annual journal of the late middle ages which publishes articles *only* on the subject of the announced theme for each volume. Preferred length for scholarly articles is 4,000-12,000 words and for research notes is under 2,500 words. Review essays will be assigned by the editors; please contact us if you might wish to be assigned a topic. We are also very committed to publishing bibliographies; please contact us if you are interested in compiling one. For review essays, inquiries from younger scholars or those working on dissertations in the field are particularly welcome. Although the preferred language of *Disputatio* is English, we will consider articles in all major European languages and Latin. All articles not in English must be accompanied by a substantial abstract in English. Manuscripts must conform to MLA style. Although contributors are requested to use hard copy for initial submission of manuscripts, final copies of accepted manuscripts must be submitted on disk (Windows *only* -- we *cannot* use Macintosh disks). Authors should send three copies of the manuscript and a stamped self-addressed envelope when submitting work. All articles will receive blind review by specialists in the field; final decisions concerning publication, however, rest exclusively with the editors.

Topics for Subsequent Volumes
1999: Late Medieval Grammars and Grammarians. Deadline: 1 Nov. 1998.
2000: Late Medieval Disputations. Deadline: 1 Nov. 1999.

Address all editorial correspondence to:

North American contributions:	All other contributions:
Carol Poster, Editor, *Disputatio,*	Richard J. Utz, Editor, *Disputatio,*
English Department, Wilson 2-176,	English Department, Baker 115
Montana State University,	University of Northern Iowa,
Bozeman MT 59717-0230	Cedar Falls IA 50614-0502
e-mail: poster@english.montana.edu	e-mail: utz@cobra.uni.edu

Book Reviews (from all locations):
Georgiana Donavin, Book Review Editor
English Dept., Westminster College
1840 East 1300 South
Salt Lake City UT 84105 USA
e-mail: g-donavi@wcslc.edu

Address subscription inquiries to:
Northwestern University Press
Chicago Distribution Center
11030 South Langley Avenue
Chicago IL 60628
Phone: 800-621-2736 or 312-568-1550
Fax: 800-621-8476 or 312-660-2235